WESTMAR COLLEGE

W9-BWQ-731

GARIBALDI.

From a photograph, probably ten years later than the siege of Rome.
See illustration, p. 117 below, for his dress during 1849

GARIBALDI'S DEFENCE OF THE ROMAN REPUBLIC

1848-9

BY

GEORGE MACAULAY TREVELYAN

LATE FELLOW OF TRINITY COLLEGE, CAMBRIDGE
AUTHOR OF 'THE LIFE OF JOHN BRIGHT,' ETC. ETC.

*WITH SEVEN MAPS
AND NUMEROUS ILLUSTRATIONS*

NEW IMPRESSION

GREENWOOD PRESS, PUBLISHERS
WESTPORT, CONNECTICUT

DG
798.5
.T8
1971

All Rights Reserved

Originally published by Longmans, Green, and
Company, London

Reprinted with the permission
of David McKay Company, Inc., New York

First Greenwood Reprinting 1971

Library of Congress Catalogue Card Number 76-156214

SBN 8371-6165-7

Printed in the United States of America

96940

TO THE IMMORTAL MEMORY

OF

GIUSEPPE GARIBALDI

THIS BOOK IS DEDICATED

BY THE CITIZEN OF A COUNTRY WHICH HE LOVED

AND WHERE HE WAS LOVED

PREFACE TO THE NEW EDITION

A NUMBER of small changes have been made in this new edition; the more important can be detected by students on pp. 39, 50, 157, 214, 301, 305, 311–313, 352–353, 362–363. In the forth-coming Italian translation of this book, published by Zanichelli & Co., there is some additional matter which I do not think it worth while to introduce into the English book; reference is made to these passages in the notes on pp. 214, 311, and 312, below. A list of books which I have consulted since the Third Edition appeared will be found as Addenda to the Bibliography, pp. 373-374 below; the centenary year 1907 was naturally rich in Garibaldian literature in Italy.

Feb. 21, 1908.   G. M. T.

PREFACE TO THE SECOND EDITION

FOR the improvements which I have been able to make in this edition I am indebted to various persons, among others to Signor Luzio at the Archivio di Stato, Mantua, who pointed out to me several sources of information, including the documents about Cesenatico and Magnavacca recently published in Italian peri-odicals; to Mrs. Hamilton King, who lent me the very rare tract, Uccellini's ' Garibaldi sottratto dai patrioti Ravegnani alle ricerche degli Austriaci,' the best authority on the escape from S. Alberto as far as Forlì, and Gualtieri's ' Ugo Bassi,' the best authority for the events attending his martyrdom; and lastly to Miss Forbes, who lent me the papers of her father Col. Hugh Forbes, which I have called the ' Forbes MSS.' The principal alterations and additions based on these and some other new data will be found on pp. 38, 252, 287, 295, 305–306, 307–309, and in Appendices M, N, O, and the last page of Appendix L. The Bibliography has been enlarged and brought up to date.

June 22, 1907.   G. M. T.

PREFACE

TO

THE FIRST EDITION

THIS year is the centenary of Garibaldi's birth, which took place on July 4, 1807. It is not on this account that the present volume has been written and published, but the coincidence may be an additional reason why some Englishmen should be curious to read about the man for whom their fathers entertained a passionate enthusiasm, pure of all taint of materialism and self-interest. On the occasion of his famous visit to our country in 1864, the ovation which he received was so universal and so overwhelming that there was nothing in the nineteenth century like it, except perhaps the Jubilee procession of the Queen herself. The feeling for Garibaldi had by no means become universal among the English in 1849, the year with which this book is concerned, but even then Italian sympathies were stronger here than anywhere else in Europe.

We English retain to this day the lion's share of Italy's gratitude. Nor is the reason far to seek. Though England was not the country which actually accomplished most for Italian freedom and unity, it was the country in Europe where the passion for that cause was, beyond all comparison, strongest and most disinterested, and where it will be for ever connected with such names as Byron and Shelley, Palmerston and Gladstone, Browning and Swinburne.

The attachment of our fathers to Garibaldi grew out of
their Italian sympathies, but it grew also out of something
in his personality peculiarly captivating to the English,
who saw in him the rover of great spaces of land and sea,
the fighter against desperate odds, the champion of the
oppressed, the patriot, the humane and generous man, all
in one. He touched a chord of poetry and romance still
latent in the heart of our city populations, so far removed
in their surroundings and opportunities from the scenes
and actions of his life. Whether his memory will now
appeal to the English of a generation yet further removed
from nature, and said to be at once more sophisticated
and less idealist than the Victorian, I do not know. But
I doubt whether we have really changed so much.

Certainly the help and encouragement in my task which
I have received from English people leads me to suppose
that the name of Garibaldi can still stir many hearts in
this island. Foremost among them I must thank Lord
Carlisle; then Mrs. Hamilton King; Mr. A. L. Smith,
of Balliol; Dr. Spence Watson; Mr. Hubert Hall of the
Record Office; the editor of the 'Illustrated London
News;' Mr. Brand, the Librarian of the Admiralty; Dr.
F. S. Arnold; Mr. J. A. Bruce; the Rev. F. W. Ragg;
Mr. Bolton King; Mrs. Humphry Ward, and many others,
some of whom are mentioned by name in the notes of this
book. Three persons have read the proofs of the whole
book at a cost of time to themselves from which I have
greatly profited—Mr. Hilton Young, my companion on the
last part of the 'Retreat'; my wife; and Count Ugo
Balzani.

Count Balzani, whose time has been lavished upon me
with a kindness which I can never forget, not only aided me
in a hundred ways himself, but introduced me to many of
my now numerous Italian friends; for their work on my
behalf I am all the more grateful because it was largely

inspired by an enthusiasm which we have in common. Without trying to distinguish between the various services which they have each rendered me, I will merely name *Signori* Carlo Segré, G. Guerrazzi, and G. Stiavelli of Rome; Sign. Pier Breschi and General Canzio himself of Genoa; Sign. Luigi Torre of Casale Monferrato; Sign. Cantoni of the Museo Civico, Bologna ; Count Alessandro Guaccimanni of Ravenna ; Sign. Ermanno Loevinson (the author of *Garibaldi e la sua Legione*) and Cav. Ernesto Ovidi of the Archivio di Stato, Rome ; Sign. Mario Menghini of the Bib. Vitt. Em. ; Captain Carlo Paganelli of the Ufficio Storico ; Major Eugenio de' Rossi of the Bersaglieri ; and Lt.-General Saletta, Chief of the Staff of the Italian army ; the family and friends of Nino Costa ; Count and Countess Pasolini and Count Pasolino Pasolini ; and the Signorina Dobelli of London.

I do not know whether to thank my friend Mr. Nelson Gay more for putting his splendid *Risorgimento* library at my disposal, or for giving me so much of his valuable student's time, which he spends with such zeal on behalf of Italy.

I am indebted to Mr. R. M. Johnston of Harvard for a correspondence which has been to me both pleasant and useful.

I heartily thank Commandant Weil of Paris for his friendly offices, and the French Ministry of War for a liberality of which I am most sensible. I trust they will not think that I have abused their kindness ; no one is more aware than the author of this book of the courage, discipline, and humanity of the French troops in 1849, or of the immense debt that Italy owes to the First Napoleon, and, in spite of Rome and Mentana, to the Third.

G. M. TREVELYAN.

CHELSEA : *March* 1907.

CONTENTS

PART III

GARIBALDI'S RETREAT AND ESCAPE

LIST OF PLATES

* From Rear-Admiral Winnington-Ingram's *Hearts of Oak*, from original sketches on the spot by the author.
† From the original pencil drawings for the famous *Don Pirlone* cartoons, which drawings are now in the possession of Mr. A. L. Smith of Balliol, who kindly lent them to me. All these four pictures appeared in the newspaper ; see *Don Pirlone*, Jan. 15, 25, May 21, 29, 1849.
‡ From the *Illustrated London News* of May–July 1849, with kind permission and assistance of the present editor. The pictures facing p. 100 were made from actual sketches of particular individuals ; the figure on the right, with arms folded, is very probably Mameli, whose portraits it resembles. Lord Carlisle tells me the pictures were done by George Thomas.

LIST OF PLATES

XV

PAGE

LIST OF MAPS

GARIBALDI'S DEFENCE

OF THE

ROMAN REPUBLIC

INTRODUCTION

MOST of us, when we visit Rome, go up on the morning
after our arrival to the heights of the Janiculum, and,
standing on the terrace in front of San Pietro in Montorio,
look back across the Tiber at the city spread beneath our
feet, in all its mellow tints of white, and red, and brown,
broken here and there by masses of dark green pine and
cypress, and by shining cupolas raised to the sun. There
it all lies beneath us, the heart of Europe and the living
chronicle of man's long march to civilisation ; for there,
we know, are the well-proportioned piazzas with their
ancient columns and their fountains splashing in shade
and shine around the sculptured water-gods of the Renaissance ; the Forum won back by the spade ; and the first
monuments of the Christian Conquest. There rise the naked
hulks of giant ruins stripped of their imperial grandeur long
ago by hungry generations of Papal architects ; and there, on
the outskirts of the town, is the Pyramid that keeps watch
over the graves. As we look down we feel the presence of
all the centuries of European history, a score of civilisations
dead and lying in state one beside the other ; and in the
midst of their eternal monuments mankind still swarms
and labours, after all its strange and varied experience,
still intent to live, still busily weaving the remote future
out of the immemorial past.

B

And then, raising our eyes to the far horizon, we see the well-known shapes of those hills of great name, shapes moulded by the chance spasms of volcanoes, as they sank namelessly to rest long ago, leaving against the sky ridges and peaks to which in after days Consuls, Emperors, and Popes of Rome looked every morning as on familiar faces. There, to the north, is the spine of Soracte, famous for no great reason except that Horace saw it from Rome—and yet so famous ; to the east, grey, gaunt Lucretilis pointing at the blue sky and hiding the valley of his Digentian farm ; to the south, the Alban Mount itself, the shape of which, never long out of sight, is like the presiding genius of the city—Alba haunting us still [1]—as it haunted Romulus and those who left its wooded slopes to colonise the Tiber bank, and Garibaldi as he ordered the battle day by day for a summer month on this very Mount Janiculum.

Across the fifteen miles that lie between the roofs of the capital and this great semi-circle of sacred hills, rolls sea-like the Campagna in waves of bare, open country. Over it, from the day when the Consul Aulus led out his host to the Porcian height yonder, to the day when Italy entered Rome under Victor Emmanuel, the armies of many nations, in many ages, for many causes, have come and gone, and each could have been seen slowly crawling over the vast plain. In the solemn hush of the distance on which we gaze, through the clear morning air, it seems as if that semi-circle of mountains were the seats of a Greek theatre whereon some audience of patient gods were watching an endless play, as if Rome were the stage on which their looks were centred from the distant hills to north and east and south, while behind, in the west, meet sea and sky, a background before which the short-lived actors move. It was in this, the greatest theatre in the world, the Eternal City, ' *Sul teatro delle maggiori grandezze del mondo, nell' Urbe,*' as Garibaldi called it,[2] that the most significant and moving scene of the Risorgimento was played out.

---

[1] See Clough's *Amours de Voyage*, end of Canto I, written during the Siege, 1849.   [2] *Mem.* 223.

And yet among the English visitors who go on from the platform of San Pietro in Montorio to view the colossal equestrian figure of Garibaldi which holds the Janiculan sky-line, not many are aware how very close to this statue raged some of the fiercest fights in which he ever took part. For his sake, or for Italy's, turn aside a few steps to the Porta San Pancrazio. Standing under its archway we look out of Rome westward, up a country road, which runs straight for two hundred yards, and then splits off to right and left. At the forking of the ways our view from the city gate is blocked by the entrance to a beautiful garden, the grounds of the Pamfili-Doria. Inside that garden we see a slope of grass, with a path running up it to an ornamental arch, which now stands where the Villa Corsini once stood. Between the Porta San Pancrazio and this other archway on the hill top, some four hundred paces away, Italy poured out her best blood. On that narrow white road, and up that green slope, and in the old battered Villa Vascello on the right of the roadway (still left like Hougoumont in honourable ruin) were mowed down the chosen youth of Italy, the men who would have been called to make her laws and lead her armies, and write her songs and history, when her day came, but that they judged it necessary to die here in order that her day should come. It was here that Italy bought Rome, at the price of their blood—here at the San Pancrazio Gate, in 1849, that her claim on Rome was staked out and paid for; twenty-one years passed, and then, in 1870, the debt was acquitted.

That there should ever have been a time when Mazzini ruled Rome and Garibaldi defended her walls, sounds like a poet's dream. In this book I wish to record the facts that gave shape to that dream, to tell the story of the Siege of Rome, than which there is no more moving incident in modern history ; and, in the last six chapters, to narrate the events that followed as an epilogue to the siege—the Retreat and Escape of Garibaldi, a story no less poetical and no less dear to Italy's heart, though more neglected

by English writers, because of its smaller political importance. These later events are the march of Garibaldi
across Italy, hunted by the French, Spanish and Neapolitan
forces through Umbria and Tuscany, into a network of four
armies of Austrians spread over northern Umbria and the
Romagna; the extraordinary feats of skill and energy
with which the greatest of guerilla chiefs again and again
disentangled his little band of followers from surrounding
hosts, and carried them across the Apennine watershed to
the Adriatic sea-board; the final hunting of them into
the territories of the Republic of San Marino, by Austrians,
close on their heels, cruel as the dragoons of Claverhouse,
killing or torturing all those whom they caught. Then the
disbanding of the bulk of the Roman forces on the friendly
neutral territory of the hill Republic, and Garibaldi's
rush to the coast, through the enemy's cordon, with the
last two hundred, who would not, merely to save their
lives, give up the sacred war so long as Venice held out;
their midnight embarkation in the fishing boats at Cesenatico; their fatal meeting, on the way to Venice, with the
Austrian gun-boats; the re-landing, among the lagoons
north of Ravenna, of Garibaldi with his dying wife in his
arms, in company with Ugo Bassi and Ciceruacchio, who
were destined in a few days to fall into the hands of the
hunters and perish. Not so Garibaldi. I shall tell how the
man of destiny, wandering in the marshes and the pine-
forest of Ravenna, among regiments of soldiers seeking for
his life as for the prize of the war, was preserved by the
strange working of chance, by the iron courage and endurance of the worn Odysseus himself, and by the craft,
energy, and devotion of the Romagnuols, who guarded him
at peril of their lives, as the West countrymen after Wor-
cester fight guarded a less precious treasure.

All this, and his escape back across the breadth of
Italy to the Western sea, and embarkation in the Tuscan
Maremma for lands of refuge where he could await his
great day, will, together with the siege of Rome, form the
principal theme of the book. The first half-dozen chapters

must serve to introduce the subject to those who are not
familiar with the history of Italy and of Garibaldi.

I have concealed nothing prosaic and nothing discredit-
able—neither Garibaldi's mistakes during the siege, nor the
misconduct of some of his associates, nor the hostility with
which part of the rural population regarded the red-shirts.

Hoping to make the story of the defence of Rome,
of the retreat of the Garibaldians and the escape of their
chief stand out in all its details of place and colouring,
I have not only visited the scenes in the capital and near it,
but have walked along the whole route traversed by
Garibaldi's column from the gate of Rome to Cesenatico
on the Adriatic, and have visited the scenes of his adventures
near Comacchio and Ravenna. It would, perhaps, be
impossible to find in all Europe a district more enchanting
to the eye by its shapes, its colours, its atmosphere, or one
more filled with famous towns, rivers and mountains, than the
valleys of Tiber, Nar, Clanis, Metaurus and Rubicon, across
which they marched. Through this land of old beauty
I have followed on foot their track of pain and death, with
such a knowledge of where they went, and how they fared
each day, as is not often the fortune of pilgrims who trace
the steps of heroes.[1] To come, in solitary places, upon the
very wayside fountains at which, as the survivors have
recorded, they slaked their raging thirst, and at other turns
of the road upon springs where they found no water that
terrible July ; to stand on the hill whence they last saw the
dome of St. Peter's, and that other hill where the face of
Garibaldi brightened at sight of the Adriatic ; to traverse
the oak woods through which they marched under the stars ;
or where they slept through the long Italian noonday ;
to draw breath in the quiet monastery gardens, perched
high over hills of olive and plains of vine, wherein they
tasted brief hours of green coolness and repose ; to scale
the bare mountains up which they dragged their little piece
of cannon, and descend the gorge where at the last they

[1] This extremely detailed knowledge we owe, mainly, to two men, Hoffstetter
and Belluzzi. (See *Bibliography* below.)

let it lie when the Austrians were hard upon them ; to see
the streets and piazzas in which the citizens held last
festivals of the tricolor in honour of their passage, and the
villages where the rearguard fought, and where the laggards
were killed by the pursuers ; to hear the waves breaking on
the mole whence the last of the army put to sea in the
midnight storm ; to stand on the lonely beach and sand-
dunes where Garibaldi waded ashore with his Anita in his
arms, and in the room of the farmhouse where he watched
her die, while the Austrians might at any moment have
been knocking at the door ; to see these places and to find
that the story is very dear to rich and poor, learned and
ignorant, in a progressive and a free country, conscious
that it owes progress and freedom to these heroes, both
those who perished and those who survived—this has taught
me what cannot be clearly learnt from the pages of Ruskin
or Symonds, or any other of Italy's melodious mourners,
that she is not dead but risen, that she contains not only
ruins but men, that she is not the home of ghosts, but the
land which the living share with their immortal ancestors.

CHAPTER I

THE TRAINING OF GARIBALDI

And other spirits there are standing apart
Upon the forehead of the age to come ;
These, these will give the world another heart,
And other pulses.   Hear ye not the hum
Of mighty workings?—
Listen awhile, ye nations, and be dumb.—*Keats* (1817).

IN these words one who never lived to see it prophesied
the new world.   It was two years after Waterloo, a time
of disillusion and of fainting by the way, when Europe,
bled white by the man who was to have been her saviour,
was again prisoner to kings whom she no longer reverenced.
But, in fact, as Keats' instinct told him truly, the fields
were ready for sowing, and the sowers were there unseen.
The long unyielding sod had been broken up by the Revolutionary ploughshare, and now that the all too efficient
ploughman was at last under lock and key, ' great spirits '
already ' on earth ' were ' sojourning,' each destined to
cast seed of his own into the tumbled soil.   If we think
whom the young generation contained undistinguished
in its ranks when Keats published these lines in 1817,
we shall see that he was speaking more truly than even he,
in his poet's ardour and optimism, could have dared to
hope.   In England alone, where Shelley's genius was on
tip-toe for its flight, there were at that moment, unknown
to the world, and unknown to themselves, Darwin, Carlyle,
Mill, Newman, Gladstone, Macaulay, Cobden, Dickens,
Tennyson and Browning.   The work of all these men taken
together was to give our English world ' another heart and
other pulses.'
  Nor would it be hard to draw up such a list for Con-

tinental Europe, headed by Heine, Victor Hugo and Wagner.
But the strangest, if not the richest, handful of fate's
hidden treasures was ripening beneath the Italian sky.
In the year that Keats wrote there might have been seen
in the harbour of Nice (then the Italian city of Nizza) a
sailor's boy of ten years old, playing amid the cordage of
his father's vessel—by name Giuseppe Garibaldi. A hundred miles further along the Riviera, in a doctor's house,
in one of those narrow, picturesque alleys that crowd the
hillside above the busy port of Genoa, was another boy of
twelve, Giuseppe Mazzini. These two Josephs, whom
neither birth nor favour had placed above their brethren,
were destined to place themselves among the great Four
who liberated Italy. And it was these two sons of the
people who were to make that liberation worthy of the
Muse, raising the story of Italian freedom to a pinnacle
of history far above common nationalist struggles, which
after a few centuries are forgotten by all save students.
The sailor's and the doctor's sons made the history of
Italy's Resurrection a part of the imperishable and international poetry of the European races. And, as regards
their effect upon their own time, if they did not actually
create, at least they ennobled and intensified, the liberal
forces which it was given to one wiser and more cunning
to wield. For there was already in the world, in 1817,
another boy, a nobleman's son, by name Camillo Cavour.
The fourth of the great liberators, the man whom these
three were between them to make King of Italy, was not
yet born.

So Keats prophesied, and shortly after died in Rome.
And still, over the plains and mountain roads of Italy, the
Austrians in their white coats and shakos moved unceasingly,
on their fruitless, mechanical task of repression ; stared
at with a vague but growing antipathy by the common
people, with horror by Shelley, and with disgust by Byron ; [1]

[1] Byron to John Murray, Ravenna, February 16, 1821. 'As or news, the
Barbarians are marching on Naples, and if they lose a single battle, all Italy will
be up, . . . *Letters opened!*—to be sure they are, and that's the reason why I

SWITZERLAND

AUSTRIA

Brenner Pass

Tirol

ITALY
Spring 1848 and Autumn 1849

English Miles

0 20 40 60 80 100

Kilometres

0 20   100   200

Austrian Territory shaded thus:- ////
The Quadrilateral underlined thus:- Verona

N

Gt.St.Bernard Pass
Luino
Lit.St.Bernard Pass
Mt.Cenis Pass
Mt.Geneura Pass

Savoy

FRANCE

PIEDMONT

LOMBARDY
Bergamo
Brescia
Morazzone
Novara
Milan
Mantua

VENETIA
Verona
Peschiera
Legnago
Venice

Turin

Nizza (Nice)

Liguria
Genoa
Chiavari
Spezzia

PARMA
MODENA
Bologna
Romagna

Comacchio
Ravenna
Pola

LUCCA
Pisa
Livorno
(Leghorn)
Florence
Arno

TUSCANY

SAN MARINO

The Marches

Umbria

PAPAL STATES

Tiber

Corsica
(to France)

Civitavecchia

Campagna

Rome

NAPLES

Naples

Caprera

Sardinia
(to Piedmont)

Palermo

KINGDOM OF THE TWO SICILIES

Calabria

Messina

X 1860
Calatafimi

X Aspromonte
1862

The Quadrilateral underlined thus:- Verona
Land below 1500 ft. shown thus:- ....

St.Gotthard Pass

Simplon Pass

The A l p s

In the Brenner Pass

Mt.Rosa
L.Maggiore
L.Luino
L.Como
L.Varese
Varese
Morazzone
Bergamo
Brescia
L.Garda
Verona
Peschiera
Roverbella
Custoza
Legnago
Venice

Novara
Milan
Mantua

Turin

Plain of Lombardy

Genoa
Chiavari

Bologna

Emery Walker sc.

while the other army of invaders, the English 'milords,' swelling with the pride of Waterloo, each with his carriage, family, footman and 'Quarterly Review' complete, looked with an indifferent contempt on Austrians and Italians, priests and patriots, and with hostile inquisitiveness at the rebel poets of their own race and caste. In such a world, Mazzini, Garibaldi, and Cavour grew up, each among his fellows.

Giuseppe Garibaldi was born at Nice, in a house by the sea shore, on July 4, 1807, as a subject of the great Emperor. On Napoleon's fall he became, as did Mazzini in Genoa, a subject of the restored royal house of Piedmont, which afterwards condemned him to death for treason in 1834, was obliged to hand over his native province to France in 1860, and in the same year received Sicily and Naples at his hands. The inhabitants of Nice were in part French and in part Italian by race. But Garibaldi's family was pure Italian,[1] having come from Chiavari beyond Genoa, about thirty years before he was born. During his boyhood, Nice had not yet been completely captured by the invalids and the wealthy of all countries,[2] but still belonged to the natives, and Giuseppe's father, Domenico, an honest and simple merchant captain, owning the little vessel in which he traded, was typical of the best sort of native, though himself an immigrant from Chiavari. Like Hans Luther, Domenico Garibaldi gave his son a better education than his slender means could well afford. But he was buying costly seed for a stony soil, and it was with difficulty that Giuseppe's parents and masters managed, until he was fifteen, to keep him intermittently at his desk. For there were the mountains behind the town, where he roamed truant,

always put in my opinion of the German and Austrian scoundrels : there is not an Italian who loathes them more than I do.'—(*Byron*, v. 245.)

[1] If, as the name is held to indicate, one of his remote ancestors was sprung from the Teuton conquerors in the dark ages, he was none the less an Italian than a man of the name of Beauchamp is, for that, less an Englishman. For details about his family see *Guerzoni*, i. 5–10; *Mario, Supp.* 2–8.

[2] *Mem.* 9.

sometimes far afield, with a cousin, a borrowed gun and a game pouch ; there was the harbour with the ships and the sailors from far countries, whose presence there and daily business were to youth a standing recommendation of romance as the common and natural avocation of man ; and above all there was the sea, always before his eyes, always in his thoughts, calling its child to its bosom.

Forty years on, a playmate of Garibaldi described his recollections of these old days :—

'Though Peppino (Giuseppe) was a bright, brave lad who planned all sorts of adventures, played truant when he could get the loan of a gun or coax one of the fishermen to take him in their boat, went oyster-trawling, never missed the tunny festival at Villafranca, or the sardine hauls at Limpia, he was often thoughtful and silent, and when he had a book that interested him would lie under the olive trees for hours reading, and then it was no use to try to make him join any of our schemes for mischief. He had a beautiful voice, and knew all the songs of the sailors and peasants, and a good many French ones besides. Even as a boy we all looked up to him and chose him our umpire, while the little ones regarded him as their natural protector. He was the strongest and most enduring swimmer I ever knew, and a very fish in water.' [1]

And so the education of books, which came to an end in 1822, never amounted to very much, partly through the limitations of the father's purse, but still more through the boy's want of eagerness for learning. He was taught a little Latin, which he afterwards forgot.[2] He neglected the opportunity to learn from one of his masters what he calls ' the beautiful tongue of Byron,' and picked up English only in later years when he became, as he says, ' the Benjamin of the lords of the ocean.' [3]   But he learnt

[1] *Mario, Supp.* 9-11, and *Mario,* ed. 1905, p. 3 ; *Mario, Vita,* ed. 1882, p. 3. See also his own *Memorie,* 7-9. Both Garibaldi (*Mem.*) and Mrs. Mario's informant state that the first of the sixteen occasions on which he saved human life from drowning was when he was eight years old and saved a washerwoman who had fallen into a deep ditch ! *Guerzoni,* ii. 639.

[2] *Mem.* 13.

[3] *Mem.* 8, 343. *Rule of the Monk,* i. 103, and *passim.* His love of the English became with him a romantic passion, answering to his hatred of priests.

reading and writing, and a little mathematics, and conceived
a devotion at least to the 'idea' of the great Italian history
and literature of the past. Since it did not require much
application for a *Nizzardo* to read French almost as well as
Italian, he was enabled to taste Voltaire and to commit
some of his verses to memory. But he loved better those
of Ugo Foscolo, the liberal poet of his own race and epoch,
whose glorious lines were often on his lips from the beginning to the end of his career, and whose melody often
soothed him in hours of pain. Garibaldi's companions in
South America observed that ' music and poetry had a
magical power over him.' [1] He himself often expressed
his own emotions in verse. In short he had acquired just
enough book learning to feed his naturally freedom-loving,
romantic and poetical disposition, but not enough to
chasten it, or to train his mind to wide understanding
and deep reflection. It was largely owing to this, that
his ' native hue of resolution ' was never, either for good
or evil, ' sicklied o'er with the pale cast of thought,' and
that his ' enterprises of great pith and moment ' were
never known to ' lose the name of action.' [2]

Such was the boy whom his parents, fearful of the
dangers of the sea, strove to bring up as a solid landsman.
But they had entered on an unequal contest, for not only
had they no moral case (the father being himself a sailor),
but they had to contend against a character which, when
roused, was the most obstinate in Europe, and a nature
whereof every part was united in rebellion against the

It is to be remembered that he was principally conversant with two classes of our
countrymen, the sea-going population and the active sympathisers with Italy.

As to his knowledge of English, it was a late growth. When he was first in
North America, in 1850, he tells us he only ' knew a few words of English.'
(*Mem.* 265.) Dr. Spence Watson says that when he was at Newcastle, a few years
later, ' he spoke English,' but it was still ' very imperfect.' Sir Charles Seely, his
host in the Isle of Wight in 1864, writes that he then spoke English ' sufficiently
well to be understood when conversing with one or two people quietly,' but that
he often found it difficult to follow a general conversation in English ; ' I see him
now with a puzzled expression on his face.' My father tells me that he fell
readily into English, when he met Englishmen by chance in Italy in 1867.

[1] *Cuneo*, 14 ; *Vecchi's Caprera*, 121.   [2] *Guerzoni*, i. 13–19 ; *Mem.* 7–9.

prospect of an unadventurous life. And there was yet a third party in the family disputes, the sea, always present, with voice and look encouraging the rebel.

At the age of fifteen Garibaldi took the decisive step. Let him tell the story in his own most characteristic fashion :

'Tired of school, and unable to endure a sedentary life, I propounded one day to some companions of my own age, to run away to Genoa, without any definite plan, but meaning in effect to seek our fortune. No sooner said than done, we seized a boat, embarked some provisions and fishing-tackle, and sailed eastward. We were already off Monaco, when a vessel sent by my good father overhauled us and brought us back deeply humiliated. An Abbé had revealed our flight. See what a coincidence ! An Abbé, the embryo of a priest, perhaps saved me, and I am so ungrateful as to persecute these poor priests ! All the same, a priest is an impostor, and I devote myself to the sacred cult of truth.

'My comrades in the adventure, whom I recall, were Cesare Parodi, Raffaele Deandreis ; I have forgotten the others.

'Here it gives me joy to bring to mind the young men of Nice : agile, strong, brave, splendid social and military material, but unfortunately led on the wrong path, first by the priests, then by depravity brought in from foreign parts, which has turned the beautiful Cimele of the Romans into the cosmopolitan seat of all that is corrupt.' [1]

But the foiled revolt had taken effect as a demonstration, the paternal government surrendered, and Giuseppe was sent to sea with all proper constitutional formalities, apparently in the year 1822. The last voyage of Shelley was in the same year and on the same coast as the first of Garibaldi.

From the age of fifteen to the age of twenty-five he worked his way up from cabin-boy to captain in the merchant craft of Nice. He applied himself strenuously to all the learning that is useful to one who commands a ship

[1] *Mem.* 9. I generally quote Werner's translation of the *Memorie*, though not in this case. The references in the notes are always to the authorised Italian edition (1888).

—mastering the necessary mathematics, geography, astronomy and commercial law. ' I set to work with books by myself, and all my practical knowledge I owe to my first captain, Pesante ; the rest came of itself.' [1]

And so the sea became the real school of Garibaldi ; it was there that his body and mind were drilled to endure every hardship, and his qualities as a man of action trained as only the sailor's life can train them. But while his powers were developed in a practical direction, his ideas became more than ever romantic. For on what manner of seas, in what ships was he sailing ? Not on the well-policed ocean of to-day, more orderly than a London street, but in the Levant during the Greek War of Independence ; in the seas of old romance, of pirates, Turks and revengeful Giaours with long guns and knives, and fierce, dark faces ; among old historic tyrannies cruel as fate, and new-born hopes of liberty fresh and dear as the morning ; among the sunburnt isles and promontories that roused Byron's jaded passions to splendour, that were even at that moment witnessing his self-immolation and apotheosis ; in those waters young Garibaldi caught, not from books but from the words, gestures and stories of men in earnest, the only true gospel of Byron, the idea that was constructive of the coming epoch—the belief that it is better to die for freedom than to live a slave.[2]

Three times on these seas he was captured and robbed by pirates.[3] It was a world of which Scott or Stevenson would love to tell enchanted tales. In outward appearance, too, the crews and the ships with which Garibaldi sailed had about them all the colour, poetry and grace of the old world. From his own loving recollections of the ship in which he made his first voyage, it would seem that she bore little resemblance to the famous paddle-steamers that long afterwards took him and his Thousand to Sicily :

' How beautiful wert thou, O bark "Costanza," whereon

[1] *Mario, Supp.* 10.   [2] *Cuneo*, 16.   [3] *Denkwürdigkeiten*, i. 13.

I was to plough the Mediterranean, and then the Black Sea, for the first time !

'Thy ample sides, thy lithe masts, thy large deck, and even thy broad-breasted female figure-head, will remain for ever engraved on my imagination.   How gracefully thy San Remo sailors, true types of our brave Ligurians, swung themselves about.   With what delight I sought the forecastle to hear their songs of the people, their harmonious choruses !   They sang of love, and softened or excited me with an emotion that I was then too young to understand.   Ah ! that they had sung to me of our country—of Italy, of rebellion, of slavery.   Alas ! none had taught them to be Italian patriots, champions of the dignity of mankind.   Who was there to tell us young men that there was an Italy, a country to avenge, to redeem ?   Who ?   With the priests as our only instructors ! ' [1]

Garibaldi had not been brought up at home in the idea either of liberalism or of Italy.   His father and mother were genuinely pious and indifferently conservative, and the Nizzard sailors had not been touched by Carbonarism.   It was on his voyages in the Levant that he first came across men with the passion for liberty, and it was beyond the sea that he first met Italian patriots, exiles who instructed him that he had a country, and that she bled.   He, too, like these Greeks, had a country for which to fight.   What a thought !   Nay, what a passion !   It seized him in early youth, like first love—the revelation of life.   Henceforth he was a man devoted, with an aim ahead that had in it nothing of self.   Italy first, Italy last, and always Italy ! Nor till the day of his death did his zeal and love once waver.   He believed in Italy as the Saints believed in God.

The second of his numerous voyages was a short one, coasting along Italy in his father's own little craft (*tartana*). They touched in the Papal States, and Domenico took his boy to see Rome.   Little did the good man know what he was doing.   The emotion with which the most poetically

---

[1] *Mem.* 9, 10.   The system of clerical education and espionage was one of the reasons why liberal ideas made so little headway in the territories of Piedmont before Mazzini began the 'Young Italy' movement of 1831.   'Priests were almost the only schoolmasters and professors.'—*King*, i. 47.

minded of the world's famous warriors looked for the first time on the Coliseum, and the other ruins of his country's greatness, has been described by himself. That emotion was only intensified by memory and years of longing in exile ; it became inextricably associated with political ideas which were, one suspects, not quite so fully developed in the mind of the youth at eighteen as the man afterwards thought.

' The Rome,' he writes, ' that I beheld with the eyes of my youthful imagination was the Rome of the future—the Rome that, shipwrecked, dying, banished to the furthest depths of the American forests, I never despaired of ; the regenerating idea of a great nation, the dominant thought and inspiration of my whole life.' [1]

He was, in fact, to spend his long and splendid manhood in trying to fight his way back to Rome. The second time that he saw the city was more than twenty years later, when, in 1848-49, he came armed to defend her. Then another eighteen years went by, and he saw her once more, from afar, in the Mentana campaign, but could not enter. Finally, as an old man, he followed in, when Victor Emmanuel had opened the way. And now, from his pedestal on the Janiculum, he seems to take his fill of the sight, of which he dreamed all his life long.

At the age of twenty-four (February 1832) he qualified officially as a merchant captain. But those were not times when such a man as Garibaldi had now become would long pursue a peaceful calling under a despotic Government. It was the era of the English Reform Bill ; of the Revolution that finally drove the Bourbons from France ; of the Carbonaro risings in Central Italy, associated in history with the name of the patriot Ciro Menotti. It was once again a moment such as 1789 had seemed to Wordsworth, when it was ' a joy to be alive '—though there

---

[1] *Mem.* II, 223. *Cuneo,* 15, shows that he had, before 1850, spoken to his friends of the profound impression made on him by this first visit to Rome. (See *Rule of the Monk,* i. 12, 13, on the Coliseum.)

were many Italian Liberals who did not experience that particular form of pleasure for long. The Austrians put down the momentarily successful revolutions in Central Italy, with the usual hecatomb of martyrs. Brave Menotti was hanged (1831). But on the ruins of the Carbonaro lodges the Association of ' Young Italy ' was at once formed by Mazzini, the student of Genoa.

The back-wash of these great events and movements of Western Europe met Garibaldi far across the waters of the Levant. In 1832 the young captain fell in with a group of Saint-Simonians, exiled from France, who indoctrinated him with their gentle revolutionary mysticism. Next year, in a port of the Black Sea, he found a man whom he was better fitted to assist, a young Genoese named Cuneo, one of Mazzini's original group, who told him of ' Young Italy,' and that it was his duty to join the Association. ' Columbus,' he says, ' was not as happy at the discovery of America, as I at finding a man actually engaged in the redemption of our country.' Cuneo, snatched thus suddenly to Garibaldi's heart, remained one of the best and closest friends of his early life, both in Europe and America, and in the year 1850 became his first biographer.[1]

On his return from this momentous voyage, Garibaldi hastened to Marseilles, where Mazzini was already living in exile after his first imprisonment. The two met here for the first time, and Garibaldi joined ' Young Italy assuming for the purposes of the Association the *nom de guerre* of ' Borel.' [2]

In the ' Manifesto of Young Italy,' issued by Mazzini in 1831,[3] we read that Italy must be founded on ' the three inseparable bases of Independence, Unity, and Liberty '— that is, the Austrian must go, the various small States must be united in one, and democratic government with liberty of opinion must be established. This dream has become solid fact, largely because of the zeal with which the missionaries of ' Young Italy ' in the 'thirties and 'forties secretly

[1] *Mem.* 14 ; *Cuneo*, 5, 6, 16 ; *Guerzoni*, i. 31–35.
[2] *Denkwürdigkeiten*, i. 17 ; *Mazzini*, i. 96, *note.*   [3] *Mazzini*, i. 67-9.

pushed their prohibited writings throughout the length and breadth of the Peninsula. Men who had never learnt from the Carbonari anything more definite than a passion for liberty, now heard of Italian unity, of democracy, of social reform. But the Mazzinian cult was more than a political programme, it was a religious and ethical movement, compelling men to a new life of self-sacrifice. It was as a publishing agency for its Chief that the 'Young Italy Association' did its great work. As a society for organising revolutions it was even more futile than the old Carbonari.[1]

One part of the new programme, which Mazzini considered essential, was destined to failure. The form of democratic government, he said, must be republican. Now, in the 'thirties constitutional monarchy was impossible for Italy, because there was no constitutional monarch; Cavour and Victor Emmanuel had not yet appeared, and indeed the first efforts of 'Young Italy' were actually directed against the House of Savoy, in whose Kingdom of Piedmont the movement had its birth. Victor Emmanuel's father, King Charles Albert, though he hated the Austrian and had visions of the ghost of Italy, had also strong clerical leanings, and was in his political nature autocratic rather than constitutional; at present he was fully in the league of Italian Governments, for the surveillance and suppression of Liberalism. He continued the censorship in the clerical and reactionary interest, so that in his dominions men read the books and papers of Liberal France at their peril, and by stealth. It had long been considered an offence in Mazzini that 'he walked by himself at night absorbed in thought'; the Governor of Genoa had complained of it to his father, saying: 'We don't like young people thinking without knowing the subject of their thoughts.'[3] In fact the Government was less odious than in other parts of the Peninsula, only because it was independent of the Austrian,

[1] *Farini* (i. 86) says of 'Young Italy,' to which he was hostile: 'A portion of the youth' (of the Roman States) 'learned its spirit and its formulas, and adopted its creed without enlisting in the sect.'
[2] *E.g., Roman MSS., F.R.*, 7, 17. [3] *King's Mazzini*, 18.

C

and because, ruling over a more conservative people, it had less often to resort to violence and espionage. But if ever Charles Albert was met by the spirit of revolt, he could show himself as cruel as a Bourbon, though, with characteristic uncertainty of purpose, the mystic allowed his conscience to brood over his cruelties even while he was committing them. And so, when in 1833 'Young Italy' began to conspire against him in earnest, a series of executions and tortures by courts-martial, which seem to have left a permanent shade of melancholy over the life of the King who ordered them, shocked Europe, and goaded the Mazzinians to a desperate attempt.[1]

The main plot began to ripen soon after Garibaldi joined the headquarters of the exiles at Marseilles. There were hopes that the soldiers would join the rebellion, for in the Piedmontese army, as in the French army of that date, there were liberal elements, originating in that contempt for the *ancien régime* and its representatives which victory under Napoleon's banners had taught to the Italian veterans. If in youth one has trampled on kings and monks, from Lisbon to Moscow, one does not crouch to them readily in later years. Besides, many to whom Napoleon had opened the career had been degraded in rank after the Restoration.[2] Relying on assistance from such malcontents, Mazzini, in February 1834, invaded Savoy from Swiss territory, with a cosmopolitan crowd of enthusiasts—Italians, Poles, Germans and French. Meanwhile the seductive Nizzard captain, with the open countenance and long curling locks of chestnut-gold, had been sent to Genoa to win over the fleet to revolution ; he deliberately entered the Royal Navy with the object of corrupting it from its allegiance.

Although Garibaldi undertook his first venture against tyranny with the readiness that he so often showed when asked to run his head against a wall, this was not one of those walls that so miraculously fell before him. As no one rose, either in the sea-ports or on the

---

[1] *Della Rocca*, 30, 36.   [2] *Ibid.* 12.

Swiss border, Mazzini in a few days was back in Switzerland ; while Garibaldi, disguised as a peasant, escaped from Genoa and stole across the mountains to Nice, and thence safely into France. The first time he ever read his name in print was when, on reaching Marseilles, he saw in the papers that the Piedmontese Government had condemned him to death, a proceeding which it is difficult to blame if we consider that he was known to the authorities only as a sailor who had entered the Royal service in order to betray it. When we think that if a few turns of the dice had gone differently, the father of Victor Emmanuel would have succeeded in snuffing out the lives of Mazzini and Garibaldi at this point, we may see that history is something far more wonderful than a process of evolution which science can estimate or predict.

When, in 1864, Garibaldi came to our island to receive, as the redeemer of Italy and the chosen hero of England, an ovation so tremendous that it frightened Europe and even Palmerston himself, on one of those festal occasions he ' looked through all the roaring and the wreaths ' where sat a certain patient, neglected figure, come among the rest to honour him, and his heart went back thirty years to the days when, as a young merchant captain, he had first seen Mazzini at Marseilles. Since then bitter quarrels had divided them; but the sight of his old friend overwhelmed all meaner thoughts of him.

' I rise,' said Garibaldi to the assembled company, ' to make a declaration which I ought to have made long since. There is a man here amongst us who has rendered the greatest services to our country and to the cause of freedom. When I was a youth and had only aspirations towards good, I sought for one able to act as the guide and counsellor of my youthful years. I sought such a guide as one who is athirst seeks the water-spring. I found this man. He alone watched when all around slept, he alone kept and fed the sacred flame. . . . This man is Joseph Mazzini: he is my friend and teacher.' [1]

[1] *Mario, Supplement*, 372. During the same visit of 1864, they met in the Isle of Wight. ' As soon as Garibaldi saw Mazzini he greeted him in the

Having made the ports of Europe too hot to hold him, Garibaldi disappeared from the Old World for twelve years (1836–48), to reappear famous when next his country had need of him.   Shortly after the fiasco at Genoa, he found it best to carry his fortunes to South America, whither, then, as now, Italians, discontented with their prospects at home, often betook themselves.   The Pilgrim Fathers of that epoch, who showed modern Italy the way to her New World, were not numerous, but they were choice.   Many were political exiles.   As the friend and hero of these, Garibaldi there learned war and leadership :

> Having first within his ken
> What a man might do with men.

Scarcely had he landed in South America (1836) when he formed one of the great friendships of his youth with the Genoese exile Rossetti.   They became like David and Jonathan.   Having set up together in Rio Janeiro as merchants, for nine months they traded in a little vessel along the eastern coasts of the Continent.   But Garibaldi was already discontented with 'the inglorious arts of peace.' 'We are destined for greater things,' he wrote to Cuneo, in December 1836.[1]   At length, on the invitation of another Italian exile, he took service under the infant Republic of Rio Grande do Sul, which was then beginning a struggle for independence against the Brazilian Empire.[2]   As the Republicans had not yet got a ship at sea, the appeal touched Garibaldi's sympathies to the quick, and so in his thirtieth year, for the first time in his life, he turned his hand to war, as a buccaneer with letters of marque from the rebel government.   He and his friend Rossetti armed a

old *patois* of the lagoons of Genoa.   It affected Mazzini, to whom it brought back scenes of their early career, when the inspiration of Italian freedom first began.'—*Holyoake*, i. 239.   *Guerzoni*, ii. 352, 360.

[1] *Cuneo*, 18 ; *Epistolario*, 3.

[2] 'A strong Spanish element existed in that province (Rio Grande), and it was not disposed to settle down quietly under Portuguese Imperialism, when their co-patriots a few miles farther south (in Uruguay) were enjoying Republican Institutions.'—*Winnington-Ingram*, 93.   Brazil conquered, after a long and exhausting struggle.

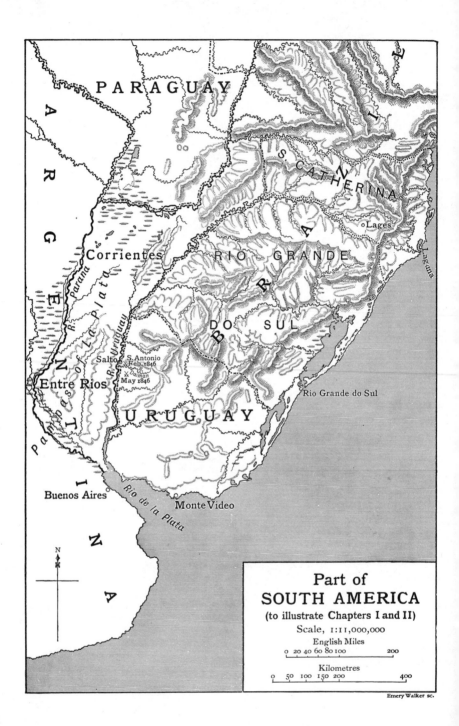

Part of
SOUTH AMERICA
(to illustrate Chapters I and II)

Scale, 1:11,000,000

English Miles

0 20 40 60 80 100   200

Kilometres

0   50   100 150 200   400

Emery Walker sc.

fishing boat, and therein set out with a dozen companions
to wage war alone against the giant Empire of Brazil, 'the
first to unfurl on those southern coasts the Republican
banner of Rio Grande, a banner of freedom.'[1] Well was
the little boat called *Mazzini*. But they soon changed it
for a larger ship which they had captured, and continued
the struggle with ever-increasing success.

Gradually Garibaldi's warfare became amphibious, and
before long, celebrated as he was for his exploits at sea,
he was yet more celebrated as a guerilla chief, leading
bodies of a few hundred, sometimes a few thousand men,
across the vast upland plains and forests and river gorges
of the Continent, that lay between the Atlantic and the
Parana River. The cavalry, who were often the more
numerous arm, were natives of the wilderness, horsemen
born and bred, and magnificently mounted; hardy and
resourceful as the Boers, they had more dash, and liked
close quarters. Their favourite weapon was the lance;
though many used the sabre, together with the lasso or the
bolas, hunting the enemy and casting at him, as they had
learnt to do in pursuit of the swift-footed ostrich.[2] Otherwise the warfare must in many respects have resembled
the warfare on the veldt. It was necessary to traverse
enormous distances across country, far from the haunts
of man; to need no food but the cattle which the troops
drove with them and slaughtered at meal time, roasting
the flesh Homerically on green spits;[3] yet always to know
the whereabouts and strength of the enemy, to fall on him
when he was weaker, and when he was stronger to vanish
into space over the prairie or hide in the dense tropical
forests. Garibaldi, after he had faced the French and
Austrian armies, declared that no civilised troops were
such skilled horsemen, so Spartan in their endurance of a

[1] *Mem.* 16.

[2] More properly called the Rhea Americana; for an account of the bird and
this method of hunting it, see *The Naturalist in La Plata*, W. H. Hudson,
26, 27. See also note, p. 23 below, on ostrich hunting and the *bolas*.

[3] Garibaldi in 1849 declared that he had 'lived on flesh and water for five
years' in America.—*Roman MSS. Batt. Univ.; Garibaldi's Cantoni*, 269-270.

campaign, or so courageous in their onset, as the *Gaucho* and *Matrero* Spaniards and half-breeds, or the freed negro horse-breakers, whom he led to these nameless scuffles in the wilderness.[1]

The 'bright breezy uplands' of Southern Brazil and Uruguay are more fitted for guerilla achievements than the dead level of the Pampas proper, which stretches away south and west of the Plata River towards the Andes. For the provinces over which Garibaldi ranged and fought, for the most part consist of an undulating plateau, raised high on a barrier of precipices above the sea level, cut by deep river gorges filled with forests for refuge, and traversed by ridges whence a soldier's eye could scan vast tracts of country and locate enemies and friends.[2]

These new scenes and actions stirred Garibaldi's blood, touched his imagination, called out his latent qualities, and for awhile satisfied his exuberant being. In his old age, as he sat brooding, restless, discontented with the adoration of his countrymen whom he had freed, and the applause of the world whose heart he had made to throb, the old man looked back with fond regret on those days of youth and strength and speed, on the still virgin plains, among the noble wild animals, and the noble wild men who had followed him in war :

'The vast undulating plains of Uruguay (he says) present a landscape entirely new to a European, and more particularly to an Italian, accustomed from childhood to a country where every inch of ground is covered with houses, hedges, or other labour of man's hands. . . . The plains are covered with short grass except along the course of the *arroyos* (streamlets), or in the *canadas* (dips in the ground) overgrown with *maciega* (a tall, reed-like grass). The banks of the rivers and the sides of the *arroyos* are covered with fine woods, often containing timber of a tolerable size. These lands, so favoured by nature, are inhabited chiefly by horses and cattle, antelopes and ostriches. Man, here a veritable centaur, rarely visits them.

---

[1] *Mem. passim*, *e.g.* pt. i. chaps. xxv. xxxix. ; and pt. ii. chap. ix. p. 241.
[2] *R. G. S. P.*, viii. 364, 5, and map ; Hudson's *Naturalist*, 2–5.

'What a handsome fellow is the stallion of the Pampas! His lips have never winced at the iron bit, and his glossy back, never crossed by a rider, shines like a diamond in the sun. His flowing, uncombed mane floats over his flanks when, assembling in his pride the scattered mares, or flying from human pursuit, he outruns the wind.

.   .   .   .

'Who can conceive the feelings awakened in the heart of a buccaneer of twenty-five [1] by his first sight of that untamed nature? To-day, December 20, 1871, bending with stiffened limbs over the fire, I recall with emotion those scenes of the past, when life seemed to smile on me, in the presence of the most magnificent spectacle I ever beheld. I for my part am old and worn. Where are those splendid horses? Where are the bulls, the antelopes, the ostriches which beautified and enlivened those pleasant hills? Their descendants no doubt will still roam over those fertile pastures, and will do so till steam and iron come to increase the riches of the soil, but destroy those marvellous scenes of nature.[2]'

Garibaldi had, perhaps, the most romantic life that history records, for it had all the trappings as well as the essence of romance. Though he lived in the nineteenth

---

[1] He was really about thirty when he first visited these upland plateaus.

[2] *Mem.* 20–22. Here is an account of a typical hunt after the South American ostrich (*rhea*), *Robertson's Paraguay*, i. 238–240:

'With crest erect and angry eye, towering above all herbage, our game flew from us, by the combined aid of wings and limbs, at the rate of sixteen miles an hour. The chase lasted half of that time, when an Indian *peon*, starting ahead of the close phalanx of his mounted competitors, whirled his *bolas*, with admirable grace and dexterity, around his head, and with deadly aim flung them over the half-running, half-flying, but now devoted ostrich. Irretrievably entangled, down came the giant bird, rolling, fluttering, panting, and, being in an instant despatched, the company of the field stripped him of his feathers and stuck them in their girdles.' Garibaldi must in his day have witnessed many such chases. He and his followers in Italy in 1848–49 wore ostrich feathers in their hats, perhaps in memory of their friend the *rhea* of South America.

On p. 239, Robertson says: 'The *bolas*, next to the lasso, are the *gaucho's* most formidable weapon. They consist of three round heavy stones, each about the size of a large orange, covered with hide, and attached to three plaited thongs, which diverge from each other, and form a centre, every thong being about five feet in length. These, when thrown with unerring aim, as they almost invariably are, at the legs of an animal at full speed, twist and entangle themselves around them, and bring him with a terrible impulse to the ground.'

century, it was yet his fortune never to take full part in the common prose life of civilized men, and so he never understood it, though he moved it profoundly, like a great wind blowing off an unknown shore. He never had education, either intellectual, diplomatic, or political; even his military training was that of the guerilla chief; nor, till he was past learning, did he experience the ordinary life of the settled citizen. Though all must acknowledge that, by the secret ordering of the mysteries of birth, he had been created with more in him of the divine than any training can give, yet we cannot fail to perceive, in studying the slight records of the first forty years of his life, how much the natural tendencies of his genius, in their strength and in their weakness, were enhanced by circumstance.

And so, when in 1848 he returned to fight for Italy, in the full strength of matured manhood—at the time of life when Cromwell first drew sword—he had been sheltered, ever since he went to sea at fifteen, from every influence which might have turned him into an ordinary man or an ordinary soldier.

‑He had had two schools—the seas of romance, and the plateaus of South America. He had lived on ship-board and in the saddle. The man who loved Italy as even she has seldom been loved, scarcely knew her. The soldier of modern enlightenment was himself but dimly enlightened. Rather, his mind was like a vast sea cave, filled with the murmur of dark waters at flow and the stirring of nature's greatest forces, lit here and there by streaks of glorious sunshine bursting in through crevices hewn at random in its rugged sides. He had all the distinctive qualities of the hero, in their highest possible degree, and in their very simplest form. Courage and endurance without limit; tenderness to man and to all living things, which was never blunted by a life-time of war in two hemispheres among combatants often but half civilized; the power to fill men with ardour by his presence and to stir them by his voice to great deeds; but above all the passion to be striking a blow for the oppressed, a passion which could not be quenched by failure, nor checked by reason, nor sated by success, old age, and the worship of the world.

These qualities, perhaps, could not have existed in a degree so pre-eminent, in the person either of a sage or of a saint. Without, on the one hand, the child-like simplicity that often degenerated into folly, and on the other hand, the full store of common human passions that made him one with the multitude, he could never have been so ignorant of despair and doubt, so potent to overawe his enemies, to spread his own infectious daring among his followers and to carry men blindfold into enterprises which would have been madness under any other chief. The crowning work of his life was in 1860, when he landed with a thousand ill-armed volunteers in the Island of Sicily, to overcome a garrison of 24,000 well-armed and well-disciplined men. Moltke could no more have conquered Sicily with such means, than Garibaldi could have planned the battle of Sedan.

Such was the hero in victory. But this book is a study of the hero in defeat; it is the story of Garibaldi in 1849, and before it can be told, it is necessary to introduce the heroine, his Anita.

CHAPTER II

Oh verdi, interminabili, deserte
distese della Pampa ! oh pascolanti
saure, del fren della sua mano esperte !

Ivi ella crebbe con l' alte erbe ondanti,
ivi Ei le apparve, biondo come il sole,
e la guardò con gli occhi scintillanti . . .
MARRADI.—Rapsodia Garibaldina.

IT was part of Italy's good luck in Garibaldi, that, thanks
to his splendid physique and to his singular fortune in the
thick of battle, he survived the perils of these dozen years
of buccaneering and guerilla war, under conditions that
would have killed a weaker man, even without the inter-
vention of a bullet.[1] But her other children fell fast
around him. Rossetti, and many exiles worthy of her love
and gratitude, perished one after the other by shipwreck or
by the sword, and their bones were lost in the ocean, or
buried in the strange land. Garibaldi grieved deeply till
the end of his life that their graves were unmarked, and
their memories unknown to the country for whom they
had given up all and gone to die so far away. They were,
indeed, more truly her martyrs than martyrs of those Re-

---

[1] *Ferri N.A., April* 1889, 432. He survived the dangers, not only of shipwreck and of battle, of starvation and of exposure in those vast unreclaimed
lands, but even the tender mercies of his enemies ; once, early in his South
American career, he endured two hours of torture, hung up by his wrists from
the beams in the prison ceiling, while the jeering populace looked on through
the doorway. 'Such agonies,' he says, 'cannot be described.' When his tor-
turer (Millan) afterwards fell into his hands, he astonished his South American
followers by refusing to see the man, and by ordering him to be set free on the
spot. *Mem.* 32 ; *Cuneo,* 22 ; *Guerzoni,* i. 76 ; *Dumas,* i. 106.

publics in whose service they fell. Their forgotten names are not inscribed, like those of their successors, on the municipal tablets of famous Italian cities, for they lived in days when to love Italy was to burn with unrequited love.

Garibaldi had no fear of death, but he had a poetic horror of the oblivion that too soon overtakes the memory of the brave. Once, in the early years of his American buccaneering, when he himself, struck down on deck by a bullet, lay for several days at the point of death, he besought one of his friends to bury him on land, earnestly entreating, in the words of Ugo Foscolo, for

> ' a stone
> To mark my bones from the unnumbered bones
> Which o'er the fields and waves are sown by death.'[1]

Not long after that, he was shipwrecked, and though his famous powers of swimming brought him safe to land, several of his dear Italian friends sank before his eyes, in spite of his efforts to save them. Thrown ashore, in the Brazilian Province of Santa Caterina, he and his amphibious following at once took part as soldiers in the capture of the important town of Laguna ; they were welcomed as liberators by the Republican inhabitants, and Garibaldi was sent on board the captured fleet of the Imperialists, where it rode in the lagoon that gives its name to the city. It was in the year 1839. He paced up and down the deck of his newly acquired flagship, ' the top-sail schooner *Itaparica*, of seven guns,' but he was in no victor's mood. The recent loss of so many friends had struck him with melancholy, and he began to feel the loneliness of his life. His heart turned to the natural remedy. The ladies of the Central States of South America, both in the towns and in the up-country ranches, combined many of the exquisite graces of old Spanish refinement and courtesy with the

[1] *Mem.* 28 ; *Cuneo*, 20.

> ' un sasso
> Che distingua le mie dalle infinite
> Ossa che in terra e in mar semina morte.'
> *Dei Sepolcri*, lines 13-15.

greater freedom and hardihood of a race of settlers in a new and spacious land ; nor was the love of letters and poetry by any means wanting among them. Since this favourable opinion was formed by staid English merchants, who travelled widely in these regions, and had intimate dealings with its inhabitants, it is not surprising to find that it was also the experience of the susceptible and romantic child of the Mediterranean.[1] In the course of his roving life he had been, several times, furiously, but briefly, in love. He felt that he must now win for himself an object on which he could fix his affections. His own artless narrative is alone worthy to introduce Anita :

'The loss of Luigi, Edoardo, and others of my countrymen, left me utterly isolated ; I felt quite alone in the world. . . . I needed a human heart to love me, one that I could keep always near me. I felt that unless I found one immediately, life would become intolerable. . . . By chance I cast my eyes towards the houses of the Barra, a tolerably high hill on the south side of the entrance to the lagoon, where a few simple and picturesque dwellings were visible. Outside one of these, by means of the telescope I usually carried with me when on deck, I espied a young woman, and forthwith gave orders for the boat to be got out, as I wished to go ashore.'

The girl, whose dark features and hair, virile carriage and determined face he had examined to such good purpose through his telescope, may or may not have been watching the handsome figure on the deck. At least she knew well enough who Garibaldi was, and what deeds he had done ; for he was already to the rebels of Brazil what he afterwards became to his countrymen in Europe, and he had just taken part in the liberation of Anita's native town. Her name was Anita Riberas ; she was a maiden of eighteen years of age, and her father had betrothed, or, at any rate, promised her, to a suitor whom she could not love.

Meanwhile Garibaldi was being rowed ashore :

'I landed, and, making for the houses where I expected to find the object of my excursion, I had just given up hope of

[1] *Robertson's P.*, i. 105-7, 199-206 : *Mem.* 23-4.

seeing her again, when I met an inhabitant of the place whose acquaintance I had made soon after our arrival.

'He invited me to take coffee in his house ; we entered, and the first person who met my eyes was the damsel who had attracted me ashore. . . . We both remained enraptured and silent, gazing on one another like two people who meet not for the first time, and seek in each other's faces something which makes it easier to recall the forgotten past. At last I greeted her by saying, *Tu devi esser mia*, " Thou oughtest to be mine." I could speak but little Portuguese, and uttered the bold words in Italian. Yet my insolence was magnetic. I had formed a tie, pronounced a decree, which death alone could annul.'

The story of so sudden a wooing is out of the common ; but he and she were both very far out of the common. Garibaldi's rash pledging of himself for life to one whom he knew so little is consonant with his character, and has a close parallel in an action of his later life which chanced to be as unfortunate as this chanced to be happy. He read in Anita's face and bearing the clear imprint of all those Amazonian qualities of mind and body that made her, in fact, the only possible wife worthy, or able, to bear him company in flood and field, and mate his adventurous spirit at its own level. She, a woman most direct and valiant, highly strung, too, by the prospect of the forced marriage that awaited her, suddenly saw face to face the Hero of her time and country, with his lion-like head and flowing mane of gold, come as her deliverer, armed with the irresistible might of his will. Who, indeed, would have wished to resist, when love flashed from those ' small piercing eyes,' ' full of smouldering fire,' and sounded in that voice, so ' calm and deliberate,' yet ' low and veiled, almost tremulous with inner emotion ' ? [1]

That power of personal attraction and moral dominion over others, with which Garibaldi seems to have been

[1] 'Probably a human face so like a lion, and still retaining the humanity nearest the image of its Maker, was never seen ' (*Martinengo Cesaresco's ' Italy,'* 148). The description of his eyes and voice is from *Haweis's* recollections of 1860.

endowed beyond any man of modern times, was in great part due to something in his voice and to something in his eyes. Written and oral traditions alike record the peculiar manner in which the light of those eyes changed when he was deeply moved. General Mitre, who knew him in his South American days, wrote of him thus :

'His face was quiet and grave, and his smile appeared on it without altering that character. His blue eyes alone revealed his emotions, by taking on a dark colour like that of the sea, which while it remains quiet nurses the tempest which is brooding in its depths.'[1]

Under this spell, Anita in a moment gave away for ever her heart, her soul, and her life.

There was no hope that her other suitor would forgo his claim, favoured as it was by her father, and since in those rough times and lands possession was nine points of the law, Garibaldi, a few nights later, came back and carried her off on board his ship, under the protection of his guns and mariners. The story of that cutting-out expedition has never been told in any further detail, nor is it possible to say whether secrecy sufficed or whether force was necessary.

Such was the beginning of a love story of nearly ten years of married life which none of the world's famous legends of love surpass in romance and beauty. But it closed in the tragedy among the marshes of Ravenna. The horrors of the hour when she died in his arms, a martyr to Italy and to him, for awhile darkened his spirit, so that he failed to see how splendid he had made her life, how bright was the place her life and death would take in his country's history. In this mood he bitterly reproached himself— but no one clearly knows for what :

'I had come upon a forbidden treasure, but yet a treasure of great price. If guilt there was, it was mine alone. And there was guilt. Two hearts were joined in infinite love; but an

---

[1] *La Patria*, June 19, 1904. Dunne told Countess Martinengo Cesaresco that his eyes ' became intensely black when he was excited.'

innocent existence was shattered. She is dead ; I am wretched ; and he is avenged, yes, avenged ! On the day when, vainly hoping to bring her back to life, I clasped the hand of a corpse, with bitter tears of despair, then I knew the evil I had wrought. I sinned greatly, but I sinned alone.' [1]

The publication of these words for awhile led many to suppose that Garibaldi had gone off with another man's wife. But the evidence of his South American friends, the terms of his marriage certificate, and the traditions of the Garibaldi family, have made it clear that this was not the case. Anita Riberas was about to be married against her will to a man whom she did not love, so she was carried off by Garibaldi, and had a perfect right to go with him. But there would seem to be some mysterious event, hinted at by Garibaldi in these words, which he was never willing to explain.[2]

Anita and her lover were legally married as soon as they returned from the wilderness to civilisation, at Monte Video, after an enforced delay of more than two years.[3] Their sudden resolve to cast in their lot together, though it was the rash inspiration of a moment, was approved by time. Neither of these remarkable persons could ever have married any one else on equal terms. The elopement with Anita was the Sicilian expedition of Garibaldi's private life ; and for Italy, too, he had won a heroine and a story.

She was not by birth or nature an Italian, but had in her veins the fighting blood of the race that ruled on horse-back the deserts of Brazil. It had been the custom of her father to take her about with him on his fishing and hunting expeditions.[4] This Amazon was ' a Creole born, but with all the engaging manners of the *señoritas* of old Spain.

[1] *Mem.* 56.

[2] I have had the honour of talking on this subject to General Canzio, Gari-baldi's son-in-law, the husband of Teresita, worthy, as one of the bravest of the Thousand, of that relationship. (See *Guerzoni*, i. 94–95 ; *Mario, Supplement*, 44–47 ; *Gironi*, 8–11 ; *Anita N.A.*, Dec. 1905, p. 573, and note of *Dumas*, i. 154.)

[3] The marriage certificate is dated Church of St. Francis of Assisi, Monte Video, March 26, 1842 (*Guerzoni*, i. 152, 377–378).

[4] *Anita N.A.*, cxx. 573 (Ricciotti Garibaldi's evidence).

She had become, from the habits of her country, a splendid horse-woman, and it was a sight to be remembered,' wrote a British naval officer, who saw her in 1846, 'as she rode a curvetting animal by the side of her husband.' [1]   Like him, she was tender as well as brave, and her only uncontrolled passion was that love for which she risked her life so often, and lost it at the end.   She was an excellent mother, except that she finally chose to die for her husband rather than to live for her children.

Garibaldi's companions in arms, the cultivated Europeans in the Italian campaign, no less than the fighting men in South America, adored her, when she talked with them round the camp fires, when she nursed them in sickness, and when she rallied their breaking ranks on the field of battle.

So these two sailed away, and spent their honeymoon in amphibious warfare along the coast and in the lagoons, fighting at close quarters against desperate odds.   In her first severe action Anita was knocked down on deck by a cannon-ball, on the top of three dead men.   Her husband rushed to her side, but she was already on her feet, and as active as though nothing had happened to discompose her.[2] On another occasion, during Garibaldi's absence on shore, she was the soul of the battle until his return.[3]

Before long they were ranging the hills again, far inland, at the head of the Republican armies :

'Anita was my treasure, and no less zealous than myself for the sacred cause of nations, and for a life of adventure. She looked upon battles as a pleasure, and the hardships of camp life as a pastime; so that, however things might turn out, the future smiled on us, and the vast American deserts which unrolled themselves before our gaze seemed all the more delightful and beautiful for their wildness.' [4]

[1] *Winnington-Ingram*, 93.

[2] *Denkwürdigkeiten*, ii. 128, 129.   This book (iv.) is the only book of Part II. which is written by Garibaldi.   It gives more details of Anita's conduct than the *Memorie* (*q.v.* pp. 59, 60, chap. xix. of Part I.).

[3] *Denkwürdigkeiten*, ii. 132-134 ; *Mem.* 63, 64.   [4] *Mem.* 65.

What spaces of earth and sky, what speed, what freedom, what glory of life and love were theirs, as they galloped side by side, and slept under the homely stars.

In one of their earliest land battles, which went ill for the men of Rio Grande, she was captured by the Imperialists, and believed that Garibaldi was among the slain. She obtained leave to search for him, and turned over one corpse after another, expecting in each dead face to see the features of the man whom she loved. When she found that he had not been left on the field, she determined to effect her own escape and rejoin him at all hazards. Slipping away unnoticed from among her drunken guards, she plunged into the tropical forest on a high-spirited horse which she had obtained from a peasant, crossed sixty miles of the most dangerous deserts in America, alone, without food, swimming great rivers in flood by holding on to her horse, riding through hostile pickets at the passes of the hills and the fords of the streams, who took the wild Amazon for an apparition and ran away in panic. After four days she reached Lages, where her husband soon joined her.[1]

Among such scenes their first child was born; they called him Menotti, after the martyred leader of the Italian revolutions of 1831. Between their elopement and his birth they had had no rest and no civilised life, but had been wandering over the sea and the wilderness. Anita had been present at several battles, and endured on horseback all the worst hardships of campaigning up to the time of her confinement (September 16, 1840). Next, she had to fly into the wilderness with her infant of twelve days upon the saddle-bow. She and Garibaldi spent the rainy season wandering, with dwindling forces, in a state little better than that of outlaws, in the depth of the primæval forest, where alone they were safe from the victorious armies of Brazil. Food ran short, for in the forest the lasso was of no avail; the rain fell on them unceasingly, whether

---

[1] *Denkwürdigkeiten*, ii. 138, 140 (Garibaldi's own narrative). He had told the same story in Anita's presence in July 1849 (see p. 247 below); and it was then recorded by Hoffstetter, who was in the audience. *Hoff.* 339, 340.

they marched or camped; the infant almost died of cold.

'Anita,' writes her husband, 'was in constant terror at the thought of losing our Menotti, and indeed it was a miracle that we saved him. In the steepest parts of the track, and when crossing the torrents, I carried him, then three months old, slung from my neck by a handkerchief, trying to keep him warm against my breast and with my breath.'[1]

This sort of Robin Hood life could not go on for ever, and Garibaldi perceived that he must choose between the service of Rio Grande and his duties to Anita and Menotti. Remembering that Rio Grande was not the land that had a lien on his life and family and everything that was his, he determined, at the beginning of 1842, to return to civilisation, and seek a peaceful home in Monte Video, the capital of the Republic of Uruguay, set at the point where the ocean-going ships enter the Rio de la Plata. He managed, on his way thither, to lose a fine herd of cattle, the wages of his six years' warfare, arrived at Monte Video with nothing in the world besides three hundred cattle hides, not a dear commodity in those regions, and was fain to earn a precarious livelihood for his family as shipbroker and teacher of mathematics. But, though diligent, he was not successful in the arts of peace, and he was glad, a few months later, to be again fighting in a new quarrel.

Rosas, the celebrated 'tyrannos' of the rival Republic of Argentina (Buenos Ayres), on the other side of the Rio de la Plata, threatened Uruguay (Monte Video), whose rulers appealed to the famous stranger within their gates. He helped to make them a navy, and taught it how to fight. But that was not all. Monte Video contained a large foreign population of French and Italians, and from the latter Garibaldi raised his 'Italian Legion,' to show the jeering Frenchmen what his compatriots could do in war.

---

[1] *Mem.* 91 : *Denkwürdigkeiten*, ii. 141, 143.

1.   2.

1. ONE OF THE ORIGINAL ' RED SHIRTS.'   GARIBALDI'S, OR ITALIAN LEGION
OF MONTEVIDEO, 1846. THE BLOUSE IS RED.

2. MONTEVIDEAN SOLDIER WITH ' PONCHO' (CLOAK).

(Admiral Winnington-Ingram's *Hearts of Oak*, pp. 86, 87.)

This Italian Legion of Monte Video was the origin of the Garibaldians proper. It was the first considerable body of his countrymen whom he ever commanded on land; most of the men were political exiles; it was they who first wore the famous 'red shirt'[1]; and those of them who came back with him to Europe in 1848 imported the Garibaldian dress, tradition, and methods in war and politics. The idea with which they enlisted was to fight for the liberties of Monte Video in return for the shelter it had given them, refusing all rich rewards; but the idea behind was to prepare for another struggle, which, as Garibaldi said, he had never forgotten even ' in the depths of the American forests.' They carried ' a black flag with a volcano in the midst—symbol of Italy mourning, with the sacred fire in her heart; ' this banner can to-day be seen in the Conservatori Museum on the Roman Capitol.[2]

In the formation and training of this force, which started a tradition afterwards so important in the history of Europe, Garibaldi was assisted by the veteran patriot Anzani, to whom he deferred more than to any other man in the course of his life. An exile from his country since 1821, Anzani had fought for liberty in Greece, Spain, Portugal, and Brazil, and it was Garibaldi's belief that if he had lived to fight for Italy he would have shown the world that he was

---

[1] The reason why the red shirt was originally chosen for the Italian Legion of Monte Video is not known with certainty. But an extremely probable, because very prosaic, solution of the problem is as follows:

' Its adoption,' writes Admiral *Winnington-Ingram* (93), who was in Monte Video as a young man in 1846, 'was caused by the necessity of clothing as economically as possible the newly raised Legion, and a liberal offer having been made by a mercantile house in Monte Video to sell to the Government, at reduced prices, a stock of red woollen shirts that had been intended for the Buenos Ayres market, which was now closed by the blockade established there, it was thought too good a chance to be neglected, and the purchase was, therefore, effected. These goods had been intended to be worn by those employed in the "Saladéros," or great slaughtering and salting establishments for cattle at Ensenada, and other places in the Argentine provinces, as they made good winter clothing, and by their colour disguised in a measure the bloody work the men had in hand.'

[2] *Mario* (ed. 1905) 60, for photograph of the flag; *Mario, Supp.* 52; *La Patria*, Jan. 9, 1905, as to the authenticity of the flag.

one of the very greatest of her sons.[1]   Another of his most
trusted lieutenants was a handsome young Milanese exile, of
the name of Medici; having served his apprenticeship as a
warrior of liberty in the Carlist wars, he had been in England
and become intimate with Mazzini, and had now come to
South America to make his living as a merchant or, as he
himself afterwards declared, merely because of weakness in
his lungs which could not endure the English climate.   But,
arrived in America, he again took to fighting, attracted by
the reputation of Garibaldi, of whom he had heard as the
rising hope of the Mazzinian circle in Europe.   The chief at
once reposed his confidence in the new-comer, and never
had reason to withdraw it, throughout the wars and revolutions of many famous years.[2]   \

The Italian Legion saved Monte Video.   They took the
leading part in the battles close round the capital, when, in
1843 and again in 1846, the enemy pressed the siege hard.[3]
At other times they were pre-eminent as the heroes of the
distant war along the banks of the Uruguay River, where
unnumbered herds of cattle and horses wandered at liberty
over the vast ranches of the gauchos, the magnificent but
half-savage patriarchs of that rich wilderness.[4]   The left
bank of the river was preserved for Monte Video in the early
part of 1846, by a few hundred of the Italian infantry
under Garibaldi, who defeated Rosas' linesmen, and formed
an impregnable rock amid the swarms of wild gaucho
horsemen, who, armed with spears, sabres, and lassos,
carried on the war between the two Republics.[5]   The

[1] Guerzoni, i. 169; Mem. 190-1; Mario, Supp. 52, 53.

[2] Pasini, 7-13; Ottolini, 18, 19; Guerzoni, i. 203-5; Elia, i. 30, 31; La
Patria, June 19, 1904; Bizzoni, 262

[3] For the siege of 1846, of which less is said by Italian authorities, see the
long account by Winnington-Ingram, especially pp. 91, 92, for Garibaldi's
important part in it.

[4] Robertson's P., i. 197-257; S. A., i. 252, 253.

[5] Cuneo, 33-35.   Mem. i. chap. xlv. xlvi.; on p. 176 Garibaldi writes:
'I have heard our lads (in Europe) cry " Cavalry, cavalry ! " and, I am ashamed
to say, throw down their arms and fly, often at a false alarm.   Cavalry ! Why,
the Italians at Sant' Antonio and the Dayman (battles on the Uruguay) laughed
at the first cavalry in the world, though in those days they had nothing but bad
flint-lock guns.'

[6] Robertson (P. i. 82) describes Rosas riding at the head of ' about 6,000 as

'GAUCHO' CAVALRYMAN IN SERVICE OF MONTEVIDEO, 1846
(Admiral Winnington-Ingram's *Hearts of Oak*, p. 90.)

most notable of these actions, fought against immensely superior numbers, was the battle of Sant' Antonio, near Salto (February, 1846), the fame of which spread to Europe.

During these wars of Monte Video, Anita stayed in the capital and minded her growing family. She proved as admirable a mother and housekeeper as she had been a warrior;[1] it was a hard struggle against poverty, for her husband always shared what little he had with others, while at the same time he refused the rewards of land, rank and wealth, eagerly proffered by the state which he had saved. In 1843 one of the most respectable merchants of Monte Video called the attention of the Minister of War to the fact that

'in the house of Garibaldi, the commander of the Italian Legion and of the national fleet, the man to whom Monte Video owed its life from day to day, no light was lit after sundown, because candles were not comprised in the soldier's ration, the only thing Garibaldi had to live on. The Minister thereupon sent, by his aide-de-camp, G. M. Torres, a hundred *patacconi* (500 francs) to Garibaldi, who, keeping half this sum, gave back the other half in order that it should be sent to the house of a widow, who, according to him, had more need of it. Fifty *patacconi* (250 francs) was the only money that Garibaldi had from the Republic. While he remained among us his family lived in poverty; he was never dressed differently from the soldiers; often his friends had to resort to subterfuges to make him change his worn-out clothes. He had all the inhabitants of Monte Video for his friends; never was a man there more universally loved, and it was only natural.'[2]

Of this period several stories are told, as humorous as they are touching: how the saviour of Monte Video came home one evening wrapped up to the chin, having given away his only shirt to an old legionary who had even more need of

good cavalry as could well take the field. It was a motley group as regards uniform; but for men and horses it was beyond all doubt a most efficient corps.' 'Rosas,' adds Robertson, 'had not 500 infantry to co-operate with his 6,000 cavalry.' This was some years previous to his wars against Garibaldi.

[1] *Denkwürdigkeiten*, ii. 143.

[2] *Guerzoni*, i. 209—from 'Pacheco y Obes,' 1849.

it than he ; how Anita was almost weeping, one day, to find
that the last three little coins had vanished from the recess
where she kept the family horde, till her warrior confessed that
he had stolen them to buy their little girl a toy, and Teresita
herself appeared in the doorway brandishing the trophy in
exculpation of the offender ; how he appeared one day on
parade with his golden locks close shorn, because the
universal and passionate adoration of him by the ladies
of Monte Video distressed Anita, and he had, for her relief,
despoiled his beauty.[1]

Garibaldi often visited his friends of the British Legation, but they noticed that he always came late at night,
until at last one of them ventured to say to him : ' Why
do you not come in the daytime ? You are always sure of
a welcome here.' Garibaldi in reply flung back his *poncho*,
and revealed the scanty condition of his clothing ; though
he might at that period have been well off, he was living in
rags rather than take the money of the struggling Republic.[2]

Towards the end of his residence in Monte Video he
refused rewards of land from the Government, and persuaded his Legionaries to· endure this self-chosen poverty,[3]
partly as an example of Republican virtue, much needed in
those latitudes, and partly in order that they should always
be morally free to throw up their engagements and return
to Italy at the shortest possible notice. Garibaldi was
getting ever more impatient to be gone. He always retained
a warm feeling for the people of Uruguay as ' a very lovable
people ' (*ben caro popolo*), but he was beginning to see
through their politicians. The sordid personal ambitions,
never far below the surface in South American affairs, soon
showed themselves in such a way that even Garibaldi,
with all his idealisation of a Republic battling for freedom,
could no longer be blind to them.[4]

Ever since his landing in America, whenever he was

---

[1] *Anita, N.A.*, 577, 584 ; *Guerzoni*, i. 379.

[2] Information given to Mr. John Ward by the late Mr. Vere Foster, formerly
attaché of the British Legation of Montevideo.

[3] *La Patria*, June 19, 1904, for details.   [4] *Mem.* 168, 186.

not buried in the wilderness, Garibaldi had been in constant touch with ' Young Italy,' corresponding under his old association name of ' Borel.' And now, as the 'forties rolled by, the Montevidean exiles listened year by year ever more eagerly to the news sent by their friends in Italy and in London. In 1844 they heard that the Italian tricolor had been raised in the Neapolitan kingdom by Attilio and Emilio Bandiera, and that the two gallant brothers, together with Ricciotti, had been taken and shot. Garibaldi gave his younger son the name of Ricciotti.

But then, in 1847, came other news. The liberal and national movement had swelled so high that it had penetrated even palace walls. Under the name of Pio Nono, a reforming Pope had come to the throne; Savoy and Tuscany were moving towards constitutionalism. It was hoped that the whole land, governors and governed alike, would soon be arming for a national crusade against the Austrians in Milan; and in December 1847 Garibaldi lived in the expectation, which now seems strange indeed, that the Pope or the Grand Duke of Tuscany would employ him to expel the foreigner from the Lombard plain.[1]

Already the names of Garibaldi and his Italian Legion were household words with patriots at home. The fame of Garibaldi's achievements had been diligently nursed by Mazzini's secret agencies,[2] and, in these latter months of freedom, by the newly emancipated press of Tuscany, Rome, and Savoy. Thus, in May 1848, while Garibaldi was actually crossing the ocean, a Dutch artist, named Koelman, was sitting in a *café* in Rome, when he heard an Italian say, ' Garibaldi is coming back from Monte Video ! ' ' Who is Garibaldi ? ' said the foreigner; and forthwith supplied himself, for a few coppers, with a pamphlet, adorned by a portrait of the eagerly expected chief, recounting his

[1] *Elia*, i. 11 ; Garibaldi's letter to Antonini, Dec. 27, 1847.
[2] Any doubt as regards Mazzini's friendly attitude to Garibaldi at this time is laid at rest by Mazzini's letters to Lamberti, dated October 6, 1846, and January 29, 1847, printed in *Giurati*, 181, 209-210.

adventures and wars in the western world. Incredulity
was the first impression produced upon the artist by a story
so sensational; for he could not believe that heroes of
romance still existed, or that, if they did, they could
have any effect upon modern Europe. A year afterwards the unbeliever was constrained by love of this very
Garibaldi to risk his life in defence of a country that was
not his own, and he has left to posterity a book which
contains a living portrait of the man whom he learnt to
adore.[1]

So the Garibaldian legend was already planted in Italy
when Anita, with her children, landed at Genoa in the
spring of the year of revolutions, welcomed to her new
country by an enthusiastic crowd of citizens crying *Vivas*
for Garibaldi and ' our Garibaldi's family.' [2]

A few months later, after heart-breaking delays caused
by the fears of the Montevidean Government and the
English merchants about the defence of the State,[3] Garibaldi himself followed in the ship *Speranza*, with the fighting
men, somewhere between sixty and a hundred in number.[4]
He had sent over his wife and children first to safe quarters,
because, not knowing the course that Italian politics had
taken in the first months of 1848, he was prepared to have
to land his troops in the territories of hostile governments,
and to meet, very possibly, the fate of the Bandieras.

The *Speranza* set sail on April 15, 1848, four weeks
after the population of Milan had risen and driven Radetzky
and his 20,000 Austrians out of the city, in five days of the
hardest and most glorious street-fighting in the annals of
revolution. But Garibaldi and his companions did not
know of these actions, as their ship moved on, day by day
and night after night, through the lonely Atlantic. They
only knew that they were going ' towards the attainment of
the passion and desire of their lives.'

[1] *Koelman*, i. 179, 180; *Guerzoni*, i. 190-192; *Mario, Supp.* 71-77.
[2] Anita's letter, *Anita*, 578; *Mario, Supp.* 71-72. The three children were
Menotti, Ricciotti, and Teresita. Rosita had died in America, to the inexpres-
sible grief of her parents.
[3] *Cuneo*, 44.   [4] Garibaldi says 63; Cuneo says 100.

' That thought was the abundant reward for the perils, hardships, and sufferings incidental to a life of tribulation. Our hearts beat high with lofty enthusiasm. If the right hand, hardened in battles far away, had been strong in an alien cause, what will it not be for Italy ? ' [1]

And so these men, joyfully self-devoted, sailed to their graves and their glories in that ship. Since they were alone upon it, with no unbelievers there to mock their ceremonies, every time that the sun went down in ocean, they stood up in a circle on the deck, and ' sang for evening prayer a patriotic hymn.' Thus from the fulness of their pure hearts did those men, about to die, salute their mother. Her past and future sang in unison. Old Anzani, type of the protomartyrs who had given their lives for no meed of fame or thanks in the bitter, stifled years gone by, himself sick to death, joined feebly in the chant with the young generation who were hastening as willing victims to a more conspicuous, but not a more noble, sacrifice. And with the other voices blended the low, rich voice of the deliverer to be—till the song, without an audience, died upon the waters' waste.

[1] *Mem.* 185.

CHAPTER III

ITALY'S FAILURE IN 1848[1]

'What bloom of hope was there when Austria stood like an iron wall, and their own ones dashing against it were as little feeble waves that left a red mark and no more?'—GEORGE MEREDITH (*Vittoria*, chap. xvi.).

WHEN Garibaldi left Monte Video, in April 1848, he was still ignorant of the events which had revolutionised Italy in the opening months of the year. Fearing that the governments in every State of the Peninsula might after all prove to be on the side of ' order,' he was prepared to run ashore somewhere south of Leghorn, on the wooded Tuscan coast, and raise the tricolor standard in the wilderness, unless he received further advices from Mazzini, with whom he had made arrangements to communicate on his arrival in European waters.[2]

With such resolute purpose Garibaldi and his comrades had already sailed past the British sentinels into the Mediterranean, before news, which had for some time been stale in Europe, met them out at sea, changing the whole character of their expedition, and causing them to reshape their course for Piedmontese territory. The tidings, which they first gleaned from a passing vessel, were confirmed and amplified when they touched at a little port town on the east coast of Spain to procure fresh supplies, chiefly for the benefit of the dying Anzani. Garibaldi thus describes the scene :

'Captain Gazzolo, commanding the *Speranza*, went ashore, and quickly returned on board with news to turn the heads of men far less enthusiastic than ourselves. Palermo, Milan, Venice, and a hundred sister cities, had brought about the

<hr>

[1] For this Chapter see map, p. 9 above.   [2] *Guerzoni*, i. 203-205, 215.

momentous revolution. The Piedmontese army was pursuing the scattered remnants of the Austrian ; and all Italy, replying as one man to the call to arms, was sending her contingents of brave men to the holy war. The effect produced on all of us by this news may be better imagined than described. There was a rushing on deck, embracing one another, raving, weeping for very joy. Anzani sprang to his feet, excitement over-powering his terrible state of weakness. Sacchi absolutely insisted on being taken from his berth and carried on deck. " Make all sail ! " was the general cry. . . . In a flash the anchor was weighed and the brigantine under sail.'

And so, on June 21, they arrived at Nice, ' no longer exiles, no longer forced to fight for the privilege of land-ing' on their ' native shores.' The whole city raged with joy round the man who had stolen away fourteen years before, under sentence of death, and Garibaldi, who had little knowledge of the real state of the Peninsula, imagined that he was landing to take part in the campaign that should decide for ever the liberation of Italy. All was hope and happiness, for here, too, he found Anita and his children safely awaiting him, and his old mother whom he loved so well and had not seen for so long. Perhaps it was the last time in his life that he was altogether contented. ' Certainly my position was an enviable one,' he writes of that day. ' I am deeply touched, remembering those sweet emotions which were to end so quickly and so pain-fully.' [1]

The first grief that clouded the Italian sky for Garibaldi was the immediate death of Anzani, the only man in his company who was in some sense his equal, ' that truly great Italian, for whom all Italy should by rights have mourned. I never knew,' he wrote, ' a more capable and honourable man, or a soldier of loftier character.'

The greatest of that first generation of Garibaldians who had shared their chief's early struggles in America, Anzani, on his death-bed at Genoa, spoke his famous word to Medici, the representative of the young men who lived to achieve

[1] *Mem.*, pt. ii. ch. i; *Guerzoni*, i. 214-218 ; *Cavaciocchi*, 9- 10.

the glories of Sicily and Naples. Some dispute had already arisen : ' Do not,' said the dying patriot to Medici, ' do not be too hard on Garibaldi : he is a man of destiny; a great part of the future of Italy depends on him, and it will be a grave error to abandon him.'

Next day the old patriot was dead ; ' his body was carried through Liguria and Lombardy to be buried in the grave of his fathers, at Alzate, his native place.' He had been an exile from Italy for twenty-seven years, but when he died at last upon her soil, he must have felt certain of her approaching liberation.[1]

The good news which had met Garibaldi on the coast of Spain, although it was true, or at least had been true at one moment, was not the whole truth. Nine-tenths of the soil of Italy was, indeed, in the power of national and constitutional governments, but, although each monarch had yielded more or less to the call of his subjects for constitutionalism, neither Ferdinand of Naples nor Leopold of Tuscany, nor even Pio Nono—whose accession had given the first impulse to the movement—had the least intention of abdicating their thrones in favour of Italian unity. The instinct of self-preservation made them jealous of King Charles Albert of Piedmont, who had abandoned his reactionary policy in order to head the national crusade against his Austrian neighbour in the Lombard plain, and was already in a sense bidding for the crown of Italy, which his son was to forge and wear. The *chants du départ* of the students and workmen starting for the battle-fields of the north could not fail to sound ominously in the ears of the Pope, the Grand Duke, and the Neapolitan King, who employed the executive power in the States of the south and centre, not in organising the national crusade, but in damping its ardours, thwarting the departure of the volunteers, and preparing for reaction at home. Their attitude towards the national struggle against Austria recalled the listless inactivity of Louis XVI.,

[1] *Guerzoni*, i. 169, 224 ; *Mem.* 190, 191.

or the open enmity displayed by his consort in the first great storm of revolutionary war; but, whereas that policy was fatal to Louis, and not to France, the similar policy of these monarchs proved immediately fatal to Italy, and only after a dozen years recoiled on themselves.

And so, when Garibaldi disembarked, it was true in theory rather than in practice that a pan-Italian war was being waged against Austria on the Lombard plain. But at least the struggle in the North engrossed the thoughts of reactionaries and Liberals in every part of Italy, for all knew that their own fate was involved in the fate of Milan, the key by which alone Austria could lock, or Piedmont unlock, the whole Peninsula. Then, as in the time of Rivoli and Marengo, as afterwards in the time of Magenta and Solferino, the battles lost or won at the foot of the Alpine passes, and in the vineyards of the great northern plain, decided what must be the approaching fate of Naples, Florence, and the Papal territories.

If the Italians had then been united in purpose and in policy, as they were in 1859, they could, without aid from France or any other country, have hoisted the Austrians over the Brenner Pass in the early summer of 1848. For they were not at that moment fighting an Empire, but only an army. Austria-Hungary had gone to pieces, Hungarians and Bohemians had established their independence, and even the Viennese—for centuries the bulwark of loyalty to the Hapsburg—were expelling the Emperor from his capital. While the central fortress of Metternich's European policy was being stormed by the mob, France and Germany were in the hands of revolutionists, and a flood, not like that of 1792, flowing eastward from France, but spontaneously rising in every quarter from a thousand wells, submerged the landmarks, palaces, and steeples of old Europe.

Driven out of Milan by the heroism of its citizens, Radetzky had at the end of March fallen back into the famous ' Quadrilateral,' the four great fortresses of Verona, Mantua, Peschiera and Legnago, which guarded the mouth of the Brenner Pass, and formed Austria's *tête de pont*, whence she could debouch into Italy. Here, in the Quadrilateral, the old order stood magnificently at bay. North of the Alps the Austrian Empire had ceased to exist, but it lived in the camp of Radetzky, where Hungarians, who in their own country were Kossuthites hostile to the Emperor, were only eager to slay his enemies. The habits engendered by discipline, the fraternal bonds of *esprit de corps*, and above all that ignorant contempt for the Italians indigenous in the transalpine barbarian—a feeling old as Attila, old as Brennus—gave to Radetzky's troops a unity which was wanting to their assailants.[1]

That want of unity was felt everywhere and in everything. It was not merely that the governments of Tuscany, Rome, and Naples succeeded in making the volunteers from two-thirds of the Peninsula comparatively few and of no great service. The whole North was engaged in the war, but the North itself was divided by factions. It was split between the monarchical party, who wanted all the liberated provinces to vote at once for ' fusion ' with Piedmont, and the Republicans, who looked to achieve Italian unity through a federation of democratic States. There was local jealousy between the cities, who had not accepted, or at least had not assimilated, the new idea of national union ; and, worst of all, there was a widespread incapacity for organisation and war, inevitable in the first months of liberty among a people whose natural, native chiefs had so long been excluded from participation in government and forced to be idle slaves or secret conspirators.

But, in Venice, Manin had already shown that Italy possessed at least one great man of action. By marvellous audacity and wisdom the inspired lawyer procured without bloodshed the withdrawal of the Austrians from the city. His next step, the proclamation of the Venetian Republic, though it did much to inspire emulation of former glories, did not make for unity of spirit. It drove Charles Albert

---

[1] The patriotic part of the Italian conscripts had deserted from the Austrian army.

into premature intrigues for the formal annexation to
Piedmont of territories which were still the seat of a
doubtful war with Austria, and this policy in turn irritated
the strict Mazzinians, a small but important body who could
not forget that this king had once sought to take their lives,
and had succeeded in taking the lives of the dearest friends
of their youth. Meanwhile the Provisional Government of
Milan, distracted by these political intrigues, and wanting in
practical ability, mismanaged the business of its war department, and wasted and wearied the fervour of the Lombard
volunteers, out of sheer incapacity ; while the Piedmontese
military authorities, suspicious of democratic enthusiasm, and professionally contemptuous of irregular troops,
thwarted the volunteer movement with deliberate intent.

Charles Albert had indeed one instrument ready
sharpened in his hand, the splendid regular army of Piedmont, a match for the Austrians by the highest professional standards. But even this he could never muster
enough resolution to use in a straight home-thrust. In
March he wasted the first precious days after the rising of
Milan, while the retreating Austrians might have been cut
to pieces before they reached the shelter of the Quadrilateral ;
in May he ordered a retreat from the half-won battle of
Santa Lucia, near Verona, and then continued, with that
strange moral timidity in war which was so much in contrast to his physical courage, to let one opportunity after
another pass by.

Such was the state of things when Garibaldi arrived at
the royal headquarters at Roverbella (July 3, 4) and loyally
offered his sword to Charles Albert. He was then, and
remained all his life, a Republican; but then, as later,
he was ready to fight for popular government under other
forms preferred by the majority of his countrymen, rather
than blast the hopes of the nation by creating divisions
—a more truly democratic view, perhaps, than intransigent
sectarianism.[1] If, in 1848, Victor Emmanuel had been in his
father's place, he would have welcomed Garibaldi with open

[1] *Mem.* 277.

arms, and Cavour would have known how to exploit ' the hero of Monte Video ' for all he was worth, to rekindle through him the failing enthusiasm of the volunteers, and to reunite the Democratic parties to the throne. But Charles Albert (or his constitutional ministers, for it is difficult to apportion the responsibility) thought it enough to show courtesy to the pardoned traitor of 1834, and his services were rejected by Piedmont.[1] Garibaldi thereupon took a commission under the incompetent Provisional Government of Milan, and was sent, with a few badly armed and ill-chosen men, to Bergamo, where he had neither time nor opportunity to create the least diversion before the disaster fell on the main army.

On July 25 the royal forces were defeated at Custoza, in spite of their valour and good conduct, owing to bad generalship and the breakdown of the commissariat. The army was not destroyed, nor even routed; but in the next ten days it was forced back from one point to another, in a series of ill-conducted and bravely contested engagements, until it was finally driven into Milan. There this most unhappy king had enough sympathy with the people to be exquisitely sensitive to the hatred which he had called down on himself by disappointing all the national hopes and handing back the gallant Milanese to the tyranny from which they had freed themselves in March without his aid. On the day that the enraged populace besieged him in the Greppi Palace, his friends could see how pure and deep were his sufferings.

' He was on foot, deadly pale, and aged in face and figure (writes Della Rocca). He held his sword tight under his arm, and, when he saw me, said, " Ah, mon cher La Rocca, quelle journée, quelle journée ! " I shall never forget the tone of his voice.'[2]

On August 5, he was compelled to surrender Milan to the Austrians, partly because the Provisional Government there had neglected to make any preparations for defence, or even for feeding their Piedmontese allies.

---

[1] *Cavaciocchi*, 6–7.   *Della Rocca*, 88.

'The army evacuated the city during the night. A few desperate men fired on the soldiers, as they sadly defiled through the streets. But disaster had broken down the misunderstanding; more than half the population, it was estimated, fled with the army, indignant at Austrian rule; and, tenderly assisted by the soldiers, the terror-stricken citizens thronged the roads to Piedmont.'[1]

By their heroic 'five days' of street fighting, in March, the Milanese had won less than five months of liberty; but they had registered a claim upon the future, and Austrian rule was henceforth too odious ever again to seem a legal and settled government. Italian unity had failed to materialise because Italians were not yet united in heart and mind, and the failure had been the more sure and rapid, because the man who alone could have saved the situation lacked all the political and all the military qualities of a *Pater Patriæ*. But if Charles Albert was not the father of his country, he was the father of Victor Emmanuel.

When, four days after the evacuation of Milan, the famous Armistice was signed between Piedmont and Austria, it was scarcely unnatural, though it was unjust, in the Democrats to think that the king had betrayed the national cause by making peace, when his army was, as they believed, intact—when it certainly had not been destroyed. And least of all men could Garibaldi, and those who had come with him from Monte Video to sell their lives for Italy's freedom, be content to lay down their arms before they had seen a shot fired in anger. Kings had betrayed them; let them appeal to the peoples. The king had made peace to save his crown; let them proclaim a 'people's war.' In this mood the Garibaldians carried on a Republican campaign against Austria in the Alps. Mazzini for some days had accompanied the troops as standard-bearer, carrying a flag inscribed with his own famous watchword 'God and the People' (*Dio e Popolo*), but he soon left for Switzerland. In the short time since Garibaldi's landing at

[1] *King*, i. 260.

E

Nice, Mazzini and he had had their first quarrel, the origin of great things for Italy in years to come.

The little campaign, a personal and political protest rather than a real war, was waged for two or three weeks in the mountain villages round the south of Lakes Maggiore and Varese. Next to their leader, his young lieutenant, Medici, distinguished himself and won the soldiers' confidence. By the end of August, Garibaldi was driven across the Swiss border, but not before he had displayed to his countrymen his genius in guerilla warfare, and so ensured for himself the enthusiastic attachment of the Democrats in every State of Italy. The affairs at Luino and Morazzone were his first exploits on Italian soil, and with them the last efforts to expel the foreigner in the year 1848 came to an end. The Austrian had recovered all his Lombard and Alpine territories, and was already preparing the long siege of Manin and his Venetians in their island city.*

* In spite of his comparatively cold reception by Charles Albert at Roverbella, Garibaldi had not, upon the whole, reason to complain of his treatment by the Piedmontese authorities. The false and even dangerous position in which they had been placed in relation to the victorious Austrians by his refusal to be bound by the armistice in August, would have supplied a less patriotic government with ample excuse for closing the frontier against him when he came back a month later from Switzerland. But they allowed him to return and take up his quarters, unquestioned, among his own people at Nice. There were, indeed, men in high places in Charles Albert's service who already understood his value. 'I have visited Garibaldi,' wrote General La Marmora in September; 'he has a fine face, rough, but frank. I am ever more persuaded that in good hands he would be useful.' 'He threw himself among the Republicans to fight, and because his services were refused. I do not believe he is a Republican in principle. It was a great error not to use him. When there is another war, he is a man to employ. Garibaldi is no common man.' (*Cavaciocchi*, 85–87.)

CHAPTER IV

CONDITION OF THE ROMAN STATES UNDER THE PAPACY, 1815–46—PIO NONO AND THE REFORM MOVEMENTS, 1846–48

> ' Pur nell' Ausonia ancor egra e acciecata
> Passeggian truci le adorate larve.
> Passeggian truci, e 'l diadema e il manto
> De' boreali Vandali ai nepoti
> Vestendo, al scettro sposano la croce ;
> Onde il Tevere e l' Arno a te devoti,
> Libertà santa Dea, cercan la foce
> Sdegnosamente in suon quasi di pianto.'
>
> UGO FOSCOLO—*Ode, Bonaparte Liberatore*, 1797.

THUS the redemption of Italy, which could be effected only by the defeat of the Austrians in the North, was postponed, by the disunion of her children, for another decade. Although it was a grievous thing that ten more years of suffering in common were wanted to teach all Italians that they had but one cause, yet it was well, perhaps, that good generalship or French interference did not, in 1848, give them independence before they were ripe for union. For if independence had come to the different States of Italy without union, independence itself would have been less stable and of less value. As yet the Papacy, with its scarcely challenged claim to reign over the centre of the Peninsula, stood morally and geographically in the way of amalgamation ; even Liberals and Nationalists had not yet completely envisaged the obligation to destroy the temporal power, but dreamed, instead, that they would make it Liberal. But events were to take place in the twelve months that followed Custoza, which for ever divided the Papacy from the national cause, and prepared the minds of the Pope's subjects to throw off his allegiance, and to merge themselves in one great Kingdom of Italy.

In order that the reader may understand how it came about that, a few months after the Austrians had driven Mazzini and Garibaldi over the passes into Switzerland, they were shining before Europe as the rival *Dioscuri* of a Roman Republic, it is necessary to give some preliminary account of the new scene and the new actors, of the Roman States, and the various regions, classes, and parties, which they embraced within their limits.

The Roman States,[1] as a glance at the map (at end of book) will show, stretched from sea to sea, including the Tiber and its confluents on the south-west of the Apennine watershed, and on the north-eastern side the great plain of the Romagna, in the angle formed by the Adriatic and the Po. This seaward plain of the Romagna, studded with famous cities like Bologna, Forlì, Rimini, Ravenna, and tilled by a comparatively prosperous peasantry, was cut off by the highest range of the Apennine mountains, and distinguished by the nature of its soil and scenery and by the character of its people from the arid, backward and poverty-stricken Tiber regions, where lay the seat of the Pontifical Government.

The origin of the unnatural subjection of the Adriatic seaboard to the rule of Rome lay remote in the history of the dark ages. Romagna and the Marches, answering respectively to the ' Exarchate of Ravenna ' and the ' Pentapolis,' had been the last pieces of Italian soil preserved by the decaying Empire seated at Byzantium. When, in the eighth century, the Lombards snatched these territories from the feeble clutch of the successors of

[1] With regard to the condition of the Papal States and the methods of government between 1815 and 1846, the best general accounts in English will be found in *Johnston*, chaps. i. and ii., and *King*, i. 72–85. The reader may also get a very good idea of the Temporal Power by studying for himself the State documents of the Cardinals and their agents, published at the end of *Orsini*, and the documents in *Gualterio*. (See also *Farini* and *D'Azeglio*, for the evidence of well-informed and moderate contemporaries, who were opposed to the Democrats as well as to the Clericals ; and Cardinal *Wiseman* and the Chevalier *O'Clery* for the Papal case.) *Galeotti* also contains information in a handy form.

Augustus, the Pope called in the Frankish kings, who rescued the cities of the Exarchate and Pentapolis from the Lombards, and made them over to the only power that seemed any longer to represent the Roman Empire in Italy, namely, ' To the Roman Republic, to St. Peter and to his Vicars the Popes of Rome for ever.' [1]

From that time forward the Romagna had been retained, in theory at least, by the Pope, and at the close of the Middle Ages it had fallen completely under his sway, by the chance of war and diplomacy. But it belonged, by what the French Jacobins called ' the law of nature,' either to North Italy or to itself alone. Napoleon, who in his youth had a keen eye for realities, especially in his ancestral land of Italy, recognised this fact, and as early as 1797 joined the Romagna to the States which he was creating in the Po valley. For nearly twenty years before Waterloo the Romagnuols had enjoyed, not indeed liberty, but enlightened government by Italian laymen trained on the French model, the best code of laws then in Europe, and a system of education that was modern instead of mediæval, military and official instead of clerical.[2] It was during this French occupation that the seeds of religious scepticism were sown, and the scientific ideas of the Encyclopædists became familiar to the educated classes.[3] The Napoleonic flame was not a pure light, but in Italy it broke like the day on those who sat in great darkness.[4]

But the French rule did at least one injury. It swept away the last remnants of municipal independence within

---

[1] Hodgkin's *Italy and Her Invaders*, vii. 135-223.

[2] *C. M. H.* ix. 390-402 (H. A. L. Fisher).   [3] *Farini*, i. 8.

[4] Napoleonic rule was a revelation even to the more intelligent of the Italian nobles. For instance, it started the Liberal tradition of the Pasolini, one of the noble families of the Romagna ; we read that ' the frequent military displays at Milan, added to all the important discussions on civil government which he had heard, chiefly through his uncle, then in constant communication with the Emperor and his ministers, had great influence on the mind of Pietro Desiderio, and made him a Bonapartist in his opinions, so that he never ceased to regret and to praise the " Code Napoléon," and he was all his life a Liberal in politics.' *Pasolini*, 12. (See also *Tivaroni*, *Fr.* ii. 350-387, and *Galeotti*, 95-99, on the effects of Napoleon's rule.)

the old Papal dominions.[1] In mediæval times, though the
Pope's claims extended from sea to sea, yet in practice not
only the cities of the Romagna, but the Umbrian hill towns
of Perugia, Assisi, and at one time Orvieto, had to all
intents been sovereign communities. In the days of their
independence the towns of Central Italy flourished exceedingly ; they became famous for saintship, learning, and art,
homes of St. Francis, of Sigismondo Malatesta's scholar
court, of Perugino and Raphael. But they wasted their
life blood in mutual wars and internal feuds till, in the
fifteenth and sixteenth centuries, one by one they fell,
exhausted by their sins, under the long punishment of the
Papal rule. That government, which soon afterwards
became an embodiment of the principles of the Jesuits
and the Inquisition, effectually extinguished the vigour
and learning of the Renaissance, together with the political
and civil liberties of laymen. But a few vestiges of local
self-government lingered on until the French occupation,
when Napoleon swept them away as relics of a system not
his own. After Waterloo, when only what was bad in the
ancien régime was restored, the loss of the old municipal
independence was for the time felt as a great evil,[2] although
the ground was thereby left all the more clear for national
union.

Napoleon's rule had not been popular, but the memory
of it soon caused the Papacy to be hated. The evils of the
clerical government, perhaps never so real, were certainly
never before so much felt as between 1815 and 1846, and
they were felt most deeply and resented most effectually
in the Romagna. The Romagnuol peasantry, a proud race
of fine physique and noble bearing, were always among the
first Italians to resent oppression, whether that of French
Republicans,[3] Austrians, or priests. Their virile qualities
had marked them out as the best soldiers in Napoleon's
Italian regiments,[4] and Byron, when he lived at Ravenna,

---

[1] Umbria, and Rome itself, were annexed to the French Empire in 1809.
[2] *Galeotti*, 99–110, on the institutions of the Restoration.   [3] *Pasolini*, 3.
[4] *C. M. H* ix. 394 (H. A. L. Fisher).

loved to take a canter 'among the peasantry, who are a
savage, resolute race, always riding with guns in their
hands.'[1] But the town population of the Romagna presented, perhaps, a still finer type. Ravenna and Rimini—
which had each in a different period of history been world-
renowned as a centre of civilisation, art, and learning—and
above all Bologna, with its University and its European
fame as one of the chief cities of Italy, became, after the fall
of Napoleon, strongholds of the most undoubted Liberalism
in the Peninsula.

Over this Romagnuol community, proud of its past
traditions, and struggling towards modern progress, the
palsied hand was now again stretched from beyond the
Apennines; again there was the 'clutch of dead men's fingers
in live flesh.' The rule of the Pope was represented in
the 'Legations' of the Romagna by Cardinal Legates, who,
resembling the Turkish Pashas in more respects than one,
were not properly responsible to the central government,
which they often flouted, and were not responsible at all to
their subjects, whom they oppressed at pleasure, being able
in time of revolt to call in the Austrian troops from across
the border. 'The Turks would be better,' was a saying
in which the Romagnuols summed up their opinion of the
government.[2]

Although the scandal and anarchy were worst in the
Romagna, because there the resistance was hottest, the
principles on which the Cardinals governed the Legations
were the principles on which the priestly government was
carried on everywhere throughout the Papal States. Education, frowned on as a design of the Liberals to revolutionise
the State,[3] was so successfully discouraged that, in 1837, it
was calculated that two per cent. of the rural population could
read, and not very much more of the dwellers in the towns.
What education there was remained under the special

[1] *Byron*, v. 19.

[2] *Farini*, i. 88; *King*, i. 82, 83. (See *Gualterio*, chap. xviii., on Romagna.)

[3] *D'Azeglio*, 104, 105. He holds up to the clergy the superior example of
Austria in this respect.

[4] *Johnston*, 13, note 2; *King*, i. 80.

surveillance of the priestly rulers, affording a subject of unedifying discussion between them and their police.[1]   In the Universities, where most of the teaching had to be given in Latin, there was no fear of its being too modern ; political economy was a forbidden subject, while Dante, modern literature, and the theory that the earth moved round the sun, were all suspect, and sometimes prohibited.[2] Anyone supposed to belong to the dangerous class of ' thinkers ' was shadowed by the police, even if he had nothing to do with politics.[3]   The same vague distrust of everything not mediæval led Gregory XVI. to prohibit the intrusion of railways and telegraphs into his dominions.

The press was under a rigorous censorship, which excluded most books and newspapers of any importance, whether Italian or foreign.   So far was clerical vigilance carried, in 1845, that even the newspapers of the British Islands were divided into classes according to their degrees of impiety, and ' all the Protestant and so-called Tory papers ' were placed under the ban.[4]

The life, freedom, and property of no one who was not a friend to Government had any real security in the Papal States.   Long lists of suspects were handed about between the officers spiritual and temporal, whose functions overlapped in the most amazing way.   The houses of the suspects were perpetually being searched, and their daily goings out and in were watched and reported.   If evidence

---

[1] *Orsini*, 254, 255.   [2] *King*, i. 80, 81 ; *Farini*, i. 116, 153.

[3] ' If one may judge from appearances, he would appear strange to political intrigues. . . . Nevertheless, as some imagine that he may belong to the class called " Thinkers," I consider it my duty to acquaint your Eminence with it, in order that he may be prudently watched.'—Cardinal Legate of Bologna, to Cardinal Lambruschini, *Orsini*, 248.

[4] *Orsini*, 256–259.   ' List of the foreign papers which may be read in coffee-houses, inns, and other public places :—

English :—1. *The Freeman* ; *2. *The Globe* ; *3. *The Courier* ; *4. *Galway Patriot* ; *5. *The Observer* ; *6. *The Dublin Weekly* ; *7. *The Dublin Evening Post* ; 8. *Galignani's Messenger* ; 9. *The Catholic Herald.*

' Father Theiner has declared the English and German papers should be limited to those not marked *.'

History does not relate whether Father Theiner's view prevailed, or the larger latitude of the complete list.

was lacking, cardinals did not stick at ordering trivial circumstances to be tortured into proof,[1] and presumably the lower officials had small scruple in obeying the spirit of their instructions. Strange commands were issued to the citizens of this Church-State, sometimes to individuals, or sometimes to thousands at a time ; as, for example, that they should keep within doors between sunset and sunrise, or not go out at night without a lantern ; that they should, under compulsion, 'perform their spiritual exercises for three days in a convent chosen by the bishop,' or confess once a month before an approved confessor. Cruel punishments were enacted for neglect. The situation of a 'thinker,' driven into the confessional by the police, must have had piquancy. What did gentlemen in this interesting position confide to the holy fathers ?

Heresy, so far as it existed, was no more tolerated than infidelity. Even the English, in the hey-day of their power and reputation on the Continent, were not allowed a church in Rome, but had to be content to worship in a building outside the Porta del Popolo. The cosmopolitan artist community, which afterwards took its part in defending Republican Rome against the Pope, loved in those earlier days to stroll on Sunday morning in the Piazza del Popolo, to see the English families marching out of the gate with firm tread and Bible under arm, to this humble shrine of their proud national worship.[2]

Throughout the States fines were imposed, inns and *cafés* closed, civil rights withdrawn, at the whim of the officials. There was no pretence, as in England at the same period, that postal letters would not be opened, and their contents communicated to all Governments concerned. Worst of all, any man was liable—and liable almost in proportion to his public spirit and desire to improve the lot of his fellows—to see the inside of the secret cells of Pesaro, or of the fortress which rises on the grim rock of San Leo in the heart of the wildest Apennines. In times

[1] *Orsini*, 207, 208. Instructions from Cardinal Bernetti, Secretary of State.
[2] *Koelman*, i. 266.

when the Government was specially alarmed, the forms of
civilised justice were laid aside, as when, in 1821, many
hundreds of men and women were imprisoned or banished,
without trial and without accusation ;[1] as when, in 1824 and
1844, Special Commissions were established, presided over
by persons of the worst character, who judged with an
indifference to all rules of law, and punished with a ferocity
that shocked even the Europe of that day. Tied up by
ropes to the walls of filthy prisons, or to the ' galleys ' of
Civitavecchia, or more mercifully executed by gibbeting
or ' shooting in the back,' the Pope's enemies perished and
were forgotten.[2]

Under such a *régime*, secret societies were the only
means of promoting ideas of reform in the State, or even of
freely studying literature and exchanging views on ordinary
subjects.   The Italian genius for this kind of subterranean
life was not wanting to the occasion, and the Carbonari,
the Freemasons, and, later, ' Young Italy,' kept alive thought
and politics, which took a revolutionary trend answering
in violence to the degree of repression.

To combat the Liberal secret societies the Papal Government had various agencies ; besides the regular police-
officers, there were the Inquisition,[3] the priesthood, the
sbirri, and the centurioni.

No one could say in the Papal States where the temporal power ended and the spiritual began.   The spiritual
courts kept a large proportion of ordinary judicial business
in their hands, and in the secular courts the clergy occupied
the highest places on the bench.   Not only the ministry
at Rome, but the bureaucracy throughout the States, was

---

[1] *Byron*, v. 323-328 ; *Farini*, i. 15, 16.

[2] *Johnston*, 24, 25 ; *King*, i. 78 ; *Farini*, i. 25, 26, 128, 129 ; *Orsini*, 27-44,
280 (referring to the year 1844) ; *D'Azeglio*, 62, 68-76, 87, 88 ; *Gualterio*, chaps.
xviii., xix.

[3] In 1843 the Inquisition issued an edict against the Jews in the Pontifical
States, containing, among other insolent restrictions on their personal liberty, the
provision that ' no Israelite shall entertain amicable relations with Christians ' ;
those who violate this rule ' will incur the punishments of the Holy Inquisition.'
Gualterio, i. 438, 439, doc. cxxvii.   The spirit satirised in Browning's *Holy Cross
Day* was still very much alive among the Papal governors.

filled with clergy, and these secular authorities (if they can be so called) were in the closest touch with the purely spiritual authorities, and were constantly supplied from that source with personal information about suspects.

'While the police harried the people in their daily lives, the Inquisition collected the secrets of the confessional, and launched its spiritual thunders on the unconforming. An edict is extant by the Inquisition-General of Pesaro in 1841, commanding all people to inform against heretics, Jews, and sorcerers, those who have impeded the Holy Office, or made satires against the pope and clergy.' [1]

A bishop would receive from ' the Director of Police ' lists of those who were ' suspect ' in his diocese, accompanied by the request to send in reports of discoveries made about, them through the spiritual channels at his command,[2] and delation by a parish priest was enough to bring about the disappearance of a supposed Liberal. Under such a system it was believed then, and is in the highest degree probable, that political and religious reasons were sometimes only the cloak for the ruin of individuals who were the victims of personal jealousy, or stood in the way of sinister designs.[3]

But there were also classes of lay helpers who assisted the ecclesiastics to perform these functions. The 'spies,' then familiar figures on the Continent of Europe, as they had been in England under the *régime* of Pitt, were the special curse of Italy. They made life intolerable by their insolence, ubiquity, and treachery; they sat with men at their meals, they whispered with them in the market-place; they entered the lodges of the Carbonari and helped to hatch the plots which they afterwards betrayed. Indeed, the only way to carry on the secret societies at all was to limit the activity of the spies by putting the fear of death

---

[1] *King*, i. 79 ; *Gualterio*, i. 33 ; *Galeotti*, 145-150.

[2] *Orsini*, 218 : letter of Director of Police to Archbishop of Camerino.

[3] *Orsini*, 232 ; *King*, i. 78 ; *Johnston*, 24, 25. Byron, who knew persons and parties at Ravenna extremely well, and was regarded as ' the chief of the Liberals,' noticed that in the proscriptions (without trial) of 1821, in Ravenna alone ten persons suffered who were really supporters of the Government (*Byron*, v. 241).

into their hearts. Under the Papacy, as under the Czardom, assassination was the only means of self-defence against a government which not only did not protect liberty, property, or life, but used every instrument of force and fraud to deprive men of the simplest rights of humanity. But, for all that, the Carbonari of the Romagna were greatly to blame for the regular system of assassination which they carried on—beginning a few years after Waterloo—not merely against spies, but against governors, soldiers, and police; though in Italy more discriminating weapons were used than the bomb, that chooses its victims by chance. Byron, who was hand in glove with the Carbonari, and lived during the winter of 1820–1821 in daily hopes of a ' row,' eager to take his place in the fighting-line, was disgusted by the system of assassination which his allies employed, sometimes under his very windows. On one December night he caused his servants to carry into his own house the dying Commandant of Ravenna, with five slugs in his body, because no one else dared touch him, as he lay bleeding in the street, for fear of the assassins. A generation later, not only scrupulous Liberals like Farini, but Orsini himself—who afterwards attempted to murder Napoleon III.—regarded the assassinations in the Romagna as wicked and harmful, and helped effectually to suppress them.[1]

The rulers, at any rate, did not regard assassination as wrong in itself, for they employed it as readily as their opponents, who at least had the excuse that they possessed no other weapon. The Papal assassins, organised in the Centurioni bands, an offshoot of the famous San-Fedist society, appeared openly, in Romagna and the Marches, assuming the name and uniform of Pontifical Volunteers,[2] while in the other parts of the Papal dominions they remained a secret society, answering to the Carbonari. The San-Fedists, who protected the Holy Faith sometimes by the dagger at midnight, sometimes by open ruffianism in

---

[1] *Farini*, i. 73 ; ii. 334–7 ; *Orsini*, chap. viii. ; *Byron*, v. 133–140, 157-161 ; *Gualterio*, i. 39, and chap. iii. *passim*.

[2] *Gualterio*, i. 416–420, docs. cxv.–cxvii.

the broad day, were permitted by Government to 'beat or kill, at their pleasure, any man dubbed Liberal, Freemason, or Carbonaro.' until, to neglect attendance at mass, or even to grow one's beard, was enough to expose one to assault by these bravos.[1] Thus the tradition of the bloody feuds, which had made life intolerable in the Italy of the Middle Ages, was continued in the Romagna in the stabbing and shooting matches between the Carbonari and Centurioni. Yet it is only fair on both political parties to remember that the blood feud was custom of the country quite apart from politics: the peasantry, whom Byron loved to see riding armed, were not armed for mere show, but because at any turn of the road they might meet the wrong man.[2] In view of these facts, some may be surprised that the sporadic outbursts of terrorism that greatly marred the Democratic triumph in the Roman States in 1848–49 were not even worse than they actually were, and that it was found possible to suppress them under Mazzini's *régime* of toleration and liberty. But that recipe, if combined with stern justice to murderers, is, in truth, the only sedative in such cases of chronic inflammation.

If this abominable Government had only been the bayonet rule of the Austrian veterans themselves, it would have been less shameful to endure. But the system which

[1] *Pasolini*, 30, 31 ; *Orsini*, 6 ; *D'Azeglio*, 59–61 ; *Farini*, i. 10–14, 71–73, 78, 119, 120. The wearing of beards was the sign of advanced principles ; it was prohibited in Sicily as late as the time of the Crimean War, when the Sardinian Consul at Trapani had to invoke his consular rights to save himself from being forcibly shaved by the police (De Cesare, *La Fine di un Regno*, ii. 193).

[2] *E.g.*, Byron, v. 202 (February 14, 1821). 'Heard the particulars of the late fray at Russi, a town not far from this (Ravenna). It is exactly the fact of Roměo and Giuletta—*not* Roměo, as the Barbarian writes it. Two families of *contadini* (peasants) are at feud. At a ball the younger part of the families forget their quarrel, and dance together. An old man of one of them enters, and reproves the young men for dancing with the females of the opposite family. The male relatives of the latter resent this. Both parties rush home and arm themselves. They meet directly, by moonlight, in the public way, and fight it out. Three are killed on the spot, and six wounded, most of them dangerously—pretty well for two families, methinks, and all *fact*, of the last week. Another assassination has taken place at Cesena—in all about forty in Romagna within the last three months. These people retain much of the Middle Ages.'

the Austrians were again and again called in to re-establish over the rebels of the Romagna was not militarism, or the rule of men with like passions to the governed, but the supremacy of that strange third sex which the Roman Church creates by training men up from boyhood in a world that is not the world of men. To live under the Austrians, after they themselves had suppressed rebellion in fair fight, to see the white-coats scourging the prisoners they had taken in fight and the women who were the prize of war, was the old pain of the world known to captured Troy and Carthage. But to be first knocked down by the Austrians and then put back to live under the direct control and daily espionage of priests, to be liable to imprisonment and ruin if one displeased the black skirt, was worse than pain. It was as though some indefinable horror, at once monstrous and despised, at once eerie and most material, were in one's house and lord of it. We English, living in a land and in a generation where these things are so far away, where the spiritual guides of an honourable religious minority claim the voluntary obedience to which they have a perfect right, since it is voluntarily given, we to-day are apt to be either angry or amused at the kind of physical horror which Garibaldi and his Roman followers felt for the priests of the reactionary party. But if we honestly try to put ourselves into their place and time, we may or may not think their expressions exaggerated; we cannot think them unnatural.

Such was the government of the Roman States from Waterloo to 1846, culminating in the proverbial obscurantism of Gregory XVI., who, elected in time to suppress the movements of 1831 with the utmost cruelty, misruled for fifteen years, flouting the protests of the French and English press, and putting off the representations of the Powers of Europe by wiles akin to those of the Turk.[1]

Such, at least, was the Papal Power as it presented itself to the middle and artisan classes, and to the more intelligent and prosperous of the peasantry, especially in the Romagna.

[1] *Gualterio*, i. 208 ; *Farini*, i. 58, 66, 67.

But to the majority, perhaps, of the Pope's subjects his rule appeared in a different light, if it can be said to have appeared to them in any light at all. The men and women of the Umbrian Apennines who, bent with toil and withered by starvation and poverty, tilled the hills of olive and the valleys thinly clad with vines, or staggered down under burdens of brushwood from the grey mountains above—or the malaria-stricken herdsmen of the deserts that surrounded Rome—what did they know of liberty, or what was it to them if Italy bled ? They did not suffer from spies, for they had no politics. The censorship was no grievance to them, for they could not read. The priest was lord of their lives, but he was their only visible friend. If the Catholic Church tends by its general influence to keep people poor and ignorant, it knows how to sweeten ignorance and poverty. Anyone who has strayed off the beaten tracks in Southern Europe, especially in mountain districts, knows the strange beauty and pathos, so far removed from anything English, of a whole community living a kind of life that seems as old as the hills around them—all of them poor, all struggling unaided by modern science to wring the daily pittance from the unmastered forces of nature, while in their midst one poor priest and one poor church remain as the only help, the only symbol of the larger world outside, and of ages not absolutely pre-historic. Such isolated conditions are now rapidly disappearing, though a few valleys of the Italian Alps still touchingly show the type. But in the first half of the nineteenth century the Papal States were a preserve of such communities. The very *régime* which checked railways and prevented the development of science and manufactures, prolonged for many a parish priest the undisputed mastery of the hamlet. As a whole, the clergy of the Roman States were unfavourable specimens of their profession ; but no one can doubt that many of the village *padres* deserved the love, as certainly many enjoyed the obedience, of their fellow poor.

These conditions were not found in the rich plains of the Romagna ; but on the west side of the Apennines, and

especially in the neighbourhood of the capital, the poverty
and superstition of the people and the power of the priest
were very great indeed.   In Rome itself, where the ignorance
of the population was only slightly less than outside the
walls,[1] devotion to the Pope was the predominant feeling
until 1847, in spite of some vigorous seeds of Liberalism.
The governors of Rome still knew how to supply the populace of the capital with a modicum of *panis* and a considerable quantity of *circenses*.

'The characteristic note of this period was struck by the
feasts and holidays which were celebrated on every possible
occasion.   Amidst all this political tyranny, financial bank-
ruptcy, and administrative disorder, the populace manifested
a sceptical indifference in all matters.   As long as they were
able to enjoy the horse-races in Piazza Navona, varied by
boating, for which purpose the Piazza used to be flooded with
three feet of water, and the spectacle of fireworks and balloon
ascensions, as long as the Pope authorised the Carnival orgies
and *Ottobrate* (October beanfeasts) with their almost pagan
rites, and as long as the subventions passed on by the convents
and the houses of the Cardinals to the indigent classes were
sufficiently substantial, they were satisfied.'[2]

Napoleon's rule in the valley of the Tiber had been
shorter (1809–1814) and more unpopular than in the Romagnuol Legations.   His dramatic brutalities against the
aged Pius VII. had done more to increase the sentimental
loyalty of the Pope's Umbrian and Roman subjects than
any benefits conferred by the brief French administration
had done to shake it.   But the execrable government of
the thirty years after Waterloo forced the growth of discontent and secret association in the towns and larger
villages in every part of the Papal States.   Such was the
state of things when, in 1846, on the death of the detested
Gregory XVI., Mastai Ferretti was elected to the chair of
St. Peter, and took the name of Pio Nono (Pius IX.).

[1] It was calculated that ten per cent. could read (*King*, i. 80).
[2] *Costa*, 20.

The good man, who was to illustrate in his own person the ineffectual tragedy of Liberal Catholicism, exclaimed, when he heard what had befallen him : 'My God, they want to make a Napoleon of me, who am only a poor country parson!' But the task of reconciling the mediæval and the modern world, to which in the first months of his popedom he addressed himself amid the grateful applause of Europe, would have been far beyond the powers of Napoleon himself. All that Pio Nono could contribute to the solution of the impossible problem was a stock of mild benevolence towards everybody, which was not completely exhausted until he had been some two years on the uneasy throne. He recalled the exiles ; he let the prisoners out of the secret cells and the galleys ; he gave partial freedom of speech and press. Then he looked round for gratitude, and it came in floods of ecstatic, demonstrative Italian humanity, torchlight processions and crowds kneeling at his feet. As though to add to his popularity, the Austrians, in August 1847, occupied Ferrara as a protest against the Liberal movement in his territories. The cult of Pio Nono was for some months the religion of Italy, and of Liberals and exiles all over the world. Even Garibaldi, in Monte Video, and Mazzini, in London, shared the enthusiasm of the hour.

But that was the high-water mark of the movement for reconciling the Papacy to Liberalism, for Pio Nono had not the least idea what to do with the situation which he had created. The prisoners whom he had released, the press and speakers whom he had set talking, the exiles returning with the bitterness that exile always breeds,[1] quarrelled with his clerical ministry and wanted to put vigour and a democratic spirit into the approaching war so as to expel the foreigner from Italian soil, while the Pope only wished to defend his northern borders against the encroachments of the Austrian troops. The demonstrations of gratitude, which so much embarrassed him, did not abate, but they gradually changed their tone, becoming dictatorial, then threatening, and finally irresistible. Throughout 1847 the

[1] *Farini*, iii. 52.

agitation raged in every town of the Papal States, against
the administration which was still unreformed, and the
clerical bureaucracy which was still in power. Only the
courage and effectiveness of the governing caste were gone,
so that in many places anarchy succeeded to oppression,
the blood-feud was worse than ever, and the *sbirri* and the
San-Fedist Centurioni, being more exposed to the popular
vengeance, were fain to re-establish their waning authority
by spasmodic outbursts of terrorism.

In Rome itself the conversion of the people, from sentimental loyalty to the Papacy, to revolutionary Liberalism,
was rapidly carried on under the particularly convenient
form of the cult of a supposed Liberal Pope. The leader,
one might say the creator, of the Roman democratic party
was the good-natured and voluble dealer in horses and wine,
Angelo Brunetti,[1] better known by his pet name, *Ciceruacchio*,
given him in his infancy by his mother and her gossips to
denote his plumpness, for which throughout life he remained
famous. ' A man of the people,' handsome and strong—
half Cleon, half Rienzi—deservedly loved by his fellow-
citizens long before he took to politics, he had all the
characteristics of the famous Roman wine-carriers, who
formed a democratic aristocracy or close caste among the
picturesque mediæval population of the Rome of that day.
Ignorant, simple, enthusiastic, humorous, kind, and without
guile or malice, Ciceruacchio spoke to the *plebs* in the
natural eloquence of the Italian market-place ; at first his
theme was the Pope's goodness (and Pio Nono had no more
sincere friend), then, as the months went by, he spoke more
of the evil counsellors at the good Pope's ear, and finally of
Rome's ancient greatness, the Republican virtues and
victories that had been before ever the Pope was. His
audience, whom this honest and really simple man led so
subtly towards new ideals, consisted largely of the Trasteverines, who were to Rome what the Lazzaroni were to
Naples, its most characteristic and primitive inhabitants.

---

[1] *Ciceruacchio*, 73–82. Also *Martinengo Cesaresco*, 218 ; *Bresciani*, vi. 45.

They dwelt in those famous Tiber-side slums, crushed in between the river and the Janiculan hill, where the early Christians had first spread the faith in what was then the poor Jewish quarter of the Imperial City. The modern dwellers in Trastevere, until Ciceruacchio emancipated them, were more proud of the presence of the Pope in Rome than impatient of his despotism. During the disturbances of 1831 feeling in the capital had been on the side of Government.[1] The bad reign of Gregory XVI. had done much to prepare men's minds for change, and in the early months of Pio Nono's mild *régime* Liberalism became prevalent among the people of Rome.

All through 1847 the agitation continued, and the Pope, as his wisest friend Rossi remarked, squandered the treasures of his popularity. At last, when the news of the grant of Constitutions in Naples, Tuscany, and Piedmont, followed by the Revolution in Paris, had stirred the Roman mob to a frenzy of emulation, Pio Nono, in March 1848, was forced to concede a Fundamental Statute,[2] which did not indeed surrender the power of the Pope and cardinals, but associated with them a council of elected deputies to aid them in their legislative functions. There was a strictly limited franchise, and it was confined to persons willing to profess the Catholic faith. At the same time that he granted this not very satisfactory charter, Pio Nono changed his clerical ministry for one in which more than half the portfolios were held by laymen. While the Pope was making these concessions, the Austrians were expelled from Milan and the Lombard war began.

Two months later a more Liberal ministry was installed, in which Mamiani was the leading spirit. If he had been given a free hand, Mamiani would not only have put vigour into the war in Lombardy, but would have liberalised the domestic institutions of the Papal States, and thereby secured them from absorption in a united Italy. But this would have involved relegating the Pope as temporal ruler

[1] *Giovagnoli*, 142, 143.   [2] The text will be found in *Farini*, i. 372–383.

to a status similar to that of the King of England—a monarch
who reigns, but does not govern ; and under those conditions
Clericalism would have had to come to terms with the
people.   Consent to such a policy would have marked out
the Pope, in the eyes of the clergy and the cardinals, as the
enemy of what they called religion.   Such a position would
have been impossible for the head of the Catholic Church,
and would not have lasted for long, even had Pio Nono
desired to create it.   But he had no such wish.[1]   He was
growing frightened at the course of events, angry with the
Liberals, fearful of estranging the German Catholics, and
irritated to find that he had been forced against his will
into an offensive war against Austria.   As some 12,000 of
his subjects were taking the field in his name in Lombardy,
he cut the ground from under their feet by the famous
' Allocution,' of April 29, 1848, in which he declared that the
idea of waging an offensive war on Austria was ' far from
his thoughts.'   From that day onwards he had forfeited
the sympathy of all good Italians, and was compelled to
rely more than ever on the support of the clericals and San-
Fedists.[2]

Then came Custoza, followed by the Austrian recovery
of Milan, and the end of the Lombard war (August).   Immediately the democratic movement broke out in Central
Italy in wild agitation and alarm.   The Moderates were
discredited, having failed to carry with them the Pope and
the Tuscan Grand Duke.   The supposed betrayal of the
national cause by Charles Albert at Milan made all forms
of monarchy suspect.   A crusade of national republican
defence against Austria was preached by the extremists of

[1] Mrs. Browning, in 1848, wrote in *Casa Guidi* :—
    ' But only the ninth Pius after eight,
        When all's praised most.   At best and hopefullest,
    He's Pope—we want a man ! his heart beats warm,
        But like the Prince enchanted to the waist,
    He sits in stone and hardens by a charm
        Into the marble of his throne high-placed.'
[2] *Farini*, iii. 50, 61 ; *Gabussi*, i. 231-235 (for text of the ' Allocution ' and
comment).

the clubs, who found ready listeners at that juncture in the average Liberal, both in Tuscany and the Papal States. Now, if ever, the Mazzinian ideals would control the real course of events.

Such was the state of things in Central Italy when Garibaldi, in October 1848, appeared upon the scene.

CHAPTER V

THE DEMOCRATIC PROTEST IN CENTRAL ITALY, OCTOBER
1848–FEBRUARY 1849—MURDER OF ROSSI—FORMATION
OF GARIBALDI'S LEGION—THE ROMAN REPUBLIC [1]

> 'Yet, Freedom ! yet thy banner torn, but flying,
> Streams like the thunderstorm *against* the wind.'
>
> *Childe Harold*, iv.

IN the autumn of 1848, Garibaldi, having returned from
his brief campaign in the Alps to the Piedmontese Riviera,
was looking round for some other scene to which he and
his companions could carry the 'People's War.' His
eye fell first upon Sicily, still in arms against its king.
Ferdinand II., King of Naples and Sicily, having by force and
fraud recovered his absolute power on the mainland, was
attempting to reduce the rebellious island by those methods
of Turkish barbarism which won him the cognomen of
Bomba.[2] The residuary of the name and traditions of
the great house of Bourbon, Ferdinand stands in history
as the type of what all tyranny must come to at the last ;
from Louis XIV. to *Bomba* the step is not so long as it
seems. In 1851, after he had re-established his power
in every part of his dominions, he drew down on himself
the terrible visitation of Gladstone, and was pilloried
before Europe in the 'Letters to the Earl of Aberdeen.'
But he died upon the throne, and it was his son who, in 1860,
was chased out of his kingdoms by Garibaldi.

---

[1] For this Chapter see large map of Central Italy at end of book.

[2] *Bomba* means 'a shell.' He won the name by the destruction of Messina
by bombardment, accompanied by massacre of the inhabitants without respect to
age or sex, September 1–7, 1848. *Nisco*, 104, attributes the name to the bombardment of Palermo, January 1848. Such were the reasons why he was called
Bomba, not, as a Clerical writer of to-day tells us, 'en raison de son embonpoint'
(*Bittard des Portes*, 140) ; *King*, i. 316 ; *Tivaroni, Aust.* iii. 335–350.

Eleven years and seven months before the hour approved by fate, Garibaldi for the first time sailed from Genoa to liberate Sicily (October 1848). He had with him some seventy companions, of whom more than half had come with him from South America; since most of them were officers, they were prepared to enlist and command a legion, but were not sufficiently numerous to take the field themselves before they had recruited a force to follow them.[1] On the way to Sicily they touched at Leghorn, where the populace so strongly urged Garibaldi to land with his men that he consented to come on shore, and thenceforth, for one eventful year, was involved in the war and politics of Central Italy.[2]

Garibaldi, in yielding to the prayers of the Democrats of Leghorn, had felt that Sicily was too far from the real scene of action, that the fate of the island could not affect the fate of the peninsula, but that Ferdinand's power might, on the other hand, be given its mortal wound by a march on Naples. He had not been disembarked many hours before he sent a characteristic telegram to the Grand Duke's Ministers at Florence, asking them whether they would put him at the head of the Tuscan forces to operate against the Neapolitan Bourbon—'Yes or no; Garibaldi.'[3]

Another reason against proceeding to so remote a point as Sicily was that the war against Austria in the North might be renewed at any moment. Already Piedmont, meditating a denunciation of the armistice and a rush on Milan, had begun to negotiate for the aid of Tuscany and Rome. But the ministers of the Pope and of the Grand Duke, representing for the moment the Moderate party, were more anxious to keep down the Democrats at home than to enter on a perilous crusade in Lombardy; it was, how-

[1] *Loev.* i. 37; ii. 22–27. In this important respect the expedition differed from that of 'The Thousand' who sailed under Garibaldi from Genoa for Sicily in May 1860.

[2] Anita had sailed from Genoa with her husband, but returned to her children at Nice, from either Leghorn or Florence. *Denkwürdigkeiten*, ii. 144. *Sforza*, 9–17. She joined him again at Rieti, in the following February or March.

[3] *Sforza*, 13; *Mem.* 208.

ever, doubtful if they could resist the cry of the town populations for war. The position was the more strained because Austria was clearly unwilling to allow the existence in Central Italy of Governments even partially constitutional, and had already in August violated the Papal territory by attacking Bologna. There the invaders had been repulsed by the valour of the mob, and the Democrats pointed to the defence of Bologna as a sequel to the Five Days of Milan, another proof that the people always won when not burdened by Royal leadership. Enraged with Austria, furious with their own rulers, the clubs in the Tuscan and the Papal cities were agitating fiercely for revolution at home as a preliminary to a second Lombard crusade.

The Moderates in their last struggle to retain power were nobly represented by Guerrazzi in Florence, and Pellegrino Rossi in Rome. Guerrazzi was at heart a Liberal and a Nationalist, whereas Rossi was an administrative reformer only; but at this moment each of them, with little support from public opinion, and with no enthusiastic party behind him, was opposed alike by the Democrats who strove for an immediate victory and by the Clericals who worked for the reaction by impartially hastening the downfall of every constitutional Government. Ministers, scarcely able to maintain their footing in such a whirlwind, were exasperated by the news that Garibaldi, who was no halcyon, had come to them from the sea. Their only thought was how to get rid of him again.

Guerrazzi, for his part, readily agreed that the Garibaldians should be passed through the Tuscan territory into Romagna. He hurried them through to Florence, where they had a grand reception from the people, and thence with all haste up the passes that lead over the Apennines towards Bologna. If the warm invitation to land given to Garibaldi by the inhabitants of Leghorn had raised in him hopes of recruiting large numbers for his Legion in Tuscany, he was disappointed. The somewhat cosmopolitan sea-port where he had been pressed to disembark was more Democratic than the average Tuscan town,[1] and in the rural districts, the peasants, under the influence of the priests and nobles, were afraid of a strenuous anti-Austrian policy which would involve conscription, taxation, and war. The Tuscans were not like the hardy Piedmontese or the fierce Romagnuols.[2] Their Grand Duke Leopold had been for many years the least unpopular monarch in Italy : all that Robert Browning, in his capacity as Republican of Florence, could find to say against him, was to call him a dotard.[3] So, by the time that Garibaldi and his officers reached Filigare, on the borders of the Tuscan and Papal territory, they and their Legion did not muster much more than a hundred men all told.[4]

[1] *Farini*, ii. 356, 357. But even in Leghorn he got very few recruits.

[2] Mrs. Browning, who saw the whole course of revolution and reaction in Florence, in 1848–49, from *Casa Guidi Windows*, speaks, in Part ii., with scorn of the unwarlike character of the Tuscan Revolutionists, of whom she had expected greater things when she wrote Part I. :—

> ' You say we failed in duty, we who wore
> Black velvet like Italian democrats,
> Who slashed our sleeves like patriots, nor forswore
> The true republic in the form of hats ?
> We chased the archbishop from the Duomo door,
> We chalked the walls with bloody caveats
> Against all tyrants. If we did not fight
> Exactly, we fired muskets up the air
> To show that victory was ours of right.
>
> .   .   .   .   .   .
>
> ' We proved that Austria was dislodged, or would,
> Or should be, and that Tuscany in arms
> Should, would dislodge her, ending the old feud ;
> And yet, to leave our piazzas, shops, and farms,
> For the simple sake of fighting, was not good—
> We proved that also.'

It was this sort of thing that made Garibaldi sometimes feel and speak so bitterly of some of his countrymen, in spite of his devotion and gratitude to the heroes to whom he owed his successes. He came back from South America from among a sparse and turbulent population of rough-riders, always ready for the hardships of campaign and the dangers of battle, and, in contrast to them, he naturally found some of the Italians of Europe ' unwarlike.' *Mem.* 241.

[3] ' When the hour is ripe, and a certain dotard
> Is pitched, no parcel that needs invoicing,
> To the worst side of the Mont Saint Gothard,
> We shall begin by way of rejoicing.'
>
> *Old Pictures of Florence.*

[4] *Sforza*, 20, 23 ; *Mem.* 208 ; *Loev.* i. 23, 37, 38 ; ii. 22, 23.

On entering the Roman States, Garibaldi found an opponent worthy to be measured against him. Pio Nono had now for some time broken with the Liberal ministry of Mamiani; and in the middle of September he committed his affairs to the man who might have done much to save the Papal authority if he had been trusted twelve months before. Pellegrino Rossi,[1] an Italian by birth, but in training and ideas a Genevan and French publicist of the conservative school of Guizot, had recently been diplomatic agent for France at Rome, and had in that capacity won the personal confidence of the Pope. He was detested both by the Clericals and by the Democrats; for his object was to preserve the Temporal Power, with but a slight infusion of the principle of self-government, by reforming and modernising the clerical bureaucracy. He was confident that any State could be saved, any political problem solved, by enlightened administration. He represented a type commoner in the days of Napoleon I., or in more recent Imperialist times, than in his own day, when fervid Liberalism struggled with obscurantism for the possession of the world. He certainly knew what good administration was, but he disbelieved in self-government, and he was unnecessarily offensive and unsympathetic towards those whom he despised. It can easily be imagined that one who had discussed political theory with the grave oligarchs of Geneva and sat at the feet of Guizot, had not much respect for the men who at that moment led the Democratic party in the streets of Rome and in the Council of Deputies. He was not likely to admire the merits of Ciceruacchio, and he was certain to be disgusted by his faults; while such a man as Sterbini deserved all his contempt.

Entering on office late in September 1848, Rossi at once took the State in hand. He inaugurated schemes for telegraphs and railways, began to reform the finances at the expense of the clergy, and attempted to clean out the corrupt civil service. These steps would have been enough

---

[1] For Rossi see especially *Giovagnoli, Fabrizi, Johnston, Farini, Bratti, Roman MSS. Ris.* 90 (his undelivered speech). See also *King* and *Bertolini.*

to alienate the Ultramontane party, even if he had not been a notorious 'thinker' with a Protestant wife. But with no less vigour he proceeded to alienate the Liberals. He was against Italian unity; he cultivated the friendship of King Ferdinand, driving Neapolitan refugees out of the Papal States [1]; he disliked Piedmont, and had no real intention of helping to win North Italy for Charles Albert,[2] so that the Albertists soon realised that he was the most serious obstacle to the realisation of their hopes. With the Democrats he kept no terms even in appearance, but proceeded to put down the agitation in the Roman States by a strong coercive policy. Much of his work in this respect was salutary, consisting of the suppression of anarchy and violence; and this part of it was taken up again six months later by Mazzini. But Rossi meant not only to suppress disorder, but to stop the agitation and to crush the Democrats.

In pursuance of this policy, Rossi had first to turn his attention to Bologna, which he himself had the honour to represent in the Council of Deputies. The second city in the Papal States, it was even more unanimously Liberal than Ravenna and Rimini, and perhaps for that reason was less addicted to feuds and to political crime.[3] But, unfortunately, after the splendid repulse of the Austrians by the Bolognese on August 8, their town fell for a short time under the domination of a set of bloodthirsty rascals, many of them the wreckage of the defeated armies drifting homewards from the Lombard campaign. Under a more or less sincere pretence of taking popular vengeance on the *sbirri* of the old *régime*, the Terrorists hunted their enemies along the arcades that adorn the streets of Bologna, and massacred them in the open day. The terror was, indeed, suppressed, largely by the efforts of the Moderate Liberal Farini, and with the grateful assent of the populace;[4] but, when Rossi became minister at Rome, Bologna was still

---

[1] *Fabrizi,* 18; *Roman MSS. F. R.* 7, 24.
[2] *Bratti,* 10; *Giovagnoli,* 326; *Johnston,* 183, 184.   [3] *Farini,* ii. 129.
[4] *Farini,* ii. 330–337.

in the power of the more respectable part of the Democratic mob, under the leadership of Father Gavazzi.

The allegiance of the Bolognese was at this time paid to two remarkable churchmen, both of the Barnabite order—Gavazzi and Ugo Bassi. Gavazzi was a native of the town, Bassi of the district, of Bologna. Both had been profoundly impressed by the wrongs of Italy, and by the sins of the Church to which they belonged. Both used their powers of eloquence, not only to call sinners to repentance, and Italians to patriotic sacrifice, but also to denounce the evils of Rome in a manner hearty enough to have satisfied her traditional enemies. But there was a difference between the two men, in character, if not in opinion. Ugo Bassi was a saint, and had been well known as such to the cholera-stricken population of Palermo long before his political career began ; he is well worthy to be the hero of the beautiful historical and religious poem of Mrs. Hamilton King.[1] But in Father Gavazzi, besides much that was strong and genuine, there was a certain strain of vulgarity ; after the extinction of Italian liberty, in 1849, he went on starring tours in the Anglo-Saxon world, and fed the British public on highly seasoned food, during the campaign against ' Papal aggression ' which our grandfathers were then enjoying. However, it is only a question of taste, for Gavazzi was a true patriot and a genuine enthusiast.[2]

---

[1] *The Disciples.*

[2] See the three orations delivered to Scotch Protestant audiences in 1851, printed at the end of Nicolini's *Life of Gavazzi.* Dr. Spence Watson, who recollects Father Gavazzi at Newcastle in the 'fifties, writes to me :—

' He was far too eloquent not to be verbose, and he certainly was violent. I remember little of what he said in his lectures. His description of the prisons of the Inquisition and of the immorality of the priesthood was exceedingly vivid ; but he struck me, after all, as being a genuine man, with the faults which one would expect to find in a clergyman who had certainly a strong love of his country and had gone through much for it, but who had become so used to stirring great audiences that that which was a means to excite interest in the matters in which he absolutely believed, in the first instance, had become in itself an end. He lectured in a long black gown, and the great action that he used, and the way in which he threw this gown about him and off again was very theatrical, but it had a certain effectiveness.'

Young Mameli (see below pp. 186, 187) had the strongest aversion to Father

STATUE OF UGO BASSI, BOLOGNA.

These two members of the Church militant and rebel-lious had established their hold over Bologna in the Easter of 1848, when they preached the crusade calling the youth to arms for the first Lombard war. It was a memorable scene, for the place, the audience, the occasion, and one at least of the two preachers, were not unworthy to rouse the best feelings of the historic Italian race which Savonarola had stirred to a like brief fury of moral and political enthusiasm. The Bolognese assembled in the Piazza of their town surrounded by the stately symbols of its past greatness—the mediæval Municipio on one side, and on another the broad façade of San Petronio, left unfinished since the generation capable of such splendid scuplture had passed away. In that great open space (where to-day Victor Emmanuel rides in bronze, and the doves sit a score at a time on his saddle and his horse's mane, as though the *Re Galantuomo* were carrying them to market) the people of Bologna stood and listened in that first Easter of Italy's hope. From the steps of San Petronio Gavazzi and Ugo Bassi preached, stirring the crowd to paroxysms of emotion, of which much, no doubt, was passing and sensational, but much also profound and lasting. Men offered their lives, mothers their sons, and those who could not go to the war their wealth.[1]

A sad half-year had now gone by, and the soldiers and the preachers of the crusade had come back defeated. But Gavazzi was still, in the autumn of 1848, the uncrowned king of Bologna, and Rossi had no sooner assumed power at Rome than he determined that the preacher should be crushed. He sent for his friend General Zucchi, an old

Gavazzi, whose theatrical manners and eloquence he could not abide ; *Luzio*, 193. (See also other pamphlets mentioned under the title *Gavazzi* in the Bibliography.)

[1] *Zironi*, 96–100 ; *Gualtieri*, 68–71. It was when Bassi preached at the *Due Torri* (not at San Petronio) that the most famous incident took place—*viz.* a girl who had nothing else to give to Italy's war cut off her long hair and handed it to Bassi. The scene of this incident is indicated in a contemporary picture in the *Museo Civico*, Bologna, and oral tradition of those who were present asserts the same. For Bassi and Gavazzi, see also *Martinengo Cesaresco*, 210–242 ; *Venosta*; *Gavazzi*; *Johnston*, 356 ; *Facchini* ; and *Gavazzi, In Memoriam*.

soldier of the First Napoleon, and commissioned him to go to Bologna and put down the Democrats.

When, therefore, Garibaldi, coming from Florence in November 1848, descended on this city, he was touching the most sensitive spot in the body politic of the Roman States. It was not likely that General Zucchi would welcome the *cadre* of a formidable Democratic army, bent on recruiting and agitation ; when, therefore, the Garibaldians arrived at Filigare (November 9) they found their descent into Papal territory blocked by some 400 Swiss mercenaries. Even if their chief had been willing to commence civil war, he had not the force to cut his way through. The plains of the Romagna, the recruiting ground at which he was aiming, lay in front of him like the promised land. But how could he reach it ? He was indeed in evil plight. His men, ill clothed and fed, were exposed on the mountains in snow a foot deep. Guerrazzi refused to let them return through Tuscany ; Zucchi barred their advance. Was it for this, Garibaldi bitterly exclaimed, that they had crossed the Atlantic, to be starved and betrayed by their country- men ? He had, indeed, as little cause to love the Moderate governments as they had to love him.

At this critical juncture in his career, the populace of Bologna, led by Father Gavazzi, came to his rescue. Taking advantage of the momentary absence of General Zucchi at Ferrara, they rose in formidable numbers to protest against the exclusion of their hero, and cried out to the officer in command : ' Either our brothers come here, or you come down from that balcony.' So Garibaldi was allowed to enter Bologna alone, and was conducted in torch- light procession to the famous Hôtel Brun. A few days later he was permitted to fetch down his men from Filigare ; they did not enter the city itself, but turned off outside the gates along the road to Ravenna. During his stay in Bologna their chief had been in deep consultation on the subject of recruiting with the rich young radical, Angelo Masina—who was himself raising his gallant squadron of lancers—and with other leaders of the Democratic party whose local information and influence did much to enable Garibaldi to enlist in Romagna his legion of ' men who knew how to die.' [1]

The compromise to which General Zucchi had been forced by the Bolognese to consent, was that the Garibaldians should pass through the Romagna to Ravenna, and there take ship for Venice, which was holding out under Manin against the Austrians.[2] Masina and his lancers were also to sail for Venice from Comacchio. In this way Rossi would be well rid of the fighters : with the talkers he would know how to deal.' But Garibaldi and Masina, who were determined to stay near Ravenna at least until they had recruited formidable bodies of men, were not anxious to sail at all if any better opportunity offered, preferring, if possible, to head an invasion of Austrian or Neapolitan territory rather than go to Venice merely to die there in the last ditch. Rossi and Zucchi were no less resolved that they should sail forthwith, and there is every reason to suppose that the dispute between characters so determined would have been settled in the streets of Ravenna by a battle in which the Garibaldians and the populace would have fought together against the Swiss regiments sent there to enforce the embarkation.[3] Meanwhile, Father Gavazzi had been arrested by Zucchi, at Rossi's orders.[4] But the civil strife imminent in the provinces was averted by a base crime in Rome. News reached Ravenna, on November

[1] *Loev.* i. 6–15 ; *Ovidi*, 240, 241.

[2] We learn from *Zucchi*, 147, 148, that Rossi had sent orders to this effect as early as November 6, received by Zucchi November 9. And yet Zucchi would not have allowed Garibaldi to leave Filigare if he had not been compelled to do so by the Bolognese mob. I suppose that, as the man on the spot, he formed the opinion that if Garibaldi once got into the Romagna it would be more difficult to get him out again than Rossi supposed. Nor was he far wrong.

[3] I do not base this conjecture on the alleged letter of Zucchi to Rossi, promising to cut up the Garibaldians by grapeshot (*Nicolini*, 73), the authenticity of which is impugned by *Johnston*, 187, note 2. I take my ground on the general situation, and on the hostility to the Garibaldians expressed in undoubtedly genuine parts of the Rossi-Zucchi correspondence. (*Giovagnoli*, 258, 259, 406.) See also *Mem.* and *Loev.* i. *sub loc.*, *Zucchi*, 145–149 ; *Bonnet*, 5–11, and p. 289 below.

[4] *Zucchi*, 147, 148 ; *Loev.* i. 16, 17, and note.

18, that, three days before, Pellegrino Rossi had been murdered.

The last letter that Rossi ever wrote to General Zucchi, thanking him for his efforts against the Democrats in Romagna, breathed stern resolves of coercion :

'It seems (he wrote) that the disaffected will attempt some folly at the opening of the chambers. So much the worse for them if they carry out their plans. The Government is determined to imitate you. Farewell, dear friend.' [1]

In this spirit Rossi introduced a strong force of loyal Carabinieri into Rome, and paraded them along the Corso, while his proclamations took a menacing tone. On the other side the Democratic press attacked him fiercely, and stirred up feeling on behalf of Garibaldi, whom they declared to be treated disgracefully.[2] The revolutionary party, of which Ciceruacchio was the leading spirit, had won over many of the troops, both volunteers and regulars, and in the capital, as at Ravenna, street fighting seemed about to commence,[3] when the dagger took the place of the sword.

The history of the assassination plot against Rossi is hard to unravel; but there is a concurrence of first-hand testimony as to the man who did the deed. The murderer was Luigi Brunetti, the elder son of Ciceruacchio, acting with or without his father's knowledge, as may be, but certainly at the instigation of the vile politician, Sterbini, and with the co-operation of some of the *Reduci* volunteers.[4]

November 15 was the day fixed for the opening of the new session of the Council of Deputies, in the Palazzo della Cancelleria, when Rossi was to speak on behalf of the

[1] *Zucchi*, 149. [2] *Nicolini*, 72, 73. [3] *Giovagnoli*, 325 ; *Fabrisi*, 9–16.
[4] *R. I.* 1898, iii. 109–115 (Caravacci's evidence), and iii. 356–358 ; *Costa*, 37–39 ; *Giovagnoli*, 268–272, 327, 342, and chapter vii. *passim*, and *Brancaleone*, i. 6–10. Giovagnoli's work is based on the extensive documents of trials arising out of the murder. See particularly the evidence of Testa about Sterbini, *Giovagnoli*, 367, 368. I am not certain of Ciceruacchio's innocence, but the only direct evidence there is absolves him of complicity before the fact (*R. I.* iii. 112).

Government. The first warning [1] of danger was the news brought him when he was about to start, that the crowd round the entrance was in a hostile and even dangerous mood, but it was late to make new arrangements, he was a brave man, and he determined not to keep Rome waiting. The Piazza in which he dismounted from his carriage was closely packed by a concourse of the mixed character usual on such an occasion,[2] but in the entrance lobby of the Palace and at the foot of the staircase, a group of blackguards were conspicuous in the uniforms of the Volunteers returned from the Lombard campaign, and known as the *Reduci*— a corps that contained better elements. As Rossi's tall figure drew near them, they raised a yell of execration, but he pushed his way through to the staircase, showing on his pale, intellectual features the scorn he felt for such enemies. He had his feet on the lowest steps, when a man struck him on the side, and as he turned his head Luigi Brunetti on the other side took advantage of this move- ment to stab him in the neck. No second blow was needed.[3]

The *Reduci* were in possession of the place, and protest was dangerous. But two young Democrats who had come on purpose to prevent the murder—Nino Costa, the artist afterwards so famous, and his friend Grandoni, who from his close connection with the *Reduci* had heard enough to fear that a crime was intended—raised loud cries of anger, and barely escaped from the throng with their lives.[4] Even Costa never did a braver or better thing for Italy.

It would have been well if the same spirit had been shown elsewhere. The Deputies in the Chamber above, who had not yet produced a Democratic chief capable of saving the State or even of leading a party with decency,

---

[1] *Giovagnoli*, 272, 273. He denies (271) the dramatic stories told by *Pasolini,* (99–100), and others, of warnings conveyed to Rossi by priests, &c.

[2] *Giovagnoli*, 272–275.

[3] *Giovagnoli*, 277 ; *Roman MSS. Ris.* 97.

[4] *Costa*, 37–38 ; *Giovagnoli*, 357, 358 ; *R. I.* 1898, iii. 115. Grandoni was afterwards unjustly condemned for the murder, in May 1854, and died in prison June 30 of that year. *Roman MSS. Ris.* 97.

G

dispersed in bewilderment and fear, without reprobating
the murder done at their door or making any demonstration
to discourage the assassins.[1] During the rest of the day
the authorities and the mass of the people—Democrats,
Moderates, and Clericals alike—remained inactive: many
were relieved that Rossi was gone, and nearly all were
afraid of those who had despatched him. So little was done
in the interests of order and common humanity that, at
nightfall, a small crowd—rather more than a hundred in
number—ventured to howl brutalities under the victim's
house, so that his widow must have heard the odious
incantation :

> 'Benedetta quella mano
> Che il Rossi pugnalò.'[2]

It was not a proud day for the Senate and people of Rome.

To posterity few political murders appear more execrable ;
but, at the time, the democratic and the nationalist spirit,
which Rossi had set himself to curb, ran so high that the feeling was that of relief, if not of joy. An analogy to the state
of public sentiment can be found in the rejoicings throughout
England at the murder of Buckingham. The political
situations in the two cases were not wholly different, and in
the matter of taking human life Italian civilisation was,
perhaps, at very much the same stage of evolution in 1848
as English civilisation had been two hundred and twenty
years before, when the 'killing affray' was only just in
process of dying out.[3]

So general was the sense of relief throughout the Papal
States that it affected persons who, if they had consulted
their private conscience alone, would have been deeply
indignant at the murder. Margaret Fuller, the friend of
Emerson and Carlyle, the flower of Bostonian intellect in its
great days,[4] wrote to her mother, from Rome :

[1] *Farini*, ii. 408 ; *Giovagnoli*, 281.
[2] 'Blessed be the hand which stabbed Rossi,' *Giovagnoli*, 288, 289 ; *Pasolini*,
102.
[3] See p. 61, note 2 above (Byron).
[4] There were, however, irreverent Bostonians capable of poking fun at her in
their private correspondence. *Story* (Henry James), i. 105, 106.

'For me, I never thought to have heard of a violent death with satisfaction; but this act affected me as one of terrible justice.' [1]

But it is much more sad to have to record the words of Garibaldi's *Memorie* :

'The ancient Metropolis of the world, worthy once more of her former glory, freed herself on that day from the most formidable satellite of tyranny, and bathed the marble steps of the Capitol with his blood. A young Roman had recovered the steel of Marcus Brutus.'

It is true that he also says :

'As a follower of Beccaria, I am opposed to capital punishment, and therefore I blame the dagger of Brutus.'

Nothing illustrates more clearly than this passage the intellectual confusion of Garibaldi's mind, and the mass of unassimilated theories and historical ideals that fermented there.   His only reason for rejecting the classical examples of tyrannicide, which the youth of his age and country were brought up to admire as the model of ancient virtue, is, so he tells us, his objection to all capital punishment. Yet nothing was more characteristic of the discipline which he maintained in his Legion than the readiness with which he had his men shot for acts of theft or violence,[2] a readiness which, being tempered with humanity, was useful and even indispensable.   The restraint which he managed to impose upon the turbulent spirits under his command, among whom the element of ' Jacobinism ' was always latent, was largely due to his employment of this extreme rigour.   Officers who accompanied his retreat from Rome in the following summer tell us that on that march ' he had two punishments: reprimand and death.' [3]   How then could he disapprove of political assassination on the ground that he objected to the death penalty ?

On the other hand it would not be fair to deduce, from his foolish words about Rossi's murder, that he ever had

<hr />

[1] *Fuller*, iii. 186.   [2] *Hoff.* 330, 365 ; *Loev.* ii. 182, 183.   [3] *Hoff.* 333.

anything to do with assassination plots, or that he was callous in taking the lives of his enemies. The very opposite is the established truth. It must be laid to the credit, not of his head, but of his heart, that the brutal school of South American warfare, the cruelties of Austrians, Papalists, and Neapolitans, the low standard of some of his own Italian followers, and the violent sentiments natural to the revolutionary party of which he became the leader, had no deteriorating effect on his action. His political passions never led him to commit a deed inconsistent with the tenderness of his nature and his constant perception of the brotherhood of man. The priests, against whom he is perpetually inveighing in his *Memorie*, were safe in his hands.[1] He constantly spared disguised military spies who, by the law and custom of war, had fairly forfeited their lives.[2] It was his special care to save the lives of his enemies in battle, and for the vanquished foe he was all tenderness and respect.[3] In the long course of his many campaigns and dictatorships he kept himself singularly free from the unnecessary shedding of blood ; and foul murder, like that of Rossi, was as far from his methods of action as anything could be. The tenderest of the brave, he took thought not only for men and women, but for the joys and sufferings of animals ; ever since the day when, as a child, he had cried over the wounded grasshopper, he was brother to every living thing. He could not endure that a bird should be caged, nor allow an animal to be struck in his presence. It pained him even to see flowers plucked, or a bough wantonly broken, because ' the great Spirit of Eternal Life is in everything.' During his Dictatorship in Naples, in 1860, he spent, in trying to remedy the condition of the cab-horses, much time which others thought he should have given to tasks of government in time of crisis ; and in the following year, when he was the most

[1] The negative evidence of this throughout his career is complete. He had already, at Forlì, severely rebuked the mob for raising the cry ' morte ai preti.' *Lazzarini*, 45.

[2] *Hoff.* 397, 400, 401 ; *Belluzzi*, 36.

[3] *Mem.* 61, 175, 291, 438 ; *Rug.* 37 ; *Vecchi's Caprera*, 54, 55.

famous man in Europe, he thought it natural to go out at night in the rain to seek a strayed lamb among the rocks and brushwood of Caprera.[1]

And yet, under the influence of passion and sentiment, he could write foolish stuff about Rossi's murder. No wonder there were men who said that he had ' a heart of gold and the brains of an ox.'

Though the method of Rossi's removal from power alienates much of our sympathy with his opponents, it should not blind us to the fact that the minister was trying to apply the *juste milieu* to a situation which was revolutionary in all its passions and in all its opportunities. He discouraged the forces making for vigorous initiative and national war against Austria, and tried to execute a domestic reform in the Papal States while putting down the reforming party.[2] Even his personal supporters, the enlightened men who led the small Moderate party, much as they disliked the Democrats, seem to have recognised his mistake in refusing to join Piedmont in the attack on Austria. Pasolini and Minghetti, summoned to the Quirinal a few hours after Rossi had fallen, were consulted as to the formation of a new ministry. Though filled with the first grief and horror at the murder of their friend, they mastered their passionate resentment against the slayers enough to tell the Pope that no Government could be carried on ' which persisted in holding aloof from the war of national independence.'[3] But if Pio Nono had been unwilling to fight for Italy before Rossi's murder, he was not likely to consent now, and the voice of such a man as Pasolini was never again to win credence in those counsels. The long reign of a more sinister influence had begun : for the shock which Rossi's death gave to Pio Nono hastened the last stages of a process, which from the moment of his

---

[1] *Mem.* 7 ; *Melena*, 23, 24 ; *King*, ii. 174 ; *Chambers*, 100; *Vecchi's Caprera*, 8, 44, 66, 67, 75, 76 ; *Guerzoni*, ii. 650–3.

[2] *Giovagnoli*, 325, 326.

[3] *Pasolini*, 101 ; *Minghetti*, ii. 125. Rossi himself had once said the same, but, in office, had acted in an opposite sense. (See *Giovagnoli*, 326.)

accession had been sure and rapid—the supposed Liberal of two years back had become as other Popes, and had taken Cardinal Antonelli as his counsellor and guide.

If anything more was lacking to fix the supremacy of Antonelli's will over the weak mind, it was supplied by the conduct of the Roman mob on the day after the murder. On November 16 they demonstrated against the Quirinal, fired at the Swiss Guard, and tried to coerce the Pope by the same methods of personal intimidation which the mob of Paris had employed on their famous visit to the Tuileries, in June 1792 ; but Pio Nono showed the same powers of passive resistance to outrage as Louis XVI.

The situation was not one that could last long, and, on November 24, the Pope fled, disguised as a simple priest. The flight from the guarded Palace in the heart of the capital to the frontier of the State closely resembled the flight to Varennes, except that it was ably and successfully conducted. The French Ambassador, D'Harcourt, though a party to the plot, appeared to some extent as its dupe, for the carriage containing the fugitives drove, not towards Civitavecchia and France, but southwards along the Appian Way to Gaeta in Neapolitan territory.[1]   The choice of route was significant of the fact that henceforth the Papacy stood for all that was most opposed to Italian aspirations, for all that was most retrograde in politics and in religion.   Pio Nono had gone to become the guest of King *Bomba* ; to put himself, as a clerical writer of the day justly said, ' under the filial protection of a pious and ever celebrated monarch.' [2]

The news that the Pope had gone was to many of the illiterate populace of Rome much what the news that the Ka'ba had disappeared would be to the people of Mecca. The consternation was great.   Many of the Trasteverines, newly converted to the radicalism of Ciceruacchio, still regarded the Pope much as the African savage regards his idol ; they would beat their fetish if he refused to do what they wanted, but they still vaguely believed in his thauma-

---

[1] *Spaur*, 18-23 ; *Maguire*, 61-66 ; *Johnston*, 203.   [2] *Montor*, 80, 81.

SCENE IN ROME, WINTER, 1848-49.

turgic powers, and felt for him a kind of family affection
growing out of an intimacy fourteen centuries old. Besides,
from a commercial point of view, the Pope was to Rome
what Diana was to Ephesus. In fact, it is thought that
if Pio Nono had been ready to treat, he would have been
welcomed back in a few months.[1] But from Gaeta he asked,
not for terms, but for submission, and this policy put the
game into the hands of the stronger spirits in Rome,
whose Republican propaganda gained ground every day.
Indignation with Antonelli and the Neapolitan gang that now
surrounded the Pope gave popularity to Mazzini's doctrine
that Rome would not lose in ceasing to be the capital of
the Catholic world, if she became instead the capital of
the Republican world, and more particularly of the Italian
Republic. The Mazzinian dream was presented in the
glowing colours of oratory to that impressionable populace,
which was capable, to a degree scarcely to be understood
by the English mind, of sympathy with murder one month,
and of exalted idealism the next. The word was passed
round, and the Republican chiefs came flocking to Rome
from all parts of Italy.

These events at Rome had their effect on the growth
and fortunes of the infant Legion in the Romagna. After
Rossi's murder, the voyage to Venice could safely be
postponed, since Garibaldi and his infantry at Ravenna,
Masina and his lancers in the island city of Comacchio,
could now be easily protected by the inhabitants from
the discouraged soldiers of Zucchi. Indeed, they were
soon strong enough to protect themselves, for Masina
and Garibaldi became fast friends, and, on November 23,
united their forces: the forty-two lancers, in their red
fezzes and picturesque uniform, came to join the Legionaries, and acted thenceforth as the Garibaldian cavalry.
Meanwhile the work of enlistment proceeded so rapidly
in the best of all possible recruiting grounds, that, at the

[1] This very common impression is confirmed by the impartial and well-informed
observer Admiral Key. (*Key*, 184.)

end of November, the Legion left Ravenna more than 500 strong.[1]

This regiment, which was to play the principal part in the Garibaldian epic of 1849, was known as Garibaldi's or the First Italian Legion, in memory of the Italian Legion of Monte Video, from which it was descended. Among the officers, the majority were natives of Piedmont or the Austrian provinces of the north ; and as many as twenty-two were Italians who had come home with their chief from Monte Video, besides two of South American extraction.[2] Of the sergeants and men the predominating element at this early stage was Romagnuol, and, until the end, the region best represented was the Romagna. But there were also many from Austrian Lombardy and Venetia, and later on from Umbria and the Tiber Valley.[3]

There were few peasants in the Legion.[4] The great majority belonged to the commercial and artisan classes, from whom were chosen out, by a process of voluntary natural selection, the most intelligent and enthusiastic partisans of Reform, together with the most adventurous spirits and the lovers of a roving life. There were a large number of 'students' in the ranks. The young men of the Universities, who played so great a part in the wars and politics of the *Risorgimento*, were individually and collectively conscious of the many ways in which the retrograde Italian Governments closed the various professional careers open to the educated middle class in France or England.[5] Their studies, too, led them to believe that

---

[1] *Roman MSS. Ruoli Gen.* 81 F. 1, show that on November 22 there were 512 Legionaries at Ravenna, and *Ruoli Gen.* 82 F.F. 10, 12, show that Masina's lancers were forty-two strong, counting officers.

[2] *Loev.* ii. 26, 27, 226–274. Other members of the staff, who were not officers, also came from America, and wore the red shirt. The orderly pictured on plate opposite p. 100 is one of these.

[3] *Loev.* i. 22–42 ; and ii. 22–27.

[4] With regard to the classes from which the Legionaries were drawn, my evidence is *Mem.* 219 ; and the list of 162 prisoners (taken at sea off Magnavacca) giving the trade or profession of each one. Of these 162, many belonged to the Legion, and the rest were probably much the same class of person. (*Bel.* App. I.)

[5] *King*, i. 104.

Italy was the heir of great glory, and that freedom had
been the watchword both of the classical Republics and
of the mediæval cities in their best days. Therefore, by
interest and conviction alike, the students were partisans
of the movement of emancipation, and not only supplied
the prophets, theorists, and statesmen who redeemed Italy,
but offered themselves by scores and hundreds as the common
food for powder.

One element in the Legion, which gave its enemies a
right to blaspheme, consisted of a few convicts whom
Garibaldi had admitted, under the characteristic delusion
that to fight for Italy would cure all moral diseases—a
point on which some of these gentlemen eventually undeceived him.[1]

But, on the whole, he was not far wrong when he called
his Legionaries 'the cultivated classes of the towns.'[2]
And these shopkeepers, workmen, and students were quite
equal, as the event proved, to pass the severest physical
tests of war, which must indeed have tried the pluck of the
numerous lads of fourteen to sixteen years of age, who were
in this, as in subsequent campaigns, a familiar feature in
the armies of Garibaldi. Sufferings were more readily borne
because of the example set by a chief who, even in the midst
of plenty, ate and drank most sparingly, and accepted the
return of privation as the natural lot of man. His followers
were ready to endure much at the request of a famous
soldier, the more so since he, being himself a man of the
people, and withal of a most tender and human heart,
was able to speak with them on terms of equality about
those whom they loved, to share their private griefs
and hopes, especially when they were wounded, and to
show a particular care and kindness for the younger
volunteers who had run away from school to fight for

[1] *Loev.* ii. 15–21.
[2] The Dutch artist, Koelman, describes how, at a midnight watch at one of the
old gates of Rome, in May 1849, he was thrilled by hearing the common
sentry (of Garibaldi's Legion) sing to the stars a stanza of Tasso's *Gerusalemme
Liberata.* *Koelman,* ii. 35–40.

Italy, and to whom he stood in some sort in place of a father.[1]

From the first the Legionaries had much to endure, since their chief had as yet no war-chest, and no support from Government. When they left Ravenna they were ill-armed, ill-clad, and without uniform—except Masina's handful of Bolognese lancers, equipped at their own expense and that of their wealthy Colonel, and the red-shirted staff officers and orderlies from South America, who alone represented the pomp and circumstance of war.[2]

And so this ragged regiment of fine fellows wandered about for the rest of the winter through Umbria and the Marches, spreading the democratic gospel, and creating for themselves a reputation of many colours. When they entered a town, the inhabitants, instructed by the fears of priests and of Moderates, looked anxiously from their windows at the entrance of the 'bandits,' though they often became friendly when they had seen and spoken to the young men, who were above the average of education and intelligence.[3] But the decided and often unpleasing manner in which the Legionaries expressed their Repub-licanism gave offence to some; others were alienated by the insults occasionally offered to monks, priests, and their relics, though Garibaldi punished such conduct most severely. By the discipline of the pillory (*berlina*), prison and capital punishment, he restrained the plundering propensities of his corps within closer limits than those usually observed by the soldiers of the period. But though his privates were not allowed to rob, the official requisitions which he was forced to make, as General, from the half-willing *communes* in order to feed and pay his men at all, and the uncertainty whether the Central Government would ever reimburse the localities, made it difficult to be enthusiastic for such expensive guests.[4]

---

[1] *Loev.* ii. 201–204; *Koelman*, ii. 109–114, for 1849. Garibaldian literature *passim*, and private information from old Garibaldini, about later wars.

[2] *Loev.* i. 43–51 and *passim*; *Guerrazzi*, 760.

[3] *Mem.* 219; *Foglietti*, 2.

[4] *Loev.* i. and ii. *passim*, especially ii., chap. xiv., where the whole question

In the middle of December, Garibaldi, accompanied by Masina, left his men for a few days and paid a flying visit to Rome, which he had not seen since his memorable journey with his father twenty-three years before. He now once more went to gaze on the Capitol and the Coliseum, which to him were the symbols, not merely (as they are to us) of time at war with human splendour and permanence, but of the past and future of his own dear land, and of the cause which inspired his life. These ruins were to him the title-deeds of Italy.

But he had the good sense to forbid the Clubs to conduct him in procession to the Capitol. Such triumphs, he said, had first to be won ; when Italy was freed, he would himself invite them to come with him. The rebuke was well timed, for it was his part to teach the Italians, and the Romans not least, how much of the bitter bread of war and suffering was needed to justify the intolerable deal of sack represented by so many speeches, processions, and classical allusions. He made friends, however, with Ciceruacchio and the other Republican leaders. The Provisional Government, not yet completely in touch with democratic sentiment, looked askance at him, and would do little to help his Legion, which was again suffering from want in the cold of the Apennine winter. So he returned, discontented, to his men at Foligno in Umbria.[1]

But events were moving inevitably towards a Republic, to which form of government, since the Pope would not treat, there was no alternative. In February a Constituent Assembly was summoned, and Garibaldi again went to Rome, as representative of the City of Macerata,[2] where his presence with the Legion had won him popularity. On February 8,

of the discipline of the Legion is discussed *in extenso* and in great detail from very numerous documents. For the system of paying the Legion see *Roman MSS. Ruoli Gen.* 80 F.F. 1-3, and *Loev.* i. 42 ; ii. 77-81.

[1] *Loev.* i. 66-75 ; *Mem.* 218, 219.

[2] In the Marches, south of Ancona ; not Macerata Feltria. (See *Foglietti, passim,* on his stay there.) Outside this town there is a particularly fine statue of him as he looked in 1849, with long hair.

1849, he took an enthusiastic part in the proclamation of the Roman Republic.

One of the first acts of the new State, carried by a unanimous vote of the Assembly, was to naturalise Mazzini, who at the beginning of March arrived in Rome, welcomed as its latest and greatest citizen. The sordid period of the Democratic revolution was over, and its period of idealism and heroism had begun. Mazzini speedily removed the elements of crime and coercion from the popular Government, and replaced them by a spirit of tolerance and liberty almost unexampled in time of national danger. Garibaldi gave to the warfare of the extreme Republicans something of the spirit of Thermopylæ, so often mouthed by orators whose stock-in-trade was classical history, but at last brought by the red-shirts into the region of fact. Little as they liked one another, these two men between them turned a rather limp revolutionary movement, begun in murder and frothy talk of the Clubs, into one of the great scenes of history. The Roman Republic showed the faults, but it showed yet more abundantly the virtues, of its origin as the work of an extreme faction. Its history is full of that appeal to the ideal in man that often guides the life of individuals, but finds little direct representation in the government of the world, except in those rare, brief moments of crisis and of concentrated passion when some despised ' ideologue ' is lifted to the top of the plunging wave.

' I entered the City one evening (writes Mazzini) with a deep sense of awe, almost of worship. Rome was to me as, in spite of her present degradation she still is, the Temple of humanity. From Rome will one day spring the religious transformation destined for the third time to bestow moral unity upon Europe. As I passed through the *Porta del Popolo*, I felt an electric thrill run through me—a spring of new life.'

approach of unity, by giving a new character to the local
pride of the Romans, and marking out Rome to all the
world as the capital of Italy and the only acceptable goal
of the national aspirations.

Desperation was the mood of the hour. The Kings and
the Moderates, said the Republicans, have betrayed the
People : let the People take their cause into their own
hands—let us have no more half measures. ' Dare ! and
dare ! and dare again ! ' So Danton had said when the
Austrian armies threatened the life of the mother of modern
Republics. And so now, in effect, said the Roman Democrats ; but theirs was the daring of men who, at bottom,
have little hope of immediate success. The ardour for the
Mazzinian Republic was less forcible and effective than
the French fury of 1793, but it was purer in its moral
conception. It was less effective, because it was strong
only in the towns ; the peasant of the Apennines could not
be roused to take arms, as Jacques Bonhomme had been
roused, to form the battalions of national defence. But
the Roman Republic was not cruel, and its advent was
followed, not by the increase, but by the suppression of
terrorism. In the first months of 1849 the new State fell
under the influence of men much better than the Sterbinis
and Carlo Bonapartes who had been prominent in Rome
at the time of the murder of Rossi. The newly elected
Constituent Assembly was a finer body, or, at any rate,
had far better guidance, than the late Council of Deputies.
Armellini the Roman lawyer, Muzzarelli the Liberal prelate,
and the gentle Saffi from Forlì in the Romagna, led the
Assembly in the early weeks of the Republic, and at the end
of March ungrudgingly yielded the real power to Mazzini, when
the triumvirate was formed. Until then he was only a mem-
ber of the Assembly, but from the moment of his first entry
into Rome he was its leading citizen and its real political chief.

It was the hope of Mazzini, with which he inspired the
people of Rome, to unite the whole peninsula in one Republic.
He dreamed that the work of liberation, starting from
Rome, would spread from State to State, in an order of

geographical expansion exactly the reverse of that by which Italian unity was in the end effected.

Tuscany and Naples were the nearest neighbours. The Tuscan Republic had been proclaimed ten days after that of Rome, and Mazzini, on his way south, had stopped to take a leading part in the revolution, effected at a meeting held under Orcagna's loggia in Florence (February 18), though he failed to persuade the Tuscans to incorporate their Republic with that of Rome. It was clear that they would be of little help in the coming death struggle against the armies of old Europe, for the forces of reaction within Tuscany itself were enough to render the overthrow of the Democrats probable even without foreign interference.

On the side of Naples, the foe was already in arms at the gate, for King Ferdinand, rejoicing in his new moral position as protector of the Pope, hoped to forestall Austria and France in the race to re-establish the Temporal Power. Had not his large, though not very efficient armies been already threatening the Roman border, the Republic would perhaps have granted the request of Garibaldi and his men to be allowed to go to the assistance of King Charles Albert against the Austrians, in the fatal Novara campaign (March 14–23).[1]

Charles Albert, who, in fighting and suffering with Italy in the Lombard war, had learnt too late to sympathise with the people, was a Liberal, perhaps for the first time in his life, during the six months that followed the surrender of Milan to the Austrians and the armistice of August 1848. Though he himself was safe in Turin, he could not forget those scenes of the retreat through Milan, and the cries of a people thrust back into slavery. He was a haunted man, and his naturally diseased imagination turned from religious to political visions. He too ' ate Austria in his bread.' Radetzky's brutal punishment of those who had trusted him to save them stirred him like a personal insult, and at length he found that neither he nor his Piedmontese subjects could any longer endure to watch the agonies of

[1] *Loev.* i. 128, 129.

Lombardy. But when, on March 14, 1849, he denounced the armistice, and gathered his forces for a last rush on Milan, Radetzky was better prepared than he. Crossing into Piedmontese territory, the Austrians won the decisive victory of Novara (March 23), where, once more, brave fighting and bad generalship distinguished the Italian army.

Charles Albert had vainly sought death in the battle. To obtain better terms for his country, he abdicated the throne and rode away disguised through the Austrian lines. Before that summer was ended, he had died in a Portuguese cloister, his heart broken for Italy. Much is forgiven him, because he loved her much. He had long imagined, in his religious and mystical melancholy, that God had set him apart to procure her liberation, on condition that he himself became a sacrifice,[1] and that unselfish thought may well be repeated by history as her final judgment of his life.

Young Victor Emmanuel, left to cope with triumphant enemies and mutinous subjects, inherited the allegiance of a still formidable army and the attachment of a small band of servants of the House of Savoy, as Liberal as the Whigs of the Reform Bill, but as loyal as any Swiss guard. He saved Piedmont from conquest, partly through the assistance of very serious threats made by France against Austria, partly by consenting to abandon for the time the Democratic parties in the rest of Italy. Austria insisted, as a matter of course, that he should leave Venice to its fate by the withdrawal of his fleet from the Adriatic—an act of necessity which the Republicans throughout the Peninsula factiously charged against him as a crime. But there was one thing which he would not surrender, and that was the Constitution granted by his father to Piedmont. All the tempting offers made by Radetzky to induce him to ' modify ' the great charter, which was destined to become the law of the kingdom of united Italy, were met by his staunch refusal, now celebrated in Italian popular art, which loves to depict the young and spirited king turning

---

[1] *Della Rocca*, 28.

GIUSEPPE MAZZINI.
From a Portrait by Madame Venturi about 1847.

away in indignation from the offers of the white-haired enemy of freedom.

The news that Piedmont was once more laid low reached Rome at the end of March. Although it had been necessary to keep the Garibaldians on the Neapolitan border, a few Roman troops had been sent towards the seat of war, but had not arrived in time to share in the disaster. The first result of Novara was that the Roman Assembly proclaimed a dictatorship of Mazzini, Saffi, and Armellini, under the title of ' Triumvirs,' with full executive power. Mazzini, however, directed the policy of his two colleagues as absolutely as the First Consul Bonaparte had directed the policy of Siéyès and Ducos. But his was the domination, not of supreme efficiency and egoism, but of an almost superhuman virtue, of an other-worldliness which long years of suffering and self-surrender had suffused through his being, so that those who looked on him and heard his voice were compelled to reverence the divine in man. While Garibaldi was being fashioned into a hero on the breezy uplands of Brazil, the more painful making of a saint had for eleven years been in process amid the squalid and fog-obscured surroundings of a London lodging-house. And now at last the finished product of so much pain and virtue shone before Europe in Italian sunlight, on the great stage of Rome. The saintliness which Carlyle had so fully acknowledged, though he would never yield to its persuasion, now cast its spell over the Roman people. They carried out Mazzini's behests in letter and in spirit, under the pure constraint of his nobility, laying aside sloth and cowardice, and abjuring at his appeal even the passion of revenge. ' Here in Rome,' he told the Assembly, ' we may not be moral mediocrities.' If Carlyle had had any eyes for the events of his own day, he would have seen in the friend whom he had so often made ' very sad ' by vociferous scorn of schemes for the moral redemption of Italy the grandest illustration of

H

his own theory that asserts the natural domination of Man over Men.[1]

In almost every town of the Peninsula, great or small, there was some group of young men who had been roused by Mazzini's appeal to devote their lives not to themselves, but to their country and their fellows. It was a process nothing short of conversion—for it was moral even more than intellectual. Garibaldi, before he went to America, had been one of the first thus awakened by the call of Mazzini ; but he was not altogether one of the ' disciples.' The form of religion on which Mazzini based his moral appeal to live for others was pure Deism, tempered by a loving respect for the Catholic form of Christianity from which he had separated ; he attached great import-ance to the bare belief in God. His watchword was *Dio e Popolo*, ' God and the People.' But Garibaldi, it is said, would sometimes call himself an Atheist,[2] when

---

[1] On June 17, 1844, the *Times* had protested finely against the opening of Mazzini's letters by our Government, but had rather ostentatiously de-clared its ignorance of Mazzini himself, saying that he ought not to be so treated, even if he was the most contemptible of mankind. Two days later a letter appeared in its columns signed ' Thomas Carlyle,' containing the follow-ing passage : ' It may tend to throw light on this matter if I now certify to you . . . that Mr. Mazzini is not unknown to various competent persons in this country ; and that he is very far indeed from being contemptible,—none further, or very few living men. I have had the honour to know Mr. Mazzini for a series of years ; and whatever I may think of his practical insight and skill in worldly affairs, I can with great freedom testify to all men that he, if I have ever seen one such, is a man of genius and virtue, a man of sterling veracity, humanity, and nobleness of mind, one of those rare men, numerable unfortu-nately as units in this world, who are worthy to be called martyr-souls ; who in silence piously, in their daily life, understand and practise what is meant by that.' On the other hand, Carlyle was most contemptuous of Mazzini's ideals and schemes. *Margaret Fuller* (iii. 100–101) records how, when the conversation one day turned on ' progress ' and ' ideals,' Carlyle was fluent in invectives on all our ' rose-water imbecilities.' ' We all felt distant from him, and Mazzini, after some vain efforts to remonstrate, became very sad. Mrs. Carlyle said to me, "These are but opinions to Carlyle ; but to Mazzini, who has given his all, and helped to bring his friends to the scaffold in pursuit of such subjects, it is a matter of life and death." '

Bolton King's *Mazzini* is a very noble delineation of the man. ' The Chief' in Mr. Meredith's *Vittoria* and the Dedication of Mr. Swinburne's *Songs before Sunrise* are the tribute of English literature.

[2] Only, indeed, in later life, and but seldom then. ' One night at a crowded Fulham party (1864) Mazzini was contending, as was his wont, that an Atheist could

he was particularly incensed against the ordinary type of priest, who he declared 'taught the peasants to hate Italy.' But more usually he spoke of ' God, the Father of all nations ; ' of 'the mighty power of a living God,' seen in nature ; or pantheistically of ' the soul of the Universe,' and of the great Spirit of eternal Life in everything.' He disliked ' miserable materialism.' He 'venerated the doctrine of Christ, because Christ came into the world to liberate the world from slavery.' [1] Christ was to him ' the virtuous man,' ' whom the priests had made God.' The general tone of his thought resembled that of Shelley, except that he was no philosopher, and had no consistent theories ; he had, instead, strong, primitive feelings, both positive and negative, that linked him to the Italian people and to human life.

It was not in Garibaldi's nature either to learn or to teach. Men, he declared, are reformed ' by example more than by doctrine.' And so his doctrine was of one word— '*Avanti!*' But on his lips it had as much power to transform the minds and souls of men as the studied wisdom of the theorist or politician. The magical effect of his voice and presence was such that, although as yet he had won no great victories for Italy, the worship of Garibaldi already rivalled that of Mazzini. During the spring of 1849 his influence was potent to enlarge the moral tone of the Republic and to animate its defenders.

From the end of January to the middle of April the Garibaldians were stationed at the border town of Rieti, in face of the Neapolitan enemy. It was here that the Legion rose in numbers from 500 to about 1,000 men, and at length obtained discipline, organisation, and equipment.[2] There were frequent quarrels between the Garibaldians and the National Guard at Rieti ; but the Legion was on

not have a sense of duty. Garibaldi, who was present, at once asked, " What do you say of me ? I am an Atheist. Do I lack the sense of duty ? " " Ah," said Mazzini, playfully, " you imbibed duty with your mother's milk "—which was not an answer, but a good-natured evasion. Garibaldi was not a philosophical Atheist, but he was a fierce sentimental one, from resentment at the cruelties and tyrannies of priests who professed to represent God.'—*Holyoake*, i. 220, 221.

[1] *Jack la Bolina*, 238 ; *Vecchi's Cap.*, 76, 88 ; *Mem.* 255, 291; *Guerzoni*, ii. 653.
[2] *Loev.* i. 113–141, ii. *passim.* *Roman MSS. Ruoli Gen.* 81, F. 3, f. 7.

H 2

the whole the most popular regiment with the Liberal party in the Republic because it represented in a concrete form the national and democratic idea. ' Italy,' said Ugo Bassi, who was sent by Mazzini to act as Garibaldi's chaplain—' Italy is here in our camp ; Italy is Garibaldi ; and so are we.' [1]

At Rieti a strong and beautiful friendship was formed between Ugo Bassi and Garibaldi, dating from their first sight of one another. Thenceforth, till the martyrdom of the friar, they were constantly together, on the battlefield, the march, and the bivouac. Garibaldi persuaded Bassi to change his clerical dress for the red shirt [2] which distinguished the other officers of the staff, and in that costume he continued his apostolate, much to the satisfaction of the Legionaries.

The rank and file were not, till near the end of the siege of Rome, dressed in the red shirt, but they had now obtained a uniform consisting of a loose dark-blue tunic and green cape, and the tall ' Calabrian hat' of operatic fame, with its turn-down brim, often adorned with black ostrich feathers. In that romantic and magnificent headgear, greatly preferable to the ugly little *képi*, they performed their deeds of arms in 'forty-nine.

It was clear that the military defenders of the new State would have no sinecure. Spain, Austria, and France were competing with Naples for the honour and advantage of restoring the Pope, although the Republic, whose destruction was regarded as the moral duty of the first Catholic power that could send enough troops to Rome, not only gave no diplomatic justification for interference, but set up within its own borders a standard of freedom and toleration entirely new in the history of Governments beset with foreign and domestic danger. Accusations of terrorism and confiscation were made against it by the reactionary parties,

---

[1] ' L' Italia è qui nel nostro campo, l' Italia è Garibaldi ; e siamo noi !' *Martinengo Cesaresco*, 229. It seems to have been a favourite cry of the time, as *Vecchi*, ii. 299, records that on July 2 the people in the Piazza of St. Peter's cried out at Garibaldi and his men, ' Voi siete l' Italia.' For Rieti see *Sassetti*, 90, 99-100.

[2] See letter of Ugo Bassi printed in *Bel.* 11, 12.

TYPES OF THE DEFENDERS OF ROME, 1849.

ORDERLY OF GARIBALDI IN ROME, 1849.
(Red blouse, Calabrian hat and ostrich feather.)
(These pictures are from the *Illustrated London News* of that date, by kind permission.)

now recovering power all over Europe. Mazzini was vexed [1] that these misrepresentations were repeated loudly in the English ' Times,' which declared that the aims and methods of his Roman Republic were identical with those of the ' reds ' of Paris,[2] although, in fact, his methods of preserving the State in time of danger were a strange contrast to those of the old French Jacobins, and his individualist legislation on behalf of the poorer classes went on different principles from the French Socialism of the day. The theory and practice of the Government are accurately expressed in the following ' Programme,' published by the Triumvirate on April 5 :

' No war of classes, no hostility to existing wealth, no wanton or unjust violation of the rights of property; but a constant disposition to ameliorate the material condition of the classes least favoured by fortune.'[3]

Regardless of the truth, the Clerical party proclaimed to Europe that their enemies were communists and socialists —names then as odious to the propertied classes as the name Jacobin had been fifty years before. ' Who does not know,' wrote the Pope in his Allocution of April 20, ' that the city of Rome, the principal seat of the Church, has now become, alas, a forest of roaring beasts, overflowing with men of every nation, apostates, or heretics, or leaders of communism and socialism ? '[4] But the only proof with which the charge of ' communism and socialism ' could eventually be maintained by Papal pamphleteers after the fall of the Republic, was the irrelevant fact that the villas Corsini, Valentini, Spada, and Barberini had been destroyed in battle (half by the French and half by the Italian guns), and that a few other houses outside the walls had been removed by the Triumvirate to facilitate the military defence of the city.[5]

And, indeed, all property was safe, except the enormous estates of the Church, which the mildest reform could not

[1] *Clough, P. R.* 147.
[2] *Times* leading articles, *e.g.* March 30 and May 11.
[3] *Mazzini,* ii. 61 (Atti della Rep. Rom.).
[4] *Allocuzione del sommo Pontefice.* [5] *Gli ultimi sessantanove giorni,* 165.

have left untouched. In other countries, Catholic and Protestant alike, the wealth accumulated by the mediæval Church had undergone large curtailment by a process of which the propertied class had been the chief beneficiaries. But it was not for squires, courtiers, or capitalists that Mazzini laid his hand on ecclesiastical property. It was for the benefit of the poorer peasants that he decreed the employment of confiscated Church land, as small holdings leased to cultivators at nominal rents ; it was for the benefit of the poorer parish priests that he joined in the movement to equalise the emoluments of ecclesiastics.[1]   If Mazzini had been permitted by Catholic Europe to carry out these edicts, he would have done much to relieve the poverty of the peasants, and something to rectify the distribution of salary among the clergy. Such changes, besides being good in themselves, would have made the Church both more efficient and less unpopular.

No change in doctrine, no State interference in ecclesiastical Government, above all, no persecution of cult, such as had marked the relations of the first French Republic to the Church, was dreamed of by the authorities at Rome. Mazzini was determined to give the necessary guarantees for the Pope's spiritual authority, and they were expressly granted in the admirable Constitution drawn up by the Assembly, which had not time to come into force before the Republic was murdered by France.[2]   When, shortly after the establishment of the Triumvirate, there occurred several cases of robbery of churches, the Government forbade the sale of any kind of clerical moveable property, arrested a Belgian landscape-painter in whose house such goods had been found, placed a guard in every church, and so effectually stopped the thefts.[3]   The services of the Church were freely and honourably conducted, libels against the priests were suppressed, and their persons were protected

---

[1] *Mazzini*, v. 371–374, *Official Acts of the R. R. King*, i. 328, 329.   *Tivaroni*, *Aust.*, ii. 381, 382.   The offices of the Inquisition were converted into tenement dwellings for the poor families of Rome.

[2] *Farini*, iv. 216–223, for text of Constitution.

[3] *Koelman*, i. 251, 252.

by Government. It was only after the unprovoked interference of France on behalf of the Clericals, that one or two particularly atrocious murders occurred in Rome, of priests supposed to be aiding the foreigner.[1] But the action of the authorities, the example and continual exhortation of Mazzini, put a stop to these crimes which might very easily have become contagious. Mazzini's own religion was unorthodox and mystical, but his sympathy with all religion and his belief in toleration were profound and sincere.

He took for the watchword of his Government : ' Inexorable as to principles, tolerant and impartial as to persons.' The enemies of the Republic, both clerical and lay, enjoyed the protection of Government for the hatching of plots against it within the walls of the capital. Mazzini knew what they were doing, and deliberately let them be. He ruled a State in time of foreign invasion and domestic crisis, ' without prisons, without trials, without violence.' [2] This was the ' bandit ' Government against which *Bomba* and the French Catholics were marching in the name of outraged morality.

The mildness of Mazzini's rule had this disadvantage, that, where the moral appeal failed, he had no physical force on which to rely. He persuaded the people of Rome to behave admirably as a whole, but those who, like the murderer Zambianchi, would not listen to the voice of his charming, did too much of their own will. And in the more distant provinces, removed from the sphere of his personal influence, the ability of the Government to enforce order was not always on a level with its desire. In Romagna and the Marches, where the blood-feud was custom of the country, greatly enhanced by long years of Papal misrule, the Civil Service was full of adherents of the old order, and the lay administration, without which but little could be done, had yet to be created. When we consider that the

[1] I relate these events below, pp. 149, 150, in their proper chronological order.
[2] *Tivaroni, Aust.* ii. 429 ; *Johnston,* 294–296 ; *King,* i. 329 ; *Pisacane,* 9 ; *Mazzini,* i. 182 ; ii. 61, 91,—*Note Autobiografiche, Lettera al Ministero Francese,* and *Atti della Rep.*

Republic was left to grapple with a population holding mediæval ideas as to the sacredness of human life, by means of a mediæval instrument of Government, we may well admire the rapid steps towards a better state of things which were made in the few months before the Austrian and French troops put an end to the new *régime*. At Ancona, the worst centre of anarchy, where the terrorists were committing assassinations at the rate of half-a-dozen every day, order was restored by the courage and severity of the Government agent Orsini, afterwards renowned for a darker deed.[1]

The worst side of the Republican administration—apart from a general want of vigour in the members stultifying the good intentions at the head—was the hopeless welter in which finance remained. Here Rossi might have done something to extricate the State from a condition which the clerical Government had created, and with which the Republicans were quite unable to contend, save by the reckless issue of paper. Refusing the temptation to adopt the most odious of revolutionary expedients, they left the property of the *émigrés* to Gaeta untouched ; they also removed some of the more oppressive of the indirect taxes that fell heavily on the common people. But while they knew what taxes to avoid, they did not know so well what to impose, or how to save the State from financial disaster.[2]

On the whole, the Republic grew more popular with the various classes of the community as its intentions and character became more clear. At worst it stood for Italy, and where one man was a zealous Republican, ten were good Italians. Some friars and priests, in spite of the Pope's excommunication, rallied to the tolerant and national Government ; the middle classes and working men of the towns became daily more enthusiastic ; the peasants, except where the influence of reactionary priests was strong, grew friendly in some parts, and ceased in others to be actively hostile ; in the Romagna, they were staunch for the Republic.

[1] *Orsini*, 79–80 ; *Johnston*, 361–365 ; *Monitore Romano*, April 30 ; *King*, i. 330, 331 ; *Tivaroni*, *Aust.* ii. 379, 380.
[2] *Valeriani*, 89, 90, 133–138 ; *Johnston*, 245, 246 ; *King*, i. 328.

The Trasteverines and other inhabitants of Rome were growing every day more strongly opposed to the restoration of clerical rule. Even the upper-class leaders of the Moderate party, deeply as they had been alienated by the Democratic violence of the last winter, much as they still disapproved of the ideas upon which the Mazzinian State was founded, could not, with returning spring, view without admiration a stand so gallantly made for Italy against a European league of her oppressors.[1]

While the Republic was daily strengthening its authority and improving its moral position, the armies of Austria, Naples, Spain, and France were hastening by sea and land to its overthrow. The Austrians who, after Novara, sent large bodies of troops southwards, began slowly to occupy the Romagna. But the French were in a position to strike a blow at the heart. On April 25, some eight to ten thousand French troops under General Oudinot (son of Napoleon I.'s Marshal), landed at Civitavecchia, forty miles north-west of Rome. The orders given to Oudinot by his Government spoke of the Roman Republic as an unpopular usurpation, which would soon be removed. He was not to recognise the Triumvirate or the Assembly, but he was to treat their members with courtesy as individuals; he was to effect the occupation of the capital as a friend, although, if the inhabitants were so absurd as to object to the entrance of a foreign army within their walls, he must employ the necessary amount of force.[2] His own somewhat illogical proclamations, though deceptive in the assertion that the French would not coerce the Roman people, did not conceal the fact that they came to overturn the existing Government and restore the Papal authority in some form or other.

The executive òf the French Republic was more responsible than the legislature for this novel development

[1] *King*, i. 331, 332. Farini's attitude towards the Democrats becomes much more favourable during the last months of the Republic. (See *Farini*, iii. 422, 423, and *Dandolo, passim.*)

[2] Orders printed in *Moniteur* of May 8.

of the nation's foreign policy, which diverted the channel
of its interference in Italy from the Lombard plain to the
Roman Campagna—from friendship with the Liberal cause
to alliance with its worst enemies. The French Assembly,
though it did not effectually oppose the action of the Government, contained strong elements of genuine Republicanism;
some of the Ministers, on the other hand, were partisans of
the clerical and military reaction which had first grown out
of the anti-Socialist panic, and was now fast drifting towards
autocracy, under the influence of the President, Louis
Napoleon. Men of all parties were agreed that an Austrian
monopoly of the Italian peninsula must not be allowed, and,
after Novara, France had flung her shield over Piedmont
because she could not afford to have Austria master of all
Italy up to the French border. The new President, heir to
the traditions of Rivoli and Marengo, and never entirely forgetful of his own youthful adventures among the Carbonari,
had some genuine sympathy with Italy—in so far as the
inhabitants wished to be freed from the Austrian yoke. But
his *rôle* as 'saviour of society' from Socialism made him in
France the ally of reaction, dependent on Clerical support
in the country; nor was he yet in a position to cross the
policy of those members of the Government who were more
Clerical at heart than he.

The Ministers saw in the situation at Rome, and in the
appeals of the Pope for help, an opportunity of combining
a check to Austria with an anti-Liberal policy which would
ensure for them the Catholic vote in France—then a more
considerable item in elections than it is to-day. If they
could regain for France the religious hegemony of the
Catholic powers, they would at once fulfil the desire of the
Clericals and satisfy the pride of the nation. 'It was the
beginning of the long chapter of fraud and insolence, for
which the French Catholics are more responsible than
Napoleon, which, beginning in a kind of perverted national
pride, ended by sacrificing the nation to the Papacy, and
had its pay at Sedan.' [1]

[1] *King*, i. 334.

Pio Nono, by taking refuge with Ferdinand of Naples, had inflicted a severe diplomatic defeat on the French, but the lost ground would be handsomely recovered if they could open for him the gates of Rome, while his Neapolitan friends were still hesitating on the frontier, afraid to attack Garibaldi. Military and naval preparations had been on foot even as early as the time of the Pope's flight to Gaeta, and some troops had actually sailed early in December, only to be driven back by storms.[1] After that there had again been hesitation on the part of the Government, until the final departure of the French expedition was precipitated by the news of Novara, which made it certain that the Austrians would soon start on the same race for Rome.

There was still enough Republican feeling in the Assembly and in the streets of Paris to compel the more reactionary of the Ministers to use the language of respect for those principles of popular government on which it was their intention to trample. For this reason they raised the cry that 'foreigners come from all parts of Italy' were oppressing the people of Rome, and French historians of the Clerical party[2] are not ashamed to repeat this astounding defence of the French interference. The 'foreign demagogues' of this theory are Mazzini and Garibaldi. These historians, not recognising the right of Italy to be a nation, consider that soldiers from Paris were less alien to Rome than the men of Genoa, Nice, and Milan. But even if we were to grant, as self-evident, the proposition that a native of Piedmont has less rights in any Italian city than those which everywhere belong to a French soldier, there remains the fact that 193 members out of 200 in the freely elected Constituent Assembly, which established the Republic and the Triumvirate, were natives of the Roman States.[3]

But it is not necessary to take very seriously the

---

[1] *Paris MSS. 33ª*, 206, 207 ; *Précis Hist.* II, 12.

[2] *E.g.,* La Gorce, *Seconde République Française*, ii. 75, 80, 203. One would gather, alike from the text and the foot-notes, that in composing his book he had not consulted Italian authorities any more than M. Bittard des Portes.

[3] *Johnston*, 232–236.

hypocritical arguments about 'liberating' Rome from 'foreigners,' and effecting a 'reconciliation' between the Pope and his subjects, which were employed as a blind to the Italian and French Liberals. The 'reconciliation' ended, as all had foreseen, in the restoration of the Papal autocracy, and all the worst evils of clerical rule ; nor could it have ended otherwise, for the Pope, though he was pre- pared to accept his restoration at the hands of France, was determined to abolish every vestige of constitutional freedom and lay government, however much the French might ask for some show of reform. Louis Napoleon, whatever he might pretend to himself or to others, was reviving, in his attitude towards the Papal States, the policy of the Holy Alliance, except that his position was more isolated than that of Alexander and Metternich, and his attitude less friendly to the other maintainers of ' order.' It was not so much a Holy Alliance as a Holy Competition for the advantage of policing Central Italy.

The one thing that can be truly said in excuse for the expedition to Rome is that the French Government, when they despatched their troops, had persuaded themselves that they would be welcomed as liberators. But they had arrived at this conclusion by the simple process of believing what they wished, and even if they had expected resistance, they would not have acted differently, except in sending a larger force. For when they found out how complete was their mistake—how ready were the citizens of the Roman Republic to die for their independence—they did not hesitate to restore, over unwilling subjects, the most odious Govern- ment in Christian Europe, and to shed the blood of the inhabitants of a State over which they had no shadow of suzerainty, whose borders did not march with their own, whose policy it was to cultivate the friendship of France, and whose governors continued, even after the fighting had begun, to pray most earnestly for a renewal of kindly rela- tions. Such action would be in the highest degree repugnant to the conscience of the French Republic of our own day, as it was then repugnant to the conscience of many of the best citizens of France, who vainly protested in the Assembly and in the streets of Paris against the great clerical and military plot to suppress liberty abroad. The murder of the Roman Republic foreshadowed, not obscurely, the approaching doom of free institutions in France.

In the last days of April, while Oudinot was traversing the forty miles between his port of disembarkation and the suburbs of Rome, the Triumvirs could look round and see that they were alone against the world. Already (April 11) the Democratic Government of Tuscany had 'gained what no Republic missed'; the Grand Duke had been recalled to his throne by the popular voice, in time to prevent a forcible restoration by the Austrians.[1] Piedmont was wisely keeping friends with France, and retiring to leap better on some distant day. The long agony of the siege of Venice still dragged on, but the end was certain. Every other power actively interested in Italy was leagued against Mazzini. England, with a passive interest, was delivering disregarded lectures to all parties. Palmerston, if not the Cabinet as a whole, was an academic friend to Piedmont and a foe to Austria, but even Palmerston did nothing to support the Roman Republic. Not realising the now intractable attitude of the Pope, he advised Mazzini to negotiate for Liberal institutions under a restored Papal rule.

But another large body of opinion in England was at this date altogether anti-Italian; the 'Quarterly Review,' true to its anti-Jacobin traditions, praised the fine old times of Gregory XVI., lauded Ferdinand of Naples, and compared Mazzini to Robespierre.[2] The 'Times' was no less strongly on the side of *Bomba*, the Pope, and the Austrians against their respective subjects. It complained

---

[1] The internal reaction in Tuscany was due partly to the Conservatism of the peasants, partly to the quarrels of the various Liberal parties in the towns, and not a little to the hatred of the Florentines for the men of Leghorn, the overbearing leaders of the revolution. *King*, i. 325, 326 ; *Dupré*, 176, 177.

[2] *Quarterly Review*, lxxxv. 230, 238, 253.

of the French expedition only in so far as it limited the action
and invaded the privileges of Austria, and took Oudinot to
task because he did not at once declare his real purpose, the
restoration of the Papal despotism.[1] The 'Times' correspondent remained within the French lines, and his thirst
for blood could not be satisfied by Oudinot's tardy and
comparatively humane operations.[2] The sneers of the
great newspaper at the 'degenerate remnant of the
Roman people,' who 'will believe they are heroes,' revealed that remarkable form of pride in British institutions which used to consider it an insult to ourselves that
any other race should aspire to progress and freedom.[3]

But the better England was well represented on the right
side of the walls. George Thomas, the artist of the leading
illustrated paper of the day, was sending home his sketches of
the Garibaldini which I have been most kindly allowed to
reproduce in this book. These pictures and the sympathetic
comment in the text of the 'Illustrated London News'
may be said to have laid the first foundations of the Garibaldian cult in our country,[4] a plant of slow but eventually
of enormous growth. Arthur Clough was also in Rome,
gathering the impressions which he dressed up in the
'Amours de Voyage.' His proverbial hesitation did not
extend to the field of Italian politics, and he watched the
martyrdom of Liberty with the eye, not of a sceptic, but of a
poet.[5] The Bostonian Margaret Fuller, as an old and dear
friend of Mazzini in England, was even more whole-hearted
in her devotion, and felt that the new Rome of the people
was the visionary country of her heart.

---

[1] *Times* leading articles, from January 18 onwards, *e.g.* April 17, April 19,
May 11.

[2] *Times*, June 6 and 12. He said the leaders in Rome, though not indeed
Mazzini, desired ' to secure a well-filled purse ' : poor Garibaldi ! The *Quarterly*
stated that most of the Roman soldiers were not Italians ! (lxxxv. 237); there
were really about 400 non-Italians out of some 17,000 or more.

[3] *Times*, May 11, June 30.

[4] I know two Englishmen, afterwards great sympathisers with Italy, who
severally recollect the lasting impression these pictures made on them as boys,
when they knew nothing of Italian affairs.

[5] His letters (*Prose Remains*) show this even more strongly than the *Amours
de Voyage.*

Thus, with only the gods on their side, the Romans armed for the fight. Outside the city, friends and foes expected that they would surrender : ' Italians do not fight,' was the word passed round in the French camp, and even those who knew the North Italians had never heard of Roman valour in the history of the modern world.   But a great moral change had taken place.   When, on the afternoon of April 27, Garibaldi, the long-expected, entered Rome at the head of his bronzed Legionaries from the northern provinces of the Republic, there was little doubt of the spirit of the citizens through whom they pushed their way. ' He has come, he has come ! ' they cried all down the Corso. He had come, and the hour of Rome's resurrection had struck.[1]

' The sculptor Gibson, who was then in Rome, describes the spectacle offered by these wild-looking warriors, as they rode in, as one of the strangest ever witnessed in the Eternal City. The men, sunburnt, with long unkempt hair, wearing conical-shaped hats with black, waving plumes ; their gaunt, dust-soiled faces framed with shaggy beards ; their legs bare ; crowding round their chief, who rode a white horse, perfectly statuesque in virile beauty ; the whole group looking more like a company of brigands out of some picture of Salvator Rosa than a disciplined military force.' [2]

The combined effect of the presence of Mazzini and of Garibaldi in Rome was to exalt men's hearts and minds into a region where it seemed base to calculate nicely whether there was any hope of victory in the defensive war which they were undertaking.   And in such magnificent carelessness lay true wisdom.   There are times when it is wise to die for honour alone.   If Rome had submitted again to Papal despotism without a blow she could never have become the capital of Italy, or only as the despised head of a noble family.   Historians who blame the defence of Rome overlook this point, which surely is one of immense

[1] *Loev.* i. 155, 156.
[2] *Costa,* 43 ; *Martinengo Cesaresco's Italy,* 148.   Their ' bare legs ' are not mentioned by other authorities.   They usually wore long trousers.

importance. The end of the present war might be scarcely doubtful, but the end for which they were about to fight lay in the distant future. ↕If it is asked why the Romans were urged to undertake the struggle, let Mazzini answer for himself :

'With those who have said or written that the resistance of Rome to her French invaders was an error, it were useless to discuss.

'To the many other causes which decided us to resist, there was in my mind added one intimately bound up with the aim of my whole life—the foundation of our national unity. Rome was the natural centre of that unity, and it was important to attract the eyes and the reverence of my countrymen towards her. The Italian people had almost lost their *Religion* of Rome ; they, too, had begun to look upon her as a sepulchre, and such she seemed.

'As the seat of a form of faith now extinct, and only outwardly sustained by hypocrisy and persecution, her middle-class living, in a great measure, upon the pomps of worship and the corruption of the higher clergy, and her people, although full of noble and manly pride, necessarily ignorant, and believed to be devoted to the Pope—Rome was regarded by some with aversion, by others with disdainful indifference. A few individual exceptions apart, the Romans had never shared that ferment, that desire for liberty which had constantly agitated Romagna and the Marches. It was therefore essential to redeem Rome ; to place her once again at the summit, so that the Italians might again learn to regard her as the temple of their common country. It was necessary that all should learn how potent was the immortality stirring beneath those ruins of two epochs, two worlds. I did feel that power, did feel the pulsations of the immense eternal life of Rome through the artificial crust with which priests and courtiers had covered the great sleeper, as with a shroud. I had faith in her. I remember that when the question as to whether we should resist or not first arose, the chief officers of the National Guard, when I assembled and interrogated them, told me sadly that the main body of the guard would not in any case co-operate in the defence. It seemed to me that I understood the Roman people far better than they, and I therefore gave orders that all the battalions should defile in front of the Palace of the Assembly on the following morning in order that the question might be put to the troops. The universal shout of *Guerra* that arose from the ranks drowned in an instant the timid doubts of their leaders.

'The defence of the city was therefore decided upon : by the assembly and people of Rome from a noble impulse and from reverence for the honour of Italy ; by me as the logical consequence of a long-matured design. Strategically I was aware that the struggle ought to have been carried on out of Rome, by operating upon the flank of the enemy's line. But victory, unless we were to receive assistance from the other provinces of Italy, was equally impossible within and without the walls ; and since we were destined to fall, it was our duty, in view of the future, to proffer our *morituri te salutant* to Italy from Rome.'[1]

[1] *Mazzini,* v. 200–202. (Italian Ed. i. 175, 176, *Note Autobiografiche.*)

CHAPTER VII[1]

THE THIRTIETH OF APRIL

'And the world passed by her, and said
(We heard it say) she was dead ;
And now, behold, she hath spoken,
She that was dead, saying, " Rome." '
SWINBURNE.—*The Halt before Rome.*

BUT Mazzini alone could not have inspired the heroic
defence. If Garibaldi had not, at the eleventh hour, been
brought into Rome by the agency of his admirer Avezzana,
the new Minister of War,[2] the resistance to Oudinot would
have been very feeble. All Italian accounts of the siege
make this abundantly clear, while French and Clerical
writers regard his ill-omened arrival at the last moment
as the reason why the Italians were ' terrorised ' into dying
for their country. The truth is, that his presence during
the two days of preparation, before the battle of April 30,
exalted the fighting spirit of the troops and of the populace
by the exercise of that personal magic felt equally by all
classes. The workman, the student, the employer and the
landowner were all brothers-in-arms in the ranks of the
volunteer regiments. To this people, singularly free from
what in our island we know only too well as ' snobbery,'
it was all one whether Garibaldi was the son of a nobleman
or of a poor sailor : he was an Italian—no one asked more.

'In Italy (wrote one who saw the workings of this remarkable
epoch in her history) the classes of society are far less distinct
than elsewhere, so that, when once they are brought into

---

[1] For this Chapter see map p. 125 below.
[2] Garibaldi's own belief, right or wrong, was that Avezzana was the first real
friend he had in high quarters at Rome. *Garibaldi's Cantoni,* 180; *Mem.* 224,
and information given me by General Canzio.

contact, or unite for the accomplishment of any object, they instantly find themselves less different, and less uncongenial than might be anticipated from their disparity of condition. Thus it was with the early volunteers of 1848.' [1]

And thus it was at Rome in 1849.

Although Garibaldi was not commander-in-chief, ' whoever heard the conversations of the people, or took a more or less active part in the fortification of the town, had occasion to notice at every moment that Garibaldi, and no other, was recognised as leader.' [2] Barricades were being thrown up in the streets with the same zeal of young and old, the same fraternity of rich and poor as the Parisians of 1790 had shown in digging out the theatre of the Champs de Mars for their revolutionary pageant. The patrician ladies of Rome, soon to distinguish themselves in the hospitals under the republican Princess Belgiojoso, were conspicuous in their elegant dresses, handling the spade ; and Garibaldi himself came round to visit the work and encourage the diggers. ' Hardly,' wrote a stranger who was present at one of these scenes,

' hardly had the General, with his melodious penetrating voice, spoken a few words, when an uproarious cheering arose. . . . The General continued his way, again followed by hundreds of people, all of whom wished to catch, be it a single glance of the popular hero, or to hear a single word from his mouth. Among this multitude were men and women of all classes, youths and boys, nay, even mothers who held their children up to show them the man whose name was on all lips.' [3]

But the political enthusiasm of the diggers at the barricades did not always imply very hard work, according to Anglo-Saxon standards. In some places the American, William Story, saw ' the labourers leaning picturesquely on their spades, doing nothing,' or ' sometimes pitching a shovelful of gravel into a wheelbarrow ' ; his party ' voted the workmen too lazy to live.' [4]

---

[1] *Dandolo*, 294 (Letter to the translator).   [2] *Koelman*, ii. 5, 6.
[3] *Koelman*, ii. 5–8.   [4] *Story*, i. 134, 153.

The Dutch artist, Koelman, has recorded his own first impression of the Garibaldini and their chief, when, in these last days of April, he visited their quarters at the convent of San Silvestro in Capite. 'One of these afternoons,' he says that he and his artist friends

'found the piazza before the convent of San Silvestro filled with a crowd eager for news. In the distance we saw lances and bayonets glittering, and were thinking of a parade or review, when, on coming nearer, we noticed an entirely new uniform. We were accustomed to the variegated dress of the soldiers, the bear-skins, the ugly shakos, the braid and horse-tails, the red, yellow, white, gold and silver stripes and embroideries, and now we saw a troop in dark blue [1] coats hanging on their bodies in wide folds and tied up with black belts. . . . On their heads they wore small black felt hats with broad turned-down brims.[2] Those of the officers were trimmed with black feathers. On their backs all of them carried black knapsacks. Part of these soldiers were armed with lances having long points,[3] others with muskets, and in the belts of all, instead of a sabre or sword, stuck a heavy poniard. " What soldiers are these ? " we asked. " Garibaldini," was the answer.

'It was the first Italian Legion founded by Garibaldi in South America.

'Before the gate of the convent two carriages were standing. Four or five nuns were just coming out of the convent gate, their hands folded and eyes cast down. Praying, they were led into the carriages,[4] which were afterwards filled up with boxes and little chests, and the five sisters evacuated the vast building which they had hitherto occupied, for the two thousand [5] *briganti*, as the Clericals called them, under the command of Garibaldi. . . .

[1] Only the principal officers, and the orderlies, chiefly those returned from South America, as yet wore the *red* blouse, in which the whole Legion was dressed at the end of June. The description (accurate for the month of April) of the *blue* Legionary uniform lends credit to Koelman's recollections.

[2] The ' Calabrian ' hats.

[3] The ' lancieri a piedi.' (See *Roman MSS. Ruoli Gen. 81, F. 14*).

[4] They were being conveyed to Santa Pudenziana. The details given in *Roman MSS. F.R.* 67, 10, and *Loev.* i. 158, bear out in a remarkable way the recollections of the Dutch artist.

[5] Really under 1,500.

GARIBALDI IN 1849.

This contemporary print does not give his features so well as the photograph of some ten years later (Frontispiece of this book); but it gives his long hair and long red shirt as he wore them in 1849. To judge by other pictures, the tilt of his hat is exaggerated.

'The gate, formerly always closed, was now wide open, and on the piazza (of San Silvestro) people from all classes of society, anxious to see the Garibaldini, jostled each other. . . .

'We entered the gate. " Is it allowed ? " we asked, to make sure, of the sentry who was sitting carelessly on one of the beautifully carved mediæval seats in the vestibule.

' "*Sicuro*," he answered—" of course." We saw, indeed, that others, just as ourselves, were taking this opportunity for viewing the interior of the convent. . . . We had to go somewhat aside, which was not very easy, the floor being covered with Garibaldini, who had thrown themselves on bundles of straw to rest from the fatigues of the preceding day. . . .

'Instinctively we looked round, and Garibaldi entered through the gate. It was the first time I saw the man whose name everyone in Rome knew and in whom many people had now already placed their hopes. Even now he is before my mind, as I saw him that first time. Of middle height, well made, broad-shouldered, his square chest, which gives a sense of power to his structure, well marked under the uniform— he stood there before us ; his blue eyes, ranging to violet, surveyed in one glance the whole group in the vestibule of the convent. Those eyes had something remarkable, as well by their colour as by the frankness—I know no better word for it— of their expression. They curiously contrasted with those dark, sparkling eyes of his Italian soldiers, no less than his light chestnut-brown hair, which fell loosely over his neck on to his shoulders, contrasted with their shining black curls. His face was burnt red, and covered with freckles through the influence of the sun. A heavy moustache and a light blonde beard ending in two points gave a martial expression to that open oval face. But most striking of all was the nose, with its exceedingly broad root, which has caused Garibaldi to be given the name of *Leone*, and, indeed, made one think of a lion ; a resemblance which, according to his soldiers, was still more conspicuous in the fight, when his eyes shot forth flames, and his fair hair waved as a mane above his temples.

'He was dressed in a red tunic with short flaps ; on his head he wore a little black felt, sugar-loaf hat, with two black ostrich feathers. In his left hand he had a light plain horseman's sabre, and a cavalry cartridge-bag hung down by his left shoulder.

'It must not be supposed that the appearance of the General caused a sudden commotion. Far from that—even the sentry remained on his little bench, half sitting, half lying, and none of the soldiers stirred. We alone took off our hats, and Garibaldi answered our greeting superficially.

'For one moment he spoke to the officer and the vision was past, but the impression it made on us was ineffaceable. . . .

' "Is that the usual thing with the Garibaldini, to take so little heed of their commander ? " I asked the officer.

' " *Caro mio*, the General demands discipline on the battle-field, not in the barracks," was the short answer he gave me, with a smile.' [1]

Rome was then a rival to Paris as centre of the cosmopolitan artist world, both because it had some vogue as a school of art, and because before the photographic era there was a large demand by the English and other *forestieri* for copies of famous pictures, and for sketches of the sights which they had come to see, and of which they wanted some memento to take home.[2]   The artists, living together on the usual terms of free but close comradeship, worked all the morning, but ' in the afternoon strolled about in the town or went to the *café* of the artists, where,' as Koelman says, ' we then heard politics talked, read the resolutions taken by the new Government, or amused ourselves with the follies of *Don Pirlone*,' the Democratic cartoon journal. Garibaldi carried the heart of this Bohemian world by storm. English, Dutch, Belgians, even one Frenchman, and the Italian artists almost to a man, enlisted during the days that followed his arrival, if they had not done so before, either in his own Legion, or in the Civic Guard, or in the special Students' Corps, which consisted of three hundred University men and artists.   Taking life and death with a light heart, they fought splendidly for Rome, and after every day of battle the survivors met to congratulate each other at jolly suppers in the *cafés*.[3]

---

[1] *Koelman*, i. 310–314. (*Cf.* App. A. below. *Dress and appearance of Garibaldi.*)

[2] Lord Carlisle tells me this.

[3] *Koelman, passim, e.g.* ii. 8, 9, 16.   Mr. A. L. Smith, of Balliol, tells me

GARIBALDI'S LEGION IN ROME.

Central group of three officers from South America, with red blouses and long hair. (*Illustrated London News*, 1849.)

One of the Italians in after years told the story of his conversion, to the Rev. H. R. Haweis. He had come out, he said, with his artist friends, to see what was going on, one day, when Garibaldi was recruiting in a public place in Rome.

'I had no idea (he told the English clergyman) of enlisting. I was a young artist ; I only went out of curiosity—but oh ! I shall never forget that day when I saw him on his beautiful white horse in the market-place, with his noble aspect, his calm, kind face, his high, smooth forehead, his light hair and beard— every one said the same. He reminded us of nothing so much as of our Saviour's head in the galleries. I could not resist him. I left my studio. I went after him ; thousands did likewise. He only had to show himself. We all worshipped him ; we could not help it.'

It was no passing emotion of youth, for eleven years after- wards the narrator was fighting for Garibaldi in Naples.[1]

On the morning of April 29, two days after the arrival of the Legion, there marched into the city the Lombard Bersaglieri, a regiment representing very different military and political traditions from those of Gari- baldi's men, but not less devoted than they to the Italian cause, and destined to play a part no less memor- able than theirs in the defence of Rome. The commander of the Lombards, the gallant Luciano Manara,[2] was a young aristocrat of Milan, who had distinguished him- self in the Five Days of street warfare that drove the Austrians out of his native town, and had been a leader of volunteers in the unhappy campaign that followed. After the recapture of Milan by the Austrians, and the armistice of August 1848, Manara formed the brigade, usually

that his uncle, Arthur Strutt, a well-known English artist in Rome, who fought for Garibaldi during the siege, used to relate the same thing as regards the suppers after the battles. Their valour is established by much testimony other than their own.

[1] *Haweis*, see Bibliography below.
[2] Luciano Romara, in George Meredith's *Vittoria*, 'was built on Manara.'

known by his name, out of the pick of the Lombard exiles
in Piedmont. They took the oath of military allegiance to
the House of Savoy; but, after Novara, Victor Emmanuel
was in no position to harbour them in his territory, and since
they would not return to Lombardy to be flogged and shot
by Radetzky, Manara found himself and his soldiers wandering about in ' the paradise of the Riviera, as if we were
under the ban of God and men alike.' [1]   Under these
circumstances he and six hundred others elected to sail for
Rome, more because they had nowhere else to go than
because they felt any enthusiasm for the Republic.[2]   The
majority, according to one who accompanied them on the
voyage, were gentlemen of Milan and Pavia.[3]

In the port of Civitavecchia the French not only refused
to allow them to land, but made them prisoners, against
all law and equity. ' You are Lombards,' said Oudinot,
' what, then, have you to do with the affairs of Rome ? '
' And you,' replied Manara, ' do you not come from Paris
from Lyons, or from Bordeaux ? '   Finally they were permitted to proceed to Porto d'Anzio, sixty miles further
south, and disembark there, on giving their word that they
would remain neutral, and not enter Rome until May 4, by
which date the French confidently expected to be masters
of the city.   But when, on landing, the Lombards received
orders from Avezzana to come at once to Rome, they obeyed
him, and thereby broke the letter of the promise which the
French had exacted only by a violation of international
law ; but they kept the spirit of their engagement by
refraining, much against their will, from taking any part
in the fighting of April 30.[4]

And so it came about that, on April 29, the eve of the
battle, the Lombards entered the capital, wearing the dark
uniform of the Piedmontese Bersaglieri, which, with its
round broad-brimmed hat carrying the plume of black-

---

[1] *Manara MS., Letter of April* 14.   [2] *Dandolo*, 183–190; *Hoff.* 15–18.
[3] *Rusconi (Ferdinando),* 25.
[4] *Mannucci,* 168–173 (169, Manara's protest); *Torre,* i. 246 ; *Dandolo,*
192, 193 ; *Rusconi (Ferdinando),* 26, 27 ; *Spada,* iii. 437 ; *Gaillard,* 167, 168 ;
Bittard des Portes, 37, 45, 54 ; *Vecchi,* ii. 194.

green cock's feathers on the side, is to this day a symbol in the eyes of all Europe of the army of the Italian King.[1] The presence of men thus royally attired, and with the Cross of Savoy on their belts,[2] side by side with the blouses and Calabrian hats of Garibaldi's Republicans, changed the defence of Rome from the act of a party to a national undertaking. Monarchists, devoted to the King of Piedmont, from whom alone they looked for the deliverance of their native Lombardy, the 'Aristocratic Corps,' as it was called in Rome, came with no friendly prejudices in favour of the Mazzinian Republic. Nor did they come prepared to admire the military virtues of irregular troops. Lombard volunteers in origin, Manara's Bersaglieri had acquired the self-restraint, the discipline and the professional traditions for which the Piedmontese regulars were famous; most of the regiment, indeed, had been trained in former years as conscripts in the Austrian army.[3] It is no wonder, therefore, that their first impression of the Republic and its motley soldiers was unpleasing, and the rapidity with which they came round to a favourable view, not of Republicanism, but of the Republicans, is a genuine and impartial testimony to the defenders of Rome. Emilio Dandolo, the warrior historian of the Brigade, has described the feelings of his companions-in-arms when they entered the city, on the eve of the first battle, in which they themselves felt bound, by their promise to Oudinot, to take no part:

'To the varied and somewhat affectedly loud *evvivas* which saluted us on every side, our men, accustomed to maintain the reserve and self-command befitting soldiers, made no answer— a circumstance which somewhat cooled the ardour of a population who had hitherto seen that volunteers under arms embraced every opportunity of making a profession of their political creed. Previously to our being lodged in the quarters assigned to us, General Avezzana reviewed our battalion. He thought

[1] See Illustration p. 223 below for their uniform.
[2] *Dandolo*, 191; *Hoffstetter*, 17, who says the plumes on the men's hats were black horse-hair, and only the officers' hats had the green feathers.
[3] *Manara MS.*, *Letter of April* 19.

proper to dismiss us with an oration ending with *Viva la Repubblica!* The soldiers remained silent and motionless at the word.

'"Present arms! Viva l'Italia!" shouted Manara, perceiving the General's embarrassment. "Viva!" was the unanimous reply; and the soldiers broke up their lines and retired to quarters.

'The first impression which most of us experienced on entering Rome was that of indefinable melancholy. Our own sad experience had rendered us but too much alive to the first symptoms of dissolution in a government or in a city, and in Rome we recognised with grief the very same aspect which Milan had presented during the latter few months of its liberty. We seemed to observe the very same overweening regard to trivial matters, whilst those of vital importance were neglected. There was the same superabundance of standards, of cockades, of badges of party, the same clanking of swords along the public streets, and those various and varied uniforms of officers, not one matching with the other, but all seeming fitter for the embellishment of the stage than for military service; those epaulettes thrown, as it were, by chance on the shoulders of individuals, whose very faces seemed to declare their unfitness to wear them; whilst, in addition to these things, the applause of an unwarlike population, echoing from the windows and from the coffee-houses, seemed to us to indicate but too clearly that we had arrived only in time to be present at the last scene of some absurd comedy. Accustomed for some time past to judge of these matters with the eye of regular troops, all this array of warriors in glittering helmets, with double-barrelled guns and with belts armed with daggers, reconciled us but little to the scanty numbers of real, well-drilled soldiers.

'In the evening, when, fatigued by our long march, we gladly answered to our names, in hopes of taking some repose, the drums beat all of a sudden to arms, and the whole city was in movement to resist the approach of the French. Whoever could have had a glimpse of Rome that night would not have recognised the city which he had seen in the morning, and we rejoiced in having reason to change the opinion which had so depressed us on our first arrival.

'In all the streets in the neighbourhood of Porta Angelica and Porta Cavalleggieri were bivouacked small but admirable regiments of the line, two magnificent battalions of carabineers, with four or five parks of field artillery; two regiments of cavalry were stationed in Piazza Navona; numerous bodies of volunteers kept watch on the walls; and the whole of the National Guard were all in perfect order at their respective quarters. Then, as might be expected, the fantastic costumes were lost sight of, and every one who wore the national colours grasped in his hand the weapon which was to defend them. We passed the night in the great square of St. Peter's enchanted with the spectacle, and with finding ourselves in the midst of soldiers, and of a confiding and resolute population. We then saw that Rome was capable of offering a noble resistance, and we thanked Heaven that, in the midst of the shame and calamities of Italy, a field had been opened to us, in which we might show that our hard fate had been unmerited.' [1]

The forces, which even before the battle thus extorted the slow approval of their Lombard allies, amounted to about 7,000–9,000 men and were composed of four distinct elements.[2]

First there were the regular Papal troops of the line, and the Carabinieri. They had joined the revolt against their employer, partly because they shared the sympathies natural to all laymen and to all Italians, and partly because, as soldiers, they had perpetually suffered neglect, being left by the Papal Government in rags and penury, while the Swiss regiments, always dearer than the natives to the heart of unpopular despots, had enjoyed higher pay and more handsome uniforms.[3] Of these regulars there were some 2,500 now under arms in Rome.

Secondly there was the Garibaldian or First Italian Legion, now numbering nearly 1,300 men, most of them, as we have seen, raised in the Papal provinces, particularly the Romagna, and all of them native Italians, except perhaps two score of officers and men. Since their arrival in Rome they had accepted some excellent recruits, especially artists,

[1] *Dandolo*, 194-197.   [2] See App. B below.
[3] *Farini*, i. 111, 152; *Carletti*, 197, 198. Two Swiss regiments had been raised by Gregory XVI. to keep down the Romagna. See *Ravioli, passim*, on the line regiments.

among whom was Nino Costa. In the same category—volunteer regiments raised in the provinces of the Roman States who had not yet seen actual fighting—may be placed the three hundred *Finanzieri*, that is, Gagers (custom house officers) under Callimaco Zambianchi, a rascally officer who obtained for his men a bad name for violence against priests.

Thirdly, there were about 1,400 men of the volunteer regiments raised in the city and the provinces, who, after taking a gallant but unfortunate part in the Lombard campaign against Austria, had capitulated at Vicenza and returned to Rome. These were the *Reduci* (600)—of whom the *mauvais sujets* had disgraced their uniform by taking part in the murder of Rossi—and the Roman Legion, a fine regiment with no such stain upon its honour.[1]

The fourth element in the defence consisted of inhabitants of Rome who had had no previous experience of war, enrolled in various volunteer bodies—such as the 300 students, the 1,000 National Guards, together with several hundreds of unbrigaded citizens who flocked to the walls, or were kept inside to guard the barricades, with whatever weapons they could find.[2] The Trasteverines, their native fury now turned full against the priests and the French, were noticed on the morning of April 30, fierce figures with spears and shot-guns in their hands and knives in their teeth,[3] pouring out from their riverside slums up the steep ascent that leads to the Janiculum.

For it was against the Janiculan and Vatican hills, the defences on the right bank of the Tiber, that the attack of the French army, coming from Civitavecchia on the north-west by way of Palo, must necessarily be delivered. The lesser Rome that stands upon this western bank is surrounded by a line of walls comparatively modern in date; the existing fortifications of the Vatican and Borgo were

---

[1] *Carletti*, 261–271; *Costa*, 29–33.

[2] *Torre*, ii. 25, 26. *Saffi*, iii. 292, says many of the National Guard were kept at the barricades. So, much to his disgust, was Hoffstetter, the Swiss volunteer just arrived.

[3] *Beghelli*, ii. 171; *Saffi*, iii. 291, 292.

built in the latter part of Michael Angelo's lifetime, as the result of the scare caused by the sack of Rome by the Constable de Bourbon; while the Janiculan walls from the Porta Cavalleggieri to the Porta Portese, though begun in the sixteenth century, were mainly the work of Urban VIII., who erected them towards the close of the Thirty Years' War (circa 1642).[1] These walls had not hitherto been the scene of any famous defence, like the walls of the Emperor Aurelian upon the other bank, which, having served Belisarius' legions to repel the Goth, were still the only protection for the main part of the city.

The Papal walls which were now to have their share in history, may be considered in three sections. First, the projecting circuit that runs from the Castle of Saint Angelo to the Porta Cavalleggieri, enclosing the *basse-ville* of the Borgo, together with St. Peter's and the high gardens of the Vatican. Secondly, the Janiculan Mount, the key to Rome, whence the whole city can be commanded by cannon, rising high above the Trastevere quarter, and defended by that part of the wall which runs up from the Porta Portese on the riverside as far as the Porta San Pancrazio on the height. Thirdly, there was the straight line of wall between these two positions, joining the Porta San Pancrazio to the Porta Cavalleggieri; over this central portion rises, to-day, the colossal statue of Garibaldi on horseback.

The fortifications erected along these lines by Urban VIII. and his predecessors would have been considered formidable specimens of the defensive art by Oliver, if he had come with his English buff-coats, as Andrew Marvell prophesied, ' to Italy an Hannibal '; and, though out of date ever since the time of Vauban, they still offered a more serious obstacle to the siege guns of 1849 than the Aurelian walls on

---

[1] The Vatican wall of the Popes of the sixteenth century surrounded or replaced the walls with which Leo IV. (847-855) had first defended the Borgo against the Saracens. But the ground lying between the Porta Cavalleggieri and the Porta Portese was enclosed for the first time by Urban VIII. (except for the much smaller enclosure of Aurelian). *Gregorovius*, iii. 97, 98. *Ranke*, iii. 34, 35, note ; *Quarenghi*, chaps. xiv.-xviii. ; *Lanciani*, 81-84, 86, 87. Maps, *Rocchi*.

the other bank of Tiber.   Those walls, built a thousand
years before the era of gunpowder, had galleries to carry
infantry and catapults, raised on perpendicular curtains
which could not resist, and small square towers where it
was impossible to mount, the cannon of modern times.   The
Papal walls, on the other hand, which the French had now
to attack, sloped backwards from the base as far as the
stone lining of the rampart, and their bastions had broad
platforms of earth, serving to give solidity to the brickwork
of the face, and ample standing room for the batteries.[1]

But although the besieged might rejoice in the comparatively solid and serviceable fortifications of Urban
VIII.'s engineers, the position had one irremediable defect.
The ground immediately outside was as high as the defences ;
indeed the Villa Corsini was even higher than the Porta
San Pancrazio ; so that a besieger could erect batteries at
a height equal to or greater than those of the besieged,
at distances only a few hundred yards from the line of
defence.

This defect, which was to prove fatal in June, was
guarded against on April 30 by the energy of Garibaldi ;
who, being entrusted with the defence of the Janiculum,
saw that it must be conducted, not behind the walls, but
on the high ground of the Corsini and Pamfili gardens
outside the San Pancrazio gate.   He had with him his own
legion, over 1,000 strong, the regiment of 250-300 students
and artists of Rome, and 900 other volunteer troops of
the Roman States, including the *Reduci*.   Behind him
Colonel Galletti was in reserve inside the city, with about
1,800 men, partly regulars of the old Papal line and partly
volunteers.   The walls round the Vatican were held by
Colonel Masi with some 1,700 of the Papal line and 1,000 of
the National Guard.[2]   These dispositions had been made by
Avezzana, the Minister of War, to whom Garibaldi, the

---

[1] *Quarenghi*, 204–206 ; *La Gorce*, ii. 156 ; *Vaillant*, 23–27. (See p. 173
below for a picture of one of these bastions.)   The Papal walls, like those of the
Emperors, are made of thin bricks.

[2] *Torre*, ii. 25, 26 ; *Vecchi*, ii. 193, 194.   See App. B below, *Number of
troops engaged on April* 30.

hero of the day, attributed its successful issue. Garibaldi took up his station on the high terrace of the Villa Corsini, whence, looking across the valley of vineyards that lay between, he could watch the approach of the enemy and the delivery of their first attack upon the Porta Pertusa, at the projecting angle of the wall that crowns the Vatican hill.[1]

Oudinot, having left a small body to guard his communications with the sea, was advancing on Rome with some six or seven thousand infantry, and a full complement of field guns.[2] He had been easily persuaded by his Clerical informants in Rome that his somewhat contradictory and deceptive proclamations, which, if they meant anything, meant that he would procure a Papal restoration with certain safeguards against the worst forms of reaction, had given the inhabitants the excuse for which they were waiting to open the gates to his troops. He therefore came without siege-guns, or even scaling ladders, and advanced in column to within grape-shot of the walls. There had not, indeed, been wanting signs, as the French drew near to Rome, that resistance was to be expected, for the roads and houses were empty of inhabitants, and were decorated with notices in large type, giving the text of the fifth article of the existing French Constitution,[3] which ran as follows :

 'France respects foreign nationalities ; her might shall never be employed against the liberty of any people.'

Whatever the private soldiers thought, the irony was wasted upon the officers, who for the most part were not Republicans at heart and wished nothing better than to see every article of the French Constitution sent to the devil.[4]

Although these wayside phenomena alarmed the more cautious, no order to reconnoitre or to deploy was given by

---

[1] *Mem.* 225, 227.   [2] See App. B below.   [3] *Vaillant,* 8.

[4] A young English Naval Commander, who saw a good deal of the French expeditionary force in the next two months, says : ' I have not found one republican in the French army or navy. All are something else—they know not what, but they do not wish the (French) Republic to last.'—*Key,* 206.

those in command, who still expected that a whiff of grape-shot would be the utmost required to procure an entry. The advance-guard marched straight for the summit of the Vatican hill, crowned by an old round tower of the dark ages, which served as a sky sign to guide them to the attack.[1] Immediately under this tower stood the Porta Pertusa, by which they were to enter Rome. The scouts, only a few yards ahead of the column, had just reached a turn in the road where the Porta Pertusa becomes suddenly visible at little more than a hundred paces distance, when a shower of grape from two cannon on the walls gave warning that Rome would resist. It was now almost the height of a sweltering Italian noon, and the troops, who had been suffering during the march under their heavy shakos, and gazing with envy at the shade offered by the strangely shaped ' umbrella pines ' of Italy,[2] were glad of any change in the order of the day. A French battery was unlimbered on the spot, and a fire of musketry and cannon opened against the Vatican wall. But the assailants were in the open, the Roman cannon on the bastions were well served, and no progress could be made.

The plan had been to enter by the Porta Pertusa, but, now that the time had come to blow in the gate, it was discovered that the gate did not exist. It had been walled up for many years past, but the change did not appear on the charts of the Parisian geographers.[3] After one desperate rush at the impenetrable wall, the French took refuge behind neighbouring dykes and mounds, whence they continued to fire at the ramparts overhead.[4]

The attack on the obsolete Porta Pertusa had perforce

---

[1] It was a relic of the fortifications of Leo IV. to protect the Vatican from the Saracens.

[2] *Bittard des Portes*, 71, 72.

[3] *Vaillant*, 8–10; *Bittard des Portes*, 72, 75; *Plan topographique de Rome Moderne*, by Letarouilly, Paris, 1841. It is not improbable that Oudinot possessed the latter, which has every appearance of being modern and accurate, but contains this fatal error. *Paris MSS. 33ᵉ*, 208, describes this first incident of the battle before the Porta Pertusa, and gives the time as 11.30; the *Historique* of the 20ᵉ says the first shot was at 11.20.

[4] *Paris MSS. 33ᵉ*, 209; *Miraglia*, 177; *Précis Hist.* 26.

therefore to be changed into an attack on the Porta Cavalleggieri, a change of plan which involved passing down a
steep hill across 1,000 yards of open vineyard country,
under a hot flank fire from the regulars and National
Guard thronging the wall, and from the Roman batteries
on the bastions near St. Peter's.[1]   The Porta Cavalleggieri
proved indeed to be a 'gate in being,' but situated at
the bottom of a deep valley, and in a retreating angle
of the wall, so that its assailants were exposed to a
double fire at close range from the battlements on either
side of the approach to the gate.[2]

Meanwhile, another column and battery had started
from near the Porta Pertusa to go round outside the Vatican
gardens in the other direction, with a view to obtaining an
entry by the Porta Angelica, near the Castle of St. Angelo.
The motive of this false military step was political, for
Oudinot had been wrongly informed by his agents that the
Clericals were in that quarter sufficiently strong to open
the gate.   The troops sent on this circuitous march, prolonged by the steep descent and the bad roads, were exposed
to a fire of terrible severity, from the hanging gardens on
their right flank, because the only path by which their
artillery could travel at all ran painfully close to the
city walls.[3]   The slaughter was such that a surgeon who
had been through the African campaigns declared that he
had never seen his countrymen in so hot a corner before.[4]
Under these conditions the attack on the defences of the
Vatican, both to north and south, was doomed to failure.
It was said that a desperate attempt to climb up by means
of 'spike-nails'[5] showed in what a pass want of preparation
had left the gallant French army.

By noon, or soon after it, the enemy had been foiled

---

[1] *Vaillant*, 10 ; *Torre*, ii. 29.

[2] See an interesting picture of the attack on the Porta Cavalleggieri in the
Illustrated London News of May 19.

[3] *Gaillard*, 177 ; *Bittard des Portes*, 79–83 ; *Vaillant*, 10, 11 ; *Précis Hist.* 28.

[4] *Gazette Médicale de Paris*, November 3, 1849.

[5] *Key*, 197.   For two gallant attacks on the gateless curtains see *Paris
MSS. Historique 33ᵉ*, 209, and *20ᵉ* (2ᵉ bataillon), 227.

in their attempt to storm the city, but had not yet been driven off the ground. Garibaldi, who from the Corsini terrace had watched their first repulse at the Pertusa and Cavalleggieri gates, determined to assume the offensive from his yet unassailed position on the Janiculum, and to convert the check under the walls into a defeat in the open. To effect a *débouchement* from the Corsini and Pamfili gardens into the vineyards on the north, it was necessary for his troops to cross the deep, walled lane [1] which connected the Porta San Pancrazio with the main road to Civitavecchia. Up this lane were coming about 1,000 infantry of the 20*me ligne*, sent forward by Oudinot to protect the rear and flank of the main attack,[2] and there the first clash of arms in this quarter took place. Garibaldi's advance-guard, consisting of the two or three hundred Roman students and artists brigaded in a regiment of their own, were clambering down out of the Pamfili garden into the deep lane, when, under the arches of the Pauline Aqueduct, they stumbled upon the advancing French column. It was the young men's baptism of fire. Before the ardour of their attack the French at first recoiled, but discipline and numbers soon prevailed, and the students were driven back into the garden.[3] The enemy followed in upon their heels, and the Garibaldian Legion was hurried up to the rescue.

A confused fight at close quarters ensued, in which, before the onslaught of the veterans of the 20me, the main body of Italians was pressed back, leaving behind them small groups holding on in occupation of various points near the Pamfili villa.[4] Among these Nino Costa, a youth of twenty-two, as yet unknown to fame as an

---

[1] Now known as the Via Aurelia Antica. Called *Deep Lane* in map, p. 125 above.

[2] *Paris MSS. 20ᵉ*, 224. Eight companies in all, of which we are told (p. 222) that five contained 700 men.

[3] *Roman MSS. Batt. Univ.* ; *Carletti*, 269. The crossing of the high wall into or out of the deep lane was difficult, and resulted, in the case of one of Koelman's friends, in a sprained ankle. *Koelman*, ii. 18.

[4] *Carletti*, 269, 270 ; *Torre*, ii. 30.

artist, but already so well known for gallantry in the Lombard campaign that Garibaldi had specially invited him to join his staff, defended a house near the villa with a handful of legionaries, amid the victorious advance of the French.[1]

At last Garibaldi, seeing part of his Legion thus holding on in the Pamfili, and part of it driven back under the very walls of Rome, sent into the city to call up the reserves under Colonel Galletti ; that officer left the regulars of his division behind him within the gates, to guard against a surprise of the wall,[2] and marched out of the Porta San Pancrazio at the head of the Roman Legion, consisting of 800 seasoned volunteers, burning to retrieve the misfortunes which they had suffered last year, through no lack of valour, in the Lombard campaign.[3]

The crisis of the battle was now at hand, and the flower of the Democratic volunteers were to prove whether they could dislodge regular troops posted behind villas and vineyard walls. Garibaldi, putting himself at the head of his own men, reinforced by the Roman Legion under Galletti, led the decisive charges by which it was hoped to recover the positions now held by the French on either side of the deep lane.[4]   The first operation was to recapture the Corsini and Pamfili.

Except at Tivoli and Frascati, there are few places within many miles of Rome with more of the charm of Italy than the northern edge of the Doria-Pamfili grounds, where the heat of early summer is shaded off into a delicious atmosphere, redolent of repose and dreams, where birds sing under dark avenues of ever-green oaks, and no other sound is heard.   The wall of the northern boundary, along the top of which runs a terrace walk, drops sheer for many feet into the dark lane below, and, parallel with it for some

---

[1] *Costa*, 44.   [2]*Carletti*, 270.   [3] *Costa*, 28–33.
   [4] See App. C below.   Three days after the battle William Story was credibly informed that 'the Romans were a little timid at first, but grew hotter and fiercer as the battle continued, and at last were full of courage and confidence, even to heroism.' *Story*, i. 156.   This would apply well to the troops on the Janiculum, who first lost and then recovered the Pamfili.

distance, stretches the old Acqua Paola. Across the lane
and the arches of the aqueduct the eye can range over
the neighbouring vineyards, the dome of St. Peter's, and
the distant hill villages beyond the Campagna, till it
rests at last on the shapes of Lucretilis and Soracte.
Such a scene and such an atmosphere make it easy to
understand why Italians are in some danger of spending
their days in the too passive reception of impressions. But
on this day there came Italians—artists and shopmen,
workmen and aristocrats—who had been inspired by the
moral resurrection of their country to ideals nobler than
pleasure and receptiveness ; who were ready to give up the
privilege of life, even of life in Italy, so that Italy might be
free over their graves.

Swarming over the Corsini hill, and across the little
stream and valley that divide it from the Pamfili grounds,
the Legionaries came crashing through the groves. The
Garibaldian officers, ' the tigers of Monte Video,' with long
beards, and hair that curled over their shoulders, were
singled out to the enemy's marksmen by red blouses, falling
almost to the knees. This was the day that they had
waited for so long in exile, this the place towards which they
had sailed so far across the ocean. Behind them Italy came
following on. And above the tide of shouting youths, drunk
with their first hot draught of war, rose Garibaldi on his
horse, majestic and calm—as he always looked, but most
of all in the fury of battle—the folds of his white American
poncho floating off his shoulders for a flag of onset.[1]

And so they stormed through the gardens, fighting with
bayonets among the flowering rose-bushes in which next
day the French dead were found, laid in heaps together.[2]
Costa and his company in the house, relieved in the nick of
time, made captive some of their assailants, among others
a gigantic drum-major whose fine proportions pleased the

---

[1] *Roman MSS. Batt. Univ.* for eyewitnesses' account of Garibaldi during this
charge. (See also *Miraglia,* 186, 258 ; coloured pictures of Garibaldi charging,
and App. A. below).

[2] *Koelman,* ii. 16.

artist's eye.[1] The enemy were thrust out of the Pamfili grounds back to the north of the Deep Lane, across which for some time the two sides fired at one another, until the Italians finally leapt down over the wall, clambered up the other side, and carried the northern arches of the aqueduct.[2] Thence the Legionaries and students broke into the vineyards beyond, and after fierce struggling, body to body, with guns, and hands, and bayonets, put the French to flight.

During this victorious advance they surrounded several hundred men of the 20me *Ligne* who had not retreated in time from the Villa Valentini and the farmhouses north of the lane. Masina's handful of lancers were brought up to the Valentini, and when the French began to cut their way out, a charge of horse secured them as prisoners to the Garibaldian Legion, several of the officers giving up their swords to the gallant Masina.[3] The Roman Legion made many other captures in the houses round about,[4] so that, in all, three or four hundred French surrendered to these two regiments.

Garibaldi had received a bullet in the side, and the wound, though it did not incapacitate him, caused him much pain during the next two months of constant warfare.[5]

The afternoon was now well advanced, but the victory had been won. When a sortie was made from the Porta Cavalleggieri, Oudinot, whose retreat from before that gate was threatened by the Garibaldian advance, hastily drew off his men from between the two fires and made off by the road to Civitavecchia. The victorious Legionaries pressed the pursuit from the direction of the Pamfili, against the 33me *Ligne* and French artillery, who covered the retreat.[6] By five o'clock, after nearly six hours' fighting,[7] the whole French army had been driven off the field, with a loss of 500 men killed and wounded, and 365 prisoners.[8]

---

[1] *Costa*, 44.   [2] *Koelman*, ii. 18.

[3] App. C below, *Capture of the French Prisoners, April 30*. See also App. D.

[4] *Carletti*, 270.   [5] *Loev*. ii. 198.   [6] *Paris MSS. 33^e*, 210.

[7] *Monitore*, May 1 ; *Rusconi*, ii. 233–235 (Triumvirs' report) ; *Saffi*, iii. 291, 292.

[8] *Bittard des Portes*, 94, 95. From the *Historiques* of the various regiments.

That night the city was illuminated, the streets were filled with shouting and triumphant crowds, and there was scarcely a window in the poorest and narrowest alley of the mediæval slums that did not show its candle. It was no vulgar conquest which they celebrated. After long centuries of disgrace, this people had recovered its self-respect, and from the highest to the lowest ranks men felt, ' We are again Romans.' [1] On April 30, Garibaldi, being put to the test, had secured the position which had already been instinctively accorded him in the popular imagination of his countrymen.

[1] *Hoff.* 19 ; *Gabussi*, iii. 357. (See *Manara MS., Letter of May* 1. The honour of Italy, Manara declares, has been saved. It is the first time since Novara that he expresses anything but shame and despair for his country.)

CHAPTER VIII[1]

GARIBALDI IN THE NEAPOLITAN CAMPAIGN—PALESTRINA AND VELLETRI, MAY 1849

'Say by what name men call you,
    What city is your home?
And wherefore ride ye in such guise
    Before the ranks of Rome?'
        MACAULAY, *Lays of Ancient Rome.*

THE first of a series of quarrels between Mazzini and Garibaldi, which marred the fraternity of the Roman Republic, arose on the question whether or not the victory of April 30 should be turned to full military advantage. Garibaldi, advising well as a soldier, wished to follow it up and drive the retreating French into the sea. But Mazzini, relying on those elements of genuine Republicanism in France of which he had some personal knowledge, though he did not know how fast their strength was ebbing away, hoped to propitiate the one country whose friendship might yet save the State, and preferred to turn the Roman armies from further pursuit of the French to the more congenial task of expelling the Neapolitan and Austrian invaders. It is not necessary, in this matter, to find fault with either of the Chiefs, for although Mazzini's policy was tried and failed, Garibaldi's root-and-branch remedy would have made the French all the more determined to send another and larger expedition to retrieve their military honour; so that, whatever had been done, the Republic must sooner or later have fallen a victim to the combination of the Catholic powers.[2]

Mazzini's magnanimity at least had the effect of putting

---

[1] For this Chapter see map p. 141 below.
[2] *Saffi*, iii. 294-297, 300-302.

the French more than ever in the wrong, and afforded a pleasing occasion for a display of the gentleness and human sympathy which have so large a place in the Italian character. The French wounded were nursed with such 'enlightened and devoted' tenderness that Oudinot declared himself 'profoundly grateful'[1] for it ; the prisoners were fêted and set free to return unconditionally to their regiments. The treatment accorded to them was prompted by sentiment as well as policy, and, though initiated by the rulers, was carried into effect by the people of Rome. Captain Key, who had come up on a visit from Civitavecchia to provide for British interests in the capital, wrote home that he had seen the French prisoners

'brought out into the streets and received with every mark of good feeling by the people, who cheered them, gave them food, and showed them round St. Peter's and the monuments, the French in return saying,' as no doubt the occasion demanded, 'that they had been deceived ; having entered the Roman territory with the idea that they were to join the Romans against the Austrians and Neapolitans.'[2]

But the rest of the French army and the Home Government would not so easily relent, and Mazzini was to find that it is dangerous to play with coals of fire.

For the present, however, it was not safe for Oudinot to show further hostility. In return for the several hundred men restored by the generosity of their friendly enemies, the French felt bound to set free a body of Bolognese volunteers under Colonel Pietramellara, whom they had made prisoners in Civitavecchia at the time of their disembarkation.[3] They also released Ugo Bassi, who, unarmed, but in the

---

[1] De Lesseps, 120, Doc. No. 14. See App. D below.

[2] Key, 198 ; Gabussi, iii. 366, 367 ; Saffi, iii. 311–313, describes the scene, and adds that the French wounded, when visited by Mazzini and himself in the hospital, expressed the same sentiments in acknowledging their gratitude for so much kindness ; Vecchi, ii. 201. See also Précis Hist. (Pièce just. No. 6) for Picard's evidence to extraordinary kindness shown to them in Rome, which he calls attempts at seduction.

[3] Bittard des Portes, 115. Précis Hist. 38. There were 400 of them, as is proved by Mannucci, 137, and many other sources.

red blouse of the Legion, had been captured in the Pamfiii grounds, while pursuing his spiritual office among the wounded, in the ebb and flow of the bayonet charges.[1] After this exchange of courtesies, Oudinot settled down to wait for reinforcements. Until their arrival the Triumvirs could spare a part at least of the troops in the capital, now rapidly on the increase, to meet another foe who, if not actually at the gates, was now literally within sight.

The Alban Hills, whence, in prehistoric times, the original settlers of Rome had come down to the plain and pushed on to the river-side, still seem to enjoy a *patria potestas* over the city, by the place which they hold in any prospect from Roman streets or gardens ; when we catch a glimpse of the country outside, it is less often the low-lying Campagna than the more distant Alban Mount that heaves in view. Among those hills—where of old lay the chief strength of the cities of the Latin League, Rome's cousins and earliest enemies—rises the Porcian height, and there, too, is the high plateau on which once shone, a dangerous rival :

> the white streets of Tusculum,
> The proudest town of all.

Its site is now swept bare, save for a few ruins, and Rome sees instead the harmless village of Frascati poured out over the hillside below.

In Frascati, and in Albano by the lake, was encamped Ferdinand King of Naples, with an army of 10,000 men, eager not to assist, but to forestall the French, who for their part would not consent to any co-operation with the Neapolitans, regarding them, apart from diplomatic rivalry, with the utmost personal contempt.[2] The Pope, who was heart and soul with Ferdinand, distrusted, more than need was, the half-hearted words of Oudinot's proclamations, and thought the conquest of Rome by the Neapolitans the best security for that unlimited restoration of clerical

---

[1] His favourite horse had been killed under him earlier in the day. *Gualtieri,* 171 ; Bassi's letter to his mother.

[2] *Torre,* ii. 122, 123 ; *D'Ambrosio,* 18 ; *Johnston,* 277-281, 292 ; *Roman MSS. F. R.* 36, *j.* 23.

despotism which in the end he obtained from the French.
Early in the year there had been some demonstrations
in favour of Pio Nono on the southern frontier and in the
Alban Hills, but the feeling at the back of this movement
did not long survive the arrival of *Bomba*, who at once
initiated a political proscription after his manner, and
made the inhabitants long for delivery by the Republican
armies.[1]

To keep these invaders in check, Mazzini consented
that Garibaldi should cross the Campagna, at the head of
a small force which, in its numbers and in the half-civilian
character and training of the men who composed it, somewhat resembled the citizen armies which the earliest Roman
Consuls had led over the same ground to battle with the
Latin League.   Not more than 2,300 troops [2] could safely
be spared while Oudinot's attitude was still doubtful, and
they consisted almost entirely of the volunteer regiments
—Garibaldi's own Legion, the Students, the Gagers, the
Emigrants and Manara's Lombard Bersaglieri—together
with a few dragoons.   Since it was impossible for Garibaldi
to make a frontal attack on the Alban Hills, guarded by an
army four times as numerous as his own, he determined
to threaten the right flank of the Neapolitans and keep it
sufficiently engaged to prevent them from advancing on
Rome.   His object, therefore, was to move on Palestrina, a
suitable base for such a campaign.

As a master of guerilla war, where the chief art is the
concealment of movements and the deception of the enemy,
he made it a custom frequently to march at night, and
to go first in some direction other than that of the real
point of attack ; hence, though destined for Palestrina, his
column crossed the plain in the direction of Tivoli on the
night of May 4–5, and next day encamped in the grounds
of Hadrian's villa.   Here, in the most beautifully situated

[1] *Key*, 198, who visited Albano on April 8; *Dandolo*, 221 ; *Johnston*,
278 ; *Hoff. passim* ; *MS. Lanza*, on the system of arrests.

[2] *Torre*, ii. 370 (Doc. xcii.).   This document is a better authority on the
numbers than *Hoff*. 20.   In *Miraglia*, 306, an officer who was on the expedition says 2,500.

of all the ruins of Imperial Rome, lying amid its groves
of orange and fig,[1] like an oasis in the desert Campagna,
but close beneath the olive-clad base of the steep Sabine
Mountains, and only some two miles

> From the green steeps where Anio leaps
> In floods of snow-white foam,

the Lombard Bersaglieri had their first opportunity of
observing the conduct in the field of their strange General,
who soon brought them to love him, against all their prejudices, and almost against their judgment. 'I am going
with Garibaldi,' Manara had written on May 4; 'he is a
devil, a panther.' His men are 'a troop of brigands,' and
'I am going to support their mad onrush with my disciplined, proud, silent, gentlemanly regiment.'[2] Exactly a
month later Manara became Chief of the Staff to this 'devil
and panther,' whom he had so quickly learnt to love.

Emilio Dandolo has also recorded, in a vivid and impartial sketch, the first impression made by the Garibaldians
on the Lombard Bersaglieri :

'We encamped on the magnificent site of the villa of Hadrian,
and the numerous fires which glistened among the ruins, and
lighted up their subterranean caverns, produced a strange and
picturesque effect. The singular aspect of the camp seemed
in unison with the wildness of the scene. Garibaldi and his
staff were dressed in scarlet blouses, with hats of every possible
form, without distinctions of any kind, or any pretension to
military ornament. They rode on American saddles, and
seemed to pride themselves on their contempt for all the observ-
ances most strictly enjoined on regular troops. Followed by
their orderlies (almost all of whom had come from America)
they might be seen hurrying to and fro, now dispersing, then
again collecting, active, rapid, and indefatigable in their movements. When the troop halted to encamp, or to take some
repose, while the soldiers piled their arms, we used to be surprised to see officers, the General himself included, leap down
from their horses, and attend to the wants of their own steeds.
When these operations were concluded, they opened their

---

[1] *Hoff.* 26.   [2] *Manara, MS. Letter of May 4.*

saddles, which were made so as to be unrolled, and to form a small kind of tent, and their personal arrangements were then completed. If they failed in procuring provisions from the neighbouring villages, three or four colonels and majors threw themselves on the bare backs of their horses, and, armed with long lassoes, set off at full speed through the Campagna in search of sheep or oxen; when they had collected a sufficient quantity they returned, driving their ill-gotten flocks before them;[1] a certain portion was divided among each company, and then all, indiscriminately—officers and men—fell to, killing, cutting up, and roasting at enormous fires quarters of oxen, besides kids and young pigs, to say nothing of booty of a smaller sort, such as poultry and geese.

'Garibaldi in the meanwhile, if the encampment was far from the scene of danger, lay stretched out under his tent. If, on the contrary, the enemy were at hand, he remained constantly on horseback, giving orders and visiting the outposts; often, disguised as a peasant, he risked his own safety in daring reconnaissances, but most frequently, seated on some commanding elevation, he passed whole hours examining the environs with the aid of a telescope. When the General's trumpet gave the signal to prepare for departure, the lassoes served to catch the horses which had been left to graze at liberty in the meadows. The order of march was always arranged on the preceding day, and the corps set out without any one ever knowing where they might arrive the day after. Owing to this patriarchal simplicity—pushed, perhaps, somewhat too far—Garibaldi appeared more like the chief of a tribe of Indians than a General; but at the approach of danger, and in the heat of combat, his presence of mind and courage were admirable; and then by the astonishing rapidity of his movements he made up, in a great measure, for his deficiency in those qualities which are generally supposed to be absolutely essential in a good General.'[2]

A little incident of one of the first days of this campaign, narrated by one of the Students' battalion, is characteristic of Garibaldi's relations to his young men. Some of the Students had turned into a house to get wine. Garibaldi

---

[1] Garibaldi admits that he had no hesitation in commandeering the cattle of the Cardinals' great estates in the region of Zagarolo. (*Mem.* 231.)

[2] *Dandolo*, 204–206.

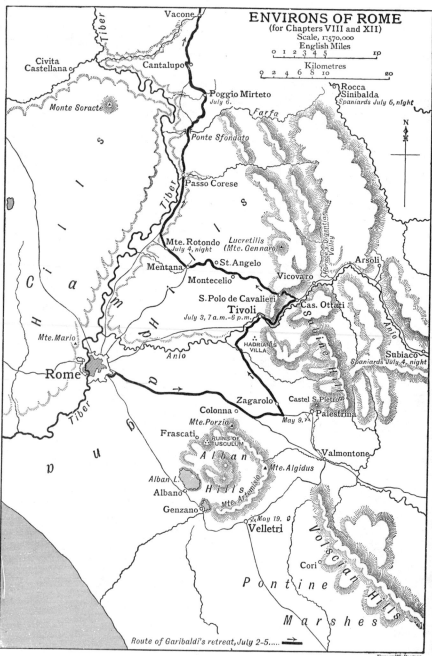

ENVIRONS OF ROME
(for Chapters VIII and XII)
Scale, 1:570,000
English Miles
0 1 2 3 4 5   10

Kilometres
0 2 4 6 8 10   20

N

Vacone

Civita
Castellana

Cantalupo

Monte Soracte

Poggio Mirteto
July 6.

Rocca
Sinibalda
Spaniards July 6, night

Farfa

Ponte Sfondato

Tiber

Passo Corese

Tiber

Mte. Rotondo
July 4, night

Lucretilis
(Mte. Gennaro)

Arsoli

Mentana

St. Angelo

Montecelio

Vicovaro

S. Polo de Cavalieri

Cas. Ottati

Tivoli
July 3, 7 a.m.–6 p.m.

Horace's Digentia Valley

Mte. Mario

HADRIAN'S
VILLA

Subiaco
Spaniards July 4, night

Rome

Anio

Sabine Hills

Anio

Tiber

Zagarolo

Castel S. Pietro

Palestrina
May 9.

Colonna

Mte. Porzio

Frascati

RUINS OF
TUSCULUM

Valmontone

Alban

Hills

Mte. Algidus

Alban L.

Albano

Mte. Artemisio

Genzano

May 19.

Velletri

Volscian Hills

Cori

Pontine

Marshes

Route of Garibaldi's retreat, July 2–5.....

Emery Walker sc.

rode up to them : ' What ! ' he said, ' you are only a few hours out of the town, and already you must call for wine ? I lived five years on flesh and water '—on the plateaus of Rio Grande and Uruguay. When they answered with shouts of ' *Evviva !* Garibaldi ! ' he stopped them at once. ' Silence ! it is no time for cheers. When we have defeated the enemy, then we will cheer.' [1]

Inseparable from the General rode the splendid negro Aguyar, his friend and bodyguard, who had followed the Chief he adored across the Atlantic. The black giant, with the lasso of the Pampas hanging from his saddle, himself wrapped in a dark-blue *poncho*, and mounted on a jet-black charger, contrasted picturesquely with Garibaldi and his golden hair, white *poncho* and white horse. The one was seldom seen without the other.[2]

From Hadrian's villa the march was diverted to the south, towards the great road that leads from Rome to Naples by the valley of the Liris. On May 7, Garibaldi took up his quarters in Palestrina, that hangs amid the ruins of its antique grandeur on the edge of the Sabine Hills—a suitable base for annoying the right flank of the enemy among the Alban Hills opposite. During the next two days various bodies of thirty to sixty men each were sent out from Palestrina, to scour the undulating plain and the wooded mountains between Valmontone and Frascati. In this guerilla warfare the irregular troops displayed a vigour, craft, and courage, in which they were by no means inferior to the Lombards. One of these small bodies, with whom rode the indefatigable Ugo Bassi in his red shirt, had a severe engagement, near Monte Porzio, with a considerable body of Neapolitans, under General Winspeare, who were advancing on Palestrina ; the handful of Garibaldians were driven off the ground, but the enemy had had such a taste of them

---

[1] *Roman MSS. Batt. Univ.*

[2] *Loev.*, ii. 192, 226–228 ; *Varenne*, 353 ; *Koelman*, ii. 72. His parents were freed negro slaves, and he had been a horsebreaker before he was a soldier.

that they fell back on Frascati.[1] On another of these encounters, Ugo Bassi rode up to the enemy, and, under a shower of bullets, addressed them on the wickedness of fighting against their country.[2]

Meanwhile another and larger force of Neapolitans, under General Lanza, were marching from Albano by way of Velletri and Valmontone, with orders to drive away the ' bandit,' who had become a thorn in the side of the royal army, delaying the advance on Rome, and striking terror by his mere name into the superstitious and timid southerners, dragged from their homes to fight in a cause which was not theirs. Lanza had special orders to force Garibaldi to retreat towards Rome, and by no means towards Naples.[3] At Valmontone he found a Republican population and municipality, planting ' trees of liberty ' and fraternising with the Garibaldian scouts. Having cut down the trees and made the requisite number of arrests, according to orders, Lanza, about noonday on May 9, advanced on Palestrina in two columns, entrusting that on the right to Colonel Novi, and himself taking charge of the left. The approach of a superior force of such an enemy caused no alarm among the staff-officers, who climbed with their Chief to the top of the mountain behind Palestrina, and from the old fortress of *Præneste* (Castel San Pietro) so famous in the wars of Sulla, watched the columns winding towards them by two parallel roads about a mile apart.[4]

Approaching by this double route, the Neapolitans in the plain below threatened the lowest side of the ancient walls of Palestrina at two points at once—at the Valmontone Gate to the south-east, and also at the Roman Gate to the south-west. The Garibaldians, however, did not wait to be

[1] *Loev.* i. 175, 176 ; *Dandolo,* 209, 210 ; *Roman MSS. Batt. Univ. Miraglia,* 306 ; *D'Ambrosio,* 25, 26 ; *Lanza MS.*
[2] *Roman MSS., F. R. 6, f. 2.*
[3] *Lanza MS.* ; *D'Ambrosio,* 25.
[4] The road on the left, followed by Lanza (Via Consolare), was a mere track, now mostly disappeared. Novi went by the main road. *Lanza MS.* ; *Hoff.* 35 ; *Dandolo,* 210 ; *Loev.* i. 177. Lanza reported his whole army as 3,000, but it was, and is usually, placed at 5,000. In either case, it was larger than Garibaldi's 2,300.

'BOMBA' AT DINNER, MAY 1849.

(Published in *Don Pirlone*, which always represents King Ferdinand as the Neapolitan *pulcinella*.)

attacked, but, rushing down the steep cobbled streets of the hill-town, sallied out to give battle under the walls. They had the advantage of the hill; and the enemy's cavalry, where his chief superiority lay, could not charge with effect because the ground was so much enclosed. Manara, in command of Garibaldi's left wing, took up his station at the beautiful Valmontone Gate, and sent down about 150 of his Lombards, supported by some of the Legion, to meet Novi's men as they advanced across the ravines and up through the vineyards, hedges, and ruins of the broken ground below the town. The Neapolitans fled, almost at once, in disgraceful rout, and the fear of the 'round hats' (*cappelli tondi*),[1] as they called the Bersaglieri, was deeply impressed on them by this engagement.

On Garibaldi's right wing, where the main attack of the Neapolitans was delivered under General Lanza himself, the fighting was more severe, and some houses not far below the Roman Gate were occupied by the enemy, who had to be dislodged at the point of the bayonet. The Legionaries, aided by another company of Bersaglieri, who had been sent up after the success on the other wing was assured, drove back the infantry, repulsed a charge of horse on the road, attacked the houses, burst in the windows and doors while the enemy's fire singed the hair on their heads, and captured the garrisons. In this operation 'the fiery Bixio' of Genoa, in after years one of the most famous of the Thousand who delivered Sicily, again attracted notice by the same impetuous daring as he had shown on April 30; and the good Swiss Hoffstetter, who had for several nights past been feeling duly sentimental about the nightingales and ruins of Italy, and taking notes of what he saw with a view to becoming the Xenophon of the Republican army, here put in the first of many hearty blows on behalf of the Italian cause.[2]

[1] *Hoff.* 47; 'capelli' is clearly a misprint of 'cappelli.' In the Italian edition it is 'cappelli.'

[2] *Hoff.* 34–57; *Dandolo*, 210–212; *Loev.* i. 177, 178; *Vecchi*, ii. 204; *Bixio*, 83–89; *D'Ambrosio*, 25–28; *Roman MSS. Batt. Univ.*; *Miraglia*, 306, 307 (Legionary officer's narrative), p. 186 (picture of the battle).

The whole battle was over in about three hours, and the enemy, in full flight, cast away their muskets as they ran.[1] The right wing of their army, under Colonel Novi, abandoned not only Valmontone, but Velletri, and did not stop till it had reached Genzano, where it was near enough to *Bomba's* headquarters on the Alban lake to feel in safety; while the left wing, under General Lanza, beat what he considered a dignified retreat to Colonna, and thence the next day to Frascati.[2] When a score of prisoners were brought into Garibaldi's presence, trembling, and with clasped hands begging their lives from the ogre of whom their priests had told them such terrible tales, their knapsacks and clothes were found to be crammed with relics, amulets, and pictures of Saints, although they had so little of the spirit of crusaders that they cried out in their dialect '*Mannaggia Pio Nono*' ('A plague take Pio Nono').[3] Such was Garibaldi's first experience of the Neapolitan troops. He was so deeply impressed by their incapacity that the recollection of Palestrina must have weighed in his mind eleven years later, when he came to his supreme decision to risk his country's fortunes, his own and his friends' lives, on the hazard of landing with a thousand red-shirts in the *champs clos* of the island of Sicily, occupied by 24,000 Neapolitan regulars.[4]

The victors remained another night and the whole of the next day at Palestrina, where the citizens, who had helped to barricade the streets against emergencies, now illuminated their little town in honour of the battle won.[5] They also took part in a scene of less innocent hilarity. The monks of the convent where Manara's Lombards were stationed, had locked them out on their first arrival, and had afterwards made their quarters

---

[1] *Miraglia*, 307.   [2] *Lanza MS.*

[3] *Dandolo*, 212, 213; *Torre*, ii. 126; *Vecchi*, ii. 204.

[4] The privates of the Neapolitan army fought better in 1860 than in 1849; but their leaders behaved in a more incompetent and cowardly manner in Sicily than at Palestrina and Velletri.

[5] *Hoff.* 39, 48; *Loev.* i. 177, 178; *Spada* (iii. 471) is ignorant of all the circumstances of this battle, though on most subjects he is well informed.

as- uncomfortable as possible ; but there had as yet been no reprisals. Unfortunately, however, when the victors returned after the battle, and found the doors again locked and the monks gone, the provocation was too much for the immaculate Bersaglieri, who got out of hand in the empty convent. Church, cellar, and library were saved, but the ordinary rooms were sacked; and Manara's men made merry, lighting the tapers and stalking about in the monks' clothes.[1]

The Palestrina expedition had succeeded in its object of preventing the further advance of King Ferdinand against the capital.[2] Garibaldi, recalled in haste by the Triumvirate, in view of Oudinot's doubtful attitude, made nother of his famous marches on the night of May 10–11, taking his wounded with him, skilfully avoiding contact with the Neapolitans, and reaching Rome in the morning, his men suffering horribly from thirst and exhaustion. But their return, though anxiously awaited, was rendered unnecessary by a change for the better in the attitude of the French. On May 15, De Lesseps arrived on a friendly mission from Paris, and on May 17 a suspension of hostilities was arranged, to give the French Envoy time to come to an accommodation with the Triumvirate and Assembly of Rome.

Such, at least, was the ostensible object. But the real motive of the French Government in the matter of the armistice, and of the whole mission of De Lesseps,[3] was to gain time: first, until reinforcements could be sent out to Oudinot; and, secondly, until the Catholic party in France, at present sorely beset by the Republicans in the Assembly, could obtain a majority for reaction at the elections which were due to take place within a few weeks.[4] The French Ministers neither expected nor desired the negotiations to succeed. On May 8, the very day on which the

---

[1] *Dandolo*, 208, 209, 214.   [2] *Loev.* i. 178.

[3] For which see *Mazzini, sub loc.* ; *De Lesseps, passim*, for documents ; *Clermont*, 45–146 ; and *Johnston*, 282–290, for the best analysis.

[4] *Clermont*, 53 (quotation from Odillon Barrot's *Mémoires*).

L

Minister for Foreign Affairs charged De Lesseps with his mission,[1] the President wrote to Oudinot : ' Our military honour is at stake. I will not suffer it to be compromised. You may rely on being reinforced '[2] ; and suiting the action to the word, sent out the great Engineer General Vaillant, with orders to take Rome, and powers to supersede the less capable Oudinot if it should prove necessary.[3] Louis Napoleon, personally a friend to Italian freedom, on behalf of which he had taken part in the Carbonaro movement of 1831, had not been so active as his Clerical Ministers in the first sending of the expedition ; but now that the honour of the army had been tarnished by April 30, his whole future as military dictator was jeopardised until that blot should be wiped out. It was necessary not only to con- ceal from the Romans and from the French Liberals the vengeance intended, but to conceal from the French nation the real nature of the defeat suffered, until it had been avenged. For this part of the game, Oudinot was emi- nently suited. His despatch, read to the French Assembly amid ' murmurs from the Left,' described the firing under the walls of the Vatican as a ' reconnaissance,' omitted to mention the battle outside the gates in which Garibaldi had driven the French off the field, and summed up with the declaration that ' this affair of April 30 is one of the most brilliant in which the French troops have taken part since our great wars.'[4]

But it was even more important to conceal present intentions than past defeats. To make deceit effective it is best to employ honest instruments ; and such was De Lesseps, who took his part in the comedy *au grand sérieux.* Coming to Rome full of zeal to bring about an accommoda- tion, he was soon under the spell of Mazzini, and, we may add, under the spell of the kind-hearted populace of Rome,

[1] *De Lesseps,* 15.
[2] Printed in *Moniteur* of May 10, p. 1734 ; *Vaillant,* 174, dates the letter May 5 ; but *Ollivier,* ii. 122, and *Bittard des Portes,* 119, support the date given by *Moniteur* (*viz.* May 8). On the importance of the letter, see *Clermont,* 59–72.
[3] *Bittard des Portes,* 146.   [4] *Moniteur* for 1849, p. 1750.

who throughout May treated him and all his countrymen within their gates with friendliness, and even with enthusiasm. He was man enough to feel the intellectual and moral superiority of Mazzini, who soon lured him to make concessions larger than his powers warranted—far larger than the managers of the comedy had intended.

The French Envoy found the ideals of Republicanism realised in all their impressive simplicity by the chief of the Triumvirs.

'Lodged in the Quirinal, Mazzini hunted for a room "small enough to feel at home in." Here he sat unguarded and serene, "sadly ἀδορύφορος (sic) for a τύραννος" wrote Clough (for it was a country where political assassination was a tradition on both sides), as accessible to working men and women as to his own officials, with the same smile and warm hand-shake for all ; dining for two francs at a cheap restaurant . . . his only luxury the flowers that an unknown hand sent every day, his one relaxation to sing to his guitar, when left alone at night. The Triumvir's slender stipend of 32*l.* a month he spent entirely on others.'[1]

De Lesseps was touched by what he saw of Mazzini and of Rome, and declared that the Republican leaders were misunderstood at Paris. After one quarrel, when the fiery Frenchman broke out in disgust at Roman unreasonableness, and abused Mazzini in violent terms, the negotiations were resumed and proceeded rapidly towards an accommodation.[2]

Meanwhile what was the attitude of the people, as distinct from the small body of convinced Republicans who led them ? It was summed up as follows by the acute and impartial Captain of H.M.S. *Bulldog*, who wrote, on May 12, after his visit to Rome :

'The general feeling among the Roman people appears to be in favour of making terms with the French, as they show no objection to the return of the Pope, but great repugnance to an ecclesiastical government. The leaders keep up their determination to resist . . . assuring the people that the return

[1] *King's Mazzini*, 133 ; *Clough's P. R.* 154.   [2] *Farini*, iv. 104, 120, 121.

of the Pope can only take place with the old system of a spiritual administration.'[1]

This would, perhaps, be an accurate analysis of the main current of opinion, if it were added that what the leaders said was quite true, and that the people believed them. All knew that the return of the Pope would only take place if clerical rule were restored, because he would consent to come back on no other terms. Whatever the French might wish, they had in fact no alternative between leaving the Republic alone, or restoring the hated rule of priests ; and the fixed determination of Pio Nono to recover the powers of Gregory XVI. would have rendered the mission of De Lesseps futile if it had ever been serious. It was absurd for the French to pretend to negotiate on behalf of a sovereign who refused to treat.

Captain Key, who passed freely between Rome and Civitavecchia, wrote again a few days later of the state of things round the French camp :

'I cannot speak too highly of the conduct of the French soldiers towards the inhabitants of the country. Every article of food is strictly paid for, and their behaviour has engendered a very kindly feeling for them in the people with whom they have had intercourse.'[2]

The absence of complaints by Italian writers against the French soldiery fully confirms this testimonial. But the French could not, by any amount of good behaviour, induce the inhabitants to give them any political encouragement or military assistance, and they were grievously disappointed at the absence of any sign of Papal partisans in the country which they had come to 'deliver' from the Republican tyranny ; even the few peasants, who came into their camps to sell them food, were gloomily silent on politics.[3]

The Republican Government, having successfully put down terrorism in the provinces, was faced in May by an

[1] *Key*, 199. See also *Bratti*, 78, 79.   [2] *Key*, 201.
[3] *Journal 16e*, p. 8. A very explicit statement.

outbreak of the Jacobin elements among its extreme supporters in the City of Rome itself, and this also it speedily overcame. On May 20 the mob raided two churches, dragged out the confessionals, symbols in the Pope's dominions not only of religion but of politics and police, and piled them in the Piazza del Popolo for a bonfire. Mazzini gravely remonstrated, and the objects were restored to their proper places.[1]

A more serious affair was the attempt of a few wicked men to introduce the indiscriminate massacre of priests. Callimaco Zambianchi,[2] a native of Forlì in the Romagna, had been an exile from the Papal States between 1832 and 1846, and while resident at Paris had picked up the traditions of the original Terror from the small group of men who still cherished the memory of Robespierre and Marat, and who taught him that no Republic was worth the name without its 'September.' Attracted back to Italy by the amnesty of the new Pope, he fought in the Lombard campaign, and having taken part in the reign of terror at Bologna, in August 1848, had been further embittered by a fresh imprisonment in the following month.[3] After Rossi's murder he was liberated, and, shortly before the establishment of the Roman Republic, he had very wrongly been made commander of the regiment of Gagers, in which capacity he arrested and sent to Rome out of the provinces certain persons whom he accused of treason. When he heard, to his great indignation, that the Triumvirate had at once set them free, he vowed that in the future he would himself be judge and hangman ; being called back to Rome, and posted with his men on Monte Mario during the battle of April 30, he there and then caused his men to shoot a Dominican, whom he happened to meet on the road. During the same week, in the little church and convent of San Calisto, hidden away among the

---

[1] *Spada*, iii. 555–558.
[2] This Callimaco Zambianchi must not be confused with Antonio Zambianchi, an honourable politician and servant of the Republic.
[3] At Civita Castellana. (*Roman MSS. F. R.* 7, f. 3.)

time-honoured slums of Trastevere, he and his men killed
six persons in holy orders, whom he declared to have been
preaching sedition and conspiring against the Republic.
The Government stopped the massacre and did everything in its power to prevent another outbreak of terrorism.
Its efforts of prevention were successful, but unfortunately
the crimes already committed remained in this case un-
punished, partly because the preoccupations of the siege of
Rome in June delayed Zambianchi's trial till the Republic
had fallen, and partly, perhaps, because the Gagers, who
were a ruffianly crew, seemed inclined to protect their leader.
So the chief criminal escaped, and two years later was turned
away from the door of a poor London house at which he had
the audacity to knock, by the indignant lodger, the ex-
Triumvir Saffi. It is painful to relate that Garibaldi allowed
Zambianchi to follow him in the retreat from Rome, and ten
years later to don the red shirt. The Papal Government
in January 1854 justly executed three of his accomplices ;
the scoundrels died game, refusing the offices of religion and
crying, ' Viva l'Italia! Viva la Repubblica!'[1]

The immunity of Zambianchi is a blot on the Roman
Government. But the contagion of violence was stayed ;
and if we consider the unprovoked invasion of the State
and the shooting down of the citizens who defended it by
foreign troops in league with the priests, the Triumvirate
deserves a good deal of credit, and the Roman populace a
little, for stopping the Terror in a country where assassination was indigenous. Arthur Clough wrote on May 31 to
Arthur Stanley :

[1] Whether Garibaldi could and should have given more assistance to Government to secure the arrest and trial of Zambianchi we have not evidence enough
to decide. (See *Saffi*, iii. 323 note and 324, bottom of page.) If the *Finanzieri* had
been put under the direct command of Garibaldi, as Amadei proposed to the
Government as early as March 11, these murders would certainly never have taken
place. (See *Loev.* ii. 186.) For Garibaldi's hard but successful struggle with
indiscipline and violence in his own Legion, see *Loev.* ii. 149–189.

For the Zambianchi incident, see *Roman MSS. F. R.*, 7, 3, the most authentic
evidence which I have found. *Torre*, i. 190, 330–333; *Saffi*, iii. 323–325;
Vecchi, ii. 275, 276; *Farini*, ii. 333, 334; iv. 153, 154; *Spada*, iii. 416;
Cochrane, 116, 117; *Tivaroni, Aust.* ii. 403 ; *Guerzoni*, ii. 50; *Bel.* 17, 75,
112, 157.

'Priests, by the way, walk about in great comfort—arm in arm with a soldier, perhaps ; in cafés and legnos and all profane places they are seen circulating as freely at least as government paper. Confession is still administered openly with long sticks in St. Peter's and the Apostle's toe multitudinously kissed. The Bambino also drives about to see the sick in infinite state, and is knelt and capped to universally.[1] Wandering about alone, and with the map, I have been twice hailed by civicas (National Guard) as a *spione*, but after some prattle affectionately dismissed.'

And again on June 21, in the final agony of the siege, ten days before the fall of Rome, when, if ever, anarchy might have been expected to lift its head, he writes to Francis Turner Palgrave :

'Assure yourself that there is nothing to deserve the name of "Terror." . . . Since May 4 the worst thing I have witnessed has been a paper in manuscript put up in two places in the Corso, pointing out seven or eight men for popular resentment. This had been done by night ; before the next evening a proclamation was posted in all the streets, from (I am sure) Mazzini's pen, severely and scornfully castigating such proceedings. A young Frenchman in a café, hearing his country abused, struck an Italian ; he was of course surrounded, but escaped by the interference of the National Guard and of the British Consul. The soldiers, so far as I see, are extremely well behaved—far more seemly than our regulars ; they are about, of course, in the streets and cafés, but make no disorder.'[2]

Garibaldi had for some time past noticed that the red shirt worn by himself and his staff officers had attained popularity as the symbol of the whole Legion and of the political ideas which it embodied. Fully sharing, in his emotional nature, that craving for symbolism which is at the root of so much in Italian religion and custom, he realised the advantages which might accrue from the red shirt as the outward and visible sign of the revolutionary

---

[1] *Koelman*, i. 258; and *Bresciani*, viii., 170–3, describe such a scene in detail. Some Liberals cried '*Viva il Bambino democratico !*'

[2] *Clough, P. R.* 153, 157; *I. L. N.* July 14, 1849, p. 25, ' our correspondent.'

brotherhood of Italians, and, be it allowed, as the bond of the fellowship of Giuseppe Garibaldi.   On his return from Palestrina, having wisely determined that no part in the democratic cult which he was founding should be denied to the laity, he ordered the manufacture of a red woollen blouse for every private in the regiment.[1]   The order was taken in hand, but the uniforms were not ready till near the end of June.

In making this change Garibaldi did even better, perhaps, than he expected.   For it turned out that in the *camicia rossa* the Italian Revolution found for itself a cheap   pageantry,   simple   in   gaudiness,   unmistakable, satisfying the desire of youth to flaunt its principles in some visible form.   For a few *soldi* the student or the workman could in a minute transform himself, in appearance at least, into the soldier of a redoubtable force, the semi-official missionary of a great cause.

The moral effect of the red shirt, which acted like a charm, giving a sense of brotherhood with their chief to the little band who so often fought in it against overwhelming odds, far out-balanced a slight military disadvantage in the colour, which did not escape comment. Before coming to Europe the Italian Legion had fought in this attire through the wars of Montevideo, where small bodies of troops moved over the great open prairies, each side straining its eyes so as to be the first to see the enemy. Garibaldi, it is said, found that in those regions his troops were less easily detected in the distance when clothed in red than were the enemy in their darker uniforms.   But in Italy, where much close fighting took place on a back-

---

[1] *Loev.* ii. 125, 126.   They were sometimes spoken of as 'tunics,' sometimes as 'shirts,' sometimes as 'blouses.'   During the early years in South America, and in Italy in 1849, they were shaped like a French workman's blouse, falling over the hips, as in illustrations facing pp. 117, 118 above.   In later years they were often tucked into the trousers like our English 'shirts,' as in the later photograph of Garibaldi in the frontispiece.   Sometimes they were more like military tunics of the regular army, with big buttons, etc.   See some specimens preserved in the *Museo Civico*, Bologna.

It was in the colour, not the shape, that the virtue lay.   The one thing needful in the *camicia rossa* was that it should be red.

ground of white or grey houses and vineyard walls, the red shirt was easily seen and offered an admirable mark to Neapolitans, Austrians, and French.[1]

Taking advantage of the improved relations with France, and of the rapid increase of the force under arms in Rome, the Triumvirs on the evening of May 16 sent out from ten to eleven thousand [2] of their best troops to drive the Neapolitans out of the territory of the Republic. Garibaldi was put as a General of Division in command of part of the army, but he was asked to serve under the Commander-in-Chief Roselli, a worthy but not very able soldier, whose respectability was meant as a pledge to Italy and Europe of the regular character of the Roman troops and of the war in which they were engaged.   In making this arrangement the Triumvirs fell between two stools, for neither were the methods and machinery of a regular force employed on the campaign, nor was it conducted with the energy of a guerilla war.   The army moved with the uncomfortable and jerky motion of a man with an excitable dog in leash ; Garibaldi dashed about in front, locating and engaging the enemy, and then was forced to wait till Roselli came sulkily lumbering up with the bulk of the troops.   On an expedition like this, such a general was about as fit to be put in command of Garibaldi as Parker was to be put in command of Nelson ; indeed, the case was much worse, for though himself a modest man, Roselli was surrounded by a staff of regular officers who urged him to assert himself, regarding the guerilla with a professional jealousy which none of the captains off Copenhagen felt against the victor of the Nile.[3]

Roselli, though commanding a force nearly five times as numerous as that led by Garibaldi a fortnight earlier, also

[1] *Lessona*, 421 ; *Cadolini, N.A.* May 1902, 61 ; *Loev.* ii. 125, 129, 130. See p. 35 above, note, for the origin of the red shirt.

[2] The most complete and trustworthy list of the regiments and their numbers is in *Roselli*, 50, 51.   *Torre*, ii. 128, is in substantial agreement.   *Hoff.* 63, 64, is, therefore, probably wrong.   See also *Vecchi*, ii. 235.

[3] See Appendix E below.

determined not to attack the Alban Hills in face, but to cross the Campagna towards Valmontone, and so take the Neapolitans in flank. The commissariat of the 'regular' army was so ill managed that the troops would have starved in crossing the Campagna but for the energy and foresight of Garibaldi in his capacity of cow-boy, exercised at the expense of the Cardinals' estates;[1] and even after the desert plain had been crossed, the advance of the main body was delayed pending the late arrival of the train of waggons from Rome. But Garibaldi, as soon as he had reached Valmontone, galloped out early on the morning of May 19 along the Velletri road, under the foot of the wooded ridge of Algidus and Artemisio, to see what the enemy were about. He found, as he had expected, that they were in full retreat from the Alban Hills, which they had no thought of holding when their rear and flank were threatened by a force as large as their own. The only danger was that they would escape altogether, for they were already arriving from Albano at the low hill where the ancient Volscian city of Velletri rises above its vineyards, when, about six o'clock in the morning, Garibaldi and his staff reined up their horses on a knoll commanding a near view of their proceedings.[2] Garibaldi determined to take, on his own responsibility, the measures necessary for cutting off Ferdinand's retreat—to hold him engaged with the advance guard, and to send to Roselli praying that the arrival of the central division might be hastened. This involved a gross breach of discipline, since he himself was in command of the central division, and not of the advance guard, to whom he now issued orders for battle. But it was not likely that those orders, however irregular, would be disobeyed, for the officer rightfully in command was Marochetti, one of his old comrades of America, only too proud to be superseded by the Chief, and the best half of the troops consisted of his own Italian Legion.

From the point of view of strategy and tactics he was as indisputably right as from the point of view of discipline he was wrong. The strategical situation showed a

---

[1] *Hoff.* 62 ; *Mem.* 231 ; *Roman MSS. F. R.* 22, 69.   [2] *Ciàmpoli*, 31.

demoralised enemy in full retreat, affording a splendid opportunity to strike into the front flank of his column in such
a way as to drive him off the high road away from his base.
The tactical situation involved the ability of 2,000 seasoned
guerilla troops to hold in play a despised foe who had fled
before them ten days before, until the arrival of the main
Roman army, which would certainly not be up in time to
catch the retreating enemy unless he was attacked at once.[1]
But whether the desire to seize the opportunity of the
campaign can justify any man, even a Garibaldi, in breaking the discipline of the camp is a question on which I have
no wish to pronounce.

Finding a body of troops close on their flank, the
Neapolitans were forced to turn aside and drive it back.
Garibaldi, whose scouting arrangements kept him far better
acquainted than any contemporary general of regulars
with the real intentions of the enemy, knew that this
offensive movement was only designed to cover their
retreat.   But until Roselli should arrive, the Legionaries,
posted about a mile outside Velletri, had before them the
prospect of a stiff fight for an indefinite number of hours,
holding their own against superior numbers of the enemy's
infantry and cavalry in the vineyards and undulating ground
on either side of the Valmontone road.   The chief incident
of the battle occurred on the road itself.   Masina's forty
lancers [2] had gone down it, driving the enemy in front of
them, until they met the head of a long column of mounted
men before whom they fled back at a gallop.   The young
Bolognese cavaliers, though noted for fearless gallantry,
were not seasoned veterans; their horses were young and
untrained, and Masina himself was not among them this
day, but was commanding the whole Legion.[3]   They came
bolting back at a pace which so aroused the indignation
of Garibaldi that, regardless of dynamics, he reined up
athwart their path.   Behind him sat his friend, the
gigantic negro, on his jet-black horse.   Like equestrian

---

[1] *Loev.* i. 184 and note 2 ; *Gabussi*, iii. 404-407.
[2] *Roselli*, 50, 74 ; *Roman MSS. Ruoli Gen.* 82, F. 10.   [3] *Loev.* i. 186.

statues of Europe and Africa they sat immovable.   One
moment the young lancers, vainly tugging at their frightened
steeds, saw these two loom in front ; the next, down they
all went together in a welter of beasts and men, with Garibaldi at the bottom.   The enemy's cavalry, who had some
spirit, came dashing up, and it might have gone ill for Italy,
had not a handful of Legionaries, fighting at a little distance
to the right of the road, come running to save their leader.
The rescue party were mostly boys of fourteen and upwards.

'I believe (wrote Garibaldi) that my safety was chiefly due
to those gallant boys, since, with men and horses passing over
my body, I was so bruised that I could not move.'

The Neapolitans, who had pushed forward too rashly into
the heart of the Garibaldian position, were caught between
two fires,[1] and severely repulsed, leaving thirty prisoners
on the scene of the recent cascade.   Thus the incident that
had begun in picturesque disaster, led to a general advance
of the Garibaldian infantry through the vineyards and
down the road.

'The charge of our men on the right—the dominant position,
and therefore the key of the whole—led by Masina and Daverio,
was made with such headlong impetus that our men almost
entered Velletri, swept away among the flying enemy.'[2]

So little, indeed, had Garibaldi imperilled the safety
of the advance guard, as he was accused of having done
on this occasion, that they not merely maintained their
positions unaided, but assumed the offensive and drove
the enemy up into the town and the Cappuccini on
the neighbouring height, before the central division began
to appear.[3]   It was well on in the afternoon when the first
detachment, consisting of Manara's Lombards, came hurrying up with loud cheers for Garibaldi, and found his men

---

[1] *Miraglia*, 200.

[2] *Mem.* 230, 231 ; *Hoff.* 69, 70 ; *Roselli*, 74, 75, 147 ; *Lazzarini*, 221–228 ;
Vecchi, ii. 236 ; *Ritucci*, 8–10 ; *D'Ambrosio*, 40.

[3] *Loev.* i. 186, 187 ; *D'Ambrosio*, 40–44 ; *Ritucci*, 10–13.

CARICATURE OF A NEAPOLITAN SOLDIER.

firing at the town and convent, from which strong positions the enemy replied with effect.[1] Roselli had been tardy in sending forward the supports, and the rest of them arrived slowly and one by one on the scene.[2] Furious at hearing of Garibaldi's indiscipline in beginning the battle without his leave, and perhaps not better pleased that the friar Ugo Bassi should have been employed to carry messages between them, the commander-in-chief rode up in the worst of tempers and positively refused to attack that evening, nor would he, at Garibaldi's suggestion, forestall the enemy's retreat by moving across onto the road to Terracina. Roselli's staff would not believe the assurances of the insubordinate guerilla Chief that *Bomba's* generals were only thinking how to effect their escape, and that their men were utterly demoralised.[3]

Many of the Neapolitan soldiers had, in fact, again been scared by the ' red devil,' whom they declared to be bulletproof ; the giant black man behind him was Beelzebub, his father. In plaintive mutiny some cried out to their King : ' You are going to Naples, and we to the slaughter.' To what extent this demoralisation had spread through the army, or how far its royal chief alone can be accused of cowardice, will always be a matter of dispute.[4] Be that as it may, Ferdinand ordered the retreat to be continued under conditions which, as the historian of his reign has pronounced, took ' from his dynasty all military prestige,' and rendered him ' so much the more contemptible to his subjects.'[5] The army with some skill took advantage of Roselli's inaction, and stole away out of the southern gate of the town, leaving its wounded and prisoners, and retreated rapidly down the road that leads across the Pontine Marshes to Terracina and

---

[1] *Manara MSS. Letter of May* 20 ; *Dandolo*, 218, 219 ; *Hoff.* 70, 71 ; *Loev.* i. 187.

[2] *Roman MSS. F. R.* 62, 8, pp. 112, 113.

[3] *Vecchi*, ii. 237, 238 ; *Loev.* i. 187 ; *Elia*, i. 155–158. That the enemy had no object but to escape to their frontier is confessed by *D'Ambrosio*, 37, 45, 47 ; thus justifying Garibaldi's opinion.

[4] *Loev.* i. 187 and note ; *Jack la Bolina*, 83. The Clerical writer *Cianfarani* minimises the demoralisation of the Neapolitans ; and *Nisco*, 272, puts all the blame on the King for ordering the retreat. [5] *Nisco*, 272.

Naples by way of the coast.   Before the grey hours, some
reconnoitring Lombards climbed over the gate into Velletri,
and, to their surprise, found the streets silent and empty,
until the townspeople began to come out of their houses,
and joyfully fraternise with the deliverers.[1]

Garibaldi was convinced that Ferdinand's throne would
not survive an invasion of his kingdom, and pressed the
Triumvirate to allow the army to advance.[2] But Mazzini,
even if he could regard the French as neutralised, had still
to think of the Austrians, who had just taken Bologna
after a gallant defence by its inhabitants, and were fast
overrunning the Romagna and the Marches.   Roselli and
half the army were therefore recalled from Velletri, but
Garibaldi was allowed to proceed with his own Legion, the
Lombards, and some other troops, advancing by the great
inland road that leads to Naples, by Valmontone, Frosinone,
and the valley of the Liris.   In the Roman States they
were welcomed as deliverers.   But when they crossed into
Neapolitan territory a curious incident took place in the
frontier town of Rocca d'Arce, related as follows by Emilio
Dandolo :

'All the inhabitants had fled and hidden themselves among
the hills ; we found the houses shut up and deserted, and not a
human being in the whole village.   The soldiers were indignant
at this want of confidence ; but, thanks to the warm admonitions
of Garibaldi, who came up at the moment with his Legion,
and to the advice of Padre Ugo Bassi (whose fervent charity
and patriotism I then learnt to appreciate), no pillaging took
place, and in that deserted village not a single door was forced.
We sat down on the ground in the square ; and, when the terrified
inhabitants observed from the surrounding heights this admirable spirit of order and self-restraint, they hurried down to
welcome us, threw open their houses and shops, and in a few
minutes the whole village had regained its accustomed activity.

[1] *Dandolo*, 219.   There were also many Clericals and indifferentists in the
town. See *Cianfarani* and General *Lanza* (*MS.*). The latter found Valmontone
more Republican than Velletri.

[2] *Nisco* (272) thinks that the loss of prestige due to the retreat from Velletri
was so great, that if the *whole* Republican army had been able to invade Naples
the King might perhaps have lost his throne.

They then related to us how many superstitious fables the Neapolitans had spread among them ; according to which we were so many ogres let loose by the devil, to devour children and burn down houses; and the fantastic costumes of Garibaldi and his followers had contributed not a little to increase the ignorant fears of the natives.' [1]

How far, under these conditions, Garibaldi would have succeeded in rousing the Kingdom to revolt was never put to the test ; for at this point he was recalled, much to his own chagrin, to save the Republic from Austrian invasion in the North. To the end of his life he believed that the march which was stopped at Rocca d'Arce by Mazzini's orders, would have anticipated the results of that triumphal progress which he made eleven years later from the other end of the Neapolitan kingdom.   No doubt the royal army was demoralised by Palestrina and Velletri ; no doubt it was much smaller in 1849 than in 1860. But, on the other hand, the general conditions of Italian politics were far less favourable, the tide was setting in the wrong direction, and Italy was tired of revolution—facts which Garibaldi, who was never tired, could not properly realise. [2] Nor, as is shown by the incident just related, was his own reputation the same, either in its nature or its magnitude, as on the day when he landed at Reggio—the world's acknowledged hero—with those miraculous Sicilian laurels fresh upon his brow.

At the end of May, Garibaldi re-entered Rome in democratic triumph, for the last time, until, as an old man, he entered the capital of Italy in peace, a third power with the King and the Pope. [3] ' Now,' wrote Manara, ' we shall go to Ancona. I firmly hope we shall beat the Austrians as we have beaten the French and Neapolitans.' [4] Most of the tired troops who re-entered Rome between May 30

---

[1] *Dandolo*, 222, 223.

[2] See p. 258 below, how he tried to rouse Tuscany even after the fall of Rome.

[3] Pio Nono said, with reference to the arrival of Garibaldi in Rome shortly after Victor Emmanuel had taken up his quarters in the Quirinal : ' Lately we were two here ; now we are three ' (*Martinengo Cesaresco's Italy*, 414).

[4] *Manara MS. Letter of May* 30.

and June 2, were hoping that before they started against
the Austrians they would enjoy a little rest after their long
month of forced marches and battles.[1] But the rest prepared for them was the grave, save for those who lived
to be mocked by the uneasy rest of exile. Even while
they were re-entering Rome, the French threw off the mask
and repudiated De Lesseps in the hour when he seemed
to have brought things to a settlement. To die for Italy
there was no need to go to Ancona.

The turn of events on which Garibaldi had fixed
his hopes—a long guerilla war over the mountains and
valleys of half Italy—was not to be. Mazzini's dream
was to be realised instead—the fiery martyrdom of the
Republic in one supreme scene of defiance and death, in
the sacred city where the memories and treasures of the
western world were heaped together. The union of Italy
was an idea which Mazzini had done more than any other
man to spread, but the last effective contribution ever
made by him to that cause, so soon to pass into other hands,
was this great demonstration, which he had organised and
inspired—the dying message of Italy slain once more,
published to the world from Rome. In this siege of Rome,
a drama of despair, a battle that was not for victory, Garibaldi, though his genius was more suited to the open field,
was to play the part of chief hero among many, and to lend
it all the nobility of his presence and the grandeur of his
name.

[1] *Dandolo,* 224, 228 ; *Hoff.* 105.

CHAPTER IX[1]

'Villa Corsina, Casa dei Quattro Venti,
fumida prua del Vascello protesa
nella tempesta, alti nomi per sempre
solenni come Maratona Platea
Cremera, luoghi già d' ozii di piaceri
di melodie e di magnificenze
fuggitive, orti custoditi da cieche
statue ed arrisi da fontane serene,
trasfigurati subito in rossi inferni
vertiginosi.'

       D'ANNUNZIO—*La Canzone di Garibaldi.*

(Villa Corsini, House of the Four Winds,
Smoky prow of the Ship thrust forward
Into the tempest, names for ever
Grand—like Marathon, Platæa,
Cremera—once ye were haunts of idleness,
Pleasure and music and frail magnificence,
Gardens guarded by blind stone statues,
Watered by fountains—all changed suddenly
Into a red infernal giddiness.)

On May 31, the day when Garibaldi re-entered Rome, De Lesseps signed with the Triumvirs terms of agreement, according to which the French were to protect Rome and its environs against Austria and Naples and all the world, but were to take up their own quarters outside the city. Since nothing was said about the Pope's restoration on the one hand, or about the continued existence of the Republic on the other, the real questions at issue were postponed to the future; but all the advantages of the present were to go to the Romans, and none to the French. In signing terms so entirely averse from the spirit and

---

[1] For this Chapter use the maps pp. 125 above and 172 below.

intentions of those whom he represented, De Lesseps had
sense enough to append a clause which provided that the
treaty needed ratification by the French Republic.[1] But the
home Government, to whom he thus appealed, had already
thrown off the mask, and had despatched a message putting
an end to his mission and bidding him return at once to
France.[2] For Oudinot's reinforcement had come to hand.
The French army was again camped within a mile or
two of Rome, within striking distance of the Italian
outposts. Twenty thousand men were on the spot,
together with six batteries of artillery, some siege guns,
and a large number of excellent sappers and engineers
prepared to carry out Vaillant's scientifically laid plans for
the reduction of the city; and 10,000 more, together with the
rest of the siege train and engineers, would arrive at fixed
dates during the month.[3] When, therefore, the man of
peace brought his treaty to the camp, Oudinot no sooner
read the clause assigning to his army quarters outside
the walls of Rome than he broke out in a violent tirade
against De Lesseps and told him to go about his business[4];
next day (June 1) he gave notice to the Romans that the
truce was at an end.

But the letter in which he informed Roselli of the
denunciation of the armistice was of the most ambiguous
character, for although he declared that hostilities could
at once be resumed, he added that, in order to give the
French residents time to leave Rome, he would not
attack ' the place ' until Monday, the 4th of June.[5] His
real intention was to surprise and capture the outposts
(the Pamfili and Corsini) in the early hours of the 3rd.
In employing the vague word *place*, which he privately
interpreted to exclude these outposts, while the world in
general supposed that he had given a guarantee to suspend
all operations against Rome until the Monday, he at once

---

[1] *De Lesseps*, 61, 62, for text of treaty.   [2] *De Lesseps*, 67.
[3] *Bittard des Portes*, 160–163, 257, 262. I take the lowest estimate of the
number of infantry from *Vaillant*, 15, 155, 156.
[4] *De Lesseps*, 63–66.   [5] See App. L below for text of letter.

lulled the careless Italians into a fatal security, and satisfied
his own conscience—for he was, as Captain Key found
at this time, ' a strict Catholic and a very religious man.' [1]

Oudinot's announcement of war, so suddenly made on
the day after the Treaty of Peace and Alliance had been
signed, woke the Italians with a start from pleasant dreams
of chasing the white-coats out of the Apennines, to the
prospect of being cut to pieces in Rome by fellow-Republi-
cans. On June 2, when the Triumvirate asked Garibaldi to
give his confidential opinion on the crisis, he suggested
a remedy on a level with the desperate nature of their
affairs, declaring that he himself ought to be made Dictator.
He gave the advice in the spirit in which it had been asked
—in perfect good faith and in the public interest ; when it
was rejected he let the matter drop, though there were many
pseudo-politicians in Rome who were only too eager to
agitate on his behalf, had he consented to lead them, and
who proceeded some way in that direction without his consent. With the simple wisdom of the sailor and warrior,
trained in no political school but that of the South American
Republics,[2] he believed that an honest dictatorship was
the best means of carrying out the democratic will in times
of supreme crisis.   From the beginning to the end of his
life, divided authority and government by Assemblies
seemed to him out of place when the foreigner was in
occupation of the soil, or a tyrant had still to be dethroned.
These views were a practical qualification of his theoretic

---

[1] The French Clerical historian, La Gorce, regards the trick by which Oudinot
obtained such easy possession of the key to Rome either as requiring no explanation or as admitting of none ; for he does not record the fact.   But the Italian
Clerical historian, Spada, agrees with the common opinion that his action was not
justified to others by the quibble with which he satisfied himself (*Spada*, iii. 584,
585).   In view of the recent attempt by *M. Bittard des Portes* to justify Oudinot
in this matter, I have consulted high military authority on the meaning which
military men would attach to his letter. (See App. L below.)

[2] When South America was first released from Spanish rule, education and
habits of self-government were so backward that the popular assemblies proved
incapable of their task ; each assembly and each party attached itself to some
military chief, and rose and fell with his fortunes. *Robertson's P.* i. 16, 17, 64-68.

Republicanism, and prepared him to accept in later years the
chieftainship of Victor Emmanuel, with that loyal self-
effacement and devoted service to the King which proved
one of the main factors in the creation of Italy.[1] But his
proposal, on June 2, 1849, that he himself should be made
Dictator, though it would have had military advantages,
would have involved political dangers, because it would
have meant the displacement of Mazzini in favour of his
rival; and, though it would have aroused much enthusiasm,
would have caused also much offence and division.

Although Garibaldi was not made Dictator, or even
commander-in-chief in place of Roselli, the defence of the
west bank was entrusted to him, and it was on that side
that the attack was again made on Rome. But before
Garibaldi took over the command in that quarter, Roselli,
on Saturday evening (June 2), visited the very insufficient
outpost of 400 men which he had placed in the grounds of
the Villa Pamfili, to tell them that there was no need to be
vigilant, since the French had promised not to attack until
Monday morning.[2] In trusting the key of the capital, and
therefore the very existence of the State, to the faith of a
foe whose whole conduct since his first landing had been
shifty and ambiguous, Roselli was guilty of an error of
the first magnitude. If Oudinot's bad faith is condémned,
no less severe a judgment must be passed on the folly of
his antagonist. Even if the French General's letter had
been perfectly explicit in its promise to postpone every
kind of operation till Monday, this vital position ought to
have been occupied day and night by several thousand
troops.[3]

Garibaldi understood better than the commander-in-
chief the immense importance of a post, which, by reason
of its height and propinquity, was the key to the Janiculum,
and therefore the key to Rome. After his victory in the
Pamfili grounds on April 30, he had proposed to fortify
them, but had had no authority to carry this plan into

[1] *Mem.* 320, 344.   [2] *Gamberini,* 6-10.
[3] See App. L below.

effect ; and Roselli, who had enjoyed the power, had not possessed the wisdom to do anything of the kind during the weeks gone by.[1] If Garibaldi had not been too unwell on the night of Saturday, June 2, to take over at once his new command on the west bank, he would very probably have done something to strengthen the guard in the Pamfili ; but as he was confined indoors, recovering from his old wound of April 30, and the bruises and fatigues of the Velletri campaign, his command was temporarily vested in Galletti.[2] All who turned to sleep that night in Rome had been given to understand by Government that Oudinot had promised not to attack till the Monday, and no one suspected that before morning the key to the city would be stolen away.[3]

The able Engineer-General Vaillant, who, like Oudinot, had served with distinction under the great Napoleon, was sent out by the new President to advise and, if necessary, supersede the commander-in-chief. No better selection could have been made, and the two old soldiers appear to have worked in perfect harmony. Although they had thrown a bridge across the lower Tiber, and occupied the Basilica of St. Paul-without-the-walls, Oudinot and Vaillant had determined not to pass over the river in force, but to confine their main operations to the capture of the Janiculum. It would, indeed, have been easy for them, if they had crossed to the east bank, to blow a breach in the ancient Imperial walls [4] as did the Italians in 1870. But the French, in 1849, had to reckon with the hostility of the Roman populace. They knew that if they entered from the low-lying Campagna on the east their difficulties would only begin when they were inside the town, because the people would take to the barricades which they had prepared, and house-to-house fighting would continue for days. How much Italian burghers could do against regular troops in

[1] *Goppelli*, 239 ; *Loev.* i. 210.   [2] *Carletti*, 273 ; *Loev.* i. 213.
[3] See App. L below.
[4] See pp. 125–6 above, on the relative strength of the Imperial walls on the east bank and the Papal walls on the west bank.

this sort of warfare had been shown the year before, in the north at Milan, and in Sicily at Messina, and, even if victory in such a contest could be considered certain, the price might be the conflagration of the Eternal City. The scandal of standing triumphant on the blood-stained ruins of Rome was such as the art-loving French could appreciate and dread.[1] The knowledge that their right of interference was questioned by all parties, liberal and reactionary alike, put them on their best behaviour, and, although they threw many shells into the streets, they showed a certain care not to do unnecessary harm to the monuments.

Military and political considerations, therefore, combined to direct their efforts against the Janiculum, for although it would take a little time to breach the Papal walls upon the west bank, they could be sure that, when once they had fought their way to the terrace of San Pietro in Montorio, Rome would lie below them at the mercy of their batteries, and would have no alternative but to surrender without further resistance. Vaillant, therefore, determined to capture the curtains and bastions close to the Porta San Pancrazio. Wiser for the experience of April 30,[2] he knew that he must make a formal approach, drawing trenches and placing breach-batteries according to the methods of scientific siege craft, of which he was a master. But he saw that it was useless to order the first sod to be turned so long as the Romans occupied the high ground of the Villas Pamfili and Corsini—a point of vantage whence the Italian cannon could sweep the district round, and a place of arms where their infantry could safely muster for sorties into flank and rear of any trenches which the besiegers could make. On the other hand, if once the French were masters of the Villa Corsini, built on a knoll which commanded the Porta San Pancrazio, it would be

[1] *Vaillant*, 27, 28. The *Times* correspondent hoped for the street fighting, see *Times*, June 6, 12. Moltke, who had been in Rome in 1845–46, examining the defences, wrote in June 1849, to Humboldt, ascribing reasons for Vaillant's choice of the Janiculum as his point of attack, closely similar to those given by Vaillant himself (*Moltke*, i. 190).

[2] *Vaillant*, 28.

impossible for troops to come out from Rome against the works, except under a deadly fire from batteries elevated and ensconced at about four hundred paces from the narrow debouchment of the gate.

Since, therefore, it was of the first importance to the French plans to capture the Villas Pamfili and Corsini, the main struggle of the siege would, under normal conditions, have been a defence by the Romans of the high wall which surrounded the woods and gardens of these two villas in one vast enclosure. But owing to Oudinot's ambiguous letter, and Roselli's misplaced security, the besiegers acquired this stronghold almost without fighting, and the Roman defence was therefore turned into an attack, carried out, as we shall see, under conditions of great disadvantage.

The capture of the vital positions was effected in the small hours of Sunday morning, June 3. One column, under General Mollière, came silently through the darkness onto the road known as the Vicolo della Nocetta, which skirts the south of the Pamfili enclosure, and began preparations for blowing a breach in the boundary wall. At 3 A.M. or shortly before,[1] the noise of the sappers' picks was heard by some Italian sentries, who discharged their muskets. Without further delay the powder was put into the hole and exploded, the French infantry poured over the ruin, and as the morning twilight came on, spread in wave after wave of men through the silent pine-woods that occupied the southern part of the Pamfili grounds. Meanwhile another division, under a General named Levaillant, had already made its way in from the west side, where they actually found a gate of the Park left open.[2] Indeed, the 400 Italians bivouacked in these vast grounds—which required a garrison of several thousands—were sleeping with perfect

---

[1] *Vaillant*, 31, says 2.30 ; but an Italian officer declared he heard the first shots at about 3.0 (*Loev.* i. 216, note 4). Oudinot had ordered the attack to be commenced at 3.0 (*Bittard des Portes*, 208).

[2] See map p. 125 above. *Vaillant*, 31, 32. Vaillant, the Engineer-General and historian of the siege, is not the same as Levaillant, the officer who led this attack. *Paris MSS. 33ᵉ*, 213, and *91ᵉ (16ᵉ léger)*, 157, 159.

confidence in Oudinot's promise not to attack till Monday, whereof Roselli himself had so rashly reminded them not twelve hours before. Here and there, indeed, sentinels were on the alert, and resistance was made at various points, particularly in the little chapel of the Pamfili. In the villa itself, and in the surrounding gardens and groves of evergreen oak, where the tide of battle had been turned by Garibaldi on April 30, the 400 Italians were surrounded and overpowered by superior numbers. Half of them were captured in the buildings.[1] But many leapt from the windows, and in all 200 escaped to the Convent of San Pancrazio and the Villa Corsini, which stood within the Pamfili enclosure, but five or six hundred yards nearer to Rome.

The flying men were closely followed by one of Levaillant's battalions, but when the gallant Bolognese Colonel Pietramellara[2] organised a strong resistance in the Corsini, and when Galletti's troops began to pour up the road from the Porta San Pancrazio, the Italians, being in somewhat greater force, were able to hold on. When the dawn was growing grey, the French battalion which had pushed on unsupported to the Corsini fell back on the Pamfili, where it joined the rest of Levaillant's men and Mollière's brigade, which had now arrived at the front. Returning to the charge, the French regiments carried the Convent of San Pancrazio, and then, with the aid of artillery, stormed the Corsini after desperate fighting, and drove the Italians down the hill to the Vascello.[3] The Villa Corsini, the key to Rome, was in the hands of the enemy.

Minutes were precious; but nearly two hours were wasted owing to the arrangements which Roselli and the civil authorities had made for the quartering of the soldiers. If the Garibaldians and the Lombards had been encamped on the Janiculum they could have rushed out by the

---

[1] *Vaillant*, 52, says 150 Italians were captured in the 'bâtiments de la Villa.' *Beghelli*, ii. 302, and *Torre*, ii. 177, 178, allow 200 captured.

[2] See last paragraph of App. F 1, below.

[3] See App. F 1, below.

Porta San Pancrazio with Galletti's men, and very possibly
have retaken not only the Corsini but the Pamfili, before
the main force of the French had been brought into the
grounds. But the principal defenders of Rome were lodged
on the wrong side of the river, and at a great distance from
the scene of action. Furthermore, the officers had been
quartered in private houses apart from their regiments.
Garibaldi's Legion was in the Convent of San Silvestro ;
several of their officers were some distance away; but
Garibaldi and Masina were staying not far off, in the narrow
streets opening on the Piazza di Spagna. There, in a
humble lodging, No. 59, Via della Carozze, the sick and
wounded General was passing the night, attended by his
friend Ripari, the surgeon of the red-shirts, who, for these
doings, afterwards tasted half-a-dozen years of Papal dungeons, and survived to be doctor to the Thousand in Sicily.
Suddenly, at three in the morning, Daverio, the chief of Garibaldi's staff, burst in, crying out that Rome was attacked.
As Garibaldi leapt from his bed the boom of distant cannon
was heard. Ripari was sent to rouse Masina in the
neighbouring Via Condotti, and in a few minutes the band
of friends—the sick man who was to live, and the hale who
were at the point of death—were hurrying to join their
troops, while, in the stillness of the long, empty Roman
streets the shadows faded out, and dawn whitened in their
faces—the last time for Masina and Daverio.[1]

Those two, being thirty-three and thirty-four years
old, had seen many more days than the other conspicuous
victims doomed for that day's sacrifice.[2] To pass thirty
was to boast a ripe age among the leaders of the defence
of Rome. Manara himself, the veteran leader of the

---

[1] For details given in this paragraph see *Mario, Vita*, 88, 89 ; *Guerrazzi*, 755 ;
Loev. i. 213–215 ; ii. 240, 241, 264 ; *Mem.* 3 (*Prefazione*). Garibaldi's horses were
stabled at the Palazzo of Prince Torlonia, in the neighbouring Via Borgognona.
Signore Marchetti (now of Halifax, England) tells me this fact ; he was a small boy
living in the Palazzo Torlonia at the time, and remembers watching Garibaldi's
horses being groomed in the yard below, and being given rides on them by the
General's black man, Aguyar, who was by all accounts a dear fellow.

[2] *Loev.* ii. 240, 243.

Lombard Bersaglieri, bore the weight of four-and-twenty
years; the famous captain of one of his companies, Enrico
Dandolo, was twenty-one; the best influence in the noble
comradeship of his regiment was that of Morosini, a youth of
seventeen. So, too, in Garibaldi's Legion : Gaetano Bonnet
of Comacchio was twenty-three, and the well-beloved Mameli
of Genoa, poet of Italy's war-hymns, twenty-one.[1] All
these, foreordained to the slaughter, were now buckling
on their swords in the dawn, and with them their more
fortunate brothers and companions-in-arms, destined to
live and to see Italy's day and to be her leaders in
arms and art—Bixio, and Medici, and Nino Costa. Such,
under Garibaldi, were the spirits who presided over that
day of fire. Men of good family for the most part—all
of high ability and moral power, bound together by ties
of the closest personal affection, they were known already
as leaders in that land where the man ripens fast out of the
boy, in that year when every quality of youth was at a
premium and crabbed caution at a discount.[2]

[1] *Dandolo,* 241, 272, and *passim*; *Loev.* ii. 234, 254, 255; *King's
Mazzini,* 136.

[2] See list, p. 325 below. The Republican idealism of these young patricians and
sons of rich bourgeois, the heroic mould of their character, and the Homeric—that
is, the personal—nature of this combat of June 3, in which so many of them lost
their lives (a battle which sank deep in the Italian imagination) were partly due,
I think, to the nature of the education which they had received. This point has
been excellently stated in the account given of the education of one of the finest
of them—Nino Costa—a Roman of the Romans, though it was much the same in
the case of the Northerners, by whose side he fought :—' In those days, especially
in Rome, education was entirely in the hands of the clergy, and at the age of six
Costa was entrusted to his earliest preceptor, a priest, Don Pasquale by name.
. . . He was an idealist and a Republican, aflame with enthusiasm for the great
deeds and heroes of classic antiquity, and he nurtured in his pupil the innate,
idealistic tendencies. The education of the period was strictly classical, and
Plutarch's '' Lives,'' Livy's '' History,'' and the Bible stories, formed the basis of
Costa's early studies ; and often, while reading of the heroic deeds of the mighty
dead, master and pupil would be moved to tears. . . . The men of that age were
steeped in classic lore ; the histories of Livy, of Tacitus, of Plutarch were to them
the realities of life, the heroes of antiquity seemed to brood over them, moulding
these moderns after their own image.' So, too, at his school at Montefiascone,
Costa was taught, by analogy, ' the same spirit of Republican enthusiasm which
had characterised the early tuition imparted by Don Pasquale. In the clerical
schools and seminaries of those years was educated the generation which, in 1848,
was to strike the initial death-blow to the Papal temporal power, and proclaim the

Garibaldi first assembled his troops on the great Piazza in front of St. Peter's and the Vatican ; riding thence to the Porta Cavalleggieri, he rapidly considered whether it would be possible to make a sortie from that gate, and so take the French in flank.   But he realised that the Pamfili grounds were now occupied in force by the enemy's army, and presented a fortress wall to any attack from the north. Indeed, if he had wasted his strength in trying to enter the Pamfili across the Deep Lane, the French would have been able to push on through the weakly guarded Porta San Pancrazio, or at least to capture the Vascello.   He therefore started at once for the Janiculum by the way of San Pietro in Montorio.

And now the bells were clashing from every campanile in Rome, and the drummers, beating the broken *motif* of the alarm, called men to doors and windows down each narrow street.   The city was alive with orderlies and officers, dashing about on horse, on foot, and in *legnos*,[1] to find their regiments, with companies of soldiers or hastily armed civilians pushing across the bridges through the cheering crowds, all, singly or in groups, making from all directions towards the foot of the Janiculum, from the summit of which sounded over the town the dull booming of the unseen strife, a magnet to the brave.   There is a steep, shady lane, called the Via di Porta San Pancrazio, that leads the foot-passenger straight up to the gate from the low Trastevere, mounting the hill by a precipitous path and steps, overshadowed on either side by old palaces and gardens hanging over mouldering walls.   This was the quickest, and for the last few hundred yards under the

triumph of free thought. In Costa's own words, the education given by the priests was of a dead age ; the pupils lived in the past, but death, the dead, are always dignified. A noble idealism, an ardent love of country, that patriotism which the ancients considered the greatest of all virtues, and above all an invincible belief in the destinies and greatness of Rome, and a longing to see her return to her pristine glory, were sown in the hearts and brains of the youth, which was to yield so rich a harvest of heroism in 1848 and 1849,' *Costa*, 4, 5, 9. On minds thus prepared in boyhood, Mazzini's no less idealistic teaching of democracy and Italian unity was grafted in early youth.

[1] *Hoff.* (107, 108). *Koelman*, ii. 61, 62.

Villa Savorelli, the only way up to the gate. During the whole of June it was a main artery feeding the battle on the Janiculum, and on this first eventful Sunday was filled from dawn to dusk with soldiers and civilians hastening up to the fight, and wounded men dragging themselves down.[1]

At about half-past five Garibaldi and his Legion arrived at the Porta San Pancrazio.[2] As he rode through the gateway he saw, opposite him, the Villa Corsini on its hill top, some 400 paces distant, on the site where the memorial arch stands to-day. That house, he knew, must be retaken, or the fall of the city was only a matter of time. No price would be too dear for it—and the price was likely to be dear enough. A fortress, cunningly devised to resist attack from the side of Rome, could scarcely have had more points of advantage in structure, outworks, and situation, than this ornate country-house of the Corsini. Above the neighbouring vineyards and villas, it rose high on the skyline, exposing its massive stone-work square to all the winds of heaven, whence it was often called the ' Casa dei Quattro Venti,' the ' House of the Four Winds.' It was four stories high, with an ornamental parapet on the top; the two lower stories had no windows on the side towards Rome, but were masked by a blank wall, and by an outside staircase leading to a balcony on the second floor; which must be ascended by any troops seeking to storm the house.[3] The flanks of the villa, too, were well protected; for not only was the neighbouring ground thickly covered with statues, trees, and bushes, but from the foot of the stairs ran in both directions a wall two feet high, on which stood a row of large pots containing orange trees, a complete cover for troops holding the line of the hill.[4] This low wall of the

[1] *Koelman*, ii. 63, and maps and pictures of *Decuppis, Werner, Andrese*. The lane is visible as a white streak leading up the hill to the Villa Savorelli on the right of the illustration, p. 211 below.

[2] His legion was at the Piazza San Pietro by 5.0, and at the Porta San Pancrazio by about 5.30 ; so he cannot be said to have wasted much time, considering that the officers had to be collected from their quarters in various parts of the city. *Loev.* i. 214-216; *Hoff.* 106, 107, 115.

[3] See App. F 2, below.

[4] *Hoff.* 119. The illustration p. 173 below shows the wall stretching on either

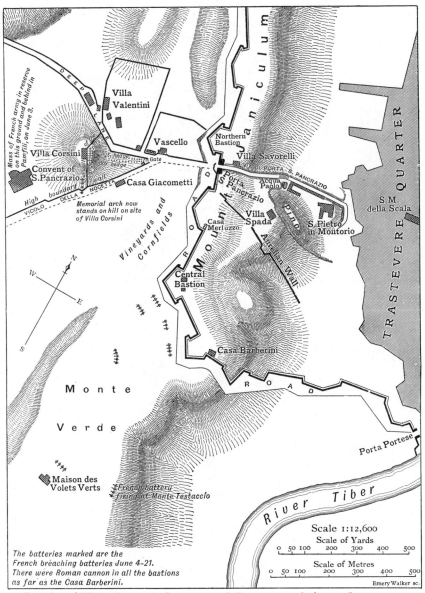

The batteries marked are the
French breaching batteries June 4-21.
There were Roman cannon in all the bastions
as far as the Casa Barberini.

Battle of Villa Corsini, June 3, and first part of siege, June 4-21

Casa Merluzzo Bastion.

Casa Giacometti.

Villa Corsini

Vascello here. Not represented in picture.

PORTA SAN PANCRAZIO FROM INSIDE ON JUNE 3, 1849

(From the *Illustrated London News* of 1849.)

orange pots ended in both directions in the high boundary
wall of the Pamfili-Corsini grounds, which, overlooking
the deep lane and the Vicolo della Nocetta, amply protected the rear of the villa on both its flanks.[1]

In front of this æsthetic fortress the ground sloped
down like a glacis towards Rome, and down the middle of the
incline, from the foot of the stairs to the garden gate,
ran a drive bordered on each side by a stiff box-hedge, six
feet high.[2] At the bottom of this box avenue, where, outside
the gateway, all the roads met in front of the Vascello,
the walls of the Pamfili-Corsini enclosure came to an end
in an acute angle. Thus the ground in front of the Villa
Corsini was a walled triangle, and exactly in its apex stood
the one garden gate by which the storming parties from
Rome had to pour in, if they were to get at the villa at
all. The Italians had therefore to move to the attack
like sand running through the narrows of an hour-glass.
It was a death angle, on which could be concentrated the
fire of all the defenders stationed in the house and along
the wall of the orange pots. On the other hand, whenever
the Italians took the villa, they had no such advantages
for holding it, for the French, if momentarily driven out,
had a wider firing line on the Pamfili side, where the breadth
of the grounds increased instead of diminishing, as it did
towards Rome. In those gardens and pine-woods behind,
in a dip of the ground affording absolute security against
the fire from the walls of Rome, their reserves were massed in
thousands, ready to feed the defenders of the Corsini, or
recapture it at need.

side of the Villa Corsini, and Hoffstetter describes it and the orange pots upon
it. (See *Dandolo*, 231, for the statues.)

[1] The illustration opposite wrongly represents the low wall stretching on either
side of the villa as if it ended in nothing, whereas it ran into the high boundary
walls on each side. The picture also does not show the continuation westward of
the boundary walls, but only the angle where the two boundary walls met at the
garden gate.

[2] *Hoff.* 113. See illustration p. 179 below. In illustration opposite the box-
hedges look more like walls, but this is an error. The illustration opposite is
good for the inside of the walls of Rome, less good for the more distant view,
though the Corsini Villa itself is well represented.

The road, up which the Italians must advance from the Porta San Pancrazio before they reached the death angle, was completely exposed to the enemy's fire. It was bordered on the left by cornfields and vineyards, not then enclosed by any wall ; on the right of it rose the Vascello, so called from its fancied resemblance to the shape of a ship. This, too, was an ornamental villa of the Roman aristocracy, a rival to the Corsini in magnificence, though, owing to its situation at the foot of the hill, it was not so prominent in the landscape. The only advantage which the Italians enjoyed in this unequal conflict was that the Vascello and its walled garden, and the two little houses on either side of the Vicolo della Nocetta, served to some extent as places of arms from which to attack the Corsini. But the advantage could not be turned to any very considerable use, because the garden of the Vascello was raked by the fire from the windows of the high Valentini Villa, already occupied by the French.[1]   The Italians had, in fact, to feed the battle from the Porta San Pancrazio by way of the exposed road, and most of the charges made against the Corsini started from the city walls.

When Garibaldi arrived the French were secure in possession of the Corsini hill, and the Italians, under Galletti, insecure in possession of the Vascello at its foot.[2]   On the bastion of the Casa Merluzzo, to the left of the Porta San Pancrazio, a Roman battery was planted. Behind this bastion, sloping down as far as the Villa Spada, there was then, as there still is to-day (1906) a vast open space of unused ground, just within the walls of Rome, where the Italian regiments, as they came panting up from the town below, were mustered under cover, and whence they were sent out, in all too small detachments, to pass under the fatal archways of the Porta San Pancrazio, and rush up the road at the Corsini. The scene here, behind the forti- fications, was spirited and even gay, lit up by the bright sun of a morning which soon turned into a sweltering, cloud- less noon. Inquisitive and sympathetic onlookers were

---

[1] *Hoff.* 112.   [2] See p. 168 above, and *Loev.* i. 218.

grouped round the inside of the gate-house, cheering the
various champions as they rode up from Rome and disappeared through the portal, and greeting the wounded
as they were brought back by their comrades in litters and
handbarrows, or slung in scarves.[1] In the bastion to the
right of the gate the band was playing the 'Marseillaise'
with all its lungs, so that the French might hear it through
the cannon roar, and be withered with the irony. At the
edge of the bastion of the Casa Merluzzo, whence the Roman
battery was firing, was a Dutch artist, taking advantage
of the incorrigible good-nature of the Italian soldier, to
peer between the sandbags, at some risk from the whistling
bullets, at the historic scene outside.[2]

Opposite to him, on the hill top, he saw the balcony
of the Corsini crowded with French soldiers, their gun-
barrels flashing in the sun whenever they raised them
to fire, and the battery which they had planted among the
trees beside the villa.[3] Close beneath him, in the open
road, sat Garibaldi on his white horse, amid his rapidly
dwindling Staff, sending up one division after another of
his Legion to dash at the garden gate of the Corsini, pour
through its narrow entrance into the death angle, rush up
the slope by the line of box-hedges, under a fire from every
window of the façade and from the low wall of the orange-
tree pots, till the survivors reached the foot of the steps.
Then, if enough were left, they would storm up the double
staircase, gain the balcony, bayonet the French in the
drawing-room, and stand for a few minutes masters of the
villa. Often the charge failed half-way up, from sheer
want of numbers. But several times the Corsini was carried,
and held for awhile, against the concentrated fire of a whole
army in the woods of the Pamfili beyond. On one of these
occasions the Garibaldians piled up their dead comrades
in the open loggias on the west side of the villa and repulsed

---

[1] *Koelman*, ii. 67–71, 74, 75 ; *Dandolo*, 241.

[2] *Koelman*, ii. 67–71. The scene is clearly represented in the foreground of
illustration, p. 173 above.

[3] *Koelman*, ii. 65–67.

the French attacks from behind that barricade, the artist Costa being in the thick of the affair.[1]

The French were in huge force, and Garibaldi as yet had scarcely 3,000 men with whom to line the wall of the city and to make the attacks.   There were his own Legionaries, with a few other small bodies of volunteers, the Emigrants, the Students, the Gagers, the remainder of Pietramellara's men, and, after seven o'clock, Medici's regiment, together with a few troops of the line.[2]   But even such force as he had it was thought that he employed in too small detachments ; whether through his fault, or not,[3] there were never enough men at hand to support the gallant bands who from time to time made themselves masters of the villa.   At 7.30 he announced in a bulletin that the Corsini was in his hands ; but it was soon lost once more.

In these early hours, when the Legion sustained the brunt of the fray, its best men and officers were swept off with frightful rapidity.   Daverio was killed, the chief of Garibaldi's Staff, the friend who had roused him that morning, of whom he afterwards said, as the highest possible praise, that ' physically and morally he was the image of Anzani.'[4]   Masina, too, before long received his first wound ; although bystanders noticed that blood was flowing freely from his left arm, he refused to retire within the walls to the field-hospital in the Church of San Pietro in Montorio, until Garibaldi had bidden him a second time : ' But I am determined that you shall go, I order thee to go ' (*Te lo comando*); whereat Masina saluted and disappeared under the San Pancrazio Gate.   An hour later he was loudly cheered as he returned on horseback with his arm bound up, indefatigable in the pursuit of death.[5]

---

[1] *Costa*, 47.   The picture of the west side of the villa in *Kandler* bears out this account of the ' open loggias.'

[2] *Loev.* i. 218, 219, 226 ; *Hoff.* 115.   Later in the day the Lombard Bersaglieri and the *Unione* regiment arrived.

[3] We have no detailed account of these early attacks before the arrival of the Bersaglieri, when Dandolo and Hoffstetter came on the scene.

[4] *Garibaldi's Cantoni*, 264, *note*.   For Anzani, see pp. 35, 43, 44 above.

[5] See App. H, part I. below.

In one of these ill-supported attacks on the Corsini, Nino Bixio, destined to play so great a part in the future history of his country and his chief, received an all but mortal wound. At the head of the Legionaries, he had galloped his horse up the outer staircase of the Corsini, charged through the drawing-room on the upper floor and emerged on the further balcony overlooking the Pamfili grounds, where horse and man at once fell under a shower of bullets. As he was borne back in a litter, Garibaldi asked him anxiously: 'Where are you hit, Captain?' 'A bullet in my left side; but I think it will be all right,' he replied. Passing within the gate, the long procession of wounded met Manara's Lombard Bersaglieri, arriving at the top of the Janiculum to the sound of their bugles, eager to restore the lost battle; young Bixio, though pale as death, 'made friendly and glad reply to their cheers and greetings.'[1]

The Bersaglieri, who had sprung to arms at the first alarm in Rome, had been standing drawn up in the Forum for two hours, chafing at the sound of distant battle, but held back by a most unfortunate order from Roselli, as commander-in-chief, which countermanded Garibaldi's divisional orders to Manara to come at once to his assistance.[2] If the Bersaglieri and the Legionaries had come fresh on the scene together between five and six o'clock, they might have done great things, instead of suffering them. As it was, when the 'round hats' arrived, about eight o'clock, the Corsini had just been lost once more, and the French were pressing down along the box-hedge to attack the Vascello, whose gardens and windows were raked by a fire, not only from the Corsini hill, but from the commanding upper stories of the Valentini.[3] For some time past the French sharp-shooters, advancing through the cornfields against

---

[1] *Hoff.* 108; *Koelman*, ii. 78; *Loev.* i. 220, describes Bixio's charge, but wrongly places it after Masina's death, which really took place ater, see App. H. *Vecchi*, ii. 260, 261, makes the same error.

[2] *Hoff.* 106, 107; *Dandolo*, 228, 229.

[3] *Dandolo*, 232, 236; *Hoff.* 112, 118, 119.

N

the walls of Rome, had opened fire at close quarters on the bastion of the Casa Merluzzo, whence the Roman battery replied with volleys of grape that bent and swayed the corn-ears like the wind.[1] Thus pressed by the concentrated fire of the French positions and the advance of large bodies of regular troops, the Legionaries, who had lost immensely, both in officers and men, were only held to their posts by the inspiration of Garibaldi's presence. The Bersaglieri officers, who came out of the Porta San Pancrazio to announce to him the arrival of their regiment, found him in the thick of the fire, his white mantle riddled with bullets, but himself miraculously untouched, spreading calm and courage wherever he appeared.[2]

Ventum erat ad triarios. It was now the turn of the Bersaglieri. The regiment was 900 strong,[3] and formed the best disciplined, and, except, perhaps, the Legion, the bravest body of men at Garibaldi's disposal. When informed of their arrival, he at once sent for one of their companies to occupy the Casa Giacometti, a small, but high and strongly built house, from whose windows the troops could fire not only down the Vicolo della Nocetta, but over the wall into the Corsini gardens and the windows of the villa. Having thus checked the French advance and prepared a protection for the flank of the storming party, he ordered up more Bersaglieri from the Porta San Pancrazio, and told Manara to capture the Corsini. It is probable that the way for this assault ought to have been prepared by another hour or more of cannonading from the bastion,[4] and of musketry fire from the houses at the bottom of the garden. But Garibaldi gave no directions to this effect, and Manara, in his eagerness to display the valour of his men, some of whom had been subject to a

---

[1] *Koelman*, ii. 68, 69.

[2] *Hoff.* 109, 116, 117.

[3] A second (weak) battalion of about 350 men had arrived from the north since the battle of Palestrina, where there had been only one battalion of 600.

[4] The cannon on the Merluzzo bastion had been forced to give their attention to the French infantry in the cornfields close under the wall, during the period preceding the arrival of the Bersaglieri. *Koelman*, ii. 68, 69.

THE DEATH ANGLE.

momentary panic under the eyes of the General, at once dashed two strong companies against the villa.[1]

With loud cries of 'Avanti! Avanti!' three or four hundred of the finest men of north Italy, led by Manara himself, Enrico Dandolo, and Swiss Hoffstetter, poured, under a storm of bullets, through the narrow gateway, where scarcely five could pass abreast, and spreading out to right and left of the box-hedges, rushed up the slope— their Bersaglieri plumes streaming behind. But the French. who were now massed in the villa and along the orange-tree wall, not being subjected to any considerable covering fire, mowed down the Italians so thickly that, at thirty paces from their goal, the assailants halted; instead of retreating, they deliberately knelt down on the open slope and opened fire at the hidden Frenchmen, while the officers stood up behind the kneeling men and partook of the massacre. Among others, Enrico Dandolo was here shot dead.[2] For ten minutes, as it seemed to Hoffstetter, Manara watched the slaughter of his men before he sounded the retreat, and until the bugle was heard not one had flinched. Then began the return down the slope, back into the death angle and through the gateway.

'And now (says Hoffstetter) as these defenceless men poured out of the garden the deadly harvest began in earnest. At first I imagined that the numbers of men falling on their faces had merely stumbled in their haste over the roots of the vines. But their motionless bodies soon showed me the truth. Those hurrying past would try, under the old impulse, to drag away a fallen comrade, to pick up the bodies; but the hand stretched out to render this last service would fly back to clutch at its owner's death-wound. Others, who had already reached the shelter of the house or of the garden-gate, would dash forward

[1] *Hoff.* 117–119. (See App. G, below. *Garibaldi's Use of the Bersaglieri on June 3.*) See also *Dumas*, ii. 187.
[2] *Hoff.* 119. An accusation of French treachery attending Enrico's death is made by his brother Emilio (*Dandolo*, 240), and is commonly repeated in Italian history. But Emilio was not an eye-witness, and the story does not appear to be very consistent with Hoffstetter's account of the scene. French and Italians accused each other very freely of these 'white-flag incidents,' as we now call them.

again to help some yet living comrade lying near at hand ; a shudder, a spasmodic movement of the limbs, and they lie beside their friend. Here, indeed, they got their first hard knock—our jolly, brave, faithful and tireless Bersaglieri !' [1]

The catastrophe was fatal to any feeble chance of victory which the Italians may have had that day, for the first strength of this fine regiment had been used up under conditions which had rendered success impossible. Now, indeed, Garibaldi caused the gunners on the walls of Rome to turn their full energies against the Corsini façade, from which large ruins ere long began to fall, while the Bersaglieri whom he posted in the Casa Giacometti and the small house at the death-angle kept the Corsini windows under a constant fire. The result was, as we shall see, that before the end of the day the villa was once more taken, though it could not be held. Meanwhile, the arrival of the Bersaglieri had at least permanently checked the enemy's advance, and made it possible strongly to occupy the Vascello and the other houses at the foot of the Corsini hill.[2]

At this stage Garibaldi was guilty of a piece of madness, of which the glory redounds to another, and the blame lies with him. Riding back through the Porta San Pancrazio, he found some of the reserve of the Bersaglieri left behind the walls under command of Emilio Dandolo, who, having parted there from his brother but an hour since, had just heard the rumour of his death. The story of what followed can best be told in Emilio's words :

'It was the first time that the tremendous idea of such a death presented itself clearly and certainly to my horror-struck mind. A sort of careless fatalism had made us feel as if it were impossible for one of two beings so closely attached to be left without the other ; " either both or neither," had been the constant expression of our vague and certainly unwarrantable hopes. But at

---

[1] The foreground of the illustration p. 179 above was the scene of this catastrophe. *Hoff.* 117–121. *Manara MS. Letter of June* 11 also describes this attack.
[2] *Hoff.* 117, 121, 122 ; *Dandolo,* 232, 233.

the moment, the dreadful scene before my eyes' (the long stream of wounded Bersaglieri being carried back from the assault) 'and the knowledge of so many lives lost, seemed to disclose to me, for the first time, the real nature of cold-blooded war in all its horrible reality, and I shuddered at the idea of outliving all that constituted my happiness in the world. I thought to myself that my brother might be breathing his last within ten paces from me, and I could not even embrace him before he died ! My duty forbade me to leave my soldiers, already agitated by so many mournful sights. I paced up and down in front of my small band, who wondered at my unwonted emotion, and convulsively gnawing the barrel of a pistol in my struggles, I strove to keep down the boiling tears, which, had they been observed, might have increased the consternation of my devoted followers. At this moment of unspeakable suffering, Garibaldi came in our direction, and I heard him say: " I shall require twenty resolute men and an officer for a difficult undertaking." I rushed forward, desirous at least to liberate myself from a state of inaction, and to suffocate in the excitement of danger the anguish which threatened to turn my brain. " Go," said Garibaldi to me, " with twenty of your bravest men, and take Villa Corsini at the point of the bayonet." Involuntarily I remained transfixed with astonishment—with twenty men to hurry forward to attack a position which two of our companies and the whole of Garibaldi's Legion, after unheard-of exertions, had failed to carry. . . .

'" Spare your ammunition, to the bayonet at once," said Garibaldi. " Do not fear, General," I replied, " they have perhaps killed my brother, and I shall do my best." This said, I hurried forwards. . . . The long deserted avenue which led straight up to the villa lay right before me ; whoever passed along would certainly furnish a mark for the enemy, who lay concealed in the garden, and was stationed behind the windows. We traversed it at full speed, but not without leaving several of our small number behind. The little band was thinned ; when we arrived at last under the vestibule I turned round to see how many of us were left. Twelve soldiers remained to me, intrepid, silent, ready for any effort ; I looked around me, we were there alone. Our own shot, from our own guns, sounded in our ears ; a shower of bullets fell fearfully round us from the half-closed windows. What would twelve men do against a place occupied by several hundreds of the enemy? I had nothing left for me but to stoop to that which more numerous forces had already done, give the signal to fire, and then retreat. When we had got half-way down the road, S—— and I were both struck in the thigh by the same ball. We returned to the Vascello, six in number, in a deplorable condition, and with the conviction that the really extraordinary courage which had just been so conspicuously and recklessly displayed would have no effect, beyond that of showing the French that Italians were still capable of fighting with temerity, whatever the fortune of war might be.'

Put out of action by the severe wound in his thigh, the hero of this extraordinary charge, who was nineteen years of age, dragged himself about for a great part of the afternoon looking for his elder brother among the dead and wounded. Many knew of Enrico's death, but none dared tell Emilio, till at last he entered the Casa Giacometti, now the most important of the Italian outposts except the Vascello. It still stands, an unnoticed memorial of that calamitous day, in an isolated position by the roadside, with a pleasant court behind opening on to the vineyards, where, under an arbour, carters take a glass of wine before they enter the walls of Rome; several ancient stones and inscriptions are built into the fine old archway at the entrance.[1] At the moment when Emilio Dandolo reached this house, Manara and Hoffstetter were within its walls, and beside them lay the body of Enrico. The Swiss officer withdrew, deeply moved. The Colonel, left alone, took Emilio's hand and said : ' Do not seek your brother any more—it is now too late ; I will be a brother to you.' The young man, sick with wounds and grief, fell fainting against Manara, who carried him out of the room in his arms.[2]

Throughout the long mid-day heat the battle settled down into a heavy cannonade and musketry-fire on both

---

[1] Present-day visitors to Rome (1906) can identify it by the word *Scarpone* written large on its walls.

[2] *Hoff.* 125, 126 ; *Dandolo*, 245, 246.

sides. The Italians held the Vascello and Casa Giacometti, supported from behind by their batteries on the wall, of which the one in the northern bastion on the right of the gate fired on the Valentini, while that on the left, directed by the French Republican and artist Laviron, kept bringing down blocks from the Corsini façade. Laviron and his artist friends in this Merluzzo bastion, watching the effect of their fire through the telescope, could see the French soldiers hurled about the ruins of the villa at each discharge, or holding on by their hands as the floors beneath them gave way.[1]

Well on in the afternoon the French fire slackened, while some retreat or change of troops took place in consequence of the terrific effect of the cannonade on the villa. Garibaldi seized the opportunity to launch another attack, headed by Masina's forty lancers in the capacity of dragoons, armed with muskets. Led on by General Galletti and their own Colonel with his bandaged arm,[2] the horsemen raced through the garden gate and up the slope, amid a gradually slackening fire from the hill-top, and then, amid frantic cheers from the Italians crowding the battlements of Rome, followed Masina in his last wild gallop up the steps of the Corsini.[3]

Meanwhile the infantry, pouring out of the Vascello and the neighbouring houses, were following close behind the horsemen, Manara and Garibaldi urging them on. At the point of the bayonet they cleared the Corsini hill of the last Frenchmen, and proceeded to occupy it in force, while some of the Lombards rushed on towards the right after Galletti and the gallant cavalry, who had already gone to make themselves masters of the houses near the Valentini and the Aqueduct.[4]

And now another wave of men came rolling up from the

[1] *Koelman*, ii. 84–86; *Paris MSS. 66⁵*, pp. 101, 102 (quoted at end of App. H. below).
[2] See p. 176 above.
[3] *Carletti*, 274, and other authorities, discussed in App. H. below.
[4] *Carletti*, 274; *Hoff.* 127; *Paris MSS. 33⁵*, p. 214.

gate of Rome.[1] The spectacle of Masina charging up the steps, the capture of the Corsini, and the evident arrival of the final crisis of the day, had been too much for the discipline of the watchers on the walls. A maddening enthusiasm, akin to panic, although its opposite, seized the crowd of citizens, artists, gunners, and the infantry of the spent regiments; flooding through the Porta San Pancrazio they swept along the road to the villa in a dense mass. Koelman, the Dutch artist, not so much running as borne through the air in the press, kept himself upright by struggling on arm-in-arm with an officer of the Civic Guard, whom he had never seen before, holding his gun high with the disengaged hand. As they passed over the bodies of the slain, through the garden gate, some riderless horses came dashing back down the slope; terrified by the shrill cries of the crowd, the first two or three of the animals swerved sideways through the box-hedges and escaped, but those that followed threw themselves head-long on the head of the column, were transfixed by bayonets and trampled under foot. When at length the mob reached the esplanade of the ruined Corsini, which they found covered with bodies, arms, and charred *débris*, they joined in the hasty preparations for the defence. It was impossible to find stations for sharp-shooters in the upper stories of the villa, for the building had been in flames, the floors had been demolished by the Italian cannon, and the French batteries were now raking it from the other side.[2] The principal defence had therefore to be made in the garden on either flank, and in the Convent of San Pancrazio, which was held as an advanced post.[3] The unregimented men, who showed much goodwill and promptness, were got into some kind of order, and made to lie down among the brushwood, awaiting the French attack

---

[1] For details of this rush see *Koelman*, ii. 89–99. Both *Hoff.* 127, and *Carletti*, 275, are agreed as to the disordered character of the supports, though both were too busily engaged in front to notice the details of the affair at the Porta San Pancrazio where Koelman was.

[2] See illustration p. 186 below. *Carletti*, 274; *Koelman*, ii. 91.

[3] *Paris MSS. 33*, p. 214.

from the Pamfili. Oudinot's well-arrayed army, regiment behind regiment, could be seen coming forward through the pine trees, which were throwing long shadows in the evening light. As the Italians lay there in rows, awaiting their fate, some of the students joked together, comparing themselves to bales of goods laid out to be sold by auction. The defence was well maintained for a short while, and the French lost severely in their advance ; but they pressed on with ever fresh men, recaptured the Convent, and finally reached the crown of the hill. The Italians fell back, still firing, from the Villa Corsini, which had proved, not impregnable, but untenable.[1]

The last to ride under the sheltering door of the Vascello was Garibaldi, whose face and bearing betrayed no emotion at the final destruction of his hopes. Behind him Manara closed the door.[2]

In the confusion, Masina had been left behind. It is not certain at what spot on the steps or in the garden of the Corsini—at what moment of the advance or retreat—he fell; eye-witnesses gave divergent accounts.[3] But his body was left lying in the middle of the slope, sixty paces from the steps up which he had so gallantly charged. During the rest of June, the Italian bullets from the Vascello, and the French cannon-balls from the Corsini, sang day after day over his whitening bones, which only after Rome had fallen was it possible to seek and bury. The leader of the *jeunesse dorée* of Bologna, he had died in the uniform of the Democratic volunteers. To future generations of his countrymen he lives in memory as a splendid cavalier riding up a bullet-swept flight of marble steps ; but to Garibaldi, to the Bonnets of Comacchio, and many others, he was a friend not less dear than gallant.[4]

Dusk had already fallen, when Garibaldi directed a

---

[1] *Koelman*, ii. 91–99, gives the only detailed account of the French recapture of the Corsini on this occasion. It is, I suspect, a little overwritten, but clearly shows that the defence was organised, and effective to the extent which I have here stated. (See App. H. III., below.)

[2] *Hoff.* 128. [3] See App. H. II., below : *The Death of Masina.*
[4] *Ciàmpoli*, 34.

last vain attack against the now shapeless ruin on the hill
top, leading on the *Unione* regiment (the ninth of the
old Papal line), who had just arrived on the scene, and
the unwearied survivors of his own Legion and of the
Bersaglieri.[1]   In this period of the battle fell Mameli,
the Genoese boy-poet, whose war-hymn was on the lips
of these warriors;[2] he was the son of the woman whom
Mazzini had loved in boyhood.   In after years Garibaldi
wrote to Mameli's mother to tell her what he remembered :

' It was towards evening, when Mameli, whom I had kept at
my side the greater part of the day as my adjutant, besought
me earnestly to let him go forward into the heat of the battle,
as his position near me seemed to him inglorious.   In a few
minutes he was carried back past me, gravely wounded, but
radiant, his face shining because he had shed his blood for his
country.   We did not exchange a word, but our eyes met with
the love which had long bound us together.   I remained behind.
He went on, as though in triumph.'

Wounded in the knee, Mameli lay for more than a month in
hospital, where gangrene set in.   Near him lay his dear
friend and fellow-townsman of Genoa, Nino Bixio, shot

[1] *Mem.* 236, 237 ; *Loev.* i. 223 ; *Ravioli*, 37–39.

[2] *Fratelli d'Italia*, written in November 1847 (see *Luzio*, 172, 173), when
the author was just turned twenty, caught the spirit of the hour and therefore
became, and remained, the Marseillaise of the Italian Risorgimento, although,
from a literary point of view, it is not so good a poem as some which Mameli
himself wrote, and some which were written by others for Italy.   One verse is
specially interesting, as it proclaims the Mazzinian notion of Italian unity, not
then generally accepted :

> Noi siamo da secoli
> Calpesti e derisi
> Perchè non siam popolo,
> Perchè siam divisi.
> Raccolgaci un' unica
> Bandiera, una speme :
> Di fonderci insieme
> Già l' ora suonò.
> > Stringiamci a coorte,
> > Siam pronti alla morte,
> > Italia chiamò.

Martinengo Cesaresco, 186–197 ; *Mameli* (Scritti) *passim ; Luzio*, 172–176.

VILLA CORSINI (QUATTRO VENTI).
The façade after the Italian cannonade. (WERNER.)

through the body. Bixio lived to command the attack on
Rome from the side of San Pancrazio in 1870, at the vic-
torious entry of the Italians on the Twentieth of September.
It was Mameli who died.[1]

At nightfall the few Bersaglieri who had held the
Valentini Villa since it had last been taken, finding themselves unsupported, at length retired. The French, therefore, ended the day in possession of the Valentini and of
the Corsini itself, while Garibaldi's men maintained themselves in the Casa Giacometti and Vascello. As darkness
closed in, the white mantle could still be seen moving
like a great moth on the roadway, amid the last flashes
of the dying battle.[2]

So ended the Third of June, which sealed the fate of
Rome. On the same day, four miles to the north, a less
important operation had taken place on the upper reaches
of the Tiber, across which the French had secured a passage
by capturing the Ponte Molle, in face of the *Reduci* and
the Roman Legion.[3] But far the greater part of Oudinot's
army of 20,000 men—seven out of nine regiments—had
been concentrated in or near the Pamfili grounds, ready
to feed the battle at the Corsini.[4] It is doubtful whether
more than 6,000 Italians in all were under Garibaldi's
orders,[5] and these had not been together in force, but had
been coming up, one regiment after another, all through
the day : the Italian Legion was more than half spent before the Bersaglieri arrived, and the Bersaglieri before the
Regiment *Unione* came on the scene. If we remember how
enormous was the force of French regulars inside the fortress
of the Pamfili-Corsini grounds, protected by a high wall
on both flanks, the complaint made by some critics that

[1] *Epistolario*, i. 250 ; *Belgiojoso*, 314, 315 ; *Loev.* ii. 254, 255 ; *Bixio*, 91 ;
King's Mazzini, 66, 67 ; *Luzio*, 179.

[2] *Dandolo*, 238 ; *Torre*, ii. 181 ; *Loev.* i. 230.

[3] *Carletti*, 275 ; *Vaillant*, 34–37.

[4] *Bittard des Portes*, 213 ; 235, 236.

[5] *Hoff.* 133. The same conclusion will be reached by a study of the numbers
of such of the regiments as are known to have been engaged.

Garibaldi did not attack the flank of the French position will appear of doubtful validity. Indeed, Dandolo has accused him of exactly the opposite fault, declaring that he wasted his slender forces by movements of his left flank, ' skirmishing uselessly among the vineyards '—an accusation equally wide of the mark if it refers to the operations which resulted in the secure occupation of the Casa Giacometti, essential not only for the maintenance of the Vascello, but for the proper preparation and support of any attack on the Corsini. The unprepared frontal attack *en masse* by the Bersaglieri, which Dandolo believed would have been certainly successful, was in fact actually tried with a third part of the regiment in one charge, and would probably in so confined a space have had no better result with the whole.[1] Those who complained that Garibaldi should have ' entrenched ' himself in the positions the moment after their capture, forget that on the Corsini hill the Italians that day had neither respite, time, nor materials for digging.[2] The entrenchment ought to have been done by Roselli during the peaceful month of May.

But Garibaldi's mistakes on this day are bad enough, when all unjust censure has been put aside. Once, at least, we know that he threw a body of twenty men, unsupported, at the villa, and he is accused in general terms of having committed the same kind of folly several times.[3] It is, however, clear that the principal attacks were made by large masses of men, and the proper criticism on the first attack by the Bersaglieri is not so much that the storming party was too small, but that the way had not been prepared by a sufficiently prolonged cannonade and musketry fire, such as afterwards drove the French from the villa.

---

[1] *Dandolo*, 236 ; *Hoff*. 120, 121. See App. G., below.

[2] *Gabussi*, iii. 431, has an excellent note on this point.

[3] *Vecchi*, ii. 261, 263, charges him with sending men to hold positions with insufficient supports, but adds, ' such was the disorder in our camp that neither the General nor his *aides* knew exactly where to find a body of men of sufficient number to feed the battle and attack the masses of the enemy.' And again, ' Garibaldi, fatalist to excess, used small bodies against the mass of the enemy, meaning to support them, and failing to do so, either from forgetfulness or want of means.'

So, too, Masina's Lancers—whose lives Garibaldi is sometimes said to have thrown away in a wild-goose chase—
took the villa by an attack admirably timed at the moment
when the French defence was weak, and held it until the
immediate arrival of the infantry.   Unfortunately, at that
late hour of the day, the discipline, though not the courage,
of the spent regiments was giving way, and the hill could
not be held by a courageous mob against the ordered attack
of superior forces.   No doubt there was a want of system
and combination both in Garibaldi's methods of attack,
and in the support of the positions when captured.   But
it may be doubted whether the force which he had under
him could, under any generalship in the world, have been
sufficient, not only to capture (as it did several times in
the day), but to hold the narrow Corsini line, against the
concentrated fire and attack of the French army, drawn
out in battle array in the broader Pamfili grounds.

Both sides fought with heroic courage, and each recognised the qualities of the enemy.   But they did not love
each other the better for that, and the trickery by which
the positions had first been won sank deep into the Italian
mind.   'I find the wounded men in the hospital,' wrote
Margaret Fuller, 'in a transport of indignation.   The
French soldiers fought so furiously, that they think them
false as their General, and cannot endure the remembrance
of their visits, during the armistice, and talk of brotherhood.' [1]   The anger of the Italians was more fierce than
on April 30 ; some French prisoners were massacred on the
scene of battle immediately after their surrender, and
others were insulted on their way into Rome.[2]

The Italians estimated their killed and wounded sometimes at 1,000, sometimes at 900, sometimes at 500 men and
50 officers.[3]   All fell in a space about 600 paces long by

[1] *Fuller*, iii. 207.

[2] *Vecchi*, ii. 262 ; *Koelman*, ii. 101.   Vecchi saw the massacre, and took part
in stopping it.

[3] *Hoff*. 129 ; *Farini*, iv. 180 ; *Torre*, ii. 184 ; *Gabussi*, iii. 433. *Ravioli*, 68,
shows that 453 wounded were taken to the hospitals ; there were also the dead
and those privately tended.   (See App. K., below.)

300 wide, outside the Porta San Pancrazio. The French officially announced their loss at 250 men and 14 officers, which is the lowest estimate.[1]

Of the killed and wounded, some 30 officers and 200 men belonged to Garibaldi's own Italian Legion.[2] Hoffstetter, who was attached to the Bersaglieri of Manara, and became an historian of their prowess on this day, admitted that the Italian Legion had won the honours. No one disputed the right of the Bersaglieri to the second place : Manara indeed claimed for them the first place, and declared that they also had lost 200 men that day.[3]

When once we have appreciated the true nature and extent of Garibaldi's failure in generalship on the third of June, which has often been exaggerated and as often unduly minimised, there is no propriety in offering excuses, such as that he was ill, or that his talent was for the open field. In the eyes of Rome, and of the survivors among the regiments which he had led to the slaughter, he needed no excuse. Manara, usually very crisp in his criticisms of men and events, describes the battle in a private letter without breathing a word against Garibaldi, and instead of calling him ' a devil and a panther,' as he had done a month before when he did not know him, only says ' the poor General lost his best officers.' [4] Everyone knew that Garibaldi had commanded badly ; no one loved him the less, and no one was less eager to fight and die under his orders. His popularity during the month of siege that followed was greater than ever, and the reason

<hr>

[1] *Vaillant*, 33 ; *Bittard des Portes*, 234, 235. (App. K., below.)

[2] *Loev.* i. 231–233; ii. 48–51. It is impossible to deduce statistics from *Roman MSS.*, *Ruoli Gen.* 80, F. 4 (hospital lists of the Legion).

[3] *Hoff.* 133, 134 ; *Manara MS. Letter of June* 11.

[4] *Manara MS. Letter of June* 11. On June 4, Manara himself, out of friendship to Garibaldi, accepted the position of chief of his staff in place of Daverio, killed. This was to identify himself with the Guerilla, and to undertake the command of the irregular troops whom, in April, he had so much disliked before he knew them. (*Hoff.* 138.) His feeling towards Garibaldi in person had undergone a great change and they were now fast friends. *Guerrazzi*, 717, and *Hoffstetter, passim.*

is not far to seek. He had given his countrymen what the national instinct craved for at that moment more than for victory—honour. It was not tactics but heroism for which Italy was athirst in that year of despair crowned and glorified by faith. If, a decade later, he had lost battles in Sicily, if he had failed to maintain his hold on the terraces of Calatafimi, if he had been driven back out of the streets of Palermo, it would have been irretrievable disaster and uncompensated loss. But, in 1849, the present was but the seedling of the future. The heroism which he had inspired in the defenders of the Republic, culminating on this day of sacrifice, made Rome splendid as the capital of the Italy to be, and rendered the Temporal rule of the Pope henceforth impossible as an integral part of Italian life—possible only as a state of interregnum maintained by foreign bayonets.

For in times when new nations and new principles of government are being formed, men are moved by appeals to the imagination—a fact too often forgotten in our modern analysis of the history of such periods. Imagination is the force that propels, though state-craft may guide. In such times statesmen, if they are as shrewd as Cavour, build their subtlest diplomatic structures on the firm base of an awakened national idealism, feeding itself on great memories and aspirations. But in order that men may aspire, it is necessary that they should have something to remember. And so the sacrifice made on the third of June, and in the month that followed, of so many of the best lives that Italy could give, had great political, because it had great spiritual, significance. The noblest Italians had recognised the eternal law of sacrifice, which Mazzini had first taught them to apply to their own politics. ' Except a corn of wheat fall into the ground and die—it abideth alone ; but if it die, it bringeth forth much fruit.'

Rome had to be won not merely from the grasp of Oudinot, but from the force of the great traditions of Catholicism which had made it worth the while of an opportunist like Louis Napoleon to send these good French peasants and workmen, dressed up in red trousers and blue coats, to shoot and bayonet their Italian brothers. They had been shipped across the seas for an idea. It was the Catholic idea, the Catholic world, that had laid its protecting hand on the Pope's throne. Against the religious zeal which the Italians had defied, they must oppose a moral force, or be beaten in the end. In claiming Rome for themselves they had outraged the Irish, the Spaniards, the Austrians, half France, and many of their own country-men. Vast spiritual agencies were at work all over the world to keep Italy out of Rome. Peter and Paul, Augus-tine and Loyola were rising from their graves to withstand Mazzini—the pale, frail Genoese, whose face was scarred with the sorrows of his country; and this shadowy host could call up armed men from the utmost ends of Europe to defend the Pope. It would never be overcome except by a more living tradition, another cycle of tales of chivalry, a new roll of martyrs; therefore the roll that had been opened in the Papal prisons was filled up on the Janiculum, and the best went gladly to the sacrifice. Some patriots, indeed, regretted that the defence of Rome was ever made, since it was so spendthrift of Italy's treasure; yet the treasure was profitably spent. Because men remembered and told with pride and anguish the story of the uncal-culating devotion of those young lives in this hopeless struggle, there grew up, as the years went by, an unconquer-able purpose in the whole nation to have their capital: there rose that wild cry of the heart—*o Roma, o Morte !* — so magical even in years of discord and derision, that soon or late the Catholic world was bound to yield to it, as to a will stronger and more lasting even than its own.

There was needed, too, a warrior hero of a new type, rival to the figures of Charlemagne and the crusaders, who should win the heart by firing the imagination of Europe. And he, too, had begun clearly to emerge, and was likely ere long to overshadow, more than was just, the fame of the Genoese who had begun it all. Garibaldi had now won Italy's devotion, and was helping to unite her divided children by their common pride in himself. Ere long he was to dazzle the imagination of Europe—even of his enemies ; and to make his greatest conquest in the heart of the least impressionable but not the least poetical of races, the northern lords of the ocean.

But the chief glory of the Third of June does not belong to Garibaldi, but to the slain—the seed that had fallen into the ground and died, and was to bring forth fruit in its season.

CHAPTER X[1]

THE SIEGE OF ROME, JUNE 4–29

'Standing by sick-beds in the hospitals,
   Where thy young warriors stricken down are lying,
Watching for thy slow shadow on the walls,
   And where for one more look of thee the dying
   Linger from hour to hour.'

Sonnet to Garibaldi (MRS. HAMILTON KING'S *Aspromonte and other poems*).

THE heroism shown by the Italians on the third of June was no spasmodic outburst of rage on the part of a race incapable of sustained valour. For nearly a month to come the regiments which had been decimated in the attacks on the Villa remained at the front, under fire every day and during many nights, exhausted in nerve and muscle by the unrelieved strain of siege and bombardment, repeatedly engaged in the fiercest hand-to-hand fighting, losing, one by one, the remainder of their officers, but still maintaining positions which, according to the ordinary maxims of the military art, had been rendered untenable by the erection of French batteries in front of the Corsini. These regiments, made up of the best of the volunteers and a few of the old Papal line, not more than six or seven thousand men, all told, held the Vascello and the bastions of the Janiculan wall. The lower parts of the city, the Vatican and the east bank, threatened and occasionally bombarded, but not seriously attacked, were guarded by rather more numerous but less seasoned troops.[2] The French army, rapidly increased to 25,000, and, towards the end of the month, to 30,000 men,[3] was supported by a train of siege guns,

---

[1] For this Chapter see maps pp. 125, 172, and later p. 210.

[2] See App. I : *Numbers of Roman army during the siege.* There were probably more than 17,000 men under arms in Rome.

[3] *Vaillant,* 155, 156.

and a fine corps of engineers directed by Vaillant himself. The Italian artillery extorted the praise of their enemies by their astonishing courage and the accuracy of their fire ; [1] but -on the scientific side the defenders of Rome had 'nothing but a few civil engineers and a battalion of wretchedly ignorant and poor-spirited sappers.' [2]

It is not possible to praise the population of Rome as highly as the *corps d'élite* on the Janiculum, who, undei Garibaldi, Medici and Manara, won renown for the city which they had taken under their protection. Many, indeed, of the inhabitants of Rome fought and fell in these ranks,[3] but the bulk of the populace, an unarmed and unregimented mob, was waiting till the enemy had forced an entrance, when it would be their part to defend the street barricades which they had erected with so much enthusiasm.[4] That intention was eventually frustrated by the capture of the Janiculan heights, which rendered such resistance impossible ; but the populace could have done something considerable for the cause, if, while the siege was still in progress, it had shown greater eagerness to labour in the trenches. Unfortunately, the soldiers were left to exhaust themselves, whenever they were not fighting, in operations with pick and shovel for which their numbers were altogether insufficient. Sometimes, indeed, the Garibaldini went down into Rome and drove up *corvées* of citizens to the task.[5] On the other hand, Ciceruacchio inspired a large body of workmen to go to the assistance of the Vascello, where many of them were shot down as they plied the spade in the most exposed part of the whole Roman line.[6]

At least there was no want of political zeal, no relenting towards the Pope. As day after day shells flew over the

[1] *Vaillant*, 108, 129, 157.

[2] *Dandolo*, 252 ; *Hoff*. 301. Amadei was a military engineer, but he and Garibaldi quarrelled, and he was put under arrest on June 12. *Loev*. i. 242–251.

[3] App. K, below. [4] *Beghelli*, ii. 308.

[5] *Loev*. i. 248, 249 ; *Gaillard*, 253, 254.

[6] *Pasini*, 122 ; from letter of Medici himself, 1872.

Janiculum and burst in the Trasteverine quarter below,
killing the unfortunate inhabitants in their own homes,
the popular hatred grew fierce against the ruler, once so
much loved, who now seemed to dispute the title of *Bomba*
with his friend the King of Naples.[1]   The citizens, as they
grew accustomed to the bombardment, greeted each pro-
jectile with the cry : '*Ecco un Pio Nono !*'—'There goes
another Pio Nono !'[2]   Women and children of the Trastevere were seen to pick up live shells and throw them into
the Tiber.[3]

  'It is the Trasteverines in particular (wrote a correspondent
on June 12), that part of the Roman populace, recently so
Catholic, who now curse and blaspheme the Pope and Clergy,
in whose names they see this carnage and these horrors committed. . . . What imprudence for the Pope to have appealed to
the Powers in order to get himself re-established on the throne
which he had himself abandoned !   It was as much as to say
" I am willing to wage against my people that war which last
year I declared that I would not make against the Croats—
against the Austrian oppressors of Italy." '[4]

The writer goes on to declare that religion is in consequence
decreasing.   Whatever may have been the effects upon
the religion of the Romans, there is no doubt what was the
permanent result of the siege as regards their political
sympathies.

  The civil authorities, and especially Mazzini, were even
more determined than the military chiefs on the Janiculum
to resist to the last, so as to be able to say : 'We did not
surrender'; but although this policy was quite independent
of any chance of success and was aimed at the far future,
they none the less cultivated the requisite spark of present
hope in themselves, and still more in the populace, by
believing, and by spreading the belief, that the newly

----

  [1] See note, p. 70 above ; and App. J, below.
  [2] *Hoff.* 198 ; *Bertani*, i. 136.   [3] Personal evidence of Costa.
  [4] Ventura's letter, *Torre*, ii. 392, 3.   Pio Nono, in his 'Allocution' of April
1848 (see p. 68 above) had refused to go to war with Austria because he felt
himself to be the 'Vicar of Him who is the author of Peace and lover of
Charity.'

'BOMBA' TEACHING PIO NONO TO BOMBARD HIS SUBJECTS.

(Published in *Don Pirlone*.)

elected Assembly in France would reverse the President's foreign policy. But on June 19 it was known in Rome that the Assembly had shown itself hostile, and that the attempted rising in the streets of Paris had been suppressed. Even then Mazzini strove to create delusive expectations of further changes in France, though he himself had little hope of anything but that the Roman Republic would make a good end.[1]

The conduct of the Italian wounded in Rome revealed some admirable traits in the national character. When carried through the streets from the scene of conflict they seldom failed to greet the passers-by with cries of ' *Viva l'Italia! Viva la Repubblica!* ' The hospitals to which many of them were taken had no proper *matériel*, and were staffed by devoted but untrained volunteer nurses. Half-way through the siege the famous doctor patriot, Bertani, did something to amend these conditions, but misery, disease, and death were all too rife, and were endured with a courage and gentleness which never failed.[2]

' Since April 30 (wrote Margaret Fuller in the middle of June) I go daily to the hospitals, and, though I have suffered—for I had no idea before how terrible gunshot-wounds and wound-fever are—yet I have taken pleasure, and great pleasure, in being with the men. There is scarcely one who is not moved by a noble spirit. Many, especially among the Lombards, are the flower of the Italian youth. When they begin to get better I carry them books and flowers ; they read and we talk. The Palace of the Pope, on the Quirinal, is now used for convalescents. In those beautiful gardens I walk with them—one with his sling, another with his crutch. The gardener plays off all his water-works for the defenders of the country, and gathers flowers for me, their friend. A day or two since, we sat in the Pope's little pavilion, where he used to give private audience. The sun was going gloriously down over Monte Mario, where gleamed the white tents of the French light horse among the trees. The cannonade was heard at intervals. Two bright-

---

[1] *Lazzarini*, 171, 188 ; *Johnston*, 305, 306 ; *Dandolo*, 256-260 ; *Spada*, iii. 634 ; *Saffi*, iii. 339, 340 ; *Clermont*, chaps. vii. and xiii.

[2] *Bertani*, i. 137, 140-143 ; *Hoff.* 134, 300 ; *Lazzarini*, 169.

eyed boys sat at our feet, and gathered up eagerly every word said by the heroes of the day. It was a beautiful hour, stolen from the midst of ruin and sorrow ; and tales were told as full of grace and pathos as in the gardens of Boccaccio, only in a very different spirit—with noble hope for man, with reverence for woman.'

Indeed, there was ' ruin and sorrow ' of every kind—death, wounds, penury, exile—overshadowing every home where high-minded men and women loved Italy ; and a year later Margaret Fuller herself was drowned at sea.[1]

In another hospital an equally notable woman, the revolutionary Princess Belgiojoso, the friend of Victor Hugo and Heine, who, as an exile from Austrian Lombardy, had long kept one of the most distinguished of Parisian salons, was working hard for her poor wounded countrymen, with untiring physical energy and great powers of organisation.[2]   When she was not wanted elsewhere, she sat long nights by the bed of the dying poet Mameli, seeking distraction from the tragedy around in reading Charles Dickens, by the light of a little oil-lamp.[3]

Although the bulk of the French army was encamped against the Janiculum, Oudinot kept a strong force beyond the river at St. Paul's Without-the-Walls, and another above the town at the captured Ponte Molle, employing them in demonstrations which occupied the attention of a large part of the troops defending Rome.   These French detachments on the east bank made it difficult, though by no means impossible, to victual the city, and to keep up communications with the Republic of which Rome was still the capital.   The French light cavalry, in their little képis,

---

[1] *Fuller*, iii. 211, 212; *Belgiojoso* (Barbiera), 311, 312.

[2] *Whitehouse*, 217–233 ; *Story*, i. 155.

[3] *Belgiojoso*, 314, 315.   Of this remarkable woman's life and character, the riddle has been best stated by Mr. Henry James in two pages of his life of *Story*, i. 162, 163.   Laura Piaveni in *Vittoria*, Mr. Meredith tells me, ' has only a portion of the character of the Princess Belgiojoso ; she was not framed on it entirely, not having in her the elements of the worldly woman, to be developed subsequently.'

which gave them a more rakish and modern appearance
than that of the infantry, still burdened with the tall shakos
recalling the Napoleonic wars, could be seen sweeping
over the Campagna to the north and east, cutting off
convoys from Rieti, blowing up the bridges over the Anio,
and on one occasion pushing out as far as the cascades of
Tivoli to destroy a powder-mill which was working there
for the Triumvirate.[1] The provisioning of Rome was a
work in which the native artist Costa was largely employed
on account of his knowledge of the ground outside the city.
In later years he used to describe the adventures which befell
him as he slipped out and in between the French and
Spaniards, for Spain also had, at the invitation of the
Pope, landed a force of 6,000 crusaders, who were now
occupying the banks of the lower Tiber, between Rome and
Fiumincino, though taking no active part in the siege.

‘ The spice of danger certainly did not make these expeditions
less attractive to the spirited young man, and he was able to
appreciate the picturesque side of these excursions into the
desolate and solitary Campagna, whose vast spaces and sweeping lines of distant purple, and amethyst-coloured hills, were to
become such a favourite note in his future artistic work. He
always remembered with a sense of pleasure one particular
occasion when, in the company of the *mercante di campagna*
(merchant farmer), Luigi Silvestrelli, mounted on horseback,
and armed with the goad, the characteristic *pungolo* of the
Roman herdsman, he drove into the City three hundred head
of wild cattle.’ [2]

But Costa also took his full share in the grim work of
the Vascello. That villa, together with the Casa Giacometti and the little house that stood between them at the
foot of the Corsini garden, formed an advanced line which
Garibaldi had, on the evening of June 3, entrusted to the
charge of the Milanese Giacomo Medici, his young lieutenant
of Monte Video and the Alps, who had received from the

[1] *Bittard des Portes,* 278, 279, 353, 357 ; *Balleydier,* ii. 257, 258.
[2] *Costa,* 48 ; *Military Events,* 320, 321.

dying Anzani the warning, ever afterwards so faithfully observed, never to abandon the destined liberator.[1] Medici had arrived in Rome from the North with a 'Medici Legion' some three hundred strong, recruited from the men who had followed him among the Alps the year before, and from other students and young men of wealthy Lombard families.[2] As his own early youth had been spent, not in the Italian Universities, but in the Carlist campaigns, he was a brusque soldier, a rough and ready disciplinarian, and above all a hard fighter.[3] With his own legion, aided from time to time by detachments from Manara's Bersaglieri, the Students, the Gagers and the *Unione* regiment, Medici held the Vascello and the two other houses, having established communication between them by means of trenches, as also with the San Pancrazio gate whence he drew his supplies. Day and night the French waged war on these Italian outposts, and the storm of lead and iron swept ceaselessly over Masina's body stretched on the neutral ground between. From the Valentini and Corsini the enemy fired down into the garden and windows of the Vascello, while their trenches, filled with sharpshooters, were pushed ever nearer and nearer. Attacks were made by night at the point of the bayonet, and a battery, ensconced in front of the ruined façade of the Corsini, pounded the Vascello walls to pieces at a range of about 200 yards. It was impossible for Medici to place cannon in the line which he held, although the battery in the Casa Merluzzo Bastion was able in the early days of the siege to direct its fire against his assailants. Under these conditions the Casa Giacometti held out for three weeks, and the Vascello (or rather what remained of its lowest story) was still untaken on June 30, when its heroic defenders retreated out of the ruins because the walls of Rome had been captured behind their backs.[4]

[1] Pp. 43, 44 above.

[2] They had flocked to join him in Florence, where he had organised his Legion during the brief life of the Tuscan Republic, February to April 1849. *Pasini*, 82–87 ; *Ottolini*, 59, 87–91 (list of names, nearly all from the north).

[3] *Pasini*, 7–10 ; *Forbes*, 142.

[4] *Beghelli*, ii. 387–392, Medici's own account ; *Hoff.* 113, 146–148, 228,

THE VASCELLO DURING THE SIEGE. (WERNER.)

From its own garden.

The unexpected resistance of these outposts delayed the fall of Rome by many days, because it prevented Vaillant from pushing his trenches forward against the face of the Porta San Pancrazio, and so capturing the Casa Merluzzo and Northern Bastions on either side of it by a direct attack.[1] But the occupation of the Corsini enabled him to reduce the Janiculum gradually from its south flank by opening trenches against the Centre Bastion and that of the Casa Barberini.

Since, therefore, the first line of French approaches was drawn from the Convent of San Pancrazio to Monte Verde,[2] its extreme right was exposed to a distant and somewhat ineffective flank fire from a Roman battery down below on the further bank of Tiber, erected on the little eminence of Monte Testaccio.[3] That strange mound, nothing more nor less than the rubbish heap where, in the days of the Cæsars, the broken crockery of the world's capital used to be thrown away, stood in 1849 surrounded by a few shabby houses, in the middle of one of those romantic deserts then occupying so much of the vast circuit enclosed by the walls of Rome, which, twenty-seven years after Shelley's death, was still—

. . . ' at once the paradise,
The grave, the city, and the wilderness.'

A battery was erected on Monte Verde to silence the Italian guns on Monte Testaccio, and, as the French shells flew over the mound, many of them passed on and burst unnoticed near a solitary and sacred spot.[4] Under the cypresses that Trelawny had planted in the shadow of the wall and of the pyramid, in the remote burying-place of the heretics, that quiet brotherhood

229, 255, 256, 273 ; *Dandolo,* 252 ; *Costa,* 48 ; *Torre,* ii. 226 ; *Tivaroni, Aust.* ii. 435 ; *Vecchi,* ii. 284, 289 ; *Pasini,* 95–111.

[1] *Moltke,* i. 191–193. See p. 212 below, note 4.   [2] *Vaillant,* 41, 42.

[3] There was also a Roman battery on the Aventine (*Vecchi,* ii. 267), but it does not seem to have played an important part.

[4] See map, p. 125, and illustration, p. 228, for the relation of the Protestant cemetery to the Monte Testaccio. There is also an interesting picture of the cemetery, as it was in 1849, in the *Illustrated London News,* July 7.

slept on and did not hear the distant roar of the battle
for Freedom ; nor could even the near bursting of the
tyrants' bombs awaken him, who, of all men that ever lived,
would have been most eager to hasten with long strides up
the Janiculum, to stand enchanted amid the shots beside
its Republican defenders, and to speak with Garibaldi and
Ugo Bassi as with friends long dreamed of and sought in
vain.

The high Villa Savorelli, towering above the Porta San
Pancrazio, had been selected by Garibaldi as his headquarters because, though exposed to the enemy's fire, it
commanded a wider prospect of the Italian and French
positions than any other house within the Roman walls.
' We officers,' wrote Hoffstetter, one of the intimate circle
of friends tried in battle who now made up the General's
staff,

' we officers lay in the great salon of the Villa Savorelli. The
General and Manara (the chief of his staff since June 4) had each
a small side room.   Night gave us little rest, because of the
constant coming and going of messengers.'

At daybreak the officers, having helped themselves to ' good
black coffee and plenty of cigars,' which were ready for
them at three every morning,

' gathered round the General, who was always the first on the
Pavilion ;[1] there he was immediately greeted by the French
sharpshooters, who gave him their particular attention all day
long. But Garibaldi, after throwing a glance at the enemy,
used to light his cigar, which was never extinguished till evening,
heard the reports, gave orders, and only left the Pavilion late
at night to seek a few hours' rest.'[2]

When the French bombardment began, the Savorelli
gradually crumbled beneath the cannon-balls ; it had been
riddled through and through before the staff, on June 21,
thought of moving elsewhere.   After the breaching batteries

---

[1] The watch-tower on the roof of the Villa Savorelli.
[2] *Hoff.* 162–164. The Pavilion at length fell in ruin, only five minutes after
Garibaldi had stepped out of it, *Bertani*, i. 138.

VILLA SAVORELLI AND BATTERY IN THE CASA MERLUZZO BASTION.

(WERNER.)

had opened fire (June 13), Garibaldi did not spend the whole of each day upon the Pavilion, but constantly went the rounds, visiting the places where the fire was hottest, and restoring the enthusiasm of the defenders, now by a word of personal sympathy, now by standing like a statue above his prostrate companions while a shell was bursting in their midst.[1] He seemed to disregard death as a weak thing that he knew by old experience had no power to touch the man of destiny before his hour ; while Ugo Bassi, equally reckless, but in a different spirit, sought death as the friendly deliverer from slavery reimposed and from the ruin of hopes too dear to be outlived. Bassi gave Garibaldi ' much anxiety,' Hoffstetter tells us :

' " I cannot tell you how that man troubles me," said the General to me one day, " for he wants to die ! " One recognised the enthusiast in Bassi at the first glance ; his mild eyes and high forehead, the waving locks of his hair and beard, his unusual dress (the red blouse and broad-brimmed black hat), his inspired language and contempt for death struck us all with astonishment. No one's hand did me so much good to shake as his. He cherished a passionate devotion to the General. " Nothing would give me greater joy," Bassi said to me more than once, " than to die for Garibaldi." ' [2]

That sentiment was now deeply implanted among all these men, some of whom, like Manara, had come to Rome with very different feelings. Their hearts beat high, but not with hope.[3]

---

[1] *Hoff.* 199, 203, 205, 231, 270-271.   [2] *Hoff.* 253.

[3] A young officer of one of the line regiments, named Count Ulisse Balzani, who took a gallant part in the defence, in after years described to his brother (Count Ugo, who told me the story) one of the deepest impressions of his life. He had been sleeping on the ramparts, where his men lay bivouacked, when at dawn he opened his eyes, dreamily half aware that a horse was stepping tenderly across his body. In that delicious state of returning consciousness, when the more prosaic aspects of daily life are still unremembered, and the objects that first meet the eyes are seen as ' in a world far from ours,' he had a vision of the rider's face looking down at him out of masses of curling golden hair. It was imprinted on his brain as one of the noblest things in art or nature which he had ever seen.

During the first seventeen days and nights of the siege (June 4–21), while the zig-zag of the French trenches was creeping nearer hour by hour, and the batteries erected under their protection were gradually crumbling the breaches in the Central and Casa Barberini Bastions, the defenders made many sorties, none very effective and some not even creditable to their arms. The want of regular training among the volunteers was felt most in the conduct of night surprises, which the Romans always failed to effect and the French sometimes carried out to perfection. In one of these sorties even the men of the Italian Legion were seized with panic, and were told by Garibaldi next morning that they were not worthy to be his companions in arms, a reproof which, if needed, was effectual. On other occasions the greatest gallantry was shown by the sortie parties, as when a detachment of the *Unione* regiment continued to maintain the fight with stones after their ammunition was exhausted. The Poles, too, conspicuous for their long moustaches and their national cap, with its four-cornered crown of red cloth,[1] were foremost in seeking death; homeless sons of the slain mother, they generously offered their blood on behalf of any nation that was at war with tyranny, whether on the Hungarian plain or before the walls of Rome. But nothing was done by the sortie parties that seriously impeded the evolution of the slow but well-laid plans of Vaillant's siege.[2]

On the night of June 20–21, when after a furious bombardment the breaches in the bastions were almost ready for the stormers to mount, and an assault on those points was expected, an attack was made instead on the Casa Giacometti, outside the walls. Closely netted by the enemy's trenches and riddled by his fire, the little outpost was still unconquerable. The sentry, the only man awake in the house, heard the storming party rustle and stumble among the vines a few yards off; he noiselessly roused his comrades,

---

[1] *Koelman*, ii. 152.

[2] *Hoff.* and *Vaillant, passim*; *Dandolo*, 250, 251; *Loev.* i. 239-241; *Ciàmpoli*, 910. The Polish regiment numbered about 200.

thirty-five men of the *Unione* regiment, who delivered a
sudden volley at close quarters, and after a fierce struggle,
in which the bayonet was used on both sides, drove off the
assailants. At dawn Medici was able to report from the
Vascello that the very outposts of his advanced position
were still intact.[1]

Garibaldi next day (June 21) celebrated the little victory
in a letter to his Anita;[2] she had last been with him at
Rieti, from the end of February until April 13, when she
had returned to her children under his mother's roof at
Nice.[3]

'My dear Anita (he wrote from the Savorelli), I know that
thou hast been and maybe still art ill. I wish to see thy handwriting and my mother's, and then I shall feel easy.

'Cardinal Oudinot's Gallic-friars content themselves with
cannonading us, and we are too much accustomed to it to care.
Here the women and children run after the balls and shells and
struggle for their possession.

'We are fighting on the Janiculum and this people is worthy
of its past greatness. Here they live, die, suffer amputation
to the cry, "Viva la Repubblica!" One hour of our life in
Rome is worth a century of common existence.

'Last night thirty of our men, surprised in a house outside
the wall (Casa Giacometti) by 150 of the Gallic-friars, used
the bayonet, killed a captain and three soldiers, made four
prisoners and a number of wounded. We had one sergeant
killed and a soldier wounded. Our men belonged to the *Unione*
Regiment.

'Get well, kiss Mama and the babies for me. Menotti has
favoured me with a letter, for which I am grateful to him. Love
me much, thy Garibaldi.'

The letter was sent, but never reached Anita, who was
already leaving Nice for Rome. When the news of the
Third of June and the approaching fate of Rome had

[1] *Hoff.* 224, 225, 228, 229; *Vaillant,* 97, 98; *Torre,* ii. 226; *Bittard des
Portes,* 317, 318.
[2] The date of the letter is June 21, not June 12 as it is usually given. See
Loev. ii. 214, 215, note.
[3] *Loev.* ii. 213, 214; iii. 331.

awakened in her the apprehension that some desperate crisis in her husband's fate was hastening on, she had formed within the tribunal of her conscience a great decision, to be carried out with that quiet, inflexible will of hers, regardless even of Garibaldi's most earnest remonstrance. This mother, again pregnant, set out for the seat of war, determined to share the extreme perils of adherence to a falling Republic with the man whom she regarded as unlike the husbands of other women, and of more value than any child could be.   She left posterity no record of her motives, and no apology for her choice, but her silent, set, immutable purpose to remain at his side until the end— whatever that end might be—pleads for her with more eloquence than words.

On June 21, while Garibaldi was writing his last letter to Anita, the Savorelli was falling to pieces about his ears. But the fire was hottest against the Central and Barberini Bastions, where a furious cannonade and musketry fire, maintained from the French trenches now within a few yards of the wall,[1] only ceased at nightfall when the crumbling breaches presented an easy slope for the assailants to mount.   The Italians made preparation against an assault that night ; piles of bulrushes were laid on the top of the ruined walls, ready to be ignited at the first alarm, so as to form a rampart of flame.   Hoffstetter, who himself came from head-quarters to place the garrison in the bastions and in the houses that stood on the wall, gave the strictest orders to the sentries, and returned with the belief that at any rate the positions could not be captured by surprise, before the reserve had time to come up from the neighbourhood of the Savorelli.[2]   But the *Unione* regiment, to whom the breaches had been entrusted, was utterly tired out by the fatigues of the last fortnight, during which they had so often behaved with peculiar gallantry. On the Central Bastion they awoke to find a French column already among them, inside the line of bulrushes, and after

---

[1] *Bertani*, i. 138 ; *Hoff.* 224-232.   [2] *Hoff.* 232-234.

a single discharge [1] they fled in panic. On the top of the other breach, some resistance was made from the Casa Barberini, and two French officers were mortally wounded under its walls. But in a few minutes the doors were broken in and the house captured.[2] The enemy were masters of both bastions.

The panic and confusion in the Italian lines was such that those who witnessed it feared that if the French pressed on at once in force they might carry the Savorelli and San Pietro in Montorio before daylight, and so finish the siege.[3] Garibaldi, with greater wisdom than many of his critics, saw the danger and refused to lead the discouraged troops to recapture the lost positions—an enterprise which would certainly have failed, and would probably have led to the loss of the inner line as well.[4] Instead of attempting the impossible, he devoted so much energy to fortifying and manning a second line of defence along the old Imperial wall of Aurelian, that when day dawned the new position was strongly occupied, and the fear of a capture of the Janiculum by a *coup de main* was at an end.

With equal caution the French generals, refusing to be tempted by the flight of the *Unione* regiment to go a step beyond the captured bastions, had used the remainder of the night in throwing up trenches on their inner side, and in mounting batteries on the top of the ruined breaches, so that they should be ready as soon as possible to bombard Garibaldi's new position.

As day dawned Rome learnt with consternation that the enemy had established themselves on the walls, ' a very fatal go,' as Arthur Clough called it in his letter home.[5]

[1] *Vaillant*, 105. The Italians thought that the French must have entered by getting themselves let in through the Italian mines, see *Hoff*. 236, 237; *Dandolo*, 254, 255. But *Vaillant*, 105, 106, disposes of this hypothesis. *Torre*, ii. 230–233; *Précis Hist.* 71–73; *Gabussi*, iii. 450, 451

[2] *Vaillant*, 104; *Bittard des Portes*, 330, 331; *Pisacane*, 7.   [3] *Hoff*. 235.

[4] *Bizzoni*, i. 423–5; *Gabussi*, iii. 450–453, and note, containing Filopanti's letter. *Hoff*. 235, 236; *Loev*. i. 253, 254. Garibaldi sent some of his own Legion to reconnoitre the enemy's positions by an attack, to make sure whether or not the newly captured bastions were being strongly held. The operation cost the Legion twenty men.

[5] *Clough's P. R.* 158. Letter to Palgrave.

Mazzini and Roselli, who knew little about the condition of affairs on the Janiculum, urged Garibaldi to recover the bastions at all costs. Mazzini, to whom it was an article of faith that the People could recapture the walls of their city, assembled the mob for this purpose, much to the annoyance of Garibaldi, who would not let them come up to cause confusion in his now circumscribed lines.

Roselli, in his capacity as commander-in-chief, and Avezzana, the able minister of war, arrived early in the morning on the Janiculum, to compel the recalcitrant divisional commander to attack. But Avezzana, when he had examined affairs on the spot, was soon persuaded that such a course was impossible.[1] Indeed, the officers of the fighting regiments, and above all Manara, had earnestly entreated Garibaldi not to send their men to another massacre more hopeless than that of June 3, since the *élan* which had inspired them on that day had now given way to a fatigue of body and an angry despair of soul; and the bravest, with the passive courage characteristic of the last days of a siege, asked to be allowed to die in the positions which they still held.[2]

Garibaldi's refusal to attack, though supported by military opinion on the Janiculum, involved another unseemly quarrel with Mazzini and Roselli, of which the populace was not slow to get wind without understanding the real nature of the dispute. The state of unrest and friction in Rome on that unhappy day (June 22) was aggravated by the action of Sterbini, who, having justly forfeited his own prestige by the abuse of his opportunities in the past winter, now plotted to creep back to power by exploiting the name of Garibaldi. Raising the cry that the General should be made dictator, Sterbini rode through the streets of Rome to raise a tumult, when the enemy was already on the walls, although Garibaldi had that very morning positively forbidden him to act, and had

---

[1] *Hoff.* 241.
[2] *Hoff.* 240–242; *Loev.* i. 253, 254, and note; *Dandolo*, 255; *Torre*, ii. 235, 236; *Vecchi*, ii. 282, 283; *Pisacane*, 7; *Gabussi*, iii. 450–453, and note.

discouraged the whole movement. Fortunately it ended in fiasco when a patriotic sculptor named Bezzi seized the bridle of Sterbini's horse in the Piazza Colonna, and threatened the life of the cowardly leader of rebellion.[1]

The second part of the siege of Rome—the nine days' defence of the Aurelian wall (June 22–30)—surprised the French and even the Italians themselves, who could scarcely believe their senses when they found each morning that the enemy had not yet stormed their untenable positions.[2] During the first part of the siege, though they had often behaved with great courage, they had been subject to fits of panic, and it might have been expected, now that a successful issue to the defence was impossible, that like other armies they would abandon a contest, the prolongation of which some of their bravest officers regarded as a criminal waste of life.[3]   And such, from a military point of view, it undoubtedly was. But the Italian character has in it something beyond the reasonable, and, when all was lost, the idea of perishing with the murdered Republic seemed to fortify the *morale* and brace the nerves of the tired men, whose conduct became now more uniformly heroic than it had been during the fortnight past, when it was still possible to indulge a shadowy hope. An English army might have held the bastions from which the Italians fled on the night of June 21–22, but an English army might well have capitulated if those bastions had been lost, seeing that there was no force in the wide world to come to their relief, and many to come to the help of the besiegers.   The defenders of Londonderry, Gibraltar, Lucknow, and Ladysmith were inspired by the practical hope of succour.   It was otherwise with the defenders of Rome.   If the Englishman does not know when he is beaten, the Italian sometimes knows it and does not care.

Though the troops were willing to continue the defence, the responsibility for giving the order to fight on rests with

[1] *Guerzoni*, i. 322, 323 ; *Loev.* i. 255 ; *Vecchi*, ii. 285 ; *Farini*, iv. 209, 210.
[2] *Dandolo*, 261.   [3] *Ibid.* 260, 268.

P

Mazzini, who was determined that the last message ' to Italy from Rome ' should be something worthier than the panic flight from the breaches. Garibaldi, no less opposed to asking terms of the foreigner, thought that the time had come to evacuate the capital and carry on the war in the mountains, but, as his advice was overruled, he continued to command the defence on the west bank.

The scene of the last struggle was worthy of the actors and of the cause. On the high ground where the ruined Savorelli stood, Servius Tullius had built the Arx Janiculensis, which had served, as the Garibaldians recalled with delight, for the outlying fort of Republican Rome when Lars Porsena had tried to bring home the *Papa-Re* of that period.[1] From this height down to the Trastevere ran the wall built by the Emperor Aurelian to keep off the trans-Alpine barbarians when Rome's grasp of the world was growing weak [2] ; behind what here remained of it lay Garibaldi's infantry. Their cannon were planted in the rear, to fire over their heads from the platform of San Pietro in Montorio, and the neighbouring Pino hill—so called because of the large pine-tree in the shadow of which the Roman gunners fought. Between the batteries on the height and the infantry below along the wall, was the Villa Spada, now Garibaldi's headquarters, a modest house standing by itself in its small garden, as it still stands to-day.[3] The Casa Merluzzo Bastion on the wall of Urban VIII. was occupied as an advanced post, and a battery was mounted between it and the Porta San Pancrazio.

This new position was bombarded from front and flank. The French guns erected on the captured breaches fired

<hr />

[1] *Vecchi*, ii. 278. Moltke, too, recalled the associations with Porsena in his contemporary letters to Humboldt.

[2] On the east bank Aurelian's walls were still, in 1849, the only defences of Rome. On the west bank they were no longer meant for use, but stood unrepaired as an inner line behind the wall of Urban VIII., on which the French had now established themselves.

[3] The Villa Spada is called the Villa Nobilia in the inscription over the entrance. It is but little changed in appearance since 1849 (see illustration, p. 223, below). I fear the same cannot be said of the new Savorelli that has risen on the ruins of the building destroyed during the siege.

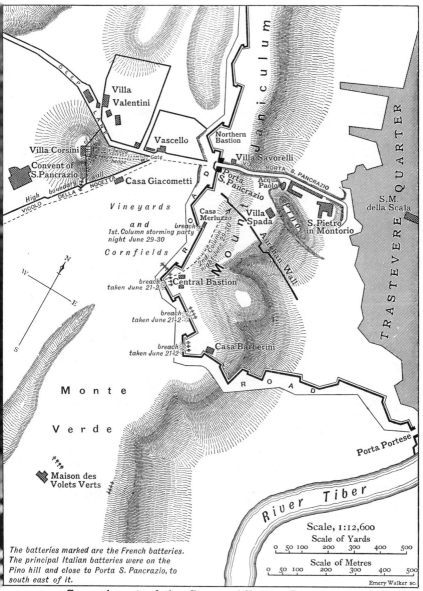

Villa
Valentini

Vascello

Northern
Bastion

Villa Corsini
Convent of
S. Pancrazio

box-hedge
box-hedge

Gate

Villa Savorelli

VIA DI PORTA S. PANCRAZIO

High   boundary
wall

Casa Giacometti

VICOLO   DELLA   NOCETTA

Porta
S. Pancrazio

Acqua
Paola

S.M.
della Scala

Vineyards

Casa
Merluzzo

Villa
Spada

S. Pietro
in Montorio

a n d
1st. Column storming party
night June 29-30

breach

2nd Column
night June 29-30

Aurelian Wall

C o r n f i e l d s

N
W   E
S

breach
taken June 21-2

Central Bastion

breach
taken June 21-2

breach
taken June 21-2

Casa Barberini

R O A D

M o n t e

V e r d e

Maison des
Volets Verts

Porta Portese

River Tiber

Scale, 1:12,600
Scale of Yards
0 50 100   200   300   400   500

Scale of Metres
0 50 100   200   300   400   500

Emery Walker sc.

The batteries marked are the French batteries.
The principal Italian batteries were on the
Pino hill and close to Porta S. Pancrazio, to
south east of it.

Second part of the Siege of Rome, June 22-30

Casa   Villa Spada.   San Pietro   Acqua Paola   Villa
Merluzzo.   Roman Battery   in Montorio   Fountain.   Savorelli.
    at the 'Pino.'   (used as
            hospital).

REAR OF SECOND ROMAN LINE OF DEFENCE, JUNE 22–30.

Taken from East bank of Tiber during June 1849.

across the wide open space and valley that divides the Villas Barberini and Spada, while the batteries near the Corsini and Convent of San Pancrazio enfiladed the Italian line from the west.[1] The enemy also drove his trenches and erected a breaching battery close up against the south angle of the Merluzzo Bastion ; this operation became possible after the night of June 23–24, when the brave garrison of the Casa Giacometti were at length withdrawn to the Vascello.[2]

For eight days the cannonade and musketry fire raged continuously. The accuracy of the Italian gunners surprised the French and retarded their attack ; indeed, on the first day of the artillery duel (June 22) the defenders had the upper hand, and under cover of the fire a small body of Medici's Legion, who happened to be within the gate of Rome, burst into the Villa Barberini, and were only driven out after a severe tussle, carrying back fifteen men wounded with the bayonet.[3] But soon the double fire of the French, from within and without the walls, began to prevail. The shells tore holes in the Spada, and exploded among the staff officers in its rooms. The roof of the church of San Pietro in Montorio collapsed. Nearly all the gunners on the Pino and by the San Pancrazio gate were killed or wounded ; their places were taken by infantry, and by artists and other volunteers from the city below.[4] The men of the Garibaldian Legion and of Manara's Bersaglieri, with indefatigable zeal consented to remain at sentry work for seventy-two hours at a time, and, with utter disregard of death, laboured in the open to pile up again the frail defences as they crumbled beneath the fire. The wounded, as soon as they were well enough to drag themselves back to the front, returned with all haste to their posts.[5]

---

[1] *Hoff.* 242.   [2] *Vaillant*, 114.

[3] *Vaillant*, 108, 157 ; *Torre*, ii. 236 ; *Beghelli*, ii. 388, 389 (Medici's account of it) ; *Pasini*, 102–107.

[4] *Hoff.* 248, 249, 252–265, 271, 274. With the gallant Italian gunners were a good many no less gallant Swiss. *Vaillant*, 129, 157 ; *Dandolo*, 264 ; *Koelman*, ii. 195–202.

[5] *Dandolo*, 264, 265.

On one of these days of fire (June 25) Laviron, the French Republican and artist, one of Garibaldi's staff, loved by all his companions-in-arms, for the first time donned the red blouse, because, as he told his friends, he observed that whoever wore it enjoyed an uncommon share of popular favour. He had scarcely shown himself at the front in this costume when he was shot through the body, fell back into the arms of Ugo Bassi, kissed him and died.[1] Death at the hands of his countrymen after the flesh had no horrors for one who was spiritually the citizen of that ideal Republic which had been dreamed of by the men of '48.

On the following day, Anita Garibaldi suddenly appeared in the doorway of the shot-riddled Spada, and her husband, with a cry of surprise and joy, sprang into her arms. She had found her way from Nice into the beleaguered city before he even knew of her intention to start upon a journey which he would not have approved.[2]

Outside the walls of Rome the storm beat with still greater fury on the Vascello. From the Corsini hill, a battery of half a dozen guns fired on it day and night, throwing into it 'not less than four hundred' cannon-balls, 'besides shells and grenades.'[3]

It was owing to the protracted resistance of the Vascello that Rome had not fallen many days before. The unexpectedly successful defence of this 'oddly shaped but very strong villa,' had, as Moltke wrote at the time, forced the French to make a lateral instead of a direct attack on the bastions next to the Porta San Pancrazio.[4] At

---

[1] *Hoff.* 252, 253; *Loev.* ii. 252, 253; *Vecchi*, ii. 286; *Guerrazzi*, 788, 789. Hoffstetter's less sensational account of Laviron's death is more likely, I think, to be correct than Vecchi's or Guerrazzi's, especially as the story told by the latter about Laviron is told about a Polish officer by Dandolo and by Hoffstetter.

[2] *Guerzoni*, i. 381, 382; *Loev.* ii. 214. The latter accurately fixes the date of her arrival, June 26.

[3] *Beghelli*, ii. 389 (Medici's account).

[4] 'Der wahre Angriff findet ohne Zweifel von Villa Corsini aus auf die Bastione zunächst Porta San Pancrazio statt.' 'Dass aber jener vortheilhaftere Angriff nicht gewählt wurde hat sein Grund wohl nur darin, dass die Römer noch immer die seltsam gebaute aber sehr feste Villa Vascello behaupten.' *Moltke*, i. 191–193. Moltke had been in Rome, 1845, 1846, studying its defences.

THE VASCELLO IN 1906.
From the road between the Corsini and Porta San Pancrazio.

INSIDE THE VASCELLO, 1906.

length, the greater part of the vast building fell with a
roar, amid a cloud of darkness, like a bursting volcano. A
score of its defenders were buried under the ruins, but
the rest, sheltered by portions of the ground-floor still left
erect, came out covered with the subsiding dust, and were
quickly reposed among the fallen masonry to resist attack.
' I wish,' said Medici to Hoffstetter, ' that I had a daguer-
reotype of these ruins.'   At night the French, with fixed
bayonets, fell upon them from every side. For three midnight hours the battle raged over the rubbish heap of what
had once been a magnificent villa. At dawn Medici was
still in possession.[1] Rome might be taken, but not the
Vascello. When the war was over the fallen ruins were
cleared away, but by good fortune the walls of the ground
floor were left standing, and now that Rome is free will
continue to stand as long as Italians have pride in their
history. On the shot-dinted wall that borders the public
road some old dusty laurel wreaths are hung, and on the
tablet which they adorn the stranger may read, in words
that here are no idle boast, that ' he who is fighting for
fatherland and freedom does not count the enemy.'

Meanwhile, within the walls, the defenders of the
Janiculum endured, day after day, the last terrible cannonade, and the other parts of the city did not altogether
escape. Not only were the inhabitants of the Trastevere
driven in crowds from their ruined houses, but the bombardment did injury on the Capitol, and elsewhere in the
very heart of Rome. The French field artillery on the east
bank shelled the city, by way of creating a diversion from the
main attack ; whenever a serious assault was intended on
the Janiculan wall, diversions were made from San Paolo
on the south and from Monte Parioli on the north ; Rome
was bombarded from both these quarters, and shells were
dropped into the Piazza di Spagna and all that neighbourhood, doing considerable damage. As early as June 25,

[1] *Beghelli*, ii. 387-392 (Medici) ; *Dandolo*, 262 ; *Hoff.* 255-257, 273 ; *Vecchi*,
ii. 289 ; *Pasini*, 108, 109 ; *Ottolini*, 77, 78.

Oudinot had received a protest against the destruction of private property and works of art, and the death of peaceable citizens, signed by the consuls of the United States, Prussia, Denmark, Switzerland, and Sardinia, at the instigation of Freeborn, the British Consular agent, whose name appeared at their head, and who was indeed too warm in his friendship for Italy to make allowance for the military needs of her enemies.[1]

While the city below was suffering more or less severely, the defences on the Janiculum were crumbling fast beneath a storm of missiles. It was clear that, in spite of the heroism of the defenders, the French would, in a few days at most, be able to storm the line of the Aurelian wall. In face of this situation the quarrel between Garibaldi and Mazzini broke out afresh. The soldier, after requesting in vain to be allowed to try to raise the siege by attacking the enemy's communications, finally urged that the Government and army should migrate from the capital, and continue the national war to the last in the mountains of Central Italy or of the Neapolitan kingdom. He had seen the Republic of Rio Grande, in time of danger, migrate in this patriarchal fashion, and he did not understand why the Roman Republic should not do the same.[2] No doubt, if he had been allowed to have his way on June 27, instead of five days later after the final storming of the Janiculum, he might have carried into the wilderness a still formidable army, including perhaps Manara and his Lombards,[3] instead of the three or four thousand broken-hearted men who left Rome with him on July 2 to share his historic ' retreat.' Mazzini's advisers, on the other hand, had perhaps a higher rationality on their side when they determined that the irrational defence of the walls of Rome should be continued to the very last. Garibaldi, finding his advice again rejected, on the evening of June 27 threw up his command, and, in an explosion of anger akin to the primitive, childish wrath of Achilles, carried off his myrmidons of the Legion from the

---

[1] See App. J, below, *Damage done by Bombardment*.

[2] *Mem.* 239; *Bizzoni*, i. 428, 436-7; *Ciàmpoli*, 40-44. In the Italian translation of this book (1908) I have given a more complete account of this quarrel.

[3] *Hoff.* 269, 307, 308.

Janiculum to the lower town. The officers of the remaining regiments were horror-struck at finding themselves deserted, and their anxiety was increased by the evident incompetence of Roselli, who, when he came in person to take over Garibaldi's command on the west bank, would not even visit the lines, but remained poring over maps in the Spada.[1] Manara hastened down to find Garibaldi, expostulated with him on his misconduct and exposed to him the fatal consequences that must ensue. Garibaldi listened to his new friend, repented and returned to his post, amid the cheers of the populace, and to the intense joy of the defenders of the Janiculum.[2] But for Manara's timely interference —the last but not the least service which he rendered to Italy —the siege of Rome would have ended in discord and disgrace, and Garibaldi would have carried through life the stigma of an ungenerous action, to which anger alone had prompted him, but which many of his countrymen would readily have regarded as betrayal.

When, at daybreak of June 28, the Garibaldian Legionaries returned to the Janiculum with their chief to share the last slaughter, the welcome they received was all the more enthusiastic because their rank and file on this occasion appeared for the first time in the famous red shirt, which had hitherto distinguished the General's staff. Indeed, many people, ignorant of the crisis that had been averted, supposed that the Legion had gone down to the town only to change the old for the new uniform.[3]

Those who donned the red shirt in the last days of the siege of Rome, and faithfully wore it during the next month, deliberately chose a dress which, from one end of the Peninsula to the other, exposed the wearer to be hunted like a wolf and shot at sight. In less than twenty years, times had so far changed, and so famous had that garb of heroes become, that poltroons sometimes chose it as the cloak of self-seeking and noisy patriotism that could not stand the stress of battle. But if, in the old age of its founder, the

---

[1] *Hoff.* 270, 271.   [2] *Loev.* i. 257–259; *Hoff.* 266–271 ; *Dandolo,* 263.
[3] *Hoff.* 270; *Loev.* ii. 126. See p. 152, above, for the order given by Garibaldi in May for the manufacture of the shirts, only now completed.

brotherhood of the red shirt partook of the decline of his powers, before he died its warfare was accomplished, and Italy was free.[1]

[1] One red-shirt expedition took place after Garibaldi's death. His son, Ricciotti, led several hundred volunteers in the Greek war of 1897. The Italians, whose generosity in going to risk their lives for the freedom of others was worthy of their dead master, behaved with courage. Some account of the expedition will be found in *Elia*, ii. 424–442. I have consulted well-known English war correspondents on that campaign, who bear impartial testimony to the valour of the Garibaldians.

CASA MERLUZZO AND BREACH OF BASTION, STORMED JUNE 29-30.
From the road outside. (WERNER.)

CHAPTER XI[1]

'Astur hath stormed Janiculum,
And the stout guards are slain.'
MACAULAY, *Lays of Ancient Rome.*

THE end was now at hand. The French artillery were
victors in the duel which both sides had waged so gallantly
for more than a week past. The Roman batteries were
'almost choked up by the tempest of hostile projectiles,'
the breastworks along the line of the Aurelian wall were
mere disorderly heaps of earth, and on the city wall proper
the breach in the Bastion sloped gently down from the
ruins of the Casa Merluzzo to the road outside, where the
assailants were entrenched not many yards away.[2]

The night of June 29–30, the Feast of St. Peter and
St. Paul, was selected by Oudinot for the final assault.
During the earlier part of the night the *festa* was celebrated
in the town in right Roman fashion, with lighting of candles
in the windows, and sending up of rockets in the streets—
functions which that mercurial people would not forgo
even under the shadow of impending doom. The Triumvirate gave official countenance to these mild *circenses*, and
the dome of St. Peter's blazed with every extravagance of
colour. The French officers, as they stood in front of their
dark columns, waiting for the signal to mount the breach,
saw below them the holy city glowing ' like a great furnace,
half-extinct, but still surrounded by an atmosphere of
fire.' Suddenly the heavens were opened in wrath, and a

---

[1] For this chapter see maps, pp. 125, 210, above.
[2] *Hoff.* 271 ; *Dandolo,* 264.

deluge of rain fell on the disobedient children of the Pope, extinguishing their last poor little fires of joy. When the torrential storm had passed away, one light alone, from the top of the great dome of St. Peter's, still shone through the thick darkness, beckoning the crusaders to the assault.[1]

But the Italians watching on the Janiculum were in no humour for the child's play that amused their compatriots below. Scarcely more than four thousand now remained of the men under Garibaldi's command. Their reserve was posted on the central height of the Pino and San Pietro in Montorio; from that point to the Porta Portese the Trastevere quarter was lined with troops; the Villa Spada, which, though half in ruins, was still the headquarters, was strongly occupied by Manara and a part of his Bersaglieri; the battery near the Porta San Pancrazio was entrusted to the Garibaldian Legion, and to the remnant of Masina's cavalry, dismounted and armed with their lances for hand-to-hand fighting.[2]   Finally, a detachment of the Bersaglieri were marched off, under a blinding storm of rain and shells, into the Casa Merluzzo bastion, to defend the house and the open breach below it. 'The poor riflemen, buried to their knees in mud, struck down by the frequent and fatal descent of the bombs, took the perilous places assigned to them in silent discouragement.'[3]   Their leader was the boy-officer Morosini, perhaps the best-loved of all the Lombard youths who served in that regiment:

'Not yet eighteen years of age (wrote the sad survivor of that band of friends) his attractive, his angelic goodness had rendered him the model and the wonder of the whole battalion. Though he was the youngest of us all, we almost looked on him as our mentor, and were used to call him our guardian angel, so great was the unsullied purity of his conduct, and the unswerving rectitude of his principles, which he sought to instil and maintain uncontaminated in those who were his friends.'[4]

[1] *Bittard des Portes*, 364; *Vecchi*, ii. 293, 294; *Journal 16ᵉ*, 27; *Koelman*, ii. 212; *Torre*, ii. 262, 263.
[2] *Hoff.* 279–281; *Loev.* i. 261; *Torre*, ii. 262.
[3] *Dandolo.* 268.   [4] *Ibid.* 272.

To both sides the long delay in the attack caused by the storm seemed an unbearable suspense. At length, more than two hours after midnight, the French columns were let loose. The rain had stopped, but the night was dark as the grave. With the impetuous but ordered valour that had marked their conduct throughout the siege, the French rushed up the breach under a heavy fire from the Bersaglieri, stormed the Casa Merluzzo, and after a severe struggle overpowered the defenders of the bastion. Morosini, gravely wounded, was carried off in the darkness by four of his men, who hastened with him towards the Spada.[1]

Meanwhile a second column of French, starting from the Central Bastion captured ten days before, passed along the inside of the walls of Rome, leaving the Casa Merluzzo on their left, till they came to the line of the Aurelian wall, which they stormed at the point of the bayonet.[2] Once within the lines of defence, this second French column obeyed admirably, in spite of the darkness and confusion, the elaborate orders which it had received. One part wheeled to the right, turning the flank of the trenches along the Aurelian wall, and rushed towards the Spada; while another part went forward to the left to capture the battery beside the Porta San Pancrazio, the guns of which commanded the Casa Merluzzo, just captured by the first French column.[3]

The orders of the second column, which had thus penetrated the Roman line, were to give no quarter, and the orders were rigidly obeyed.[4] The four Bersaglieri who were carrying Morosini to the Spada, fell in with these new enemies, who disregarded their attempts to surrender.[5]

---

[1] *Vaillant*, 137 (134–136 for Oudinot's orders of attack; also printed in *Bittard des Portes*, 359–361); *Dandolo*, 270; *Bittard des Portes*, 367, 368; *Hoff.* 281–287.

[2] See map, p. 210, above.

[3] *Vaillant*, 134–136 (Oudinot's orders); *Bittard des Portes*, 360, 369–371; *Hoff.* 285.

[4] *Vaillant*, 134–136; *Bittard des Portes*, 360, 369–371.

[5] Probably rather because of the orders to give no quarter, than because, as *Dandolo* surmised, 'they suspected some ruse.' *Dandolo* does not seem to have

' Finding themselves again surrounded and their lives
threatened, rendered ferocious by the combat, they laid down
the litter, and attempted to cut their way through the ranks
of their opponents ; then, strange to say, the poor lad was seen
to rise, and stand erect on his bloody couch, grasping the sword
which had lain at his side. He continued to defend his already
ebbing life, until, struck a second time in the body, he fell once
more. Moved by the sight of so much courage, and such misfortune, the French conveyed him to their hospital in the
trenches.' [1]

There he lingered for a day, and died, moving his captors
in the hospital to tears, and impressing them, as he
always impressed those who saw him, with that rare
quality of saintliness which in every age is the natural
inheritance of some among the countrymen of St. Francis.
Oudinot himself was moved to write a letter recounting
these things to Morosini's mother, to whom and to his
sisters the boy had been wholly devoted. When urged not
to let him go to the war, she had answered : ' I give my
country the best I have, my only and dearly-loved son.' [2]
She had not bargained for his return. ' In such mothers
Italy revived.'

The detachment, which had given Morosini his final
wound, charged along the inside of the trenches, driving
before them all the Italians they found there, until pursuers and pursued dashed up against the garden gate of
the Spada, which Manara and his Bersaglieri turned out to
defend. Not being able in the darkness to tell friend from
foe, they reserved their volley until Hoffstetter could distinguish at a few yards the epaulettes which marked the
French uniform ; then the Bersaglieri fired with terrible
effect, and the French attack recoiled. [3]

Garibaldi himself was no longer in the Spada. Starting

known of their special orders to kill everyone, which I derive from French
sources only.

[1] *Dandolo*, 270-271 ; *Torre*, ii. 268.
[2] *Hoff.* 298, 299 ; *Dandolo*, 271, 280-284.
[3] *Vaillant*, 138, 139 ; *Hoff.* 282-284.

up at the first alarm, he had sprung out, sabre in hand, crying: *Orsù! Questa è l' ultima prova* ('Come on! This is the last fight ').[1] There was need of him outside, for the first onslaught of the French columns had put to flight many of the Italians, who were rushing about through the darkness in wild panic, while others were still desperately holding their own in small groups near the Merluzzo bastion and in front of the Savorelli.[2] At this crisis, when a disgraceful catastrophe was only too probable, Garibaldi and a few gallant men behind him flung themselves headlong on the victorious French, and checked their career. Inspired by the presence of their chief, the runaways turned back, and ' the last fight ' was worthy of the siege of Rome. ' I saw Garibaldi,' wrote Emilio Dandolo, ' spring forward, with his drawn sword, shouting a popular hymn.' In the thick of the *mêlée* he sang and struck about him with his heavy cavalry sabre, which next day was seen to be covered with blood. Behind him the red-shirts pressed into battle. Along the road in front of the Savorelli, and in the battery near the Porta San Pancrazio, Italians and French fought hand-to-hand, with primæval rage. In the last hour of darkness before dawn the whole space between the Pino and the city gate was a swaying mass of men killing each other with butt and bayonet, lance and knife, to the cries of ' *Viva l' Italia !* ' ' *Vive la France !* ' The cavaliers of Bologna, who had been Masina's comrades, and were for a short while his survivors, fought on foot among the guns of the battery until nearly all had perished. Next day the French Generals saw, with admiration and pity, the ground covered with the red pennons of the lances still grasped in the hands of the slain.[3]

On such a scene came up the golden dawn, and there in the fresh morning were Soracte, and Lucretilis, and the Alban Mount, again as of old.

---

[1] *Vecchi*, ii. 294 ; *Hoff.* 284.   [2] *Vaillant*, 139.
[3] *Vaillant*, 138-140, 145 ; *Dandolo*, 269, 270 ; *Hoff.* 284, 288 ; *Loev.* i. 261, 262 ; *Vecchi*, ii. 294 ; *Torre*, ii. 263, 264.

With the first light the Italians re-occupied the line of the
Aurelian wall and the road in front of the Savorelli ;[1] but
the French, with their admirable promptitude as engineers,
were already fortifying themselves round the Casa Merluzzo.   At these close quarters a furious cannonade and
musketry fire, varied by spasmodic charges of infantry,[2]
continued throughout the early morning. The French
batteries on the Barberini and Central Bastions and the
Corsini hill renewed their bombardment of the Spada and
Savorelli, while the fire of the infantry from the newly
captured bastion raked the Italian lines.   The defenders'
cannon, all except a few guns on the Pino, were now silent.
Most of them were lying overturned, among the corpses,
with their wheels broken, and the battery near the Porta
San Pancrazio was in the hands of the French.[3]   Seeing
that the city gate might be taken at any moment, Garibaldi
at last recalled Medici and his gallant comrades from the
ruins of the Vascello, which the army of France had failed
to take by assault.   Medici and his men retired into Rome
unmolested, and in perfect order.   So little was their spirit
broken that they took the chief part in a successful defence
of the Savorelli and of the northern bastion behind it,
which the enemy had breached but now assaulted in vain.[4]

The principal efforts of the French on the morning of
June 30 were, however, directed to make the Spada untenable ; and within its walls the tragedy of Manara and
his Lombard regiment was fulfilled.   The last scene in
the little villa must always be described in the words of
Emilio Dandolo, who, though not yet recovered from his
severe wound of June 3,[5] was taking his part in the defence :

'Villa Spada was surrounded ; we shut ourselves into the
house, barricading the doors, and defending ourselves from the

---

[1] *Vaillant*, 140, 141 ; *Précis Hist.* 80, ll., 2–6 ; *Dandolo*, 273.
[2] *E.g. Hoff.* 289–290.   [3] *Vaillant*, 144; *Hoff.* 288 ; *Dandolo*, 273.
[4] *Beghelli*, ii. 391, 392 (Medici's own narrative); *Torre*, ii. 266 ; *Vaillant*,
144, 147 ; *Pasini*, 112, 122.
[5] *Bertani*, i. 147.

VILLA SPADA, DEFENDED BY MANARA'S BERSAGLIERI, JUNE 30, 1849.

windows. The cannon-balls fell thickly, spreading devasta-
tion and death, the balls of the Vincennes chasseurs hissed with
unerring aim through the shattered windows. It is maddening
to fight within the limits of a house, when a cannon-ball may
rebound from every wall, and where, if not thus struck, you
may be crushed under the shattered masonry; where the air,
impregnated with smoke and gunpowder, brings the groans
of the wounded more distinctly on the ear, and where the feet
slip along the bloody pavement, while the whole fabric reels
and totters under the redoubling shocks of the cannonade.
The defence had already lasted two hours. Manara passed
continually from one room to another, seeking to reanimate the
combatants by his presence and words. I followed him, distracted by anxiety, having had no news from Morosini; a ball,
rebounding from the wall, wounded my right arm. " *Perdio!* "
exclaimed Manara, who was standing at my side, " Are you always
the one to be struck? Am I to take nothing away from Rome? "

' A few minutes afterwards he was standing at an open window,
looking through his telescope at some of the enemy who were
in the act of planting a cannon, when a shot from a carabine
passed through his body. "I am a dead man," he said, falling;
" I commend my children to you." The surgeon hastened to
his assistance. I looked inquiringly into his countenance, and,
seeing him turn pale, lost all hope. He was laid on a hand-
barrow, and, taking advantage of a momentary pause in the
firing, we passed through a broken-down window into the open
country.' [1]

Still, after their chief had been carried off to die, the
Bersaglieri continued the defence of the villa, till almost
everyone inside its walls, as well as Hoffstetter and Dandolo, had been wounded.[2]

Finally, when the ammunition was running low, Garibaldi headed a last desperate charge of his own Legionaries
and some of Pasi's line regiment against the French positions. Again, as on the night before, it was cold steel,
and again Garibaldi fought in the front, dealing death
with his sword, reckless of his life, and against all the
chances remaining unscathed.[3] The French could not

---

[1] *Dandolo*, 273-275.   [2] *Hoff.* 293-296.
[3] *Dandolo*, 278 ; *Vecchi*, ii. 295. Vecchi fought by Garibaldi's side in this

be dislodged; gradually the firing slackened. A truce was arranged at mid-day for the gathering of the dead and wounded, and Garibaldi was summoned to the Capitol, where the Assembly was discussing the question of surrender. Although the ruins of the Spada had not been stormed, all knew that Rome had fallen.[1]

Meanwhile Dandolo and his men had carried Manara to the rear.

'After many windings and turnings we reached the ambulance of Sa. Maria della Scala, where a hundred of the most severely wounded had been already placed, it being impossible to have them conveyed to a greater distance. The moment we arrived, Manara desired me to send for his Milanese friend, Dr. Agostino Bertani.'[2]

When the patriot doctor, who had done so much during the last fortnight to mitigate the wretched condition of the wounded in Rome, arrived by the death-bed of his friend, Manara exclaimed: 'Oh, Bertani, let me die quickly! I suffer too much.' No other complaint escaped his lips during the long hours of agony.[3]

'After having partaken of the Sacrament, he did not speak for a considerable time. His first words were to commend his sons again to my care. "Bring them up," he said, "in the love of religion, and of their country." He begged me to carry his remains into Lombardy, together with those of my brother. Perceiving that I wept, he said, "Does it indeed pain you so much that I die?" And, seeing that my suffocating sobs prevented my replying, he added, in an undertone, but with the holiest expression of resignation: "It grieves me also." . . .
'A short time before he died he took off a ring, which he

last action; so his evidence as to Garibaldi's personal conduct is not mere hearsay. See also *Dumas*, ii. 238-240, for whatever it is worth.

[1] *Vaillant*, 145; *Torre*, ii. 266, for the truce at noon-day. *Hoffstetter*, *Dandolo*, *Vecchi*, and *Paris MSS.* 20[e], p. 235, give rather different accounts as to the time of day when the last stray gun was fired, but clearly there was no real fighting after noon-day.

[2] *Dandolo*, 275.   [3] *Bertani*, 147; *Dandolo*, 277.

valued greatly, placed it himself on my finger, and then drawing me close to him, said "I will embrace your brother for you. *Saluterò tuo fratello per te, n' è vero?*" [1]

So Emilio Dandolo was left desolate in the world, like many another noble Italian that year. He had lost in one month the three men whom he loved—his brother Enrico, Morosini, and Manara. And he had lost his country. With a broken heart he wrote for posterity the story of his regiment, and dedicated it to the memory of his three friends. Then he endured, distracting himself as best he might, for ten years, till his country again began to stir for her next great effort, this time with the gallant French army on her side. In February 1859, when, in the captive cities of Italy, men with secret elation sniffed the breath of coming war, welcome as the scents of spring after a northern winter, Emilio Dandolo died. *Pro solitâ humanitate suâ*, death came when at length he was unwelcome. The great demonstration at Dandolo's funeral in Milan, in the face of the Austrians, who dared not interfere, was no unworthy national tribute to the last of the band of friends who had led the Lombard Bersaglieri to Rome.

But among the rank and file of that regiment were some whom, I think, we should pity yet more than Dandolo, if only we knew their story. After they had buried their chief, over whose grave the trumpets wailed, and Ugo Bassi, himself about to perish, spoke the funeral oration,[2] the regiment was in a few days' time disbanded. But the Lombards had no home to which to return; the Austrian ruled again in their native province, and as yet Victor Emmanuel dared not harbour many of them in Piedmont. So 'these unhappy exiles, driven out

---

[1] *Dandolo*, 276, 277. It is to be observed that these officers of the Lombard Bersaglieri were not prevented by their religion (though it was orthodox and not Mazzinian) from fighting against the Pope as Temporal ruler. In Garibaldi's Legion many of the men, like their chief, were free-thinkers, though they loved their chaplain, Ugo Bassi. Manara and Garibaldi represented the two sides of the Risorgimento, not only in politics but in religion. It was the union of these elements that made the cause national, and ultimately irresistible.

[2] *Hoff.* 308, 309; *Dandolo*, 283.

of Rome, condemned to beg their bread in the streets of Civitavecchia, were driven by despair either to enrol themselves in an African (French) regiment, or to give themselves up to the Austrians,' who were certain to flog, imprison, or shoot them as rebels and deserters.[1]

'Such then (says Dandolo) was the fate of the Lombard rifle brigade—a corps which was a model of discipline and of courageous endurance in misfortune. . . . Thus was it left, after so many perils and hardships, in such infamous neglect that the survivors were often heard to envy those who, by an honourable death on the battle-field, had escaped the still more cruel alternative of being scattered as miserable wanderers over the face of the earth.'[2]

To starve in the slums of foreign cities, or serve far off under a hated flag, while the country for which a man's best friends have died has fallen back into servitude, perhaps for ever, may appear a romantic fate in the retrospect, after Italy has been redeemed, but to the actual sufferers it was bitter as the lot of Andromache.

> ' Exile, what of the night ?
> The tides and the hours run out,
> The season of death and of doubt,
> The night watches bitter and sore.'

About mid-day on June 30, while Manara was dying in the hospital, Garibaldi was galloping across the Tiber to the Capitol, whither the Assembly of the Roman Republic had summoned him to attend its fateful session.[3] He rode in haste, for though the fighting had died away, he would not consent to be absent from his post longer than one hour. He had missed death in the battle, and his heart was bitter within him. To add to his misery, news had

---

[1] *Dandolo*, 183–185, 288, 289.

[2] *Dandolo*, 289. Some of the officers managed to reach Lugano in Switzerland, where Hoffstetter found them a few months later. *Hoff.* 308.

[3] Vecchi went with him. He is far the best authority on Garibaldi's words and actions during this day.

just been brought that his faithful negro friend, Aguyar, who had so often guarded his life in the perils of war, had been killed by a shell whilst walking across a street in the Trastevere. Garibaldi, who was far above base racial pride, and regarded all men as brothers to be valued each according to his deserts, had given his love freely to the noble Othello, who in body and soul alike far surpassed the common type of white man.[1] Sore at heart, and pre-occupied by bitter thoughts, he galloped up to the Capitol, dismounted, and entered the Assembly as he was, his red shirt covered with dust and blood, his face still moist with the sweat of battle, his sword so bent that it stuck half-way out of the scabbard. The members, deeply moved, rose to their feet and cheered, as he walked slowly to the tribune and mounted the steps.

They had sent to ask his advice on the three plans, between which, as Mazzini had told them in his speech that morning, they were now reduced to choose. They could surrender ; they could die fighting in the streets ; or, lastly, they could make their exodus into the mountains, taking with them the Government and army. This third plan was that which Garibaldi had for some days past been urging on the Triumvirate, and he now pressed the Assembly to adopt it, in a brief and vigorous speech.

He brushed aside the idea of continuing the defence of Rome. It could no longer, he showed them, be carried on even by street fighting, for the Trastevere must be abandoned, and the enemy's cannon from the height of San Pietro in Montorio could reduce the capital of the world to ashes. As to surrender, he does not seem to have discussed it. There remained the third plan—to carry the Government and army into the wilderness. This he approved. ' *Dovun-que saremo, colà sarà Roma* ' (' Wherever we go, there will be Rome '), he said. This was the part he had chosen for himself and for everyone who would come with him.

---

[1] *Vecchi*, ii. 295, 296 ; *Loev.* ii. 226, 227. Aguyar, like the traditional Othello of the stage, was called a Moor, but was a Negro. On Garibaldi's feeling as regards negroes in general, see Vecchi's *Caprera*, 65, 66.

But he wished to have only volunteers, and to take no one on false pretences. He declared that he could promise nothing, and very honestly drew for the senators a picture of the life of danger and hardship to which he invited them.

Altogether it was a wise and noble speech, for it put an end to all thought of bringing further ruin on the buildings of Rome, and at the same time offered a path of glory and sacrifice to those who, like himself, were determined never to treat with the foreigner on Italian soil. Having spoken, he left the hall and galloped back to the Janiculum.[1]

In the discussion that followed, Mazzini supported the proposal of Garibaldi. But to go out and perish was the part only of the few, and the Assembly did right when it refrained from adopting the exodus as an official programme. It passed the following resolution :

' In the name of God and the People :—
' The Constituent Assembly of Rome ceases from a defence that has become impossible and remains at its post.'

Mazzini protested against the decision, refused to participate in the surrender, and resigned, together with his two fellow triumvirs.[2]

One of the last acts of the Republican Assembly was to confer on Roselli and Garibaldi, jointly and separately, plenary power in the territories of the Roman Republic. Garibaldi always considered this decree to be in force during the next twenty years of papal usurpation.   In 1860,

[1] *Vecchi*, ii. 296; *Koelman*, ii. 233, 234; *Loev.* i. 263-267; *Camozzi, Vecchio*, 116; *Gabussi*, iii. 467, 468.   Gabussi, who saw and heard all at close quarters, and took notes of Garibaldi's speech, denies that Garibaldi declared that if he himself had been Dictator things would have gone better with the Republic. According to Gabussi, Garibaldi only said, ' Errors have been committed, but it is not a time for recrimination.'   Even that might well have been left unsaid.

[2] *Mazzini*, v. 209-214.   I see nothing inconsistent in Mazzini's refusal to go out with Garibaldi, after the Assembly had refused to adopt the plan of a general exodus of the Government.   If Mazzini had gone with Garibaldi merely as a private individual, there would have been little advantage as a matter of principle, and the strained relations with Garibaldi would have been a constant source of irritation to both men, and to the army also.

CAPTURED ROMAN BATTERY ON THE AURELIAN WALL.

Monte Testaccio and Protestant Cemetery to right and centre of middle distance. Alban Hills in distance. (WERNER.)

1862, and 1867, in the expeditions that ended at Naples, at Aspromonte, and at Mentana, he still regarded himself as a Roman general-in-chief, by a vote never superseded until the people chose Victor Emmanuel as their king. He was, therefore, always ready to act on occasion, as one having authority in any part of the Roman Republic still unredeemed by Italy.[1] As the years went by, and old age drew on, the office which he still held was ever present to his mind, at once as a legal formula binding him over to break the peace, and as a mystical summons to deliver Rome.

The French troops were to make their entry on July 3. Garibaldi had little left to do on the 1st and 2nd, except to hurry on his own departure. Every man was supposed to have free choice to go with the General or to stay, but the officers of most of the old papal regiments used pressure to keep back those under their command, and many soldiers, including some of Garibaldi's own Legion, were, against the wishes of their chief, forcibly detained in the castle of St. Angelo.[2] There were searchings of heart in Rome ; mothers, wives, and sweethearts strove to keep their men from going on an expedition which would reach no point of safety by advancing, and had no base on which to retreat. The motives were very various which induced some 4,000 Italians to start on the wildest and most romantic of all Garibaldi's marches. Many went to avoid the papal dungeons, some few hoped for opportunity to plunder, and some merely sought escort and company upon their way back towards their homes in the provinces. Others went out of anger at their country's wrongs, sharing the determination of their chief never to lay down arms to foreigners on Italian ground; others nourished a delusive hope that something might yet be done ; and more still were

---

[1] *Loev.* i. 267 ; *Rug.* 9. *Guerzoni*, ii. 51, proclamation of May 1860, signed 'G. Garibaldi, General of the Romans, appointed by a Government elected by universal suffrage'—(viz. in 1849). *Guerzoni*, ii. 550, *Mem.* 426 for 1867.

[2] *Rug.* 10 ; *Loev.* i. 272 ; *Bel.* 8.

ready to follow Garibaldi blindly to the world's end, asking not for victory, but to be allowed to be with him in life and death.

It was for love of Garibaldi that Swiss Hoffstetter yet awhile denied himself the happiness of returning to his free and peaceful Alps, and risked his life again for a country not his own, in a venture which he considered hopeless.[1] On the night of July 1, the eve of the departure, he dined with the General and his wife. Anita had by now made it clear that, in spite of her husband's earnest prayers and remonstrances,[2] she was coming with him on the march.

'She was a woman of about twenty-eight (Hoffstetter observed) with a very dark complexion, interesting features, and a slight delicate figure. But at the first glance one recognised the Amazon. At the evening meal to which the General had invited me, I could see with what tenderness and attention he treated his wife.'[3]

Next day Garibaldi met by appointment the soldiers who had volunteered to come with him. The scene fixed for the meeting was the Piazza of St. Peter's, the greatest of the open spaces in the city, lying in the shadow of the most famous church and palace in the world. It was filled by thousands upon thousands[4] of the inhabitants of Rome, come to say good-bye to their heroes. The whole space enclosed by Bernini's semicircular colonnade of gigantic pillars seemed paved with human faces. The crowd stood packed up to the very doors of the Vatican. In the middle

---

[1] *Hoff*. 307.

[2] *Mem*. 240. 'La mia buona Anita, ad onta delle mie raccomandazioni per farla rimanere, aveva deciso d' accompagnarmi. L' osservazione che io avrei da affrontare una vita tremenda di disagi, di privazioni e di pericoli framezzo a tanti nemici, era stata piuttosto di stimolo alla coraggiosa donna ed invano feci osservare ad essa il trovarsi in istato di gravidanza.' See also *Denkwürdigkeiten*, ii. 144, 145.

[3] *Hoff*. 309.

[4] *Bel*. 6, 7, gives the estimate of ten to twelve thousand. It is very difficult to count large crowds, but to judge from the description of the scene by Koelman, there could scarcely have been fewer and may well have been more.

were the troops, scarcely able to keep their footing, and
quite unable to keep their order, in that tossing ocean of
men and women gesticulating in wild excitement to ex-
press every form of conflicting emotion. Garibaldi had
not yet come, and all attention was centred on the volunteers who had undertaken to share his march. Mothers
were trying to pull their sons away ; youths of seventeen
and eighteen were breaking by force from their families
and trying to hide themselves in the ranks.[1] Suddenly a
roar of cheering was heard from the Borgo. All eyes
were turned towards the mouth of the narrow street
where the waving of hats and handkerchiefs showed that
it was he.

' In the midst of the swaying crowd which discharged itself
from the Via del Borgo on to the Piazza, we saw appear (says
Koelman) the black feathers of Garibaldi ; he was surrounded,
not by his staff officers (for they were seen scattered here and
there making efforts to reunite), but by citizens and women
who stormed him from all sides. He only managed slowly and
with difficulty to reach the Egyptian obelisk, that stands in the
middle of the Piazza. Here he stopped and turned his horse,
and when his staff had joined him, he gave a sign with his hand
to stop the cheers. After they had been repeated with double
force, there was a dead calm on the square.'

In that stillness after the tempest, the sonorous, thrilling
voice was heard almost to the outskirts of the vast crowd :[2]

' Fortune, who betrays us to-day, will smile on us to-morrow.
I am going out from Rome. Let those who wish to continue
the war against the stranger, come with me. I offer neither
pay, nor quarters, nor provisions ; I offer hunger, thirst, forced
marches, battles and death. Let him who loves his country
in his heart and not with his lips only, follow me.'

' *Fame, sete, marcie forzate, battaglie e morte*,' such was
the offer, and no more. Having so spoken and appointed

[1] *Koelman*, ii. 237, 238. He was present at the scene, and gives far the
best account of it.
[2] *Koelman*, ii. 238, 239.

the Lateran for the rendezvous of departure that evening,
he rode away again, as he had come, slowly through the
frantic and sobbing crowd. Above the upturned faces of
those broken-hearted men and women rose the calm, set
features of Garibaldi, resembling a perfect type of ancient
Greek beauty, and lit up with that serene and simple regard
of fortitude and faith which gave him power to lead the
feeble multitudes of mortal men, as though he were the sole
descendant of some fabled, god-like race of old.[1]

About six in the afternoon[2] another assembly, smaller,
sterner, and more business-like, was being held within the
Lateran gate. Garibaldi and his troops had found their
way thither across the Ponte Sant' Angelo, and past the
adored ruins of the Forum and Coliseum, which few of
them ever saw again. The open space round the Lateran,
where they now held the muster-roll, hard by the gate in
the ancient wall of the emperors, in full sight of the Campagna and the Alban Hills beyond, was the part of Rome
specially dedicated by its associations to the antiquity,
power, and terror of the mediæval Popes, whose *manes*
were once more driving out to chastisement and death
these children of a rebellious generation. There rose the
Lateran Palace, the residence of the Popes from the time
of Constantine till the migration to Avignon, during the
ten centuries of their greatest power, the spot from which
they had given law to the kings of Europe, and cast out
their shoe over remotest England and Germany. And
there rose that strange monument, the Triclinium of
Leo III., displaying in mosaic work, before the eyes of the
Garibaldian democrats, the forms of popes and emperors
kneeling together to receive from the divine powers the
insignia of their right to rule the world—the thousand
year old theory of mediæval Christendom which even in

---

[1] There are, of course, innumerable variants as to the precise form of words
(as, for instance, *sole* and *fredilo* for *fame* and *sete*). But the sense is essentially
the same. See *Guerzoni*, i. 331 ; *Bel.* 7, 8. It is from *Bologna MSS. Bonnet*
that I draw the first sentence, which *Belluzzi* also accepted.

[2] *Hoff.* 315.

its decline was still too strong for these rebels.[1] There, too, was the basilica church of San Giovanni in Laterano, ' *omnium urbis et orbis ecclesiarum mater et caput*,' on the top of whose façade towered that row of colossal statues, still one of the most imposing of the sky-signs of Rome, gigantic bishops and doctors of the ancient Church leaning forward to curse all heretics—figures not of love, but of terror, holding out threatening arms to tell man that he shall not be free.

Thus, in the enchanted grounds of their enemies, the little army formed itself and waited during the last hours of daylight for the word to march. Ciceruacchio was there, kind and jolly as ever, in plain clothes, riding beside his younger son, a boy of thirteen.[2] And there was friar Ugo Bassi, with his red shirt and crucifix ; the manuscript of a religious poem that he was writing was hung in a leather box round his waist, his long hair fell to his shoulders, and he was mounted on a spirited English horse which Garibaldi had given him so that he should be ever by his side.[3] Anita came, escorted to the spot by Vecchi.[4] She was mounted and dressed like a man, in the garb of the Legion, for her last campaign. In all there were some four thousand ready to start, mostly men of the volunteer regiments.[5] Conspicuous among the rest were the red Legionaries, of whom far the greater part were there, and a hundred or more of the Lombard Bersaglieri.[6] A few units of Masina's lancers who had survived June 30, and several hundred papal dragoons, some of whom had broken out from the stables where their officers had locked them

---

[1] See Bryce, *Holy Roman Empire*, chap. vii. 115 (ed. 1904).

[2] *Bel.* 10 ; *Bologna MSS. Piva.* His elder son, Luigi, aged twenty, who had murdered Rossi, was also in the expedition, dressed in a red shirt. *Bel.* 72, *R. I.* 1898, iii. 356–358.

[3] *Dwight*, 235 ; *Bel.* 10, 11, 71 ; *Bologna MSS. Piva.* The poem, called *La Croce Vincitrice*, related the martyrdom of the Christians under the heathen empire. *Venosta*, 25, 26.

[4] *Vecchi*, ii. 299. Vecchi himself did not go on the expedition.

[5] For various estimates of the numbers, ranging from 2,900 to 4,800, see *Hoff.* 319 ; *Rug.* 11 ; *Varenne*, 376 ; *Bel.* 9.

[6] *Rug.* 55.

in,[1] formed a small but, as it proved, a very efficient scouting force of cavalry.

Here, too, a large crowd of friends had come to see them off. Men were standing on carriages, and climbing on to each other's shoulders to get a glimpse of the sad review. At last, not before eight o'clock, the word to march was given, and the troops began to pass out gradually and in order under the ancient gateway, while the *addio* of those who were left behind sounded after them down the darkening road.[2]

When the rear of the column had vanished, and the last cries had died away in the night, many a man who had come to see the departure of the Garibaldians turned home with the sick feeling that they had chosen the happier lot. They were free, and they would soon be dead. But in Rome the priest, the spy, and the foreigner were the masters before whom all must tremble for long years to come. Even before the re-establishment of the papal authorities, the comparatively indifferent French caretakers, whose troops made their unwelcome entry into Rome on July 3, took steps towards the old system of delation and arrest, though at first with but little result. General Rostolan, named military governor of the conquered town,

institued a search (as we learn from his modern compatriot M. Bittard des Portes) for the most deeply compromised of the revolutionaries. The greater part escaped, thanks to the complicity of the Consular agents of England and the United States, who had always been our enemies, and who, under cover of their passports, enabled the principal chiefs of the Revolution to pass through the French lines · and avoid the Conseil de Guerre.[3]

The anger still shared by the clerical historians of to-day was loudly expressed at the time against the British Consular agent, Freeborn, who had, indeed, by a very wide

---

[1] *Koelman*, ii. 237.   [2] *Koelman*, ii. 242; *Hoff*. 315-317; *Rug*. 10.

[3] *Bittard des Portes*, 423. The French tried to search the house of the American Consul, Brown, for political refugees, but he met them on the stairs with a sword in one hand and the Stars and Stripes in the other. *Nelson Gay, N. A.* Feb. 16, 1907, pp. 661-662. *L' Italia e gli Stati Uniti.*

interpretation of his diplomatic privileges, issued several hundred of these passes. Even Lord Palmerston felt obliged to rebuke him for his noble fault.[1] But the fact that in Italy's darkest hour many of her best sons were saved from the dungeon or the scaffold by the representative of England, in a manner however little authorised, was one of the first links in the long chain of events that now began to bind together the two countries. Nor, in spite of clerical writers, does the France of our own day any longer regard England as an enemy because of her friendship to Italy and to freedom.

Mazzini for some days walked about the streets of Rome, as a private citizen, challenging the vengeance of a people over whom, according to his enemies, he had exercised so hateful a tyranny.[2] The French, knowing how much he was loved, dared not arrest him, though they were hunting in vain for the other leaders. After about a week he, too, fled, and found his way back to England, where he remained for the greater part of his long, sad life. 'Italy is my country,' he said, ' but England is my real home, if I have any.' Before the end he had grown actually to love the fogs and the hazy London atmosphere, in which the prophet seems to have found the sorrows and shortcomings of mankind more softened and bearable, than amid the hard, clear outlines revealed beneath the Italian sky.[3]

The restored Papacy, under the guidance of Antonelli, was no longer the half-liberal policy of Pio Nono's first years, but the old clerical *régime* of former Popes. Every vestige of representative government, every trace of institutions securing person and property against absolute power, was swept away ; the Liberal press was again silenced ; the spies, lay and clerical, were again let loose on the people ; the prisons and galleys were filled with those who had consented to serve the Republic. Some of the victims of

---

[1] *Johnston*, 314. The American *chargé d'affaires*, Mr. Cass, had offered a pass to Garibaldi among others. He refused it, but recorded the fact gratefully in his *Memorie*, 239.

[2] *Mazzini*, v. 214.   [3] *King's Mazzini*, 138-141.

the restoration had, like Ripari, been guilty of doctoring the wounded ; others belonged to the Moderate party, on whose behalf the French had pretended to interfere.[1]   The rulers soon turned against themselves those classes which had been hitherto comparatively loyal to the old order :

The inferior clergy were neither friendly to the Government nor its accomplices ; the population of the rural districts were discontented with the taxes, discontented with the foreigners who disarmed them, discontented with the police which gave them up as a prey to thieves.[2]

Farini, who, as a staunch Moderate, had been bitterly hostile to the Mazzinian Republic, wrote as follows to Mr. Gladstone in December 1852 :

The Government is, as formerly, purely clerical, for the Cardinal Secretary of State is the only real Minister ; Cardinals and Prelates prevail, if not in number, at any rate in authority, in the Council of State and in the Consulta of Finance ; Cardinals and Prelates govern the Provinces ; the clergy alone have the administration of all that relates to instruction, charity, diplomacy, justice, censorship, and the police.   The finances are ruined ; commerce and traffic at the very lowest ebb ; smuggling has sprung to life again ; all the immunities, all the jurisdiction of the clergy are restored.   Taxes and rates are imposed in abundance, without rule or measure.   There is neither public nor private safety ; no moral authority, no real army, no railroads, no telegraphs.   Studies are neglected ; there is not a breath of liberty, not a hope of tranquil life ; two foreign armies ; a permanent state of siege, atrocious acts of revenge, factions raging, universal discontent ; such is the Papal Government at the present day.[3]

This _régime_ differed in no essential point from that of Gregory XVI., except that it was maintained by foreign bayonets not only in the distant provinces, but in Rome itself, and that it stood no longer as a venerable though decayed relic of the nation's past, but as a tyranny reimposed by force on the ruins of a free Government and of a people's hopes.

[1] _Farini_, iv. 322-324 ; _Mazzini_, v. 236 ; _Loev._ ii. 264.
[2] _Farini_, iv. 317-318.   [3] _Ibid._ iv. 328.

CHAPTER XII[1]

THE RETREAT, I—ROME TO AREZZO—ESCAPE FROM THE FRENCH, SPANIARDS AND NEAPOLITANS

'As Garibaldi fortunately marched out of Rome to the South at the head of his six thousand partisans, who are hotly pursued by the First Division of the French, the worst enemies of the country will probably be annihilated.'

Times (Leading Article), July 10.

'There is a Mrs. Garibaldi; she went out with him to the Abruzzi. I hope the French won't cut them to pieces, but *vice versâ.*'

ARTHUR CLOUGH (Letter from Rome), July 6.

THE column of about four thousand[2] men who, with a train of waggons and one little cannon, set out at nightfall of July 2, from under the Porta San Giovanni, had need to be across the low ground before daylight. Next morning must see them twenty miles away in some defensible post on a spur of the Sabine hills, no longer exposed in the open Campagna to the attack of the foreign soldiers who had so kindly made it their business to 'annihilate the worst enemies of the country.'

Every precaution had been taken by a chief who was a master of the art of night marches. He sent out the cavalry to scout through the darkness for the French columns, in front, rear, and flank, round the walls of Rome and along the numerous roads diverging in all directions over the plain. The infantry marched in silence at the top of their speed; the officers whispered their orders; the consolations of the cigar (that friend so treacherous in the darkness) were forbidden to the fugitives.[3] Now and

---

[1] For this Chapter see map p. 141 above, and map at end of book.

[2] Compare *Hoff.* 319; *Rug.* 11; *Bel.* 9. (Figures given by *Varenne*, 376, apparently refer to period after junction with Forbes.)

[3] *Hoff.* 318.

again a tomb of some ancient Roman, or a line of ruined
aqueduct, hove dimly in sight, and vanished like a ghost.
Hour after hour went by, and still they plodded on through
the veiled, silent Campagna. The least melancholy, perhaps, were those who were dreaming of home, hoping that
the column would pass by their native town, wondering
how easy it would be to slip out of the ranks, how the
family would receive the returned hero or prodigal, and
how much the priest would ask and suspect. Others
questioned death, whether it would seem bitter to them,
wounded and alone, high on the barren mountains. To
some who would gladly face the firing party, the prospect
of the Austrian rods, the Papal dungeons, had terrors.
But many, besides Bassi and Anita, had no thought save for
Italy, or for the safety of their chief. Garibaldi himself
revolved the vision of Venice, of brave Manin still at bay
among its lagoons, of the perilous road that led thither
by land and sea. And all had Rome to remember, what
men and things they had seen there. The Pole Müller
and the Brazilian Bueno—courageous mercenaries trusted
by the Chief—as they galloped to and fro among the cavalry
that night, were each, it is to be feared, already asking
himself how much longer it was worth while to serve a
fallen cause, a hunted outlaw, and how much gold the
enemy would give for betrayal. And so, each man searching
in the depth of his own heart, that strange army moved
in silence towards the hills.

Along a line stretching for several miles southward
from Tivoli, the Sabine mountains rise steeply out of the
Campagna, and the barrier which they here present to the
plain is clothed in a great forest of olives, that glittered
in the rising sun as the tired Garibaldians straggled up
the ascent. They reached Tivoli at seven in the morning
of July 3.[1] Of all the ancient and beautiful cities set upon

[1] The route followed from Rome to Tivoli is not certain, but probably it was
by Zagarolo. The evidence to that effect given by *Bel.* 210 is insufficient ; but, as
Major de Rossi writes to me, ' Militarily considered, the march to Zagarolo was
the only one which could have really deceived Garibaldi's enemies ' into thinking

hills, under the walls of which they camped during the next four weeks, none is more beautiful and few are more ancient than Tivoli, the *Tibur* chosen by Horace for the seat of his old age, shining above many groves and waters. For here the riotous Anio makes one leap of it from the mountain to the plain, and the trees and gardens hanging on the precipice beneath the Temple of the Sibyl are kept green by the spray and resonant with the thunder of the eternal fall. It is one of the few places in the Apennines where there is a sense of abundance of water, and where the lush verdure of a moist bank is added to all the native beauties of Italy. Above it perches the old town with its towers set to watch distant Rome. After their long night march, Garibaldi granted his men a day of sleep and recuperation among the olive-groves, terraces and gardens outside the southern gate of Tivoli,[1] where they could sleep in the shade, or gaze out over the Campagna fading indistinguishably into sea and sky beyond, with the dome of St. Peter's clearly visible, afloat above the misty distance. Looking back over this great expanse, they could see that they had given the enemy the slip, and that no army was moving after them from Rome. During this first bivouac, made sweeter by the enthusiastic and inquisitive friendship of the townspeople, and by scenes of loveliness and repose so strangely contrasted with their real situation, their Chief took stock of his position and decided on his course.

In the strange campaign which Garibaldi had now undertaken, immortalised in Italian history under the title of ' the Retreat from Rome,' he was guided by one principle, in accordance with which he pursued two military objects. The principle was never to capitulate to the foreigner on Italian soil. Of his objects, the first was to rouse the populations of Central Italy to war; the second was to

that he had gone to the Alban Hills. And such was their belief next day in Rome. (See p. 242 below.)

[1] It was just outside the Porta Santa Croce, where the tramway from Rome now ends. (*Hoff.* 318 ; *Bel.* 15 ; *Bologna MSS., Coccanari.*)

get into Venice and join Manin, before the famous siege, already nine months old, should be brought to its inevitable close.   Circumstances would decide for him which of these plans he could pursue with any chance of success.   On July 3, when he still required to be taught by experience the utter impossibility of the first plan, he determined to move northward from Tivoli, into Umbria, Tuscany, and the Romagna, because, although the Austrian armies were in occupation of those districts, the inhabitants were, in his opinion, more likely to rise than those of Naples or the Abruzzi.[1]   And such a course was at least not taking him away from Venice.

In whatever direction he had turned he would have been met and pursued by hosts of enemies.   All the hunters were out to catch the lion.   In Tuscany and the Papal States alone there were some 30,000 French, 12,000 Neapolitans, 6,000 Spaniards, 15,000 Austrians, and 2,000 Tuscans, who had no other enemy to contend with, and no other operation on hand but the chase of Garibaldi.   At Tivoli, on July 3, he was fairly in the middle of all these armies. To the North, the bulk of the Austrians were concentrated at Florence, with their faces turned in his direction ; a powerful body lay at Perugia ; another at Ancona on the Adriatic, and smaller garrisons of white-coats occupied all the coast towns whence he might have embarked his army for Venice.   To the East, besides this seaboard watch, there were Austrians at Ascoli and at Macerata in the Marches, and Neapolitans close at hand at Aquila. To the South, there was the main body of Neapolitans at Frosinone ; while the Spaniards, whose equipment and quality had surprised and pleased the reactionary courts at Gaeta, were already moving from Velletri to Valmontone to cut him off if he turned to Naples or the Abruzzi.[2]   To the West were the French in Rome, sending

---

[1] *Mem.* 241.   'Mossomi da Tivoli verso tramontana, per gettarmi tra populazione energiche e suscitarne il patriottismo . . .'
[2] See *D'Ambrosio, Kriegsbegebenheiten, Mittheilungen,* and *De Rossi,* 10, 11.

out expeditions against him, though fortunately in wrong directions.

To penetrate through so many armies, flushed with conquest and confident in numbers, Garibaldi had 4,000 men, of whom a good half were seeking home and safety rather than those fresh battles which their leader and the stalwarts had come out to seek. Every night there were desertions by the score, at first even by the hundred; and of those who remained together, it may be doubted whether as many as 2,000 had any real heart left for giving and taking blows, after the fight to a finish in which they had just taken part in Rome. This army, if it can so be called, was badly equipped, badly armed, and possessed eighty rounds of ammunition per man.[1] Far the greater part of Garibaldi's best officers had been killed or wounded, or had declined to come on the hopeless expedition.[2] As to the rank and file, his force was made up of handfuls of men from different bodies, whom he brigaded together in two provisional regiments at Tivoli. He could not therefore wish to fight a pitched battle with any large body of French or Austrians, since disaster would be the not improbable result, and even in case of success the hunted army would be obliged to leave its wounded behind.[3]

Under such conditions it is doubtful whether any other leader in the world could have penetrated right through the immense hosts of the enemy, and reached the Romagna and the Adriatic coast. Such a feat was rendered possible only by the peculiar arts of war which Garibaldi had learnt and developed for himself in South America, and by the vigour and mobility with which he managed to endow his motley force. After a few days he changed the waggons for beasts of burden, so that he could, when necessary, leave the roads and range the bare Apennines in any direction at will. From the first he adopted his South American custom of making the food of the army walk, in the shape of driven cattle. Marches of irregular length, by day and by night; the camp broken up at uncertain and unexpected

[1] *Hoff.* 319.   [2] See list, pp. 325, 326 below.   [3] *Hoff.* 402.

R

hours, often at sunset ; the feint, when in the presence of the
enemy or of the public, shortly followed by some unseen
turn in another direction ; the elaborate means by which
he set afoot rumours exaggerating his numbers, and the
genuine fear that his red-shirts still inspired by their reputation for hard fighting ; above all, his use of cavalry—the
perfect system of scouting which kept him informed of
what the enemy was doing scores of miles away, and the
moving screen of horsemen with which he bewildered the
minds of the opposing Generals as to his own position and
movements—these were the means by which he carried
his army through from Rome to San Marino.

In such a system, the cavalry were the most active arm.
They were always on the move in numerous detachments,
often ten, twenty or thirty miles away from the column.
The ex-Papal dragoons were, in fact, taught by Garibaldi,
and by the officers of his school, to play the part of
the American *gauchos*, and became, for all scouting and
masking purposes, vastly superior to the regular European
cavalry of that decade.   Ill-equipped, they were fortunately well mounted, and though they would scarcely have
withstood the shock of a French or Austrian charge of
horse, as scouts they completely deceived, outrode and
outwitted their slow-moving enemies.[1]

In the night march from Rome, Garibaldi had so covered
up the traces of his flight to Tivoli that Oudinot, believing
him to have gone to the Alban Hills, next day ordered
General Mollière to take a division after him in that direction.   Mollière started on the morning of the 4th, still
under the impression that he would find, near Albano,[2]
the man who had never gone there at all, and who was at

---

[1] *De Rossi*, 110, and *passim*, on this, the most important military aspect of
the retreat.   No one should pronounce judgment on Garibaldi as a soldier until
he has read *De Rossi*.   *General Saletta* fully endorses his opinions.   See also
Rug., *Bel.*, *Hoff* 319 and *passim*, Cadolini, *N.A.* (1902), 319.   *De Rossi*
regrets that the methods of employing cavalry were so much more antiquated in
the regular Italian army in 1866 than those of Garibaldi in 1849.

[2] *Paris MSS.* 20°, 236 ; 33°, 217 ; *Bittard des Portes*, 408–410.

that moment on the other side of the Campagna, racing
away from Tivoli over the lower slopes of Lucretilis towards
Monte Rotondo and the Tiber.[1]   For the great north road up
the Tiber valley, left open to the guerilla chief by the inaction
of the French Generals whom he had duped, would set him
on his way to Terni, the town best situated for the maturing
of his plans, where, moreover, he could join hands with the
last detachment of the Republic's provincial army, lying
there under the Englishman Forbes.   He had therefore to
strike westward from Tivoli onto the Terni road through
Monte Rotondo, and he must effect this movement while
persuading his enemies that he had started eastward into
Neapolitan territory.   The operation of carrying his army
from Tivoli to Monte Rotondo so swiftly and secretly that
no one in Rome found out for several days what had
happened, was the more difficult because the spurs of
Lucretilis which he had to cross were exceedingly mountainous, and the direction of the march ran athwart that
of the principal roads, all of which led to Rome.   It was
an operation of the most dangerous kind, for if the French
had got wind of his return westward they could have
poured out from Rome along any of those roads with
great rapidity, and so taken his column in flank.

For this reason, Garibaldi began his march to Monte
Rotondo with a feint in the opposite direction.   The friendly
inhabitants of Tivoli, and the clerical spies among them,
saw the Garibaldians march off before sunset on the 3rd,
by the main road leading to Vicovaro, in the direction
of Neapolitan territory.   At nightfall they encamped
somewhere off this road, but not far from Tivoli.[2]   The
report, therefore, spread far and wide, and was believed
by the French, Spanish, and Neapolitan Generals, that
Garibaldi had started for the Abruzzi.   But before daylight
next morning (July 4) his column secretly turned back to
the west and crossed by a mule-track over a high spur of

· It is essential that the reader should follow the map, p. 141, above.
[2] *Hoff.* 326, 'nahe bei Tivoli,' not near Montecelio, as *Bel.* 22 suggests.

Lucretilis, through the mountain village of San Polo dei Cavalieri, which

> 'Like an eagle's nest, hangs on the crest
> Of purple Apennine.'

A more extraordinary march can hardly be imagined for an army burdened, as they still were, with waggons. The peasants told them that no wheeled carriage could pass that way at all, and such is the first impression left on anyone who walks over the route. But Garibaldi, who, after his custom, had visited San Polo the day before, while his men were resting at Tivoli, had decided that it could be done, and so, with much cursing and shoving, the waggons were hoisted to the top of the mountain and down again on to the Campagna.[1]   After that the worst difficulties were over.   But there was still no good road leading westward to Monte Rotondo, and the mass of Lucretilis towered grey above the heads of the infantry, as they struggled along over the broken ground at its feet through the vineyards and olives that surround the hill-villages of Montecelio and S. Angelo, and afterwards on to Mentana across an open stretch of desert ground.   Meanwhile the cavalry scouted over the lower Campagna, nearer to Rome, whence, if Oudinot got wind of what they were doing, the supreme danger would come.[2]   At last, towards noon, the infantry passed through the long street of Mentana, which then meant no more to Italy and to Garibaldi than any other poverty-stricken village within twenty miles of Rome.

---

[1] *De Rossi*, 12–14; *Hoff.* 328. The route followed from Tivoli to Montecelio is not exactly described by Hoffstetter or by any authority except Gaetano Sacchi (commander of one of the two divisions formed at Tivoli). Sacchi's notes are now in the possession of Maggiore de Rossi, and are the basis of much of that officer's narrative. The description given by *Hoff.* 328 of the difficulties encountered on the morning of July 4, and the incredulity of the peasants as to the practicability of the route, bears out Sacchi's authoritative statement that they went by Casale Ottati and San Polo. (*De Rossi*, 12–14.) We have, besides, to account for the strong and universal impression of Garibaldi's enemies that he had marched from Tivoli into the Abruzzi. If he had not started out of Tivoli up the Anio he could not have set this rumour afloat; and if he started that way he could have reached Montecelio only by San Polo.

[2] *De Rossi*, 14.

Leaving there his rear-guard, he himself camped with the front division at the fine old hill-town of Monte Rotondo-which dominates the Tiber valley. Here he spent the evening of his forty-second birthday. From the grounds of the monastery, where he took up his quarters just outside the town walls, he could see Rome, and the dome of St. Peter's shining in the sunset, and there Hoffstetter watched him as he stood gazing at it in motionless, speechless sorrow and longing, while, from a neighbouring vineyard, a boy was singing 'one of those yearning melodies peculiar to Italy.'[1] Garibaldi may well have thought that it would be his last view of Rome, for though he never despaired of the ultimate liberation of his country, he could scarcely have felt confident on that summer evening that he himself, ringed round as he was by enemies, would live to see the vintage.

Next morning (July 5) the army marched off, passing beside the old gate of Monte Rotondo, which long afterwards Garibaldi burst open when he stormed the town eight days before the battle of Mentana. As the cavalry had by now reported that there were no French coming out from Rome, and that the way to Terni was open, the column boldly entered the great road, and proceeded by it northwards, up the left bank of the Tiber.

None of Garibaldi's enemies had learnt of his march to Monte Rotondo—so effective had been his feint in the wrong direction when he left Tivoli on the evening of the 3rd. The Spaniards, having heard that he had gone from Tivoli up the Anio into the Abruzzi, had started from Valmontone on the previous morning over the steep Sabine ridges, and, after a magnificent day's march, in which their hemp sandals must have assisted these hardy mountaineers, dropped down into the valley of Subiaco on the evening of the 4th, at an hour when Garibaldi, who had gone that day in a direction so unexpected, was gazing at Rome from Monte Rotondo. On the morning of the 5th, again deceived as to the road taken by the heretics, the indefatig-

[1] *Hoff.* 329.

able crusaders set off from Subiaco northwards for Rocca
Sinibalda, with a rapidity of movement in difficult ground
which far surpassed that of the French and Austrians in
this campaign. On July 5-6, while Garibaldi was marching to Poggio Mirteto on the road to Terni, the Spaniards
pushed as far as Rieti, unwittingly travelling by a line
parallel to his route and rather in advance of his column.
Thus it was entirely owing to his *ruse de guerre* at the
moment of leaving Tivoli, that they were not now falling on
him in the Tiber valley, but were trudging along, some
fifteen miles away on his right flank, on the other side
of the mountain range. The Spaniards for three days
(July 4-6) marched as well as the Garibaldians themselves,
but as their scouting was inferior, they failed to use the
chances which their energy secured to them.[1]

Deceived by the same stratagem of the feigned march
into the Abruzzi, Oudinot passed July 5 and 6 in complete
ignorance that Garibaldi had come back to the Tiber Valley.
When he discovered his mistake, it was only to fall into
another—namely, to suppose that Garibaldi had marched
from Monte Rotondo across the Tiber towards the west
coast. This deception had also been carefully arranged by
his antagonist, who had sent Müller and fifty horsemen from
Monte Rotondo to make a demonstration in the direction
of Viterbo ; they swam the Tiber and rode through all the
region round the Lago Bracciano, to spread the false news
that Garibaldi was coming that way.[2] These rumours,
which even asserted that he was threatening Civitavecchia,
so far deceived Oudinot that, instead of sending men up the
Tiber, he sent General Morris, on July 7, to find Garibaldi
in the region west of Lago Bracciano. The French marched
first by the sea-coast as far as Corneto, and only then
turned inland.[3]

---

[1] *De Rossi*, 15, 16, 18 ; *Military Events*, 321 ; *D'Ambrosio*, 67.

[2] *Hoff.* 329 ; *De Rossi*, 14.

[3] *Bittard des Portes*, 412. From the *Historiques* ; I do not think this
deviation to Corneto, due to Garibaldi's skill in disseminating false reports of his
movements, has been noticed by Italian writers.

Having thus thrown his pursuers off the scent, by a strategic feat comparable in design and execution to the great march by which, at the supreme crisis of his life, he effected his entry into Palermo in 1860, Garibaldi moved northwards, unmolested, from Monte Rotondo to Terni. On the 5th he followed the main road, first along the flat Tiber bank, and then over desert hills towards Poggio Mirteto, with Mount Soracte close in view all day across the river. Since he had determined to march through the following night, the troops were halted at noon for a siesta of seven hours, in a cool, wooded valley, beside a 'great stone bridge.'[1] Here the soldiers bathed in the river, and here they slaughtered eight of the twenty oxen which they were driving with them; the flesh was roasted Homerically on green spits plucked from the trees around, with culinary results which delighted Hoffstetter, new to these South American customs. Meanwhile Anita sat under a rock, smiling and talking cheerfully with Garibaldi, Ugo Bassi, Ciceruacchio and the staff. On these occasions she worked at a tent which she was making for herself, while Garibaldi spoke with hope and courage of better times to come, and told stories of their adventures in South America. The stirring tale of Anita's escape from her captors, and lonely ride through the Brazilian forest to rejoin her husband, he repeated in her presence to this circle of friends, made more dear to each other by the recent loss of so many comrades in Rome, and by the shadow of their own approaching doom.[2]

During the night of the 5th to 6th they marched up into

[1] The account of the place in *Hoff.* 331 does not exactly suit either Passo Corese or the Ponte Sfondato over the Farfa, a tributary of the Tiber; yet it must be one of these two places. From observations on the spot I incline to think that it was the latter, and this idea also occurred to *Belluzzi* (see his *Note-book*) when he visited the places. The Ponte Sfondato is in a wild, narrow, rocky, and wooded valley, and Hoffstetter might well call it a 'great stone bridge,' for it is the living rock through which the Farfa torrent has burrowed its way, hastening down to the Tiber. They certainly passed over it, whether they camped there or not.

[2] *Hoff.* 327, 331, 332, 337, 339, 340; *Bel.* 23, 24. For the story see p. 33 above. *Rug.* 13.

the vine-covered hills as far as the remote town of Poggio Mirteto, near which they encamped among a friendly population.[1] On the 7th, a day of great heat, they started in the morning twilight and made a long march, first over hills of vine and olive, then across an empty river-bed and past a dried-up fountain at Vacone, up a long pass, by a road skirting the bottom of the wild evergreen forests that variegate the grey mountains above. Those who have walked along these roads from fountain to fountain will realise what the army must have suffered when half the usual springs were dry. At last, after a day of unquenched thirst, the fortunate vanguard came to the roadside fountain below Confine, whose waters are caught in a series of long troughs, where men and horses drank together in crowds— so long that evil effects were expected. But they slept all the better for that draught on the top of the pass among the scattered oak-copses, below the hamlet of Confine, and next day dropped into the broad vineyard-clad plain of the Nar, and entered Terni amid the rejoicings of the population. The Spaniards, who ought to have attacked them there, remained inactive near Rieti, in close touch with the division of Neapolitans coming up from Aquila, and utterly deceived as to Garibaldi's movements by the Italian cavalry outposts who were set to watch and bewilder them.[2]

Having reached Terni, and there effected his union with the 900 men under Colonel Forbes, Garibaldi had done all that was possible. And yet he was bitterly disappointed. It grieved him sorely, though it did not surprise others, that even in the friendly towns no recruits would join the forlorn hope, and that desertions were constant. He found European soldiers wanting in hardihood, for he judged them by comparison with the half-civilised *gauchos* and horse-breakers of Rio Grande and Uruguay :—

' In my own heart ' (he wrote of these first days of the retreat) ' I often recalled the steadfast endurance and self-abnegation

[1] *MS. Poggio Mirteto.* Henceforward consult map at end of book.
[2] *De Rossi*, 16, 109 ; *Bel.* 25, 26 ; *D'Ambrosio*, 67, 68.

of those Americans among whom I had lived, who, deprived of
every comfort of life, content with any kind of food, and often
with none at all, kept up a war of extermination for many years
in deserts and forests, rather than bow the knee to a tyrant or
a foreign invader.' [1]

The child of the Ocean and the Pampas now for the
first time realised the physical limitations of the ordinary
inhabitant of Europe, the idealist was reading hard fact,
and the sanguine patriot was discovering that all Italians
were not of the same temper as the best, and that his
countrymen were not the race of impossible warrior-heroes
of whom he had dreamed for a dozen years in the American
wilderness. But he showed no outward sign of dishearten-
ment or of rage ; to his followers he was all dignity, kindness and courage, and as they watched him riding ' grave
and quiet' past the monuments of antiquity along the
deserted roads of the Roman States, many felt the greatness of the time, the country and the man, nor would they
have changed, for a more commonplace and hopeful expedition, their armed pilgrimage through Italy under this strange
leader to some unknown fate beyond the mountains.[2]

Though half his army served him splendidly on the
retreat, he had much to embitter him. Most of those who
stole away at night left their muskets behind and went
innocently back to their homes[3] ; but some were thieves,
who took with them their horses and arms, and went about
in small bands requisitioning and robbing in the name of the
chief whom they had deserted, and the cause which their
conduct disgraced.[4]

It may be well here to inquire what was Garibaldi's own
system of treating the various classes of inhabitants on his
passage, and what was his method of provisioning the
troops who remained under him during the July of 1849.
It was a difficult problem, for he had no base and no

[1] *Mem.* 241.   [2] *Hoff.* 348, 349.
[3] *Rug.* 16 ; *Mem.* 241.
[4] *Rug.* 17 ; *Bel.* 50-52 ; *Military Events*, 328, 329 ; *Mem.* 244 ; *Farini*,
iv. 233.

supplies, and his war-chest only contained the now value-less paper-money of the slain Republic.   He solved it by taking loans and requisitions of food from almost every town or large village near which he camped, acting in his right as General of the Republic with plenary powers. The municipal bodies and the townsmen gladly gave their wealth for the use of the men, who, as they felt, were acting as their proxies in patriotism ; if they were sparing of their own blood, they were not niggardly of their money for the national cause, even now when all was lost.   Sometimes, indeed, the municipality registered a touching claim for repayment in years to come, when Italy should be free. The monasteries, on the other hand, paid their shares most unwillingly, being on the other side in politics, and ex-pecting anything rather than reimbursement under future Liberal governments.[1]

By means of these loans the Garibaldians were able to pay the peasantry for everything which they took on the road, and the General enforced this rule by the only effective means : ' The soldiers feared, as well as loved him, for they knew that he would order them to be shot without taking his cigar out of his mouth.' [2]   The oxen which they drove with them, having been bought from *contadini*, had been paid for, cash down.[3]   And so, in effect, Garibaldi made the towns and the monasteries pay the tillers of the soil for what he needed to take.   It was a just distribution of the burden, because the poorest suffered the least, and his con-duct in this respect is the more to be commended, since the *contadini* in the outlying districts, unlike the townspeople, were hostile to the national cause, and sometimes turned out under the leadership of priests and Sanfedists to cut off the stragglers.[4]   But Garibaldi would not rob the poor, merely because they were misled.

The only criticism that could be made of this system of

---

[1] *Hoff.* 323, and *passim* ; *Bel.* 35, 73, 74, 96, 97, and *passim* ; *Bolsi* ; *Bologna MS. Cetona.*
[2] *Hoff.* 333 ; *Bel.* 27–29.
[3] *Hoff.* 331 ; *Bel.* 63, 125.   [4] *Rug.* 29.

maintaining the war was its heavy incidence on the religious communities. In that respect he showed himself, not the bandit, but the Revolutionary soldier. His men, says one who witnessed the retreat, 'were excellent towards private individuals, and scrupulously paid for whatever they took from the peasants, but were in like degree hostile and fatal to the monasteries.'[1] This was true, at least in the sense that while the lay townsmen paid their quotas willingly, the religious corporations had often to be forced to reveal their hidden wealth. But these inquisitions were not roughly conducted, and were sometimes made palatable by kindly chaff; in a dispute over the alleged resources of a monastery at Castiglione Fiorentino, a bottle of Vino Santo, judiciously fetched up from the cellar, induced the Garibaldian officer to take his pen and write 150 *scudi* for 200, and crack a good-natured joke, which the monk recorded in his diary.[2]

The other grievance of the religious was that Garibaldi generally quartered his men in their grounds, because he preferred, for the better discipline of his troops, to camp outside the walls of the friendly towns, on some neighbouring eminence, either in an olive grove, or, by preference, among the cypresses and laurels of the garden of the local San Francesco, of which also the cool cells and cloisters were in much request at mid-day halts. The behaviour of the troops in the monasteries was not bad upon the whole. Only in one place was there looting of convents on the retreat, and nowhere any personal violence.[3] Indeed, the relations, though strained, were courteous,[4] except on occasions when the men of religion fired from their windows or loosed the mastiffs on their unwelcome guests, or when

[1] *Bologna MS., Manfredini.*

[2] See the monk's own story, in *Bolsi.* The officer, pocketing the 150, said with a laugh : ' *Ah frate! cinquanta scudi hai, ma gli hai specolati con una bottiglia di Vino Santo.*' ' Il Padre Ugo Bassi,' ' dressed like an officer,' then confessed himself to one of the fraternity. A *scudo* = 5 *lire* (*Bel.* 220).

[3] For conduct at Citerna see *Magherini*, 27 ; *Bel.* 123.

[4] The statements in this paragraph are deduced from scores of individual incidents recorded in *Bel.* (*e.g.* 39, 61), *Hoff.*, and the *Bologna MSS.* (See also *Rug.* and *Bolsi.*)

the lean red-shirts seasoned their repast in the refectory by lecturing the brothers on their life of ease and want of patriotism.[1]

While the French had been accomplishing the reduction of the capital, the Austrians had destroyed the provincial armies of the Republic, of which the last remnant, under Colonel Hugh Forbes, was stationed at Terni, on July 8, when Garibaldi entered the town. The Forbes family were British citizens, resident in Tuscany; Forbes, who had begun his military career more than twenty years before in the British Coldstream Guards, now a spare, grizzled man of forty, had taken the field on behalf of Italian freedom. He had served first the Venetian and then the Sicilian rebels during the past twelve months, and now he and his boy were in Terni, quarrelling with its citizens, who found the Colonel too arbitrary. Hugh Forbes was *italianissimo* but not *simpatico*—at any rate, not to the people of Terni. Garibaldi's arrival restored concord, and the soldiers of both armies fraternised with each other and with the citizens in a grand *festa* of the Italian tricolor. Forbes and his men now became part of the column of retreat, and Garibaldi soon learnt to admire, as a ' most courageous and honourable soldier,' ' the eccentric Briton,' who cared so little about the garniture of war, that he went through the campaign in the summer suit and white chimney-pot hat of his class and country.[2]

But the 900 men, who had only in the last few weeks been committed to the charge of Forbes, were not all of the same kidney as their officer. When the rest of the Republican regiment, of which they had formed a part, disbanded on the news of the fall of Rome, these soldiers, who were chiefly Swiss and other ex-Papal troops and employees, remained in arms, but not entirely out of

[1] *Rug.* 17–19, notes; monasteries some miles north and west of Todi.
[2] See App. N., below, *Hugh Forbes*; also *Hoff.* 342, 414; *MS. F.O. Papers*; *Bel.* 30–34, 230; *Vecchi*, ii. 315; *Ovidi*, 127; *Bologna MS. Piva*; *Mem.* 241 : *De Rossi*, 7, note. Neither Hugh Forbes nor his son is identical with Capt. C. S. Forbes, R.N., author of the *Campaign of Garibaldi*, 1861.

patriotic enthusiasm, for they were subsequently distinguished on the retreat for the rapidity with which many of them deserted, in order to pillage the country in the name of Garibaldi. Since a large number of the men whom he had led from Rome to Terni remained behind in the town, he cannot be said to have quitted it with his strength seriously increased.[1]

More than twenty-four hours were spent at Terni, while the troops were rested and reorganised, and while the arms abandoned by the deserters were disposed of to local patriots who could be trusted to secrete them, be it for months or for years, until another wave of revolution should sweep over the Papal States. Before leaving the town, Garibaldi had, moreover, to determine once for all the direction in which he was going to break away. For Terni was the central point on which his enemies were converging from three sides. The Austrians at Perugia were sending out forces towards Foligno and Spoleto ; the Spaniards still occupied Rieti, backed by the Neapolitans at Città Ducale ; the French, under Morris, were at last turning inland from Corneto towards Civita Castellana and Viterbo. But since Garibaldi's energetic cavalry so imposed on the Spaniards and on the Austrians as to check their advance, and at the same time kept their chief informed of the movements of the French, he was at leisure to decide on his direction, and determined to go north-west into Tuscany before the French should block his route thither by seizing Orvieto. His troops, therefore, left Terni by the northern road.[2]

The march out of the plain of the Nar to the upper valley of the Tiber was made under comparatively easy conditions, though Forbes' men were astonished to find that not even the General slept under a roof, and that everyone had to do without supper. Garibaldi, Ciceruacchio, and the staff gave to the soldiers the little water which was procured for themselves on the way, and Anita made a

[1] *Pianciani*, 10, 11 ; *Farini*, iv. 233 ; *Rug.* 16 ; *Forbes MSS.*
[2] *Hoff.* 344, 345 ; *De Rossi*, 19, 20 ; 105–107 ; *Mem.* 241 ; *Bittard des Portes*, 412 ; *Bel.* 34 ; *Rug.* 14, 15, 22 ; *D'Ambrosio*, 67.

like sacrifice, though she was in far greater need of comforts.[1]
On the morning of July 11, they reached Todi, which rises
far-seen above a gorge of the curving Tiber. A few hundred
yards outside the gate they were welcomed by the citizens
with the inevitable band of music, and lodged in the garden
of a pretty little white-walled and red-roofed convent on a
hill by the roadside, where, amid the Franciscan laurels,
cypresses and fruit trees, the soldiers built for Anita a straw-
hut in which she received the visits of the ladies of Todi.[2]
From the garden there was a broad view up the Tiber
Valley, which opens out to the north, so that she could see
the hill of Perugia where the Austrians lay in force twenty-
five miles away, and even the dim outline of the crater of
Lake Trasimene.

Leaving his troops outside, in the convents, to make
friends with the friars, as they very soon managed to do,
Garibaldi, with his staff, entered Todi. The red-shirted
horsemen clattered up the narrow street which pierces three
concentric circles of ancient fortification in its way up to the
centre of the town. So steep and straight is the ascent
that no wheeled carriage can mount to the mediæval
piazza, which, with its fine Cathedral, Town Hall, and
Government House, resembles that of Perugia in style
and beauty, though not in spaciousness. Here, where his
statue stands to-day, Garibaldi transacted business with the
patriotic municipality, and obtained from it freely both
money and provisions. The column of retreat was so
badly armed that it was considered advantageous to exchange 200 of their firearms for those of the Civic Guard of
Todi.[3]

The march westward into Tuscany was now to be carried
out. The cavalry were sent great distances in all directions,
to find and bewilder the various hostile armies, and had
orders to rejoin the column near Cetona in five or six days'
time.[4] The infantry started for Orvieto, where they had
need to arrive before the French, if they did not wish to

[1] *Rug.* 19.   [2] *Hoff.* 359, 360; *Bel.* 37–39.
[3] *Bel.* 37–39.   [4] *Rug.* 22, 23; *De Rossi*, 10

be caught in a trap.¹ The difficulties of the way thither
were great : it was necessary to cross the Tiber by the Todi
bridge and scale the mountains to Prodo ; but the good road
that now runs that way did not exist in 1849. A roughly
paved bridle-path then climbed steeply through the thin
oak copses of the mountain, and enough of it still remains
for the modern pedestrian to experience for himself parts of
the route by which the half-starved and thirsty men made
their way, driving and dragging ninety heavily laden beasts
of burden, and in the worst places walking in single file
and bearing on their shoulders the beloved piece of cannon
they had brought from Rome. The waggons and Forbes'
two pieces of artillery were wisely left behind at Todi.²

The night of July 13–14 was spent in a crevice of the
naked mountain, above the thick forests that slope down
into the Tiber gorge below. Here, in this 'gash of the
wind-grieved Apennine,' below the old castellated hamlet
of Prodo, that seems to shiver with the fear and poverty
of centuries, Anita slept in the tent which she had made.
Near by trickled a half-dried fountain, and around lay the
tired soldiers. Her husband, alert at daybreak, rode off to
reconnoitre, and, seeing a shepherd, approached to question
him as to the route. The half-savage fellow in his sheep-
skin shuffled off for the woods in panic. Hoffstetter would
have threatened him, but Garibaldi forbade all show of
force, and riding up to him soon won his friendship. 'What
do you fear ? Do we speak *Tedesco* ? We are fighting for
you. We are your countrymen.' New words these, full
of difficult matter for the poor thick head ; he and his
ancestors, toiling here among the mountains for unnumbered
centuries, have heard of a God and of a Lady who care for

¹ At Todi, Garibaldi learnt from his cavalry that the French were *en route* for
Viterbo, and probably, therefore, for Orvieto. (*De Rossi*, 109, 111.)

² *Hoff.* 362 ; *Bel.* 46–55. Besides Hoffstetter's account of the path, see
Murray's Central Italy, 1850, which calls it a 'bad mountainous bridle road.'
See also all contemporary maps, and especially the large-scale map in the
Municipio of Narni, for the absence of any great road from Todi to Orvieto. The
'great road' down the Tiber gorge spoken of in *Hoff.* 361, 362, as purposely
avoided by them for fear of the French, only began after Prodo ; it is not possible
to go along the bottom of the gorge of the Tiber running south-west from Todi.

their sorrows, but never before of a country that was theirs, of a cause that was the people's, of soldiers who were not the natural enemies of the poor. But this armed horseman is kind, and has a voice that is not like other voices, so the sad, frightened face of toil melts into a smile, and the poor man answers gladly in his uncouth dialect, and even offers to lead the way. Whereat, other shepherds, who have been watching from behind cover, come up, their Italian inquisitiveness conquering fear, and in a few minutes the stranger has won all their hearts, and each is clamouring to be his guide.[1]

After Prodo * the track was no better than before, save that it began soon to turn down-hill, and that the march was cheered by the sight of old Etruscan Orvieto rising on its acropolis of tufa rock above the junction of the Paglia, the Clanis, and the Tiber, while behind lay green vistas of Tuscany and of Monte Amiata stretching into the western distance. The race had been won, and the French had not yet arrived from the south. In Orvieto, famous since the twelfth century for its internal feuds, there were two parties among the citizens; but the Democrats got the upper hand, invited Garibaldi and his staff to come up on to the rock, illuminated the city in his honour, and gave supplies and money for his army encamped in the valley below.[2]

But the French were close at hand; so close, indeed, that the food consumed by Garibaldi's soldiers had been prepared by order for those of General Morris. But before their arrival the retreat was resumed, on July 15, by the road that leads over the mountains to Ficulle. Garibaldi hoped to pass through Città della Pieve, but it was found by the cavalry to be closed and garrisoned by Tuscan troops, and large Austrian forces might be expected to arrive there from Perugia. He, therefore, turned west at Santa Maria,

---

[1] *Hoff.* 362–365. Even in this wilderness, where there was none to bear witness if they wronged any one, a soldier was shot for stealing a hen. (*Hoff.* 365.)   * See Garibaldi's Prodo despatch at end of chapter.
[2] *Bel.* 55–57; *Hoff.* 369.

and on the night of July 16-17 crossed the canalised plain of the Clanis (Chiana) towards Salci. The night was pitch black, the rain fell in torrents, the mules floundered into the ditches, the men lost their way on the miry tracks and bridges of the canals, and the inhabitants roused at midnight were hostile and unhelpful. But at last the night came to an end, and the column reunited on *terra firma*, at the fortified village of Salci—a curious relic of mediæval life consisting of a score of peasants' houses, built in a square, with the gates and defences of a walled city.[1]

That morning (July 17), as they crossed the border into Tuscany, everything smiled on them. The morning was warm, sunny, and fresh after the tempestuous night, the Tuscans were friendly, and their wine was good ; the landscape, bounded on the west by the ridge of Monte Cetona, and on the east by the distant hills round Lake Trasimene, was rich with fruit, and wine, and oil.[2]

By the terrible march of the last night, Garibaldi had finally thrown off the French, whom he did not again see for ten years, and then as his allies for the deliverance of Italy. In crossing the Tuscan border he left behind all the armies of the Latin races ; but there remained ahead of him a foe more formidable than the Spaniards and Neapolitans, more cruel than the French—the *Tedeschi*, waging their war of extermination on Italian rebels. The network of Austrian armies, stretched across Italy through Florence, Siena, Perugia, and Ancona, had yet to be passed before he could reach the Adriatic, and stand by Manin in Venice.

---

[1] *De Rossi*, 114, 115; *Hoff.* 377-380 ; *Bel.* 56-66.   [2] *Hoff.* 380, 381.

* The following despatch of Garibaldi's—one of the very few despatches of which the originals are now remaining, that were written on the retreat—is addressed to ' Col. Hugh Forbes, commanding the 2nd Legion,' and dated ' Prodo, 14 July, 1849, 9 A.M.' It is among the *Forbes MSS.* (see App. N. below) : ' Citizen Colonel, I have received yours of yesterday with the enclosure and thank you for it. At this moment I am marching the cavalry for the Paglia bridge, as there is not here enough water to give the horses to drink. I shall start towards afternoon by the same route with the rest of the column. I have demanded rations at Orvieto. I have no news of the enemy. Yours, G. GARIBALDI.'

S

CHAPTER XIII

THE RETREAT, II.—FROM TUSCANY TO THE BORDERS OF
SAN MARINO—THROUGH THE AUSTRIAN ARMIES

'Fuga di cauto leone inseguito
che si rimbosca, cupido di strage,
contenendo nel gran petto il ruggito,
e sbarrando nel buio occhi di brage.'
MARRADI.—*Rapsodia Garibaldina.*

GARIBALDI, when he turned westward to cross the Tuscan
border, hoped to rouse another revolution against the
Grand Duke Leopold, and another war against the foreigner,
in a State whose inhabitants had failed to do very much
for Italy, even when times were far more propitious. He
was quickly undeceived. When, at Montepulciano, on
July 19, he issued a manifesto calling Tuscany to arms
against the Austrian invaders, it met with no response.
For all knew that, after Novara and the fall of Rome, a
popular rising in Central Italy had no chance of success,
in the face of the whole power of Austria and of France.
Moreover, in spite of the unwelcome entry into Florence
of the Austrian troops,[1] as the protectors, or rather now as
the task-masters, of the restored Grand Duke, that pliable
and kindly old man was not actively disliked by his subjects ; indeed, Leopold still hoped to make his rule popular,
in contrast to the Papal tyranny in the neighbouring
State, of which he spoke with disapproval to the British
Minister.[2]

---

[1] For the entrance of the Austrian troops into Florence, see Mrs. Browning's
Casa Guidi Windows, Pt. II.
[2] *F.O. Papers, MS.* Letter of Sir G. Hamilton to Lord Palmerston,
August 19, 1849. The Grand Duke was, however, in the habit of saying one
thing to one man and another to another.

And so the leader of revolution marched through eastern Tuscany, generously aided with money and provisions by the municipalities, and loudly welcomed by the populace, sometimes with the strange cry *Viva Garibaldi, Re d' Italia*, yet all the while bitterly disappointed at the absence of recruits. But the young men to whom he appealed vowed themselves to the service of their country in future years, and as he passed on he left the inhabitants of each little town devoted to the legendary hero who had ridden through their streets, drunk at their fountain, and spoken to the mothers and children thronging round him of the time to come when the motherland would need those young lives.[1] Stories of what he had said and done, passing from mouth to mouth, worked in secret for ten years, and prepared the season when Italy was indeed created by the irresistible impulse of all her populations. Although as a military operation the retreat was foredoomed to failure, it served as a mission of political propaganda in the highest sense of the word.

In this way they marched on through Cetona[2] and Sarteano, through Montepulciano, famous for its wine and its view of Lake Trasimene, through Torrita, with its pretty towers of red brick, through Bettolle and Fojano, right across the central plain of Italy, tramping to the monotonous chorus of frogs from the half-dried ditches that distribute the canalised waters of the Clanis among the vineyards— on towards the north-eastern mountain wall on which hangs Cortona. The Tuscan regular troops, who might have resisted their passage of the plain, shrank away and let them pass, merely skirmishing with their scouts at Clusium. So, on July 21, they reached the edge of the mountains and entered Castiglione Fiorentino.

Now that his extravagant hope of rousing Tuscany to

[1] *Rug.* 30, 35, 38; *Bel.* 63, 77, 90, 91; *Magherini*, 13, 14.
[2] See map at end of book for this chapter. At Cetona the Garibaldians were quartered in houses, for the first time since Rome. They were hospitably received, and some, I hope, partook of a certain brand of the white wine of the district. Here, too, Anita changed her man's dress for a woman's.

war had been dissipated, Garibaldi determined to strike
across the highest ridges of the Apennines, descend
on some Adriatic port, and there embark for Venice.
Four armies of Austrians (under the supreme command
of General D'Aspre), amounting to 15,000 men or more,[1]
occupied the whole ground over which he would have
to manœuvre.   Two of these armies—that of Archduke
Ernest at Ancona, and that of Hahne at Bologna—
lay on the other side of the *massif* of the Apennines,
ready to catch him as he descended on the Adriatic, if
ever he were to reach the top of the passes.   The other
two were on either flank of him, where he now was ;
for Paumgarten lay at Perugia, and D'Aspre himself at
Florence, each sending out strong expeditions to catch the
guerilla, and each prepared to follow with the rest of the
troops if once he were located.[2]   On July 13, D'Aspre
had written a shrewd letter to Oudinot, saying that the
threatened irruption of Garibaldi into Tuscany must be
a *ruse de guerre*, and that he would probably turn back
to the Adriatic ;[3] but a week later D'Aspre's lieutenant,
Stadion, commanding the portion of the forces despatched
from Florence to deal with the 'Bandits,' was deceived
on that very point by Müller and his active cavalry, whom
Garibaldi had sent out for this purpose from Sarteano.
Fully persuaded that the Italian army was coming into
the valley of the Umbro in order to reach the west coast,
Stadion lingered near Siena and Buonconvento during the
critical days when the Garibaldians were traversing the
open plain of the Clanis.[4]   Meanwhile, on their right flank,
Paumgarten, scarcely less bewildered than Stadion as to
their movements and intentions, kept part of his men at

---

[1] *De Rossi*, 10.   There were 10,000 Austrians in the Papal States alone by
the end of April (*Mittheilungen*, 233, 234).

[2] *Mittheilungen*, 283 and *passim* ; *Kriegsbegebenheiten* and *De Rossi*, *passim*.

[3] *Torre*, ii. 398 (letter from Florence).

[4] *De Rossi*, 116–119 ; *Kriegsbegebenheiten*, 19, 20.   After this last service the
Pole, Müller, betrayed the cause and chief whom he had served so well, and sold
himself to Stadion.   *Vecchi*, ii. 317, 321 ; *Rug.* 32 ; and *Farini*, iv. 233, dispose
of the doubts of *Bel.* 184, note.

Perugia and sent out others in ill-directed or belated expeditions to Città della Pieve, Clusium and elsewhere.[1]

Garibaldi, having thus freed himself from all immediate pressure at the moment of entering Castiglione Fiorentino on the 21st, marched along the foot of the mountains to Arezzo. His desire was, before beginning the passage of the higher Apennines, to recruit his tired troops in the chief city of the district. He also hoped, by this move on Arezzo, to deceive Paumgarten's men once more, and draw them westward, for he feared lest they should march from Perugia up the Tiber valley, and cut off his retreat at San Sepolcro, near which point he would have to pass on his way to the Adriatic.[2]

Arrived in front of the walls of Arezzo, the tired patriots underwent a cruel disappointment. The gates were closed in their faces by the officials of the Moderate party, backed by quiet citizens afraid of Austrian vengeance. The energetic Gonfaloniere of Arezzo, the poet Guadagnoli, manned the walls with a few Tuscan regulars, and ninety invalided Austrian soldiers, while he improvised and armed a Civic Guard of 260 men, partly consisting of peasants called in from outside to keep down the city Democrats. The latter, normally the strongest party in Arezzo, which had sent many volunteers to Lombardy in '48, were indignant at an act of inhospitality degrading to the reputation of their town in the annals of patriotism. They attempted a revolt, but were suppressed, and many suffered long terms of imprisonment. Meanwhile, during the greater part of July 23, Garibaldi lay encamped in front of the walls, on the hill of Santa Maria, parleying in vain for an entry. His angry troops clamoured to be led to the assault, which could not have failed, but their chief dreaded the scandal of a victory over Italians, especially as it might have been followed by looting on the part of the undesirables in his army; he also told Hoffstetter that he did not wish to leave behind a number of wounded to be shot by the Austrians, and that he feared to be caught in a trap inside the town by

[1] *De Rossi*, 119.   [2] *Ibid.* 120–122.

the arrival of Paumgarten and Stadion.   Indeed, at nightfall of the 23rd, Paumgarten's troops were already drawing
so near, that he was forced to hasten on his way up the
road leading to the Scopettone pass.   The failure to enter
Arezzo had a demoralising effect on his men, who now felt
too clearly that they were no more than fugitives.[1]

This impression was enhanced by the horrors of the
night retreat, when the rearguard went astray and became
engaged with the Austrians under the walls of Arezzo; when
all over the hills and up to the pass, deserters, stragglers, and wounded were hunted down by bands of peasants
under the leadership of friars and priests, dispatching
their countrymen or handing them over to the Austrian
butchers.   So strong was the reactionary sentiment among
some of the *contadini* in the mountains behind Arezzo,
that during the same week a traveller saw cottages illuminated, and heard rude voices chanting festal hymns in
honour of the Austrian Emperor, who was not even legally
their lord.   The hills resounded with

' Evviva la corona
Del nostro Imperator,'

till the astonished gentleman could believe himself in
Tyrol rather than Tuscany.   Such, in its effect, was the
political teaching of the Church in the era of Italy's resurrection.[2]

Meanwhile the main body of Garibaldians, having slept
at midnight on the top of the Scopettone Pass, descended,
next day, the long gorge beside the clear Cerfone torrent,
the rays of the July sun falling pitilessly on their heads, until,
on the afternoon of the 24th, they crossed out of Tuscany
into the Papal States, and emerged into the valley of the
Upper Tiber.[3]   This reach of the great river, where it first
leaves its mountain cradle, has a peculiar effect on the

---

[1] *Salaris*, 9-25; *Bel.* 99-106; *Rug.* 39-44, 56; *De Rossi*, 245; *Hoff.*
402, 403; *Guerzoni*, i. 342.   *Torre*, ii. 400 (D'Aspre's letter).
[2] *Corsi*, i. 186, 187; *Rug.* 29, 44; *Hoff.* 403-407; *Bel.* 108, 122, 123.
[3] *Hoff.* 407, 408.

imagination, for the valley, several miles broad, through which it flows, combines the freshness of an Alp with the wealth and spaciousness of a populous country-side. It is studded with small towns, of which San Sepolcro is the chief; and through the thick web of vines that nets the plain runs the line of a poplar wood shading the course of the Tiber—not here a yellow flood, but a clear stream of blue and silver eddies. The whole valley is shut in on the south-west by the mountains, covered with oak forest, out of which Garibaldi emerged; and on the other side by the central ridge of the Apennines—the Monte Luna, and the precipitous ascent to the Trabaria pass, by which alone his hunted army could now hope to escape to the Adriatic.

The spirals by which this road winds up the mountain, and the whole panorama of the valley below, were clearly visible from the old walled village of Citerna, whose ruined keep crowns an olive-clad hill, enclosed on three sides by tributaries of the Tiber.[1] In this position, dominating the plain, and too strong to be stormed except by overwhelming numbers, Garibaldi remained for more than forty-eight hours, to reorganise and rest his exhausted troops, and prepare for the passage of the water-shed of Italy. From Citerna hill, on the second day of the bivouac, he watched the Austrian divisions, numbering many thousand men, pour one after the other into the valley below. Some came on his traces from Arezzo; others, as he had feared, up the Tiber from Perugia; and finally, Stadion's men began to enter from the opposite direction, behind Anghiari.[2] He could observe the white columns crawling in different directions over the green plain, each ignorant of the other's movements, but all as clear to him as pieces set out on a war map; he could see the road climbing up the mountain wall on the further side of Tiber—a ladder to the foot of which he must attain by passing between these various hostile bodies; and he was thus enabled to lay his plans

[1] See illustration, p. 269, below.
[2] *Kriegsbegebenheiten*, 21, 22 ; *De Rossi*, 247–249 ; *Bel.* 114, 115 ; *Magherini*, 23, 24 ; *Rug.* 45, 46.

according to what he saw himself, as well as by the reports of his outposts, who were watching and skirmishing all along the valley.[1]

Until the word to move was given, the hours of repose were passed in pleasant quarters. Most of the troops were bivouacked inside the walled grounds of two small monasteries, situated upon the ridge of which Citerna crowns the summit. The Cappuccini, a pretty little white building, is set in a large garden that slopes half-way down the hill, where

> ' all the flowers and trees do close
> To weave the garlands of repose.'

In July the flowers of spring were gone, but cypresses and stone pines, figs and fruit trees, besides oak, brushwood and exotic plants, gave that look of dark coolness in the midst of lucent heat which is the most prized of the beauties of Italy. Here Anita slept under a bower of evergreens.[2] And here Garibaldi interviewed the patriots of the Tiber valley, who came up the hill to offer him their services at no small risk to themselves. ' This time things have gone badly,' he told a deputation from Città di Castello, ' but the blood shed at Rome will be productive, and I hope that in ten years at most Italy will be free.'[3] It was, in fact, not till September 1860, that the Bersaglieri of Victor Emmanuel, set in motion by the victories of the redshirts in Sicily, marched gaily down this way to Perugia, amid the wild rejoicings of the liberated people, who had never forgotten, and whose descendants will never forget, Garibaldi's passage across their valley in July 1849.[4]

During the long encampment on Citerna hill, some of the men looted in the rooms of the monasteries—almost the only case of such misconduct that occurred during

[1] This is evident to anyone who has stood on Citerna hill.

[2] The edge of Anita's bower of evergreens, together with the monastery itself, can be seen in illustration opposite. (*Hoff.* 408, 409 ; *Bel.* 109.)

[3] He repeated this strangely correct prophecy two or three days later at Mercatello (*Magherini*, 14 ; *Bel.* 112, 113, 131), and again at Gatteo (*Modoni*, 86, 87). Salvagnoli made the same prophecy of ' ten years.' *Tabarrini*, **9.**

[4] *Della Rocca*, 180–184 ; *Magherini, passim* ; *Bel.* 124, 125.

MONASTERY OF CITERNA,
WITH EDGE OF ANITA'S BOWER.
Halt of July 24-26.

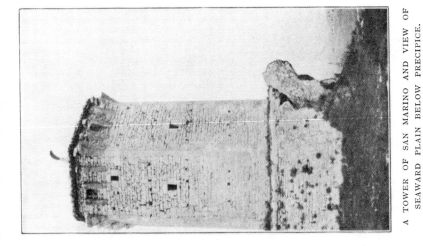

A TOWER OF SAN MARINO AND VIEW OF
SEAWARD PLAIN BELOW PRECIPICE.
Halt of July 31.

the Retreat. Ugo Bassi's *bonhomie* was not altogether unsuccessful in consoling the victims, who received much sympathy from the officers when the fault was discovered.[1]

About a mile distant from Citerna lies Monterchi, another little town on a lower hill to the south. Here the Austrians lay in force, and Garibaldi, watching from the garden of the Cappuccini their preparations to attack or surround the Citerna hill, and their guns planted against him, determined that it was time for him to be gone. Indeed, his escape northwards across the valley might be closed at any moment by the troops from Città di Castello and Anghiari, some of whom were already in the neighbourhood of San Sepolcro. The forces of the Austrians within a few miles of Citerna were three or four times as numerous as his own, and their generals believed themselves to have blocked every road by which he could escape out of the Tiber valley; this error arose from the dependence of their Staff on a map which did not show the great road up to the Bocca Trabaria, though it was in full sight of Garibaldi at Citerna.[2] At its foot lies San Giustino, and he determined to reach that town by a secret march on the night of July 26–27.[3]

To effect this he had first to escape from the Austrians in Monterchi, and then to pass through their other armies on the line of the Tiber. The attention of the former was engaged by a false attack on Monterchi during the afternoon of the 26th, and by a screen of men left on Citerna hill, while the main column secretly descended its steep northern slope and began to cross the plain in the falling dusk. Through the night they made a forced march to San Giustino, one division going round by the road and bridge of San Sepolcro, and the rest moving in a straight line across the sandy fords of the Tiber.[4] In the poplar

[1] *Magherini*, 27; *Vecchi*, ii. 319; *Bologna MS. Manfredini.*

[2] *Corsi*, i. 189; *Rug.* 46; *De Rossi*, 247–249.

[3] The date, about which an erroneous statement is made in *Bel.* 110, is correctly given in *Bel.* 119; and is proved by *Bologna MS. San Giustino.* (*Magherini*, 27, 28; *De Rossi*, 249, 250; *Rug.* 46, 47.)

[4] *Bologna MS. Piva*; *Magherini*, 31, 37; *Hoff.* 410, 411; *Rug.* 46;

grove on its banks there was a struggle with the fat friars of Citerna, who complained bitterly at the necessity of wading up to their knees; it had been thought prudent to take them along, because if left in Citerna they would have found means to warn the Austrians in Monterchi of the escape of their common enemies.[1]

Marching through the darkness, often in single file, by the narrow tracks of the vineyards and the rough fords of the streams, the army left behind—besides many baggage animals and much of their scanty stock of ammunition— a number of men who lost their way in the darkness, and were picked up in the following days by the Austrians. Many, when asked to what corps they belonged, although they knew that death or torture was awarded to all who followed Garibaldi, confessed him to the drum-head court-martials as their 'chief and father.' Some were shot, and others flogged with that revolting cruelty which did so much to turn against Austria the sympathies of our country, happily forgetful that, fifty years before, she had been guilty of the same form of wickedness in Ireland.[2]

At dawn of the 27th the column of retreat reached San Giustino, but, too fatigued by the night march to begin at once the scaling of the great mountain, they remained during the greater part of the day at the foot of the pass, while the Austrians, only a few miles away, on three sides, left them strangely unmolested. This inactivity surprised the Italians then, and has surprised their historians since. The truth is that Garibaldi's enemies, all through July, were unduly afraid of him, being deceived by his devices into supposing him stronger than he was; and at this moment their troops were utterly exhausted by the forced marches that had brought them from Perugia, Arezzo, and Siena. But when all is said, the Austrian generals were very stupid, and the best excuse for their inaction at this

Vecchi, ii. 320; *Bel.* 110, and *Belluzzi's Note-book, Bologna MS.*; *De Rossi*, 250.

[1] *Magherini*, 28; *Bel.* 111.

[2] *Rug.* 47, 48; *Magherini*, 29. (See also *Bel.* 114.) See App. M, below, *England and Austrian atrocities.*

crisis—namely, that they thought 'the bandit' could not escape because they did not know of the important road over the Bocca Trabaria—in itself shows by how much they were inferior to their antagonist in personal activity and observation, as well as in the use of scouts. The Austrian officers were well aware that he was more than a match for their chiefs; as day by day they urged their tired men over fresh mountains, they cursed and admired the man who led them such a dance. 'This devil,' they said, to an Italian gentleman, 'will lead us to Africa at least.' [1]

On July 27, after a long halt at San Giustino,[2] about 2,000 men who still followed the desperate fortunes of Garibaldi began to move up the road to the Bocca Trabaria by 'gigantic spirals,' like those which join valley to valley in Hoffstetter's fatherland. The Switzer, riding in front with the Staff, looked back to watch the army winding up from below, 'like a long beautiful snake,' through the scattered oak copses, corn-fields and farms sprinkled over the steep mountain side. In the front Garibaldi rode beside Anita —his white poncho streaming out on the mountain breeze. Then came the few remaining lancers of Masina's devoted squadron; then the baggage-mules, now reduced to forty, and then, moving with deliberate steps, a majestic herd of white bulls with long, curved horns, destined to be the provisions of the army on the foodless mountains. Below, the red shirts of the Garibaldian Legion, and still further down, the light summer suits of Forbes and his boy were visible among the darker uniforms of their companions.[3] At the bottom of all lay the broad, green valley, the scene of their night march, across which the last patrols and rearguard were hastening to the foot of the pass, and the white Austrian columns were still aimlessly in motion. The size and nature of the hunted army, the driven cattle, the wild scenery into which the war was being carried, the near

---

[1] *Corsi*, i. 193, 194; *Rug.* 46, 47; *Bel.* 35, 36, 104; *Torre*, ii. 398.

[2] *Bologna MS. San Giustino* and *Bel.* 126, say they started at 6 P.M.; while *Hoff.* 412, and *De Rossi*, 250, say it was in the morning. But all agree they rested some time just outside San Giustino. (See also *Rug.* 48, 49.)

[3] *Hoff.* 413, 414.

prospect of death, were the same for Anita and Garibaldi, this day, as when, nine years before, they had ridden thus side by side in the Brazilian mountains, near the time of Menotti's birth. Nothing was changed, except that love, which then was young, was now rich in memory.

After this first climb they traversed several miles of flat road along a high barren ridge, and night had fallen before they reached another spiral ascent. When they had mounted it they were on the top of the water-shed of Italy. Here, on the Bocca Trabaria, they slept at midnight, though many watched from thirst and sorrow. The carpet of primroses, crocuses, and blue squills, which beautify this remote place in spring time, had vanished with the summer heats ; there was no sign of vegetation or of any living thing, but a hungry wind was moaning among the rocks. All were glad when the dawn sprang up over the grey mountain-tops below them, and lighted their way down towards the Adriatic. At first their road ran by a wooded gorge of one of the head-springs of the Metaurus; till after many miles the river opened into a broad valley, in the middle of which lay Sant' Angelo in Vado. Entering its streets on the evening of July 28, they found, to their dismay, blocking their further descent a short distance below the town, another Austrian army under Archduke Ernest, whom D'Aspre had ordered up from Ancona, through Urbino, to cut off Garibaldi if by chance he should succeed in crossing the water-shed. The Italians, who had been greatly elated at the skill with which their leader had extricated them from the Tiber valley, saw themselves once more entrapped.[1]

Retreat was impossible, for the enemy were following them from behind, while on both sides the mountains shut them in, and in front lay the new foe. But once more Garibaldi found a way overlooked by the slow Austrian generals, where, three minutes walk below Sant' Angelo in Vado, a rough road diverges to the left, leading over the hills into the Foglia valley. Since the enemy, who would

---

[1] *Rug.* 47-51 ; *De Rossi*, 247 ; *Kriegsbegebenheiten*, 21.

ST. ANGELO IN VADO.
Action of Juiy 29.

CITERNA ON THE HILL.
Halt of July 24-26.

have had time to occupy the foot of this important pass, if they had known of its existence, had drawn themselves up a mile or so lower down the Metaurus, Garibaldi on the morning of the 29th made a false attack on their position, as if he intended to force their line, and under cover of this feint took the strategic turn to the left, and carried his column over the hills to Pian di Meleto.[1]

Again the Italians had escaped, but not quite unscathed. A rearguard of cavalry, left in Sant' Angelo in Vado after the main column had started, were surprised by Hungarian hussars, following from the Tiber valley, who galloped in under the unguarded western gateway, sabred the Republicans in the street, and dragged them out of the houses. It was a general massacre, no quarter being given.[2] Indeed, the murder of prisoners, if they belonged to Garibaldi's band, was the rule approved at the head-quarters in Florence by D'Aspre himself.[3] A man-hunt was instituted in Sant' Angelo and the surrounding hills, in which the peasants were forced to assist by threats of burning their houses and crops. In the town itself some of the soldiers were hidden, and afterwards smuggled away in disguise by patriotic citizens, who risked their own lives by these acts of mercy. In all Sant' Angelo there was only one man, a shoemaker, who turned false ; the poor fellow whom he denounced was taken and shot ; but the traitor, unable to endure the hatred of his fellow-townsmen, went mad, and shortly died.[4]

Meanwhile Garibaldi was struggling over into the Foglia valley ; the road winds along a high ridge, whence the northern landscape in the direction of Monte Carpegna and San Marino becomes clearly visible. It is one of the strangest regions of Italy : the higher mountains, naked

---

[1] Illustration opposite is a view of S. Angelo in Vado, taken from this road by which Garibaldi escaped. *Rug.* 51–53 ; *Hoff.* 415–421 ; *De Rossi*, 254–256.

[2] *Rug.* 53, 54 ; *Bel.* 134–139 ; *De Rossi*, 255, 256 ; *Hoff.* 421, 422.

[3] *Torre*, ii. 400, 401. Letter of D'Aspre, July 31, to Oudinot, recounts that ' an officer and several men of Garibaldi's band were taken and immediately shot,' in ' the mountains of Borgo S. Sepolcro.'

[4] *Bel.* 138–142.

peaks and tables, rear themselves on the sky-line in fantastic fortress shapes, hard to distinguish, except by their size,
from the works of man—the old robber castles perched on
their summits.   The aspect of the lesser hills, skeleton ridges,
washed bare of soil and corrugated by the rain-torrents, baked
by the sun into a hard white grey, with patches of brown
or of sparse verdure, is well known in the backgrounds of
Piero della Francesca and other painters of the Umbrian
school.   The broad valley bottoms are white as snow-drifts,
being filled from side to side with the polished stones of the
dried-up river courses.   The olive is no longer seen ; thin
vineyards and corn are the only cultivation.   Such was the
country through which the Tyrolese sharpshooters followed
on the heels of the Garibaldians from Sant' Angelo in Vado
to San Marino, killing all whom they caught, and sometimes
treating even the wounded with revolting brutality.   They
were kept off from the main column by a handful of Manara's
old Bersaglieri, commanded by Hugh Forbes in his top-hat,
with a courage which won the admiration of his brother
officers.[1]

After passing Pian di Meleto, with its beautifully machi-
colated castle, the army descended the Foglia for some
miles ; the fatigues of the way were great, for the road was
not, as it is now, supplied with bridges over the numerous
torrent-beds that cross it.   Towards evening on the 29th,
Garibaldi turned to the left out of the Foglia valley, marched
up the gorge of the Apsa, and reached Macerata Feltria,
which rises on the edge of the dried-up torrent.[2]

The troops could scarcely drag themselves along for

---

[1] *Rug.* 55 ; *Hoff.* 423 ; *Bel.* 151, 152, 156.   In some rough notes on the
story of the Retreat in the handwriting of Col. Forbes himself (*Forbes MSS.*)
we read, immediately after the mention of St. Angelo : 'G(aribaldi) looks for
F(orbes).   Finds him *Rear Guard*—Go rest of retreat together to the camp.
G. and F. continue together with the last *drapello* of Rear Guard.   Such is the
spirit which animated both, instead of the petty jealousy which so frequently
reigns between the Chiefs of the same army.'
[2] See illustration, p. 272, below, in which the bed of the Apsa consists of
white stones, not water.   The photograph was taken in April, so, *a fortiori*, the
torrent must have been dry in July.

weariness, but the enemy were too close to allow of any halt at Macerata, except to eat the food provided by the friendly inhabitants. Affairs were indeed getting desperate. Bueno, the commander of the cavalry, Garibaldi's South American comrade of the longest standing—a countryman and old friend of Anita—had sold himself to the pursuing Austrians, and passed over to the Emperor's service: unlike Müller, who had deserted a week before, he was of no military value except for his courage in a charge; but Anita and Garibaldi felt that a link with their romantic past had been most cruelly cut.[1] Next, some of the Italian officers fled from the doomed army and took refuge in the territory of San Marino.[2] The morale of the 1,500 men who still held together was seriously undermined, and a general dispersion was not unlikely. Archduke Ernest was close on them to south and east, Stadion's men were pouring over the hills to the west behind Monte Carpegna, and Hahne, from Bologna, was hastening down the Via Æmilia and towards San Leo to cut them off from the north.[3] With his disheartened and exhausted troops, Garibaldi saw that he could no longer hope to capture a large port on the Adriatic and embark with 1,500 men for Venice. He therefore determined, from information received at Macerata, to make for the neutral territory of the Republic of San Marino.[4]

And so again, without a rest, they staggered on through the midnight from Macerata up the head-waters of the Apsa to the Convent of Pietra Rubbia, standing at the foot of the naked mass of the Carpegna mountain that blocks the head of the valley.[5] Hence, on the 30th, utterly exhausted by the extraordinary exertions of the day before, they turned north and crossed a high moor covered with thin grass and white stones, not unlike the tops of some of

[1] *Hoff.* 424; *Bel.* 139–141, 144, 147–149; *De Rossi*, 255; *Rug.* 56, 57.
[2] *Rug.* 55; *Brizi*, 8.
[3] *De Rossi*, 257–259; *Mittheilungen*, 283; *Kriegsbegebenheiten*, 23.
[4] *Bel.* 148; *De Rossi*, 256, 257.
[5] They did not go to Carpegna village, as is wrongly stated by *Hoff.* 430.
(See *Bel.* 154; *De Rossi*, 259.)

MACERATA FELTRIA.
Passed through, night of July 29.

CITADEL OF SAN MARINO, ON EDGE OF PRECIPICE.
Reached July 31.

CHAPTER XIV

SAN MARINO AND CESENATICO, JULY 31–AUGUST 1

'And many a warrior-peopled citadel,
Like rocks which fire lifts out of the flat deep,
Arose in sacred Italy,
Frowning o'er the tempestuous sea
Of kings, and priests, and slaves, in tower-crowned majesty.'

SHELLEY: *Ode to Liberty*.

THE Republic of San Marino, when Garibaldi drew near its
borders, was, as it is to-day, the sole survivor of the innumerable sovereign cities which nursed the free and vigorous
life of Mediæval Italy; it had outlived a hundred more
splendid sister cities, partly because the peasants who tilled
the rugged sides of the Monte Titano had never accumulated
the wealth that tempts the invader, and still more because
the market town, which serves as capital to this rural community, is enclosed by the walls of a virgin fortress of immense
natural strength.[1] The last serious attempt on its independence had been made, in 1739, by the famous Cardinal
Alberoni, then Papal Legate in the Romagna. It was the
only Italian State which Napoleon spared and befriended.[2]

On the edge of the precipice facing the Adriatic, 2,437
feet above the sea-level, stand the highest towers of San
Marino, and from their base the cliff falls sheer away for 700
feet.[3] Down below, the twelve miles of undulating, fertile
country that descend to Rimini on the coast; the stony
bed of the Marecchia river, a straight, broad, white band
through the vineyards; the ships at sea, and the towns
along the shore, are all visible, as in a bird's-eye view, from
the rock of the freemen. On the land side, the Monte

---

[1] See illustration, p. 272, above.
[2] He characteristically offered to send a present of four cannon for the rock,
and forgot his promise (*Modoni*, 5–8).   [3] See illustration, p. 264, above.

T

Titano falls away only less steeply than to seaward, and
the western view ranges far over gnarled mountains and
torn ravines, among which rises the frowning fortress of
San Leo, the Papal dungeon where the arch-quack
Cagliostro breathed his last, and where many a Carbonaro has languished for Italy and freedom, and
left neither name nor memory. Through this wild
region, on July 30, 1849, Garibaldi was coming from the
south, with the Archduke Ernest at his heels; Holzer was
approaching from the south-west,[1] and Hahne, unknown
to Garibaldi, from the north. Distant glimpses of all these
hosts might have been caught from time to time from the
piazza of San Marino, where the fathers of the city were
anxiously on the watch, divided between desire to befriend
the Roman Republicans and anxiety to preserve their
own State from the vengeance of the reactionary powers,
to whom it had for many years been notorious as the place
of refuge for the persecuted Liberals of the Romagna.[2]

The arrival of mounted Garibaldian deserters had first
warned the little community that danger was in the
air.[3] Then, early on July 30, a messenger from Garibaldi
rode up the winding ascent of the Titano, and announced
that his Chief intended to pass through the neutral territory; to which the Captain-Regent, Belzoppi, replied that
if he did so he would violate his principles by endangering
the existence of a Republic, and would not help himself,
because the Sammarinesi could see from the rock that their
dominions were already surrounded on all sides by Austrians.[4]

The next ambassador was Ugo Bassi himself, who
arrived late on the night of the 30th.[5] Having received
the same reply from the Regency, coupled with a friendly
offer to feed the troops at the boundaries of the Republic,
the red-shirted friar began to wander disconsolately about
the streets of the frightened town, looking out for somewhere to sleep, until at last 'a true Republican,' Lorenzo

[1] Holzer commanded a part of Stadion's army (*De Rossi*, 248, 258, 260).
[2] *Franciosi*, 3-6; *D'Azeglio*, 74-76; *Simoncini*, 6-9.   [3] *Brizi*, 8.
[4] *Bel.* 162-164; *Brizi*, 8, 29; *Franciosi*, 14, 15.   [5] *Brizi*, 8.

CAPPUCCINI MONASTERY, SAN MARINO.
Showing loggia where Garibaldi wrote order of the day
disbanding his army.

GATE OF SAN MARINO.
With house beyond from which Ugo Bassi saw the
Austrian watch-fires in valley below.

Simoncini, drew him into his *cafe*. This house, which became the scene of memorable events during the next thirty hours, stands close to the western gate, and overlooks the outer wall of the city,[1] in which convenient position it had often served its generous owner to entertain and expedite fugitive Liberals and Carbonari of the enslaved provinces below.[2] After a much-needed supper, Ugo Bassi went to the window and looked out at the moonlit mountains. Suddenly he started back in horror, for he had seen the watch-fires of Hahne's men stretched along the hillside below San Leo. 'My God,' he cried, ' the General is caught between two fires : he is lost. But we must save him.' Sitting down at once he wrote to Garibaldi warning him that he was headed off by yet another army from the northward, and the good Simoncini, with the unofficial aid of the Secretary of State, found an enthusiastic and capable messenger, named Balda, who in the darkness of the night picked out the rugged and difficult way across the slopes of Monte Tassona to Garibaldi's presence, and gave him Ugo Bassi's letter. Warned thus before daybreak that he could no longer pass along outside the western boundary of the Republic unless he wished to fall into the midst of Hahne's troops, Garibaldi, if he still entertained any doubt, saw that he had no alternative but to enter uninvited the territory of San Marino and throw himself on the mercy of its citizens.[3]

Therefore, at earliest daylight of July 31, his troops resumed their march along the ridge of the Serra Bruciata, and then turning north over the slopes of Monte Tassona, made straight for the towers of San Marino. Garibaldi rode on in front to explain his action to the authorities, and arrived on the piazza of the town about eight o'clock. In the Hall of Audience he was publicly received by Belzoppi and his colleagues.

[1] Simoncini's *café* is the house to the left of the town gate in the illustration on the opposite page.

[2] *Simoncini*, 8, 9.

[3] *Simoncini*, 10–12 ; 25–29 ; *Bel.* 166. It is impossible to say for certain whether the letter did more than confirm Garibaldi in a previous resolution.

' Citizen-Regent,' said the General, ' my troops, pursued by superior numbers of Austrians, and exhausted by the privations they have endured among the mountains and precipices, are no longer in a condition to fight; it therefore became necessary to cross your border to obtain bread and a few hours' repose. They shall lay down their arms in your Republic, where the Roman war for the independence of Italy now comes to an end. I come among you as a refugee; receive me as such.'

' Welcome to the refugee,' answered Belzoppi. ' General, this hospitable land receives you.'

It was then and there agreed that the Government of San Marino should mediate with the Austrian commanders, to secure the safety of all who laid down their arms.[1]

While this interview was taking place, Garibaldi's column, still several miles away, crossed the bare slopes of Monte Tassona by stony lanes, passed through the village of Castello, and at length reached, at the foot of Monte Titano, the ravine which divides the territories of Pope and Republic. Here, on the steep slopes, the little cannon got into difficulties, and since the men were unwilling to leave their favourite behind, and Garibaldi was absent in San Marino, a long delay took place, during which the advanced guard of Hahne's men fell upon their flank. A large part of the demoralised soldiers fairly fled up the Monte Titano; but Anita, as soon as she heard the first shots, rode to the point of danger, looking for her husband, and crying, ' Where is Peppino ? '[2] With the help of Forbes, she rallied a strong rearguard and checked the Austrian pursuit, until the white mantle was seen floating along the hillside above, and Garibaldi came galloping back down the spirals of the road, meeting and rallying the fugitives as he came. When he had restored such order as was possible, the remnants of the army, some 1,500 men in all, proceeded together up to the city of refuge. But the little cannon, which they had dragged with such pains and pride over so many mountain paths and river

---

[1] *Brizi*, 10, 11 ; *Franciosi*, 16, 17 ; *Bel.* 166, 167.

[2] A common abbreviation for Giuseppe. *Bologna MS. Piva* gives this detail.

beds, the whole way from Rome, was left, fallen, at the bottom of the last ravine.[1]

And so, about mid-day, they reached the summit of the Titano, a band of veritable refugees. The confusion of their ranks and the variety of their uniforms, the *ponchos*, the red shirts, the cocks' feathers, the top-hats, formed a strange medley. There were cavalrymen limping along on foot, infantry and wounded on horseback; pale-faced boys who had thrown away their arms in the last skirmish, strong men fainting with every kind of anguish and exhaustion. The citizens, moved to deep compassion, vied with each other in supplying the wants of the army. It was quartered in the Cappuccini convent on the road outside the walls, where all, especially the wounded, were treated with the utmost kindness by the non-political friars of San Marino. On the steps of this convent [2] Garibaldi sat down and wrote the last Order of the Day :—

'REPUBLIC OF SAN MARINO.

Order of the Day, July 31, 1849, 2 P.M.

'SOLDIERS,—We have reached the land of refuge, and we owe the best behaviour to our generous hosts. We, too, have earned the consideration due to persecuted misfortune.

'From this moment forward I release my companions from all obligation, and leave you free to return to private life. But remember that Italy must not continue in shame, and that it is better to die than to live as slaves of the foreigner.

'GARIBALDI.' [3]

That afternoon and evening the authorities of San Marino busily negotiated with Archduke Ernest for the safety of their guests, and, after some bargaining, obtained the offer of terms which would not have been unreasonable

---

[1] *Mem.* 244; *Rug.* 62–65; *De Rossi,* 260; *Bologna MS. Piva*; *Bel.* 158, 159; *Hoff.* 431–434.

[2] See illustration, p. 275, above. It is only a few hundred yards from the gate in the companion picture.

[3] *Brizi,* 11, 12; *Rug.* 66; *Bel.* 168, 169; *Mem.* 245; *Hoff.* 434–436. There are slight variants as to the wording of the Order of the Day, but not as to the sense of the words.

if there had been any security for their fulfilment. The
Italians were to surrender their arms to the San Marinesi,
who were to hand these over to the Austrians, and the disarmed men were to be allowed to return safely to their
homes. Garibaldi and his wife were to take ship for America.
But these conditions were not to hold good unless they were
ratified by Gorzkowski, Governor-General of the Cavalry
resident at Bologna, to whom the whole question was
referred. This delay, which left all to the mercy of a cruel
man, was eagerly seized on by Garibaldi and his Staff as
a sufficient reason for breaking off negotiations, upon which
they had entered most unwillingly and only for the sake of
their followers. That same night, at a Council of War held
in Simoncini's *café*, the faces of those present lit up with joy
when it was decided to refuse the terms, for Garibaldi was
thus set free to seek Venice with a small body of volunteers,
leaving the bulk of his disbanded army to the good offices
of the friendly Republic. But the decision was not at once
made known. Since the faithful few would have to steal
through the Austrian lines on the Marecchia before daylight, secrecy was essential ; it would have been fatal to
arouse the main body of the troops, who were sleeping on
the road between the Cappuccini and the town gate, and
equally fatal to warn the authorities of San Marino, who were
bound to prohibit the setting forth of an armed force from
their dominions. It was, therefore, not till the birds were
flown that the Regency received the following note, hastily
written in pencil :—

' Citizen Representatives of the Republic.—The conditions
imposed by the Austrians are unacceptable ; and therefore we
will evacuate your territory.—Yours, G. GARIBALDI.' [1]

This laconic statement of facts, scribbled in the hurry
of preparation for the dangerous sortie, was somewhat
brusque, but Garibaldi was deeply grateful to the San
Marinesi, and always spoke in warm terms of his debt to

[1] *Rug.* 67, 68 ; *Brizi,* 15, 16, 22 ; *Franciosi,* 19–22 ; *Hoff.* 437–439 ; *Bel.*
171–177.

'those excellent Republicans' and 'generous hosts.'
Whether his departure with the other notorious Republican
chiefs, such as Bassi and Ciceruacchio, whose lives neither
Austria nor the Papacy would willingly spare, made it
more likely, or less, that the remainder of the troops would
be well treated, it is difficult to decide. Probably, in leaving the army, which he had already disbanded, to obtain
what terms it could for itself, he by no means betrayed its
interest. But one thing is beyond all doubt : it was no
coup de théâtre, but an act of heroism requiring iron nerves
and fortitude of mind, for the man who had been in command night and day during the whole siege and retreat,
and who during the last forty-eight hours had not closed
his eyes, to start out once more from a haven of present
rest and at least of possible salvation, and face again a sea of
immediate hardship and danger, in the hope of penetrating
into Venice so as to share in its last, hopeless defence.

Late at night (July 31) the preparations for departure were made by the band of friends who were in the
secret, gathered in the *café* Simoncini, and round the city
gate. Garibaldi supped with Ciceruacchio, Ugo Bassi, and
Anita, who was showing grave signs of illness. He implored
her to remain among the kindly Republicans, in a house
whose inhabitants were already treating her with tenderness and affection. ' In vain ; that resolute and noble
heart, indignant at all my remonstrances on this subject,
silenced me at last with the words : " You want to leave
me." ' [1]

It was close on midnight. Garibaldi was sitting on
a stone outside the *café*, reading his map by the light of
a lantern, and from time to time questioning three peasants
of the Monte Titano, who stood reverently before him. He
was smoking a cigar, and listening with his usual quiet
manner to their replies as to the exact position of the
Austrian forces that surrounded the borders of the Republic.
His officers were standing round him. Suddenly he rose

[1] *Mem.* 246; *Denkwürdigkeiten*, ii. 145, 146.

up. 'Whoever wishes to follow me,' he cried, 'I offer him fresh battles, sufferings and exile : treaties with the foreigner, never '—*patti con lo straniero, non mai.* So saying, he leapt on his horse, and rode out under the gateway of San Marino, which ought by rights to have been closed by the porter, had he not been in collusion with Garibaldi. In the next minute everyone present had to determine whether to go or stay. More than 200 devoted men, and one all too devoted woman, followed after him, and in silence they began to descend the great mountain, northwards, through the night.

It was done so suddenly that even Ugo Bassi would have been left behind, had not Garibaldi remembered to ask for him at the gate. One of the officers went back to fetch the friar from the *café*, whence, in the hurry of departure, he forgot to take his collar and his writing materials; they were found lying on his bed and preserved in San Marino with great veneration, after his martyrdom.[1]

When, early next morning, the remainder of the army awoke to find their leader gone, they picked up their weapons, and rushed after him down the road almost to the borders of the Republic. Their next instinct was to return and occupy the citadel, and die defending it against the Austrians; but, finally, their remaining officers and the civic authorities brought them to reason, and induced them to surrender their arms. The negotiations with the Austrians were then resumed, and dragged on during the whole autumn, the victors securing the surrender of the arms, but giving only equivocal and ill-observed promises as to the treatment of the interned army. The good Sammarinesi spared neither efforts nor expense to help the poor fellows, gave them each a sum of money, and sent them off in civilian clothes to their homes. Some went in large bodies, others in small groups, others alone. Some were seized, flogged almost to death, and shut up for long terms in horrible prisons. Others

---

[1] The gate by which they went out is that in the illustration, p. 275, above. *Simoncini,* 15–17 ; *Modoni,* 76–80, 82 (Zani's narrative) ; *Hoff.* 440 ; *Bel.* 178, 179.

were allowed to pass, and yet more got away by avoiding the enemy, as the cordon of troops round the Republic was gradually relaxed.[1]

Meanwhile, between midnight and dawn, Garibaldi and his column had escaped through the Austrian blockade. Just outside the north-west corner of the territory of San Marino, the bed of the Marecchia, almost dry in summer, but broad as the London Thames, lay athwart their course, and the moment of greatest danger was while they were stumbling in the darkness across this quarter of a mile of white stones, pools, and sandbanks, between two bodies of Austrians, at Pietracuta above, and Verucchio below, the point of their passage. But again the enemy came up too late—only in time for his cavalry to skirmish with the rearguard under Forbes, Hoffstetter, and Ugo Bassi.[2]

Once across the Marecchia, the Garibaldians had little cause to fear being overtaken that night. Climbing the high mountains on the further bank by mule tracks, they stumbled on till dawn, up and down the sides of terrific ravines such as that of the Uso, by stony, breakneck paths of the nature of dried watercourses, difficult in the day-time, and impossible at night to ordinary soldiers. At Garibaldi's side, constantly pointing out the invisible path, rode Zani, a workman of San Marino, who used sometimes to act as professional guide, and who had volunteered for love to show the way over the northern mountains as far as the plain of the Romagna. Under these conditions not a few lost the column, and set off alone to find their homes ; Hoffstetter, left behind in a cleft of the Uso valley, sold his horse, changed his clothes, and made off, eager at

[1] *Rug.* 73, 74, 84–86 ; *Franciosi*, 27–36 ; *Brizi*, 16, 17 ; *Farini*, iv. 237 ; *Modoni*, 93.

[2] *Modoni*, 82–84 (Zani's evidence) ; *Hoff.* 440–443 ; *Bel.* 185, 186. The Garibaldians descended Monte Titano by the Acquaviva road, and crossed the Marecchia near the point where the San Marino river enters it. The bridge over that tributary must be the fine modern bridge referred to by Zani (*Modoni*, 83). If the Austrians blockading the Republican territory had kept a body of men at the place where the San Marino road and river debouch together into the Marecchia valley, Garibaldi could not have crossed their line without giving battle.

length to quit the parched Apennines for the echoing torrents of the Alps, and to become, in the leisure and freedom
of his native Zurich, the Xenophon of the Retreat from
Rome.[1]

By the time the column touched a road once more, near
the high-perched village of San Giovanni in Galilea, the
men were utterly exhausted; but they were soon cheered
by the rising sun, and revived by the fresh bread, wine,
and water-melons sent out to them by the friendly townspeople of Sogliano.[2]   All that day (August 1) they raced
on, sometimes by roads along high narrow ridges,
sometimes by mule tracks across ravines, traversing
hills that gradually became less rugged, re-entering the
region of olives, and crossing the deep valley of the Rubicon
(Fiumicino)[3] through corn and vines and fruit-trees.   In
the scattered hamlet of Musano they halted from one o'clock
till three near the pretty little parish church, which the
authorities afterwards ordered to be ' re-blessed,' because
Garibaldi and Anita had entered it.[4]   Anita, who was rapidly
growing worse, called all day most piteously for water.

After Musano they regained the high road, and passed
close by the town of Longiano, staggering along, stupid
with fatigue ; Garibaldi himself had not slept for three
nights and days.[5]   At about four in the afternoon they
found themselves standing at cross-roads, on the very
edge of the weary hills, at a spot where the traveller suddenly sees spread before him the plain in which Cæsar
crossed the Rubicon, and beyond it, only eight miles away,
the blue Adriatic dancing in the sun.   As they stood there
gazing on the sea, the face of Garibaldi the sailor lit up as
though he had arisen fresh from sleep, and his eyes kindled
darkly in their strange fashion.[6]

---

[1] *Hoff.* 444, 445 ; *Modoni,* 75–86 (Zani's evidence) ; *Bel.* 182–187.

[2] *Bel.* 187 ;*Modoni,*85.

[3] It is not quite certain whether the Uso or the Fiumicino is the ancient
Rubicon. In either case, they crossed it in the march from San Marino.

[4] The parish priest himself befriended them (*Bel.* 187, 188).   *Modoni,* 86.

[5] *Bel.* 182, 188 ; *Bologna MS. Roncofreddo.*   *Modoni,* 86.

[6] A memorial pillar and little grove now mark the spot.   It is within half a

MAIN STREET OF CESENATICO, WITH 'BRAGOZZI.'
(No change in character of street or boats since 1849.)

A 'BRAGOZZO' BETWEEN CESENATICO TOWN AND THE MOLE AT THE
HARBOUR ENTRANCE, WHICH IS NEAR THE HOUSE IN THE DISTANCE.

An hour more, and they were in the full plain of the
Romagna, crossing at right angles the great highway of
the Via Aemilia. When, late in the afternoon, they reached
the village of Gatteo, Zani's task was done ; he had led them
safely off the hills. Garibaldi took his hand and said:
' Good-bye, dear Zani ; I thank you for your work. In
ten years I hope to see you again, with better fortune.'
The faithful guide went back to his shop on the summit of
the Titano, and, in precisely ten years' time, came down into
the liberated Romagna to be welcomed by the hero of the
age, as one of those who had saved him in the hour of need.[1]

From Gatteo they hurried on, in growing weariness
and excitement, through the darkening vineyards, past Sala,
towards the sea. The goal of their extraordinary march of
twenty-two hours from San Marino, was to be Cesenatico,
where Garibaldi heard that there were many fishing boats
and few Austrians. The neighbouring municipalities were
patriotic and active, as became Romagnuols. The Governor
of Savignano sent false reports that Garibaldi was spending
the night at Longiano, and so prevented the Austrians, who
were thick along the Via Aemilia, from following to Cesenatico
until it was too late. The savage Gorzkowski, come from
Bologna to Savignano to catch Garibaldi, was unable to find
and shoot this splendidly lying governor, who had decamped,
and so had to be content with kicking the secretary.[2]

It was past ten at night, in the little town of Cesenatico.
The fishing fleet had come home and thirteen of the *bragozzi*
(or *baragozzi*) by which the inhabitants made their livelihood, were lying in the canal that runs down the middle of
the main street.[3] ' The *bragozzi* are the most picturesque
boats that traffic on the lagoons,' writes Mr. Horatio Brown,
who can make such a statement with authority. ' It is
the *bragozzi* alone that carry upon their bows those wonder-

mile of Longiano, and quite close to the high, squarely built Villa Pasolini, which
is the most prominent landmark on the edge of the hills. *Bel.* 188-190.
[1] *Modoni*, 86, 87 (Zani's evidence).
[2] *Bologna MS. Savignano* ; *Bel.* 194, 195.   [3] See illustration opposite.

ful flying figures of fame blowing a trumpet in a swirl of
drapery. Nothing can be prettier than to see them lying,
bow by painted bow, in a long row.'[1] Even so they lay
in Cesenatico that night. Their dyed sails, which had
shone in the daylight, sheets of scarlet and saffron, orange,
brown and white in curious patterns, were furled and
muffled in darkness. The tired owners were fast asleep
in the houses on both sides of the canal; half a dozen
white-coats were dozing or playing cards with guttural
exclamations in their guard-house, and a few Papal Carabineers were similarly off the watch in another barrack.
The street and the little square, and the masts of the sleeping
ships in the midst, were wrapped in peace and darkness,
when suddenly the silence was broken by a clatter of horsemen, the voice of a leader, men dismounting and hammering
at doors and scattering in all directions on their errands.
The guards were dragged, dazed and half-awake, out of their
quarters into the square (where Garibaldi's statue stands
to-day); some of the desperate band were for shooting the
officer of Carabineers—a man named Sereni—lest he should
give information after they had gone; but since Ugo Bassi
pleaded for his life, and Garibaldi would not hear of imitating
Austrian methods of warfare, it was decided to take the
prisoners on the voyage.[2]

And now the serious work of embarkation began. The
fishermen of Cesenatico were hauled out of bed, sulky and
sleepy, to take an unenthusiastic part in the commandeering
of their own boats; the municipal authorities were brought
into action, and the town was ransacked for ropes and provisions. The thirteen *bragozzi* were towed down the half mile of
canal that joins the town to the shore,[3] as far as the harbour
entrance, which consists of two piers, built of wood-piles
and stones, carrying the canal out into the sea. So far
all had gone well; but here, as Garibaldi writes in his

Life on the Lagoons, 151, 152.

[2] *Mem.* 246, 247; *Bel.* 196, 197, 201; *Guerzoni*, i. 257, 258, note; *Bologna
MS. Cesenatico, Piva's communication to the Corriere del Polesine, November* 15,
1896; *Boll. Ris.* ii. 112–113.

[3] See the lower of the two illustrations, p. 283, above.

Memorie, fortune ceased any longer to favour him that night.

'There had been a violent squall from the sea, and the breakers were so heavy in the mouth of the port that it was almost impossible for vessels to put out.

'Here I found the advantage of my seamanship. It was absolutely necessary that we should leave the port; day was at hand, so were the Austrians, and no retreat was open to us except by sea.

'I went on board each of the *bragozzi,* had ropes fastened to two kedge-anchors lashed together, and tried to get out of the harbour in a small boat, in order to drop the anchors and warp the *bragozzi* out. Our first attempts were fruitless. In vain we sprang into the sea, to push the boat by force of arm through the breakers; in vain we encouraged the rowers with cheering words and many promises. Only after repeated and laborious attempts did we succeed in carrying the anchors to the proper distance and sinking them. As, having let down the anchors, we returned to the harbour, gradually letting out the ropes as we went, the last one, being thin and made of inferior hemp, parted, and we had to do the whole of the work over again. Such mishaps were enough to drive a man crazy. At last I was obliged to return to the fishing-boats, and get fresh ropes and fresh anchors; and all this with a sleepy and unwilling crew, who could be made to move at all—not to speak of doing the necessary work—only by means of blows with the flat of our swords. At last we tried once more, and this time succeeded in taking out the anchors as far as was needful.'

In these prolonged operations of 'warping out,' Garibaldi took the most arduous part upon himself, plunging through the breakers to shove out the little boat with the kedge-anchors on board, and diving into the sea to fasten them. While he was engaged in this latter operation, his companion, unable to keep the boat still, dropped away from him, but saw him, when he had fastened the anchors, swim back with ease through the stormy water and, as dawn was breaking, leap into the boat, 'like a sea-god,' 'shaking out his long locks with a vigorous motion

of the neck.' [1]   He was in his own element once more, and
the vigil and journeying, and strain of so many days and
nights seemed to have had no effect upon his iron frame.

For seven hours Anita sat by the shore, faint and in
great pain, but propped up so as to watch her husband at
his work.[2]   Half a mile away, at the inland entrance of the
town, Hugh Forbes had thrown up a street barricade
against the Austrians, who were expected at every moment
throughout the long agony of delay.   There he stood, with
the rearguard, until all the rest were aboard.[3] *   He and his
white top-hat deserve a place in the Garibaldian epic.   The
forerunner of Peard, Dunne, and others of our countrymen
who won names for themselves under the great Italian in
less calamitous times, Forbes professed the faith ten years
too soon for prudence and respectability, and so earned
nothing but detraction, besides an excellent chance of being
set up against a wall and shot.[4]   He was by no means a
perfect character, but he appeared at his best in 1849.

At last, between half-past six and eight in the morning,
the *bragozzi* with the men on board had been ' warped out '
into the open sea, and all was ready for departure.   Garibaldi,
not without emotion, kissed the forehead of the horse that had
carried him so far and so well, and gave him to a patriot of
Cesenatico with the words : ' Do what you will with him, but
never let him pass into the hands of the Austrians.'

And so they set sail for Venice ; about an hour later the
Austrians entered the little town.[5]

' The day was already somewhat advanced when we left
Cesenatico ; the weather had turned fine, and the wind was
favourable.   If I had not been so distressed by the situation of
my Anita, who was in a deplorable state of suffering, I might
have said that our condition—having overcome so many difficulties, and being on the way to safety—could be called fortunate.

---

[1] *Bologna MS. Cesenatico, Piva's communication to the Corriere del Polesine,*
Mem. 247.

[2] *Denkwürdigkeiten*, ii. 146.   [3] *Mem.* 248, and note at end of chapter.

[4] *F.O. Papers, Tuscany.   January to December* 1849, 141.

[*5] *Bel* 200 ; *Forbes' Volontario*, 121, *note* ; *Boll. Ris.* ii. 113 ; *Citt. Cesena*,
Uccellini's Garibaldi, 9.

But my dear wife's sufferings were too great; and greater still was the misery caused by my own inability to relieve them.

'What with the stress of weather, and the difficulties encountered in getting out of Cesenatico, I had not been able to turn my attention to the provisioning of the boats. I had entrusted it to an officer, who had collected all he could; but at night, in a strange village, where we had taken the inhabitants by surprise, he had procured but a small quantity of supplies, which were distributed among the different boats.

'The chief thing wanting was water, and my poor suffering wife was tormented by a feverish thirst—no doubt one of the symptoms of her illness. I too was thirsty, worn out as I was by the night's work; and we had very little drinking-water. All the rest of that day (August 2) we coasted along the Italian side of the Adriatic, at a certain distance off shore, with a favourable wind. The night, when it came, was most beautiful. The moon was full,[1] and it was with a terrible misgiving that I watched the rising of the mariner's companion, contemplated by me so often with the reverence of a worshipper. Lovelier than I had ever seen her before, but for us, unhappily, too lovely—the moon was fatal to us that night. East of the point of Goro lay the Austrian squadron.'

[1] *Mem.* 248, 249. Full moon was on August 4 (see Almanacs of 1849).

---

* The Mayor of Cesenatico, in his official report, declared that he tried to send word to Cesena during the night, 'but all was useless, as the Garibaldians had stopped up all the exits from the town, having also barricaded the roads out of the place with carts, tables, benches, and other objects. In this way they held the town till half-past six this morning' (*Citt. Cesena*). This is borne out by Forbes himself, who says that he concealed two men in ambush, 30 yards beyond the sentries, on every road leading out of the town, and that these men and the sentries between them secured the arrest of everyone either leaving or approaching the town. Forbes believed that but for this device the Austrians would have got news, and Garibaldi and all his men would have been caught during the 'warping out,' and destroyed. *Forbes' Volontario*, 121, *note*.

CHAPTER XV

THE DEATH OF ANITA

'I cannot count the years,
    That you will drink, like me,
The cup of blood and tears,
Ere she to you appears :—
    Italia, Italia shall be free !

'You dedicate your lives
    To her, and you will be
The food on which she thrives,
Till her great day arrives :—
    Italia, Italia shall be free !

'She asks you but for faith !
    Your faith in her takes she
As draughts of heaven's breath,
Amid defeat and death :—
    Italia, Italia shall be free !'

GEORGE MEREDITH (*Vittoria*, chap. xxi.)

IN that extreme north-eastern angle of the Romagna formed by the Adriatic and the Po, lies the lagoon district of Comacchio, a southern counterpart to the more famous region round Venice to the north of the great river. Although its islands, marshes, and strips of sandy soil are seldom visited by tourists from Ravenna, owing to some difficulty of access, it has, for all who reach it, a fascination and beauty of its own. Comacchio, like a diminutive Venice, rears its beautiful red towers out of the middle of the inland sea, upon which it seems to float, a princess of the waters. Canals run through some of the principal streets, and the island city is joined by a narrow causeway road, across the lagoon,[1] to Ferrara and the western mainland on

---

[1] In the map at the end of the book, which must be used for this Chapter, the breadth of the causeway carrying the road has been inevitably exaggerated.

one side, and to the little port town of Magnavacca on the other. The district which included Comacchio and the neighbouring city of Ravenna was noted as a nursery of brave men, and its peasants, boatmen and fishermen, fine fellows as any in the Romagna, were good patriots and Liberals, alike when Byron dwelt in their midst, and when Garibaldi entrusted his life to their keeping.

The leading citizen of Comacchio, in 1848–49, was Nino [1] Bonnet, the owner of a good deal of land round the lagoon, and a man of great influence with all classes, except with the Papal Governors of the country. In November 1848,[2] he had taken a leading part in rousing Comacchio to defend Masina and his lancers against the Government troops sent from Ferrara by Rossi and Zucchi, had gone the length of erecting a barricade and a battery on the causeway over the lagoon, and had even fired the cannon to warn off the advancing column. In the following week, at Ravenna, he had seen Garibaldi and been taken into his counsels while the Legion was forming, and had, as he tells us, been won to a lifelong devotion by 'the air of nobility and heroism which radiated from that manly countenance.'[3] Since then eight months had gone by, during which two of Bonnet's younger brothers had fought, and one of them had died, under Garibaldi at Rome; while a third, named Celeste, was with Nino in Comacchio during the eventful first days of August 1849.[4]

Nino Bonnet, secretly informed by his Liberal confederates of Garibaldi's march through San Marino to take ship for Venice, was strolling along the seashore near Magnavacca on the evening of August 2, with an anxious eye on the eastern horizon, when he descried, by the last light of day, the red and orange sails of a fleet of *bragozzi* in the offing, running before a favourable wind for Venice, He knew at once who must be on board, and he knew also,

---

[1] Short for Gioacchino (Joachim), a common name, especially in patriotic Italian families at this period, in honour of Joachim Murat.

[2] See p. 79, above.   [3] *Bonnet*, 5, 6; *Guerzoni*, i. 361, 362.

[4] *Bonnet*, 20, 25, 41; *Loev*, ii. 234.   See list, p. 326, below.

from his friends in Venetia, that an Austrian squadron was cruising off the mouths of the Po. With sombre forebodings he stood and gazed, until darkness rose out of the sea to blot the view ; then, returning to his house in Comacchio, he flung himself down in his clothes, not to sleep, but to lie nervously listening for what he most dreaded to hear. Shortly before midnight the distant boom of cannon from the sea sent him leaping from his bed, and in a few minutes he was driving like a madman, back along the causeway to Magnavacca, in his little *biroccino*.[1] Arrived at the mouth of the harbour, which, like that of Cesenatico, consists of two piers carrying the canal out into the surf, he found the population of Magnavacca and 150 Austrian and Papal soldiers crowded on the mole, straining their eyes over the disturbed and moonlit surface of the sea. But nothing could be made out beyond the breakers except an occasional flash, always followed by the sullen roar of a cannon. As the night grew grey, more and more troops poured down to the beach, and the excitement became intense, as the people and their foreign oppressors watched together, but with such different feelings, the veiled spectacle of the tragedy that was enacting on the waters.[2]

At sunrise, experienced mariners in the crowd by the pier could distinguish that most of the *bragozzi* had been captured, but that three of them were running for shore some miles north of Magnavacca, pursued by pinnaces and long-boats. If Bonnet had now remained inactive, or if the Austrian commandant had at once marched a part of his men northwards to cut off the fugitives as they landed, as he certainly ought to have done, it is not likely that one of the men on board the three *bragozzi* would have survived to deliver Italy in years to come. But while the officer kept his soldiers drawn up on the pier of Magnavacca—perhaps because he did not clearly perceive what was going on at sea—Bonnet, informed by an old salt of the real

---

[1] A light one-horse gig between two high wheels, much used on the sandy tracks of the Ravenna and Comacchio district.

[2] *Bonnet*, 12–16; *Gualtieri*, 182 (Lieut.-Governor of Comacchio's report); *Benko*, 631–2 ; App. O, below.

state of the game, drove his *biroccino* along the track that runs northward, a little inland, but parallel to the shore. After travelling thus for two or three miles, till he was out of reach of the Austrians, he sent on his confidential servant with the vehicle to await him at Cavallina farm, and himself, leaving the track, made his way down to the beach. As he emerged from among the sand-dunes on to the open shore, the first things that met his eyes were the three *bragozzi*, safely aground, half a mile further to the north, and a group of men disembarking from them and rapidly disappearing into the covert of the dunes, in various directions. As he ran towards them along the hard sands by the water's edge, he saw the last two men of the party wading through the surf from the fishing boats, one of them carrying a woman in his arms. ' It is he, it is he,' the runner whispered to himself, straining every muscle to reach them before they should follow the others and disappear among the dunes.[1]

Among the men whom Bonnet had seen making off inland were Ugo Bassi and Ciceruacchio, to whom their Chief bade a hasty but tender farewell with the sure foreboding that he would never see them again. At that moment his own chance of life was even less than theirs, for the Austrians were more eager to catch and kill him than all the rest of his band put together, and he could move away from them no faster than he could carry Anita. He had ordered all to disperse and escape, but to one other man, who could himself move but slowly, he accorded the privilege of remaining with him : this was his devoted friend Captain Culiolo, commonly called *Leggiero*, who, wounded in the leg during the siege of Rome, had not been able to leave the city till July 14, but had succeeded, with the aid of good horses, in overtaking the column of retreat.[2]

The greater part of the *bragozzi*, with 162 Garibaldians on

[1] *Bonnet*, 12–16. The place of Garibaldi's disembarkation is about four miles north of Magnavacca, not at the memorial pillar near the port.

[2] *Mem.* 250, 251 ; *Loev.* i. 271, 272 ; *Bel.* 157 ; *Bologna MS. Verità ; Citt. Cesena.*

board, had been captured out at sea.[1] The fishermen of Cesenatico, less than half-hearted in performing the *corvée* imposed on them by the red-shirts, and scared by the Austrian cannonade, had shown so little activity in obeying the orders shouted by Garibaldi, that the greater part of his commandeered fleet had been easily overhauled. The Austrians, as they leapt on board, spat in the faces of the Italians, but refrained from massacre, and took them to the fortress of Pola on the Illyrian coast. There, although the female population of the town received the enemies of their Kaiser with the same charming courtesy with which they had been first greeted by their captors at sea, their lives were spared on the ground that they had been taken, not as rebels against the Pope, but as prisoners of war in Venetian waters; and after some months of severe imprisonment, they were released under an amnesty. If they had been caught in Papal territory, or if they had been landed there immediately after their capture, they would, many of them, have been shot, as were most of Garibaldi's companions who were hunted down on land during the first days of August.

Hugh Forbes was released in October, rather before his fellow-prisoners of Pola, owing to the representations of the British ministers, and the entreaties of his wife, a lady of partly Italian origin, who personally visited General D'Aspre to entreat mercy.[2] Throughout August and September, this poor woman, hourly fearing to hear that her husband had been handed over to the Papal authorities and shot, must also have had grave fears for young Forbes, who had been left behind by his father, probably at San Marino, and whom the reactionary Governments were making special efforts to arrest; however, he escaped uncaught. His father lived to devote himself to the liberation of the American negroes and of the Poles, and to take part under Garibaldi in the more fortunate Sicilian campaign.[3]

---

[1] See App. O, below.

[2] She was Forbes' second wife; his former wife, the mother of young Forbes, had been an English lady.

[3] See App. N, below, *Hugh Forbes. Bologna MSS. Cesenatico, Piva*; F. O.

But, when Garibaldi waded through the surf, on the morning of August 3, there was little prospect that he would live to win future victories. Set ashore on the Bosco Eliseo, a strip of land three miles wide by six long,[1] which was already beginning to be searched by hundreds of soldiers incited to kill him by the promise of rich rewards, himself bound, by ties dearer than life, to a dying woman clinging to his breast, and accompanied only by a friend halting on a wounded leg, he could not move a mile or find fresh water for Anita's parched lips but by the help of the peasants, who had the fear of the Austrian murderers heavy upon them. Gorzkowski, moved to brutal rage by the news of the escape from San Marino, and knowing that he himself would be held responsible if Garibaldi escaped alive, proclaimed death to all who should give bread, water, or the shelter of the hearth, to any of his following, and, with the generosity peculiar to the hunter after blood, announced that the leader might be identified at sight by the companionship of a woman far gone with child.[2]

While Garibaldi heavily mounted the nearest of the sand-hills with his precious burden, and descended towards the marsh water beyond it,[3] if he did not then think his last day had dawned, it was because he was sustained by a strong faith in his destiny. If he had such faith, it was answered, as it were by miracle. Suddenly, in that desert place, a panting but well-dressed young gentleman stood at his side, holding out his hand, with a look of earnest determination and intelligence on his face.[4] ' Bonnet ! ' cried Garibaldi, in a rapture of surprise, seeing, when he least expected him, the one man who might procure for the fugitives some means of escape through the farms on

Papers, *Tuscany and Rome, Aug.–Sept.* 1849, 3, 139, No. 147, and *Tuscany, Jan.–Dec.* 1849, 141 ; *Guerzoni*, i. 359 ; *Bel.* App. I. ; *Rug.* 87–90 ; *Vecchi*, ii. 323 ; *Forbes*, 109.

[1] This strip of land was cut off by the sea to the east, by the lagoon to the west, by the Magnavacca canal to the south, and by one of the mouths of the Po to the north. In contemporary accounts it is called the *Bosco Eliseo.*

[2] *Rug.* 72 ; *Boggio*, 17 ; *Scampo*, 9 ; *Guerzoni*, i. 358 ; *Bonnet*, 64, 65.

[3] This he must have done, as personal observation of the scene will show.

[4] See picture of Bonnet, frontispiece *Bonnet*, ed. 1887.

his land, and the intricate waterways of his native district.[1]

Scarcely had they exchanged greetings, when they became aware of a man hovering near them, whom Bonnet recognised as a character well known on the countryside under the name of *Baramoro*, a beach-comber, one of the poorest of the very poor, but none so poor as to sell his countrymen to the foreigner. '*Baramoro*,' cried Bonnet, pointing inland across the marsh to a straw-roofed hut on the edge of the cultivated ground, 'do you see that little cottage ? ' ' Yes, I see it.' ' Well, take my friends there, while I am off after some other business. The lady is ill, and needs to be carried.' While *Baramoro* and Garibaldi conveyed Anita to the hut, and *Leggiero* hobbled along behind, Bonnet ran down to the three *bragozzi* to fetch out some papers and clothes needed by the fugitives. But the Austrian long-boats, arriving in belated pursuit, opened fire, and drove off Bonnet before he had time to effect his purpose.[2]

Returning inland, he reached the hut, to find Garibaldi already dressed as a peasant. With infinite difficulty and danger—for the Bosco Eliseo was now swarming with Papalini and white-coats—they proceeded to carry the agonising woman across two miles of country to Cavallina farm, where they arrived well after midday. Here Bonnet's servant and *biroccino* were waiting, and here Anita was laid on a bed and given such nourishment as she could take. Here, too, Bonnet had time to take the chief aside and expose to him at length the utter impossibility of crossing the Po and reaching Venice, and the need, if he wished to save his own life for his country, of parting from Anita as soon as she had been placed in safety and comfort. At last Garibaldi consented to leave her, provided that he could himself bear her company as far as the house designed by his friend for her accom-

---

[1] *Bonnet*, 16 ; *Mem.* 251.

[2] *Bonnet*, 16–19 ; *Gironi*, 39. Gironi's book represents local tradition ; but where it differs from Bonnet, as regards scenes at which he was present, Bonnet is the more likely to be right.

modation—the large Zanetto farm. He agreed that after that he would try to escape, with *Leggiero*, through the Romagna and Tuscany into Piedmont, by such means as the Liberals of Ravenna should provide.[1]

About this time a large portion of the searchers had fortunately got on to the track of another party of fugitives, possibly that which included Ciceruacchio and his sons, and had followed the trail out of the Bosco Eliseo, passing close by the Zanetto farm itself and going on northwards for many miles, as far as Massenzatica, on the edge of the Austrian territory. They found along the route arms thrown away by the fugitives, and were lured on apace by false reports that Garibaldi, in company with his wife dressed as a man and mounted on a horse, had been seen among the party whom they were following.[2]

In the middle of the afternoon (August 3) Garibaldi and *Leggiero* started on again, taking Anita in a cart, towards the Zanetto farm on the borders of the great lagoon, where, at Bonnet's request, every comfort was being prepared, and where her husband might with a good conscience leave her behind. Meanwhile Bonnet himself hastened back to Comacchio to engage and despatch the boat which, according to the plan as now agreed upon, was to fetch Garibaldi away from his wife. Entering his native town at imminent risk of being arrested, he found Ugo Bassi in bed at the *Luna* inn, under surveillance as a suspect, having deliberately come to Comacchio in the belief that as he was a non-combatant his life would be spared. Bonnet, who knew better, urged him and his companion Livraghi to instant flight ; they hurried on their clothes and would have escaped forthwith, had not the Austrian soldiers burst in while they were in the act of eloping by the window, and arrested them under Bonnet's eyes. They had been denounced by Sereni, the Papal Brigadier, the very man who had been spared at

---

[1] *Bonnet,* 19–24, 35 ; *Gironi,* 39–41 ; *Itinerary.*

[2] *Gualtieri,* 184–185 (Lt.-Gov. of Comacchio's report). The map shows that they could not have got to Vaccolino without passing close to the Zanetto farm. Had Garibaldi yet arrived there when they passed its door ? Probably not.

the friar's own intercession at Cesenatico, and carried off on the voyage ; rather than take his life in cold blood, Garibaldi had set the potential informer free that morning, when they had dispersed from the *bragozzi* on the beach.[1]

Leaving Bassi to his now inevitable fate, Bonnet, with the help of his brother Celeste, despatched the boatmen to Zanetto farm, but without informing them of the character of the party whom they were transporting, and himself stole back thither, avoiding numerous parties of white-coats. At the farm he found that a new difficulty had arisen. Anita, growing hourly worse, and no longer well able to understand what was going on around her, was in agony at the idea of being separated from Garibaldi. ' Bonnet,' he said at last, ' you cannot imagine all that this woman has done for me, nor how tenderly she loves me. I owe her an immense debt of gratitude and love. Let her come with me.' After again making clear, but to no purpose, the great danger which the two men would incur by this change of plan, their friend bowed to the ruling of love, and granted that death alone should part the wife from her husband. And so, when the boat arrived from Comacchio, they laid her beside him, among the cushions in the stern, and at the moment when the *Ave Maria* was sounding over the broad, still surface of the lagoon, Bonnet watched Anita, Garibaldi and *Leggiero* float from the shore and recede into the gathering gloom.[2]

Anita, in her last hours, still held by the undogmatic religion of her husband—to which, perhaps, she had ad-hered more consistently than he. It had been noticed at Rieti, on Good Friday of that year, that, while Garibaldi pleased the population by dismounting and taking off his hat to a procession, Anita, who was at his side, remained in the saddle.[3] The minute daily records of those who watched her during the Retreat from Rome, and during her long death agony throughout the first four days of

[1] *Bonnet*, 24, 25 ; *Bel.* 196 ; *Venosta*, 136–139 ; *Facchini*, 126, 127 ; *Gualtieri*, 95–6, 183.   [2] *Bonnet*, 25–29 ; *Mem.* 252.

[3] *Loev.* i. 131 ; see also *Bel.* 86, ll. 13–16, for another incident indicating her opinions.

August, mention no sign of craving on her part for those miraculous consolations which she had rejected in her days of health and strength. Dying on the breast of Garibaldi, she needed no priest.

The land-locked sea over which Anita was taken for her last voyage, called the Valli di Comacchio, is cut into two unequal parts by the highroad causeway that joins the island city to the mainland and to the seashore— the part of the lagoon north of Comacchio, known as the Valli Isola and Ponti, being smaller than the portion lying to the south. The lagoons are again subdivided, though in less marked fashion, by long strings of narrow islands, some of bare earth and some covered with rough grass, never more than two feet above the water, and not many feet wide, but extending often for miles in length. Except the towers of Comacchio, the low black lines of these *argini*, as they are called, alone break the monotony of the lake ; and a few huts rising upon them, at intervals of many miles, serve as the only landmarks within the wide boundaries of the green, encircling shores. Under a spring sky, with larks singing above the causeway, and white cloud masses rolling along the horizon over the distant Apennines, and Comacchio near at hand rising red out of the blue waters, there is neither terror nor gloom in all the tranquil scene. But on that hot August night, danger lurked in the still lagoon, and death was companion in the boat.

They rowed safely across the northern Valli Isola and Ponti, and then, carrying Anita and their little vessel across the highroad causeway, at midnight and unobserved, they embarked upon the larger southern lake. But during the portage over the causeway something aroused the suspicions of the crew, the identity of Garibaldi was disclosed to them, and, in terror of their lives, they abandoned him, at about three in the morning of August 4, alone with his wife and *Leggiero*, in a hut upon one of the desert islands to the north of the *argine* Agosta. The sun, rising from behind Comacchio on the desolate scene, brought neither comfort nor hope ; she, it was now too clear, would in any case be dead before nightfall, and the Austrians would in all likelihood be the next visitors to the oozy isle on which they were marooned.[1]

But the boatmen had not returned to Comacchio in order to betray, and the fact that they had declined to prosecute further a task imposed on them under false pretences reached the ears of their employers and not of the Austrians.[2] At an early hour, Nino Bonnet was roused from bed by his brother Celeste's wife, who rushed into his room with the calamitous news. A few minutes later he was battering at the house of a patriotic boatman named Michele Guidi, whom he soon roused from sleep. It was neither possible nor necessary to conceal from this man the real nature of the case, and he agreed to fetch away Garibaldi and his party to a certain dairy-farm near Mandriole, whither Nino Bonnet hastened to prepare the inhabitants for their arrival.[3]

And so at eight in the morning, after five hours of terrible suspense, they were taken off the lonely island by Michele Guidi and his brother, who rowed them across the lagoon to the Chiavica di Mezzo (or Pedone), their chosen landing-place on the southern shore. They arrived here about one in the afternoon (August 4), but only to encounter fresh delays and difficulties before they could transfer the dying woman to the dairy-farm at Mandriole. It was necessary first to carry the boat across the bank which divides the lagoon from the Po di Primaro ; after that, a cart and horse had to be fetched from the farm by Michele Guidi. He and his brother worked with indefatigable zeal, for Bonnet was now absent at Ravenna, making arrangements for the further escape of the fugitives ; and the scared peasants, though friendly, and not altogether unhelpful, were afraid of doing too much, since it was easy to guess the character of such strange travellers. Not till half-past seven in the evening (August 4) did the little procession reach the Guiccioli dairy-farm, near the scattered hamlet of

<hr>

[1] *Gironi*, 43 ; *Bonnet*, 29, 30 ; *Itinerary*.
[2] There are two different accounts as to how the Celeste Bonnets were informed of the marooning of Garibaldi. (*Gironi*, 43 ; *Bonnet*, 29, 30.)
[3] *Bonnet*, 29–33.

Mandriole.[1] It is a finely built, spacious house, standing among vineyards; but the reeds and waste land of the southern marsh come almost to its doors, and from its upper chambers the tall trees of the famous pine forest of Ravenna are seen, the nearest of them scarcely a mile away. It was here that the tragedy of Garibaldi's life took place.

The last words that he had heard Anita say to him concerned the children whom she left to his care. Then, for long hours, her speech had failed. All day she was losing her hold on life, and Garibaldi could but clasp her closer in his arms, as their boat glided over the smooth surface of the lagoon. No longer conscious of anything save that he was there, the dying woman may have fancied that they were escaping once more over the well-known waters of another lagoon now all too far away; or that they were riding together to war, in the first glory of youth and love, over rolling, infinite spaces.

When they drew near the door of the farm in the long shadows of evening, she was lying in the cart, on the mattress in which they had lifted her from the boat. The good doctor, Nannini, who had been fetched from Sant' Alberto, arrived almost at the same moment. 'Try and save this woman,' said Garibaldi to him as they met. 'Then we must make a shift to get her to bed,' he replied. 'The four of us then each took a corner of the mattress,' writes her husband, 'and carried her into the house, to a room at the head of the stairs. In laying her down on the bed, I thought I saw the death-look in her face.'

It was too true. She had passed away as they bore her into that quiet chamber. Then the noble outward calm of Garibaldi, which had been proof against the thousand dangers, disappointments, and sorrows of the past months, and had inspired his fainting followers with courage, all in an instant gave way, and he burst into a flood of prolonged and bitter weeping.[2]

[1] *Bonnet*, 52 (Guidi's narrative); *Gironi*, 47; *Itinerary*.

[2] *Mem.* 251, 252; *Bonnet*, 53 (Guidi's narrative); *Gironi*, 47-49; *Uccellini's Garibaldi*, 12-14; see Appendix P, 'The death of Anita.'

CHAPTER XVI[1]

THE ESCAPE OF GARIBALDI

‘ That second time they hunted me
From hill to plain, from shore to sea,
And Austria, hounding far and wide
Her blood-hounds thro’ the country side,
Breathed hot and instant on my trace,—
.   .   .   .   .
‘ At first sight of her eyes, I said,
“ I am the man upon whose head
They fix the price, because I hate
The Austrians over us : the State
Will give you gold—oh, gold so much !—
If you betray me to their clutch,
And be your death, for aught I know,
If once they find you saved their foe ! ” ’
                    ROBERT BROWNING, *The Italian in England.*

STUNNED by the first blow of the irreparable loss, and for
awhile, as it seemed to those who were in the room, deprived
of his reason, Garibaldi no longer concealed his identity,
and in a few minutes the crowd of peasants who had gathered
outside the door of the house were whispering the name
of joy and fear.[2]   But there was not found among them
one who would sell Italy for gold.   In Romagna, the
patriotism of the *contadini* was as staunch as that of the
townspeople in Umbria, and from this moment forward
Garibaldi’s life was handed on with religious devotion from
one poor man to another, until, after many days, they had
safely transferred him out of the region where the hunt
was hottest.

It was impossible to permit him to linger in the house
of death, close to the high road, for the Austrian searchers
might arrive at any moment, and the corpse would betray

[1] See map at end of book for this chapter.
[2] *Bonnet,* 43–5. (Ravaglia’s evidence.)

them all. ' I directed the good people,' he writes, ' to bury the body, and left, yielding to the entreaties of the inhabitants of the house, whom my farther stay compromised.' Then he ' staggered along, scarcely able to walk,' accompanied by *Leggiero* and a guide, who took him, partly in the doctor's cart, to the little village of Sant' Alberto, and lodged him there in the cottage of a poor handicraftsman, where he was received with a generosity that sank deep into his heart. He himself belonged to the poor, by origin, and by the simple habits of his early life which he never abandoned ; the heroism and kindness of his hosts on this dreadful night pierced the armour of his grief, and he determined to live for a country whose humblest children were ready to die for him. Another feeling, less tender but no less wholesome as an antidote to sorrow during the crisis of his soul's malady, was roused as he looked out from the window and saw the white-coats swaggering down the village street, with their insolent airs of mastery towards the defenceless natives. Wrath choked him at the sight, and he hungered for new battles.[1]

Very early on the next morning (August 5), *Leggiero* and he, accompanied by one of the faithful men of Sant' Alberto, started back eastwards towards the coast. The Austrians were swarming close around them, but they managed to make their way down the course of the Po di Primaro, sometimes walking, sometimes hiding in the tall Indian corn, and sometimes rowing with the help of one regular

---

[1] *Mem.* 252–4. *Bonnet*, 45–6 ; *Uccellini's Garibaldi*, 14 ; *Mini*, 39–41. Garibaldi calls his host of Sant' Alberto a *tailor*, but Marie von Schwartz, who accompanied him in his pilgrimage to these scenes in the autumn of 1859, records that ' our return journey to Ravenna led us through the hamlet of Sant' Alberto, where, during his adventurous retreat from Rome in 1849, Garibaldi sought refuge and found shelter at the hands of a poor *cobbler*. This very cobbler now lay at the point of death. He had already received extreme unction. But when the shouts of the people announced Garibaldi's triumphal procession through the village, the poor man tried to leave his sick bed to welcome the hero of Varese and Como. The General was informed of this, and at once paid a visit to his former benefactor, who, as I learnt afterwards, was so strongly affected with joy by the visit that he recovered from his illness.' *Melena*, 72. He had been moved about from one house to another during the dangerous night's residence in Sant' Alberto, occupied as it was by some 200 Austrians. *Itinerary* and *Mini*, 40–1.

oar and of a big stake, picked out of the water by Garibaldi, and shaped for use with the large knives which were now the only arms borne by the two fugitives. When they had in this way approached the northern end of the pine forest of Ravenna, they stole out of the fevered marshland into the covert of that luxuriant and health-giving jungle that grows beneath the tall pine stems.[1]

The pine forest of Ravenna has been so perfectly described by John Addington Symonds, that no inferior hand need attempt the task:

' As early as the sixth century,' he writes, ' the sea had already retreated to such a distance from Ravenna that orchards and gardens were cultivated on the spot where once the galleys of the Cæsars rode at anchor. Groves of pines sprang up along the shore, and in their lofty tops the music of the wind moved like the ghost of waves and breakers plunging upon distant sands. This Pinetum stretches along the shore of the Adriatic for about forty miles, forming a belt of variable width between the great marsh and the tumbling sea. From a distance the bare stems and velvet crowns of the pine-trees stand up like palms that cover an oasis on Arabian sands ; but at a nearer view the trunks detach themselves from an inferior forest-growth of juniper and thorn and ash and oak, the tall roofs of the stately firs shooting their breadth of sheltering greenery above the lower and less sturdy brushwood. . . .

' As may be imagined, the spaces of this great forest form the haunt of innumerable living creatures. Lizards run about by myriads in the grass. Doves coo among the branches of the pines, and nightingales pour their full-throated music all day and night from thickets of whitethorn and acacia. The air is sweet with aromatic scents; the resin of the pine and juniper, the may-flowers and acacia-blossoms, the violets that spring by thousands in the moss, the wild roses and faint honeysuckles which throw fragrant arms from bough to bough of ash or maple, join to make one most delicious perfume. And though the

---

[1] *Uccellini's Garibaldi*, 14-18 ; *Itinerary* ; *Bologna MS.*, *Belluzzi's Note-book*, from personal information given by one of Garibaldi's saviours. The part of the pine forest north of Ravenna (*Pineta* San Vitale), where Garibaldi hid on August 5-6, still exists, though the larger southern forest has been mostly destroyed by a fire. The thick underwood of the *pineta* of Ravenna distinguishes it from the corresponding *pineta* on the Tuscan coast, Shelley's Pisan haunt.

air upon the neighbouring marsh is poisonous, here it is dry, and spreads a genial health.   The sea-wind murmuring through these thickets at nightfall or misty sunrise conveys no fever to the peasants stretched among their flowers. . . .

'You may ride or drive for miles along green aisles between the pines in perfect solitude ; and yet the creatures of the wood, the sunlight and the birds, the flowers and tall majestic columns at your side, prevent all sense of loneliness or fear.   Huge oxen haunt the wilderness—grey creatures, with mild eyes and spreading horns and stealthy tread. . . .

'Then there is a sullen canal, which flows through the forest from the marshes to the sea, it is alive with frogs and newts and snakes.   You may see these serpents basking on the surface among thickets of the flowering rush, or coiled about the lily leaves and flowers—lithe monsters, slippery and speckled, the tyrants of the fen.

'It is said that when Dante was living at Ravenna he would spend whole days alone among the forest glades, thinking of Florence and her civil wars, and meditating cantos of his poem.'[1]

And here, in a later age, Byron had taken his daily ride, meditating a less divine comedy, and finding strange companions under the greenwood tree.   In his diary of 1821 we read :

'Met a company of the sect (a kind of Liberal club) called the *Americani* in the forest, all armed, and singing, with all their might, in Romagnuole, " *Sem tutti soldat' per la libertà* " (" We are all soldiers for liberty "). They cheered me as I passed.'

And again :

'The *Americani* give a dinner in *the Forest* in a few days, and have invited me, as one of the *Carbonari*.   It is to be in *the Forest* of Boccaccio's and Dryden's " Huntsman's Ghost " ; and, even if I had not the same political feelings (to say nothing of my old convivial turn which every now and then revives), I would go as a poet, or, at least, as a lover of poetry.'[2]

And now Garibaldi, conducted by the sons of Byron's *Americani* through the same enchanted thickets, lay concealed for more than twenty-four hours amid these scenes

[1] J. A. Symonds. *Sketches in Italy. Ravenna.*
[2] *Byron*, v. 192, 206, January 29 and February 20, 1821.

of untamed nature, the sight of which was a talisman more
sure to touch and heal his heart, than formerly to dispel
the *ennui* of the English lord.

The beauty of the forest, the long hours of repose in its
salubrious air, varied by the occasional excitement of dodging
the Austrian searchers, had a recuperative effect upon
Garibaldi's body and mind.

' The Austrians,' he writes with a certain gusto, ' had divided
a battalion into sections, which marched in every direction
through the pine forest. . . . On one of these occasions it happened that, while I lay stretched out beside my comrade *Leggiero*,
on one side of a clump of bushes, they passed on the other—their
voices, anything but welcome, somewhat disturbing the quiet
of the forest and our peaceful reflections. They passed very
near us, and we probably formed the subject of their rather
animated conversation.'

' Several people,' he tells us, ' were in the secret of the concealment which saved me from the researches not only of the
Austrians, but of the Papalini, who were worse still. These
courageous Romagnuols—most of them young men—were
untiring in their care for my safety. When they thought me in
danger in one place, I used to see them coming up at night with
a cart, to remove me to a safer situation, many miles distant. . . .

' My young protectors had arranged their night-signals
with admirable skill, so as to transfer me from one point to
another, and to give the alarm in case of danger. When all
was known to be safe, a fire was lit in an appointed place, and we
passed on ; if, on the contrary, no fire was seen, we turned back
or took another direction. Sometimes, fearing some mistake,
the driver stopped the cart, got down, and himself went on to
reconnoitre—or else, without getting down, found some one to
give him directions at once.

' These arrangements were made with admirable precision.
Be it noted that, if anything had transpired—if my persecutors
had had the slightest hint of what was happening—they would
have shot even the very children of the people who showed
me such devotion, without trial and without mercy.' [1]

---

[1] *Mem.* 253-4. Within a few miles and a few days of this hunt for Garibaldi
in the forest, they shot Ciceruacchio's younger son, a boy of about thirteen, guilty
only of following his father on the retreat from Rome. See p. 307 below.

On the evening of August 6 he was conducted out of the
pine-wood to a little thatched hut standing in a position
of extraordinary loneliness in the middle of the strip of
marsh between the forest and the sea. ' Garibaldi's
hut,' now a small museum in the wilderness, can only be
reached by boat, for it stands amid a network of canals—
a situation which had commended it to the peasants as a
place of safety for their guest. Indeed, it was never
visited in those days except by a club of sportsmen who
shot duck there in springtime. The spot where Garibaldi
and *Leggiero* landed at its door is marked by a stone. All
around, the dark, flat, unprofitable marsh stretches away
for miles, bounded on one side by the sea, and on the other
by the beautiful curving sweep of the pine forest. Here
they remained for twenty-four hours, until the secret
preparations undertaken by Bonnet's Liberal friends in
Ravenna were in a state of readiness. During this interval
Garibaldi in his hut nursed schemes of procuring a ship
to take him to Venice, but the shore was so strictly watched
from both sea and land that the wiser counsels of his friends
prevailed. And so, just before nightfall of August 7, the
two fugitives re-embarked on the canals, and were smuggled
safely, first as far south as Savio, and then into the Sisi
suburb outside the southern gates of Ravenna.

There, in the closest neighbourhood to the Papal and
Austrian authorities, they passed nearly a week in strange
safety, moved on sometimes from one house to another,
and latterly quartered on a farm a mile or two to the south-
west of Ravenna, among the damp rice-fields of Porto
Fuori, not very far from the solitary and ancient Church of
S. Apollinare in Classe. Here Garibaldi could hear through
the door of the room where he lay concealed the conversation of the gangs of farm-labourers at their dinner ; one day,
they were telling tales of his already legendary escape, and
added the terrible story—all too true—of how Anita's
body, hastily concealed from the police in the thin sand
near Mandriole, had been grubbed up and gnawed by un-
clean animals. At that the door opened, and for a

x

moment a spectre stood gaping with horror at the feasters but was instantly pushed back before it could gather voice to speak.

Meanwhile arrangements were being made for his reception at Forlì and subsequent passage thence into the Tuscan Apennines. When all was ready, he and *Leggiero* were driven by night along the direct road from Ravenna to Forlì ; one of their most active friends, Savini, went in front to prepare the way, and succeeded in making the guards in the roadside hamlet of Coccolia so drunk that they did not wake to question the midnight travellers. When they reached Forlì, they had recrossed the plain of the Romagna, and were once more at the foot of the Apennines.[1]

While Garibaldi and his sole companion were thus escaping from the toils, some fifty or more patriots who had disembarked with them on the shore and whom Garibaldi had ordered to shift for themselves, had made off, most of them throwing away their arms, assuming disguises, and for the most part disappearing from the knowledge of history.[2]

Ciceruacchio and his two sons, with half a dozen other Italians, made northwards for Venice, and with immense difficulty succeeded in crossing several of the mouths of the Po, and entering Austrian territory ; but there, about the middle of August, they were betrayed by a fellow-countryman covetous of the blood-money, condemned by a drum-head court-martial, and shot in the market square of San Nicolò in the district of Ariano, close to the central mouth of the great river. The elder of Ciceruacchio's sons, Luigi Brunetti, who had stabbed Rossi with his own hand, deserved his fate, though he was sentenced under an *alias*, and by men who, even if they had known his real name, would have been totally ignorant that he had committed any worse crime than that of following Garibaldi. The secret of his guilt, confined to private individuals for

[1] *Uccellini's Garibaldi*, 24–36 ; *Mini*, 40–57 ; *Itinerary. Mem.* 254–5. *Bologna MS. Verità. Stocchi*, 668–672, 690, and notes.

[2] See App. O, below.

many years after his death, has only in recent times been revealed, to a generation which can look without blind partiality on Rossi and his assassins.[1] Luigi's brother, somewhere between ten and fifteen years of age, stood at his father's side to face the levelled muskets, with the innocence and courage of boyhood.[2] The public execution of such a lad among a band of 'Liberal thieves,' was not, in those months, a thing that aroused surprise or comment.

So fell Ciceruacchio, the man who first won the populace of Rome to a tardy but enduring sense of their place in the national movement. He was himself a loveable, hearty, simple-minded man, who had earned, not merely the applause of the market-place, but the admiration and friendship of Garibaldi and Ugo Bassi, and even of so respectable a person as the Whig grandee, Lord Minto, during his residence in Rome in the winter of 1846-7. The crime of Ciceruacchio's elder son overshadows the father's name in history with a doubt ; [3] if he was implicated, he paid the penalty with his blood and that of his children ; if he was guiltless, he was one of the chief of Italy's martyrs, should there be any order of precedence among those who died for her cause.

No shadow of any sinister suspicion rests on the pure fame of Ugo Bassi. After the soldiers had seized him and Livraghi in the bedroom of the Comacchio inn, on August 3, they were taken to the Government prison 'with barbarous treatment and at the point of the bayonet.' They remained in the island city two days longer, and on the wall of the prison Ugo Bassi drew in pencil 'a beautiful Christ,' with this motto—'Ugo Bassi here endured somewhat, glad of heart in feeling himself innocent. Livraghi, captain of Garibaldi, was present and with him through all.' [4]

---

[1] See pp. 80-81 above. *Pasini*, 127-130 (Braga's letter). *Bel.* 193 and *Mem.* 250 convince me (in spite of *Ortore* and *Carcani* in the *R.I.* 1898, iii. 356-558) that the absence of Luigi Brunetti's name from the lists of the party executed, does not prove an *alibi*, but only that he gave an *alias*.

[2] *R. I.* 1898, iii. 356-358. *Pasini*, 128-129. *Bel.* 10.

[3] See p. 80 above, note 4.

[4] *Gualtieri*, 97 (Bonnet's evidence).

On the fifth the two friends were carried off, bound, in an open cart towards Bologna. As the tragic procession passed along the roads, there were not wanting priests who mocked the outcast of Church and State ; at the bridge of Castenaso, a few miles east of Bologna, the parish priest of the neighbouring village called out, ' Preach your war against the Austrians now.' [1] On their arrival in the capital of the Romagna Gorzkowski at once had Bassi condemned to death on the utterly false accusation that he had been taken with arms in his hands. The sentence, which the General was anxious to have sanctioned by the spiritual power before carrying it into execution, was approved by a council held in the Palace of the Cardinal Legate Bedini, composed entirely of secular priests, nine Bolognese and three Hungarians. The Italians, whose names are on record, signed the disgraceful document ; the Hungarians refused, and were seen to leave the palace in tears.[2] That evening (August 7) Bassi was taken to the Penitentiary prison ' della Carità,' and left there for his last night on earth, in the hands of his bitter enemies the secular priests.[3] At half-past eleven on the morning of the eighth, he was led to hear his sentence, to which he merely answered, ' I am innocent.' In the afternoon of the same day he was carried to execution, like Browning's ' Patriot,' through the streets of the city where his noblest triumphs of fame and popular success had been won.[4] A mile outside the city gate, close under the Church of the Madonna of St. Luke standing on a hill visible for many miles round Bologna, the cart stopped and Bassi and Livraghi were taken out to die. Bassi's last spoken thought was of a brother-worker, whom he had

---

[1] *Gualtieri*, 185, 97-8 ; the scene of this incident shows that they were not taken by the Via Aemilia, but by cross-country roads. There is not sufficient evidence of the route traversed to render it possible either to accept or reject the story of Bassi and his captors passing close to Garibaldi's hiding-place in the Pineta (*Uccellini's Garibaldi*, 20).

[2] *Montazio*, 78. *Gualtieri*, 99-100, note. This fact alone would dispose of the ridiculous excuse of Cardinal Bedini that he had not had notice of the execution ; but indeed Gualtieri says (p. 187, note) : ' All the city was given notice of it eleven hours before it took place.'

[3] *Gualtieri*, 100, 179-181.   [4] See pp. 76 and 77 above.

perhaps known many years before in his struggle with the cholera in Palermo:—' This handkerchief,' he said, ' is not mine, but it belongs to Padre Filippo, a bare-footed Augustinian of Palermo, my intimate friend ; let it be returned to him, and tell him that it has wiped the tears of my agony.' The officer who was to give the order to fire had not the heart to do his duty ; another took his place, and a minute later the two victims had fallen, bathed in blood. That night Ugo Bassi's grave, which was dug near to the spot where he fell, was found covered with flowers and garlands ; the people regarded him as a saint and martyr ; visions of him descending from the clouds in an aureole of light were accredited by the pious and simple ; and his tomb outside the gate became a place of pilgrimage, until the Papal authorities thought it wise to dig up the body and hide it away. But that did not cause Bologna to forget him.[1]

The memory of Ugo Bassi may be revered by men of all creeds. The heroism of the saint who fought the cholera in the streets of Palermo, and of the patriot who rode unarmed in the thick of so many battles, the fiery eloquence of the prophet and reformer, were softened by a pure gentleness of soul and manner, which Garibaldi compared to that of a maiden tenderly nurtured far from such dreadful scenes as those in which this true Christian moved unstained.[2]

The news of these murders, overtaking Garibaldi during his secret peregrinations not many miles to the south, moved him to intense pity and anger. In the years to come, he always thought and spoke of the Austrians as ' the men who shot Ugo Bassi and Ciceruacchio.'[3] But time takes its revenges, sometimes with a kindly smile. The youth in whose Imperial name these and many like cruelties were committed in that summer nearly sixty years ago, is now, wary old expert that he has long since become in constitutional ways and means, urging the populations

[1] *Gualtieri*, 101–103, 179, 187–188. *Venosta*, 139–147. *Zironi*, 119–124. *Vecchi*, ii. 323–325. *Facchini*, 132–152. *Montazio*, 75–81.

[2] Letter of Garibaldi to Mrs. Hamilton King, Feb. 4, 1873—shown me by the poetess.

[3] *Mem.* 250–251, 305.

who still remain under his facile rule, to adopt the principle
of manhood suffrage.

Garibaldi's own escape from the region of the lagoons
was visited upon Gorzkowski by his removal. This event,
which has its humorous side if we consider how little the
General's failure was due to want of zeal, incidentally saved
the life of Nino Bonnet, who had been arrested on just
suspicion, and, after some delay, 'taken to be shot at
Bologna,' as the newspapers put it. Gorzkowski had
specially sent for the person whose activities had so seriously
injured his reputation as a man-catcher, and had no intention of foregoing his revenge. Bonnet was lodged in the
cell occupied a few days before by Ugo Bassi, and would
certainly have left it for the same destination, had not
Gorzkowski's disgrace occurred in the nick of time. His
successor gave Garibaldi's saviour both life and freedom,
in circumstances from which we may conclude that the
hero's marvellous escape, while it stimulated the brutality
of some of the Austrian generals, awakened the chivalrous
sympathy of others.[1]

As Garibaldi re-entered the valleys of the Apennines
and approached the Tuscan border, he was eagerly awaited
by Don Giovanni Verità, the parish priest of Modigliana,
a pretty little mountain town built at a meeting-place of
three valleys. This good man, as Garibaldi writes,

'had saved, by hundreds, the proscribed Romagnuols, who,
condemned by the inexorable rage of the clergy, had sought
refuge in Tuscany—a country whose government, though not
good, was at least less atrocious than that of the priests. Proscriptions were frequent among the unfortunate and courageous
people, and whenever, in my wanderings, I met with banished
Romagnuols, I always heard them bless the name of this truly
pious priest.' [2]

Verità, who lived long to tell his stories of these strange
times, relates that, having received instructions to expect

---

[1] *Bonnet*, 54–65 ; *Guerzoni*, i. 362, note.   [2] *Mem.* 255–256.

Garibaldi, he waited up for him night after night on the Faenza road, until at last, when that route proved to be too strictly watched, he was told that his guest would come by way of Terra del Sole. And so, on the night of August 20–21 (or possibly 21-22),[1] the good priest was waiting by the cross at Monte Trebbio in a torrent of rain, when Garibaldi at length arrived, walking beside a cart on which he had placed *Leggiero*. Verità had been led to expect the hero alone, and the need of providing for his lame companion added greatly to the difficulties of finding a passage across the Apennine summits. To this task, however, he gladly addressed himself, as he had done on behalf of many less celebrated refugees. After hiding the two in his house for more than twenty-four hours,[2] he started with them over the mountains, solving the problem of *Leggiero* sometimes by the aid of a cart, sometimes by the help of certain Liberal muleteers and horse-owners, accustomed to act as his secret service on these occasions.[3]

In this way, riding, driving, or walking beside a cart, the three friends traversed the Apennine ridges by winding and rocky paths, crossing almost at right angles the innumerable rivers that flow down into the Romagna plain,[4] until on the night of August 23–4 (or 24–25) they found themselves standing on the great road between Florence and Bologna. They had struck it at a point a mile or two south of Filigare, the village wherein Garibaldi had spent some anxious days with his infant legion, in the snows of the previous November;[5] it was therefore a district where he was only too well known by sight. Here Verità left his friends, protected by the darkness, while he went down towards Filigare to find a rich merchant farmer named Francia, whom he could trust to guide and help them. But Francia was not at home, and it was hours before the priest could find him and return. Meanwhile day had dawned,

[1] See Ap. P., in the Italian edition of this book (1908), my argument on the difficult question of the dates (Aug. 20-25) based on *Mini* and *Stocchi*.

[2] *Un par di giorni*, says Garibaldi, *Mem.* 256. Verità's statement that they remained a week or more is an error, as the known dates of the escape prove.

[3] *Bologna MSS. Verità* and *Oriani*; *Belluzzi's* note-book; *Stocchi*, 688-691.

[4] *Bologna MSS., Belluzzi's Note-book*, and *Verità*.   [5] See p. 78 above.

and its light exposed the two fugitives lingering on the high road patrolled by Austrian and Tuscan troops.[1]   No longer daring to wait about for Verità, they chartered a tumble-down country cart and the sorry jade that drew it, and drove southwards up the pass, meeting numerous Austrian columns on the way.[2]

In this adventurous manner they traversed a dozen miles of hard white road between the wooded sides of the mountains, and recrossing the watershed of Italy began to descend towards Florence.   Just below the top of the pass stands the wayside inn of Santa Lucia, then kept by the patriotic family of Baldini, and here the fugitives, cut off by their recent misadventure from all friends and helpers, presented themselves at the door and called for coffee. The mother happened to be ill in bed, and the house was in charge of her daughter Teresa, then a beautiful girl of twenty, who survived to a great and honoured old age, to tell a generation of free Italians the story of what befell her with those strange guests in the inn.[3]

The elder of the two strangers began to chat with the girl as she waited on them, and to ask the news of the country.   ' Oh,' said Teresa, ' the Tuscan and Austrian troops are out looking for you.'

' What !   You know me ? '

' You are Garibaldi.'

' Where have you seen me ? '

' Don't you remember that you passed here last November with your volunteers, on the day of Galliano fair ? '[4]

' Basta, basta.'

---

[1] There is a tradition that an officer of Tuscan cavalry, during a halt near Filigare, recognised Garibaldi, but made no sign of the discovery, and at once gave the order to mount and ride on.   *Ricciardi*, 7.

[2] *Mem.* 256.   *Stocchi*, 673–678.   *Bologna MS. Verità.*

[3] See her narrative, *Stocchi*, 678–683.   *Mem.* 256–257 tells the same story. Where there are differences of detail, Teresa Baldini's recollections are to be pre-ferred to those of Garibaldi, as it was the great event of her life, the memory of which she cherished, while to him it was only one adventure out of a thousand. The same principle applies in comparing the *Mem.* to *Bonnet, Sequi*, etc.   (See Ap. P., Italian edition of this book, for reasons why Stocchi's version of Teresa's narrative is to be preferred to Mini's.)

[4] Galliano, or Gagliano, is a few miles to the south.

An understanding was soon arrived at, after which
Garibaldi, sleepy from his night upon the hills, sat leaning
over the table, and letting his face fall forward on his arms,
dropped off into a doze.   Roused by a touch from *Leggiero*,
he looked up to see a party of whitecoats sitting down with
them to the board.   Signing Teresa to keep them in conversation, he drew a cigar from his pocket and lit it at the
lantern, which he replaced in such a position as to leave
his face in shadow; the poor room had no windows, and the
light from the door was by itself too feeble to betray him.
There he sat and smoked in silence, while the Austrian
sergeant, who found Teresa most engaging, informed her and
her guests in broken Italian that the army to which he
belonged was coming up from Barberino in Mugello, 3,000
strong, to catch ' the infamous *Garipalda*.'   At length the
Tedeschi got up and left the room, intent upon the chase.[1]

The fugitives were then placed, for their greater safety,
in a hut at Pian del Monte, just on the other side of the road,
but on ground considerably above its level, where they sat
under a chestnut-tree and watched through a telescope more
Austrians passing the inn.   Some of them handled Teresa
roughly, calling her ' Garibaldi's wife,' and threatening to
shoot her ; they treated many other women along the road in
the same manner.   Garibaldi and *Leggiero* were then supplied
with guides by their new friends in Santa Lucia, and on the
night of August 25–26 were conducted westward out of the
dangerous valley, by mountain paths south of Mangona,
over the slopes of Montecuccoli.   Travelling all night, on
the following morning they dismissed their guides and
descended off the mountain side into Cerbaja in the Valdi
Bisenzio, where they arrived, friendless once more, but once
more destined to find deliverers.[2]

[1] The evidence as to whether Garibaldi had shaved his beard is contradictory.
Guerzoni, i. 386. *MS. Verità. Stocchi*, 679 and note. Teresa's recollection
was that he wore ' only his moustache' during this dangerous interview.

[2] *Stocchi*, 678–688. *Mem.* 256–257. *Guelfi*, 40. *Sequi*, 5, 9–10. *Sequi*
states, and *Guelfi* and *Stocchi* prove by sufficient arguments that Garibaldi arrived
at Cerbaja on the morning of the 26th, and not as the *Memorie* and *Ricciardi* say,
on the former evening.   Of the places mentioned by *Sequi*, 9–10, Montepiano =
Pian del Monte, at S. Lucia ; and Calvana is a continuation of Montecuccoli.

While the fugitives were coming down from Monte-cuccoli in the early morning of August 26, a young man named Enrico Sequi set out with his dog and gun from Vajano a few miles down the valley, in pursuit of game— but of what size and species, history, fearful perhaps of alienating English sympathy, has providentially left un-recorded. About eight o'clock the sportsman took refuge from the rain in the mill of Cerbaja, which was also kept as a rustic inn by the host and miller, a jolly fellow, but no politician and above all no Liberal. Here Sequi was joined by the two travellers, and they ate and smoked together, charmed with one another's company. Being himself an active Liberal, the young Tuscan, as he took stock of his new acquaintances, at once had the thought of refugees, an idea naturally uppermost in the minds of all members of his party in those months. Partly in order to test their politics, he drew a Val d' Arno newspaper from his pocket and handed it across the table. Seeing the elder of the two laugh and show his companion the advertisement about Garibaldi and *Leggiero*, he could not refrain from ex-claiming, ' And where is our Garibaldi now ? ' ' Friend,' said the stranger, rising suddenly and advancing to embrace the young man, ' Garibaldi is in your arms.' [1]

When Sequi, having recovered from his first delight and surprise, heard that their intention was to cross the moun-tains towards Spezia in the hope of reaching the territory of Piedmont, he declared the venture too hazardous, because the whole frontier region was thickly occupied by the troops of the reactionary powers, on the watch for the passage of such fugitives ; he himself undertook to provide them with better means of escape. Leaving Garibaldi and *Leggiero* at Cerbaja, he took horse and rode in haste to Prato, the pretty little town at the northern edge of the Val d' Arno plain, where the cathedral, with its Renaissance bas-reliefs and its balcony of Donatello's dancing boys, looks out over the square to tell the traveller that he is in the enchanted neighbourhood of Florence.

[1] *Sequi*, 5–8. *Guelfi*, 1–10. *Mem.* 257.

Here Sequi made one of his friends take him at once to Antonio Martini, the chief of the Liberal party in Prato, whom they found at his midday meal. It was arranged then and there that the two fugitives should be carried southwards in a closed carriage across the Val d' Arno, and over the hills near Volterra to a solitary point on the Maremma of Tuscany, where there were good patriots who would ship them off to Piedmont. This scheme, actually accomplished during the ensuing week, speaks much for the energy and faithfulness of these Tuscan Liberals, for it was a plot in which, before all was over, a score of persons took an active share, and of which many more were cognisant. Nets of conspiracy, when they are as widely spread as that, usually become tangled or break at some one point.

Meanwhile, in the mill of Cerbaja, taking his meals with the jolly miller and his family, who seem to have suspected nothing, Garibaldi confidently awaited the return of the stranger, whom he had trusted to the death on no other security than that of his honest face and bearing. And surely after sunset the young man came back—without the police—and drove Garibaldi and *Leggiero* down the river towards the Val d' Arno, to the rendezvous with his friends. In the dead of night the various parties to the plot met in the Prato railway station on the outskirts of the town, under the nose of an Austrian sentry. There the last plans were made, the greetings and farewells were exchanged, and the two wanderers, having been transferred into an excellent four-wheeled carriage, were driven off along the outside of the city walls. Going round by the flattest road, they crossed the Arno at Empoli about dawn, and ascending the Elsa valley reached Poggibonsi at eight in the morning of the 27th, having accomplished in six hours a drive of nearly forty miles from Prato.[1]

After a short rest, they started on again at midday with a new carriage, and travelled for eleven anxious hours, with coachmen who were not in the secret. At the first

[1] *Sequi*, 10–14. *Guelfi*, 11–27, 40. *Ricciardi*, 6–8. *Mem.* 257–258.

short stage, Colle d' Elsa, they sat through a bad quarter of an hour, suffering much from the inquisitive habits of their countrymen, who happened to be collected there in great numbers for a *festa*.

' Our journey from Prato to the Maremma was indeed singular. We passed over a great extent of country in a closed carriage, stopping every now and then to change horses. Our halts in some places were rather longer than was absolutely necessary, some of our drivers being much less careful of us than others. In this way time was given to the curious to surround the carriage ; sometimes, too, we were obliged to leave it for meals, instead of having them brought to us, to conceal in some degree our exceptional situation. In small towns, our vehicle was, of course, turned into a species of pillory by the idlers of the place, who offered aloud a thousand conjectures as to who we were, and were naturally disposed to gossip about people whom they did not know, and who, therefore, in those difficult and terrible times of reaction, seemed doubtful or even dangerous characters. At Colle, in particular, nowadays quite a patriotic and advanced place, we were surrounded by a crowd, from whom our faces, certainly not those of peaceful and indifferent travellers, drew manifest tokens of suspicion and dislike. However, nothing took place beyond a few abusive epithets, which, as was to be expected under the circumstances, we pretended not to hear.' [1]

From Colle they left the valley of the Elsa and travelled westward, until their carriage had by three in the afternoon climbed onto the far-seen table mountain of

' lordly Volaterræ,
Where scowls the far-famed hold
Piled by the hands of giants
For godlike kings of old.'

Passing near the colossal masonry of its Etruscan gate and walls, they dared not look out at the town—nor even at the view which would have been to them more thrilling, of the distant western sea—but sat well back in the carriage with their hats pulled over their eyes, until they felt themselves rattling down the mountain on its southern side.[2]

[1] *Mem.* 258–259. *Guelfi*, 34.   [2] *Mem.* 259. *Ricciardi*, 8. *Guelfi*, 36.

On hearing that the village of Saline was full of soldiers, they crossed the Cecina river a little further down, making a *détour* which clearly showed the coachman that they were not the innocent merchant farmers they pretended to be. From the valley bottom they again mounted the hills by the high road that leads through Pomarance, straight south-wards for the Maremma. An hour before midnight (August 27) they entered the local health resort of Bagno al Morbo, and drew up at the door of Girolamo Martini, a sturdy old Liberal, who looked hard at their letters of introduction from his namesake and relation of Prato, mysteriously recommending the two nameless travellers to his good offices. At last one of them said, ' I am General Garibaldi and this is my companion, *Leggiero*.' ' Courage, General,' answered the old man, ' all will come right again.' [1]

Girolamo Martini now took matters in hand. Several days would be required to communicate with the Liberals of the Maremma, who were to make all ready for a speedy embarkation in the neighbourhood of Follonica. Mean-while, the fugitives, who could not safely be left to the tender mercies of the gossips and invalids of Bagno, now at the height of its season, were transferred off the high road to the remote and high-lying village of San Dalmazio, and lodged in the house of one Serafini, specially chosen for its facilities of escape into the mountain. Here Garibaldi remained more than four days, enjoying his first holiday since the siege of Rome began, while a dozen devoted adherents were guarding his neighbourhood, or at work down in the Maremma procuring a fishing boat with a faithful crew, who should carry him to the ports of Piedmont.

On the evening of September 1, all was ready for the last rush to the sea. At nine o'clock they left their moun-tain fastness, armed to the teeth for whatever might befall, walked over a few hundred yards of broken ground to their horses, rode by stony paths back to the high road at Castel-nuovo, mounted a carriage that was waiting for them a

---

[1] *Ricciardi*, 8–9. *Guelfi*, 37–44. For incidents at Bagno di Morbo and S. Dalmazio, Ricciardi is the primary authority.

little farther to the south, and were driven, during the
darkest hours of night, at a smart pace down towards the
coast.   After diverging a short while from the road, in order
to avoid passing through the town of Massa Marittima,
they entered the plain of the Maremma, and, at two in
the morning of September 2, drew up at the door of the
Casa Guelfi, a large and solitary farmhouse prepared as
their headquarters, whence the final venture was to be
made.[1]

[1] *Ricciardi*, 10-20.   *Guelfi*, 51-117.

CHAPTER XVII

THE EMBARKATION—SEPTEMBER 2, 1849

‘ Push hard across the sand,
　　For the salt wind gathers breath;
Shoulder and wrist and hand,
　　Push hard as the push of death.

· 　　· 　　· 　　·

‘ Out to the sea with her there,
　　Out with her over the sand;
Let the kings keep the earth for their share
　　We have done with the sharers of land.

‘ They have tied the world in a tether,
　　They have bought over God with a fee;
While three men hold together,
　　The kingdoms are less by three.

· 　　· 　　· 　　·

· All the world has its burdens to bear,
　　From Cayenne to the Austrian whips;
Forth, with the rain in our hair
　　And the salt sweet foam in our lips.

‘ In the teeth of the hard, glad weather,
　　In the blown wet face of the sea;
While three men hold together,
　　The kingdoms are less by three.’

　　　　　　SWINBURNE, *A Song in Time of Order.*

THE Casa Guelfi, a square house of three stories, rising
high by the side of the road that leads from Pisa to
Grosseto, is far seen as a landmark in the partly reclaimed
marshlands that stretch between the port town of Follonica
and the wooded hills of Scarlino.　In 1849 the upper stories
of the Casa Guelfi were inhabited by the inmates of the
farm, while the ground floor, then as now, was used for

---

¹ For this chapter see inset in large map at end of book.

My authority for the incidents recorded in the remainder of the book is
Guelfi, 117–147.　See also *Guerzoni*, i. 386–387 (Azzarini's narrative), and
Mem. 259–260.　I have visited all the scenes.

cattle and stores ; the house took its name from the pro-
prietor, who was one of the chiefs of the plot.   When
Garibaldi alighted at its door two hours after midnight,
greeting his hosts with a cheery 'Good-morning, friends,'
he and *Leggiero* were at once conducted upstairs, refreshed
with food and coffee, and sent to lie down for the last two
hours of darkness, while their protectors kept guard below.
The great expedition was to start at first glint of dawn.

At four o'clock Pina, one of the most active of these
young Liberals of the Maremma, knocked at Garibaldi's
door ; never was Alpine climber waked in the early hours
by the low tapping of his guide, for a more thrilling, a more
eagerly-expected day.   'In a few hours,' the wanderer must
have thought as he looked from the window, 'I shall, if all
goes well, be sniffing the sea-breeze from deck, bound for my
own Ligurian coast.'

Half an hour later, while they were all assembling and
arming for immediate departure, a strange figure at the
door alarmed the conspirators.   It turned out to be a
Hungarian, a deserter on patriotic principles from the
conscript Austrian army, who, having heard of Garibaldi's
presence at the Casa Guelfi (no one knows how, but the
web of the plot was wide), had come with the request
to be taken with him across the sea.   The general nature
of his petition was clear, but in trying to tell his whole
story he had no medium of communication except
his native Magyar, an unknown tongue to the impatient
Italians ; he obtained, however, one eager listener, for the
name of his great countryman, *Kossuth*, kept occurring at
intervals in his obscure discourse.   'This man,' said the
generous Garibaldi, 'must come with us.'   'No, he shall not,'
said Pina, who protested, not without reason, that he and
his friends were risking their lives for a great national object,
and would not jeopardise its success for the sake of an unknown foreign wayfarer.   A heated dispute arose, only
ended by Pina's declaration that the boat which they had
engaged could hold but two travellers, besides the crew.[1]

---

[1] This was quite true, as we gather from Azzarini's narrative, *Guerzoni*, i.
386-387.

The Hungarian was given a rendezvous for a later hour, and sent away, content with the assurance that his case would be attended to when once Garibaldi was safely embarked.

And so, at five o'clock, six Italians, one of them still halting a little in his gait, all attired as sportsmen, accompanied by large dogs, and each carrying a double-barrelled shot gun—charged that morning for big game—set out on foot from the back door of Casa Guelfi, and made across the low, damp farmlands towards the hills south of Scarlino.[1] Striking the great Allacciante canal which drains the fen, they marched in Indian file along the top of its western dyke for some distance. On every side of Garibaldi, as he strode along, Italy was looking her best in the morning light. Behind him lay the sombre mountains out of which he had escaped ; far off to the right stood the hill-promontory of ' seagirt Populonia ' ; in front of him, the pointed peaks of Elba rose in a bunch out of the shining sea ; close at hand to his left were the forest-clad hills above Scarlino, itself standing high on a slope of glittering olives. Its morning bells sounded sweetly over the marsh. ' What town is that ? ' said Garibaldi, who was in high spirits. ' It is Scarlino, our native town,' was the answer, ' and if you order it, General, it will change the tune,' meaning that its young men were all Liberals and would gladly sound the tocsin of revolt.

Turning to the left, they crossed the canal by a rustic bridge, ascended off the level of the marsh, crossed a country road, and entering the forests of the hills, began to traverse them in a south-westerly direction, towards Cala Martina, the bay where their boat was in waiting. At first they walked by easy paths through glades of oak, but gradually the nature of the vegetation changed to a thickly matted jungle of dark evergreens, more impenetrable than any kind of woodland known to us in Britain. The paths, too, became narrow almost to vanishing-point, and the men began to struggle like explorers in a tropical forest. Here

[1] See their approximate route marked in red in the inset of the large map at end of book.

Y

the question was raised whether they ought not to go round by way of the Portiglione coastguard station, where they could strike into the coastguard path through the jungle, and so reach Cala Martina by way of the shore. This would be a quicker and less fatiguing route, but on the other hand it would be more dangerous, because there were six coastguards in the station. It was argued, however, that the garrison of Portiglione were well known for cowards, and that even if they showed any fight they could easily be overcome. But Garibaldi, knowing that any encounter would expose his saviours to vengeance after he had gone, decided for the safer and more wearisome route. ' Not for us two,' he said, ' but for the sake of those who remain on land we must use prudence.'

And so they plunged on once again through the depth of the forest, tearing their way through the dark-green boughs, which shut from them all view of the silver sea they were approaching. After a couple of hours or more of hard work, they leapt out into the coastguard path, a broad ride cut through the jungle. Crossing it, they dashed through the last few yards of forest, down a steep slope, and stood on the sand and rocks of the little bay.

The Cala Martina [1] was an ideal spot for the conduct of a secret embarkation. A few yards from the water's edge lay the safe shelter of the jungle, stretching up over the high hills for miles and miles, in solitude uninvaded save by a few herds of swine and white oxen thrusting their way through the bushes in search of food, and by the herdsmen whose horns at evening alone break the silence of that brooding, lonely coast. The bay was out of sight alike of the guard station at Portiglione and of another station perched on the top of the Punta Martina, where another small garrison, though close at hand, was far removed from all view of what was happening on the shore below. Soon after the

---

[1] I accept the decision of *Guelfi*, 140, that the bay where the embarkation took place was the one to the north of the Punta Martina, though the one to the south of the point is, I find, often called the Cala Martina by the herdsmen of the shore. But in either case my description and story will hold good without needing alteration on that score.

new-comers emerged on to the beach, the fishing boat hove in sight, and at the given signal moved towards them, manned by four chosen mariners.   While they awaited its approach, Garibaldi's companions observed him stand, flushed with life and joy by the presence of the sea, bathing his naked feet in its ripples with the pleasure of a child, and looking out towards Elba where they were first to touch, in an ecstasy of desire to cleave the waves once more.

It was ten o'clock on the morning of September 2 when the boat reached the shore and the rapid embarkation took place.   The last words of farewell have been recorded by the actors themselves:

Garibaldi.—' Nothing could be a recompense for what you have done for me. But I hope to find you again in happier times.'

Pina.—' A piece of your handkerchief is reward enough for each of us : we shall leave it as an heirloom to our children. Our object was to save you in order to preserve you for Italy. We will willingly go with you to Genoa, if you will let us.'

Garibaldi.—' No. On the sea I fear no one. We shall meet again.'

Then they embraced, Garibaldi stepped on board with *Leggiero,* and the boat was pushed from shore.   When a few yards of water separated him from the land he loved, and from the men who had saved him and who now stood silently watching his receding form, the chief, standing in the stern of the boat, cried out in tones that vibrated for ever in their memory, ' Viva l' Italia ! '

EPILOGUE

I cannot here relate all that befell Garibaldi after his embarkation. Suffice it that he was now in relative safety, that after touching at Elba he reached the ports of Piedmont, saw his motherless children for a few hours at Nice, and was then hurried out of the country by Victor Emmanuel's government, not yet in a position to harbour him for long. Expelled once more, he passed six months at Tangier, enjoying the hospitality of the Piedmontese and British Consuls, until in 1850, feeling that he ought no longer to depend on the charity of others, he passed by way of Liverpool to the United States. He was never more noble than during the obscurity of the years that followed. He acquired none of the faults and habits characteristic of the exile, but cheerfully set about the task of earning his bread, first as a journeyman candle-maker, then as a merchant captain, and finally as a farmer, until the time came round for him to deal in the manufacture of kingdoms, and to be hailed by his countrymen as ' Captain of the People.'

LIST OF SOME OF THE OFFICERS WHO DEFENDED ROME IN 1849

(Names of those who went on the Retreat in *Italics*.)

Avezzana . The Minister of War.

Roselli . . The Commander-in-Chief.

Garibaldi . General of Division, commanding on west bank of river.

Medici . . (Giacomo), commanding a ' Legion ' of his own during the siege, though a Garibaldian red-shirt both before and after, in South America, the Alps, and Sicily. Defended the Vascello. A Genoese, æt. 32.

Pietramellara (Colonel Pietro, Marquis), commanding a regiment of his own, mortally wounded, June 5, and died in Rome early in July. A Bolognese noble.

MANARA'S LOMBARD BERSAGLIERI

*Manara . (Luciano), commanding the regiment, æt. 24; killed in Villa Spada, June 30.

Dandolo . (Enrico). Captain of a company, æt. 21 ; killed June 3, at the Corsini.

Dandolo . (Emilio). Brother of Enrico. Wounded June 3 and 30; æt. 19. Died in 1859.

Morosini , (Emilio), æt. 17. Killed June 30. The favourite of the regiment.

IN GARIBALDI'S LEGION OR ON HIS STAFF

Daverio . (Francesco). Chief of Garibaldi's staff; æt. 34. Killed June 3 at the Corsini.

*Manara . (Luciano), see above, commander of Lombard Bersaglieri, but became Chief of Garibaldi's staff, June 4. Killed June 30.

Vecchi . . (Candido Augusto). Joined Garibaldi Jan. 1849, at Ascoli, and was at his side on June 30, 1849.

Afterwards became his intimate friend, and wrote of him at *Caprera*, etc. ; æt. 35.

Masina . . (Angelo). A rich young man of Bologna, where he raised his lancers, attached to Garibaldi's Legion ; æt. 33. Killed at the Corsini, June 3.

Sacchi . . (Gaetano). Old Garibaldian of South American days ; æt. 44. Commanded one of the two divisions on the Retreat.

Bixio . . (Nino). A Genoese. (He and Medici were afterwards two of Garibaldi's chief lieutenants in Sciily and Naples, 1860.) Wounded, June 3, at the Corsini ; æt. 27.

Mameli . (Goffredo). Poet ; friend and fellow-townsman of Bixio ; æt. 21. Mortally wounded June 3 at the Corsini.

Marocchetti . (Guiseppe). Old Garibaldian of American days. wounded in siege, but accompanied the Retreat as Chief of the Staff ; æt. 45.

Hoffstetter . (Gustav). A Swiss. Attached sometimes to Manara's Lombards, sometimes to Garibaldi's staff. Wrote long and valuable account of Siege and Retreat.

Laviron . (Gabriel). French citizen and artist. Captain of the Ordnance ; æt. 35. Killed June 25.

Leggiero . Giovanni Battista Culiolo, commonly called *Leggiero*. Wounded at end of siege, so only left Rome July 14 ; but caught up the column of Retreat, and alone accompanied Garibaldi in his adventures and escape in August and September ; æt. 35.

Bonnet . (Gaetano) of Comacchio, æt. 23. Killed at the Corsini, June 3.

Bonnet . (Raimondo). Twin-brother of the above, went through siege, and accompanied Retreat as far as San Marino.

N.B.—The eldest brother, Nino Bonnet, who was at home, saved Garibaldi's life, Aug. 3, and subsequent days, when Garibaldi arrived as fugitive in district of Comacchio. In this he was assisted by a fourth brother, Celeste Bonnet.

Bassi . . (Ugo). Chaplain to Legion, æt. 47. Arrested in Comacchio, Aug. 3, and shot by the Austrians. at Bologna, Aug. 8.

APPENDICES

APPENDIX A

DRESS AND APPEARANCE OF GARIBALDI IN 1849

GARIBALDI's appearance four days after the battle of April 30 is thus described by *Hoffstetter* (p. 20) :

' He sits on his horse quiet and firm, as though born in the saddle. His dark-brown (*tiefbraune*) hair clusters thickly from under the narrow-brimmed pointed hat with the full black ostrich feather. His reddish beard covers about half his face. Over the red blouse floats lightly the short white American cloak ' (*poncho*).

This implies that his hair was dark, but this was only as it appeared to Hoffstetter in contrast to his beard, for other people called it light. *Cuneo* (p. 14), who knew him well, writing in 1849, speaks of ' fulva intonsa barba,' and ' lunghi e biondi capelli.' In the interesting coloured picture in *Miraglia*, p. 175 (anno 1850), his beard and hair are both a golden brown. So they are in a miniature of about this date or a few years later, which I have seen in the Vittoria Emanuele Library.

The descriptions which I give in this book of the dress and appearance of Garibaldi in 1849 are drawn from at least a score of different sources—*e.g. Bologna MSS. Piva* and *Savini*. See also the excellent description in *Koelman*, i. 314, quoted on p. 117, above. Garibaldi sometimes wore a cap (possibly sometimes a képi), but his most common headgear at this time was his peaked hat, which was not, however, as tall as the Calabrian hats of most of his followers. This hat was decorated by a black ostrich feather. He is wearing this in a picture of the *Illustrated London News* (where he appears mounted on his white horse, and followed by his Moor on a dark horse, as they are described in *Koelman*, ii. 72), and also in the interesting pictures

in *Miraglia*, 186, 198, 258 (anno 1850), and in a coloured picture
made from the life in Rome by Lord Mount Edgcumbe, then a
boy of seventeen—a copy of which is in my possession.   His
poncho, or South American mantle, is sometimes called white,
sometimes grey.   In Miraglia's coloured pictures it is quite white.

The illustration, p. 117, above, shows the shape and length
of his red blouse in 1849 to have been the same as it is represented in the picture of Garibaldi at Monte Video in 1846,
which may be found in Winnington-Ingram's *Hearts of Oak*.
They are, unfortunately, both bad portraits of his face.

His natural beauty was much enhanced by the unusual
feature of a nose and forehead in line, after the model of ancient
Greek sculpture.   For his eyes and voice, see pp. 29, 30, above.

APPENDIX B

NUMBER OF TROOPS ENGAGED ON APRIL 30

The troops under arms for the defence of Rome on April 30
are given as follows by *Torre* (ii. 25, 26) :

1st Brigade.—Under Garibaldi.   Italian Legion (Garibaldini),
1,300 ; students, 300 ; *emigranti*, 300 ; *reduci*, 600 ; *finanzieri
mobili* (Gagers), 250 (these latter were stationed on Monte
Mario) ; total, 2,750.

2nd Brigade.—Under Masi.   Papal troops of the line, 1,700 ;
National Guard, 1,000 ; total, 2,700.

3rd Brigade.—Under Savini.   Dragoons, 304 ; total, 304.

4th Brigade.—Under Galletti.   1st Regiment of line, 600 ;
2nd ditto, 400 ; Roman Legion, 810 ; total, 1,810.

Additional.—(Bersaglieri Lombardi, 600, under pledge not
to fight till May 4.)   Carabinieri (foot and horse), 511 ; Engineers,
etc., 450 ; Artillery, 505 ; total of available troops, 1,466.

This would give a *grand total* of 9,030 regimented troops,
besides some hundreds of unenrolled citizens.   But not all these
were actually engaged, as many—*e.g.* the line regiments under
Galletti—were used to guard parts of the wall not actually
attacked, and many of the unenrolled volunteers and National
Guard were kept inside the city to guard the barricades in
the Trastevere (*Saffi*, iii. 288–292 ; *Hoff.* 9–11).   Also the
Roman authorities give these totals as the nominal strength,
putting the real strength 2,000 lower (see *Tivaroni, Aust.*,
ii. 400).   *Farini*, iv. 18, gives the total at 9,000 or 10,000,
while *Vecchi*, ii. 194, estimates it at 8,700.

The number of the French actually engaged in the attack on Rome on April 30 was set down in the French official report (*Vaillant*, 7) at 5,800 men ; but the Liberal Italian authorities reckoned it higher—at 7,000 at least. *Spada*, iii. 436 (Italian Clerical), calls it 6,000 and twelve guns, which hardly differs from the French official statement, and is very probably correct.

I do not, therefore, think it possible to decide absolutely the number of troops engaged on each side on April 30. But the Romans, it is certain, had rather more in numbers, which compensated for the irregular and untrained character of most of those who fought on their side.

APPENDIX C

CAPTURE OF THE FRENCH PRISONERS, APRIL 30

Hoffstetter became intimate with the Garibaldian Legion immediately after the battle (in which he was not himself engaged), and he was constantly in their company for the next three months. He must have heard endless talk about April 30 from the Legionaries. It is he who twice (pp. 12–13, 413) declares that Masina's lancers charged and captured a body of French infantry on April 30. It was, he says, while the French were trying to escape from the Valentini. Confirmation is not wanting, since Garibaldi (*Mem.* 228) mentions Masina as having distinguished himself on April 30 ; in *Vecchi* (ii. 198) and *Camozzi Vecchio*, 32, we read how Masina, on April 30, himself received the sabres of several French officers and a drum-major's silver-knobbed staff, which he showed to several persons in triumph.

Some of the surrenders, on April 30, appear to have been hastened by the absence of Commandant Picard from the men under his command. Picard himself (*Moniteur*, May 30, p. 1923) declared that he had been lured away, and Torre accepted part of the story (see *Gaillard*, 178–179; *Vaillant*, 11–12, note ; and *Torre*, ii. 34–35). But Bixio declared that he, Bixio, had collared Picard, and had dragged him out of the ranks as prisoner. This story Bixio has told in great detail in his letter of August 20, 1851, to *Il Progresso*, Turin. (See also *Guerzoni's Bixio*, 85–88 and *Guerzoni*, i. 269.)

Picard's statement that he left his troops and entered Rome *because he was told by the Italians that Rome was captured by the French* (*Moniteur*, p. 1923) is, in any case, quite fantastic. If he accompanied Bixio at his own free will it must have been with a view to arrangements for surrender, as the French were losing all along the line.

Vecchi (ii. 197), following Bixio's narrative, tells the story thus :

'Nino Bixio, slanciatosi con una mano di armati verso il loco occupato dallo inimico . . . era per sforzare la porta, quando questa si aprì e mostrossi il maggiore Picard ; il quale, parve, accennasse ad una discussione sulle sue sorti. Lo animoso giovane dissegli in fretta, si arrendesse ; non aver scampo ; l' oste francese battere in ritirata ; . . . E nell' atto che il francese borbottava parole confuse, e i suoi soldati se gli facevano intorno, il Bixio lo strappava di là, mentre il Franchi, di Brescia, ghermiva il sottotenente Termelet ; ed ambedue disarmati e bendati erano condotti presso il Generale Garibaldi, questi gl' inviava al ministro Avezzana. Gli altri undici ufficiali co' 300 soldati ancor validi—scoraggiati com' erano—si arresero.'

Gabussi (iii. 356) and *Carletti* 270 say that Picard was the first to request a parley, showing the white flag from the house in which he was shut up.

The question may perhaps be raised whether Bixio should have laid forcible hands on an officer with whom he was treating for surrender. But Bixio, a man of violent passions and of great physical force and violence, as incidents in his later career showed, was quite likely to do it. On the other hand, he was quite incapable of luring Picard away by falsehoods about the French having entered Rome. To entertain such a notion for a moment shows an entire ignorance of the character of the ' fiery Bixio.' [1]

The alleged treachery of Bixio and of 1,200 of Garibaldi's men repeated in *Précis Hist.* 30, and now by *M. Bittard des Portes*, 86–89, is based on the vague implications of Picard as to what happened to his division *after* (by his own account) he had left it —in a statement which was printed in the *Moniteur* for the benefit of the French public. This story, which tells how the Italians having got close up to 300 of Picard's men by crying ' *Pace*,' and by declaring that Rome was occupied by the French army, then, apparently, hustled and disarmed them, is so ridiculous that I would not have thought it worth while to confute it had not M. Bittard des Portes resuscitated it. Is that how prisoners are made in the heat of hand-to-hand fighting ? It is, besides, denied implicitly by the quite contrary accounts of the Italian writers.

I have in my narrative of the battles and of the sieges of Rome

---

[1] Needless to say, the eminent and scholarly Italian historian, Signor *Luzio* (231), has no hesitation in taking, on this matter, the word of Bixio, ' la lealtà fatta persona.'

refused to record (except on one occasion to impugn, p. 179, note 2, above) any of the numerous declarations made by Italians who took part in the fighting, to the effect that the French soldiers, while charging, cried *amici*, and so prevented the Italians from firing on them until the French were upon them with the bayonet. Battles are not lost or won by 'white-flag incidents.' And I think it absurd of M. Bittard des Portes to believe that 300 French soldiers allowed themselves to be surrounded and disarmed in battle, on such a tale as that their comrades had entered Rome, and that peace was established !

Whatever Bixio did or did not do, one thing is certain—that the capture of three or four hundred French infantry took place *during the recapture of the Pamfili and Valentini grounds in fair fight*, and as a result of their comrades having been driven off the field. Picard's omission of the all-important fact of Garibaldi's successful charge (*Moniteur*, May 30, p. 1923) is quite inexcusable, and the repetition of his error by modern clerical historians is due to the fact that they do not study the Italian authorities. M. Bittard des Portes' account of the action in the Pamfili is therefore highly misleading. He commits a grave error, and one, moreover, that he could easily have avoided, when he implies (as he does on pp. 86–89 of his work) that the surrender took place as a result of deliberate fraud on the part of the Italians, while the French were still in victorious occupation of the Pamfili after their first successful advance. He omits altogether to state that the Italians drove the French out of the Pamfili, and off the Aqueduct and across the Deep Lane, *in fair fight*, and that that was why there was any question of Picard's surrender. The recovery of those places by a series of charges is established by all Italian authorities, including numerous persons who took part in the affair—*e.g. Torre*, ii. 30, 31 ; *Loev.* i. 163 ; *Costa*, 44 ; *Koelman*, ii. 16–19 ; *Carletti*, 269, 270 ; *Hoff.* 12, 13 ; *Vecchi*, ii. 197 ; *Mem.* 227, 228 ; *Roman MSS. Batt. Univ.* ; *Triumvirs' Report* (reprinted *Spada*, iii. 440). These and, so far as I know, every other Italian authority, make it perfectly certain that the Italians advanced again and recaptured the Corsini, and Pamfili, and Valentini *in fair fight*. The most detailed and interesting account of the action is given by *Carletti*, 269, 270, *Fatto d' armi del* 30 *Aprile*, in connection with the charge of the Roman Legion. But there is no evidence in M. Bittard des Portes' work that he has studied any Italian book on the subject of the siege of Rome, except *Loevinson* (whom he deserts whenever he wishes, as in this case).

Altogether M. Bittard des Portes' account of April 30 is worthy of his statement about *Bomba* (p. 140) : ' Le roi *Bomba*, comme on l'appelait en raison de son embonpoint.' His ignorance of Italian history and of the authorities for it is very great, and is on a par with his dislike of modern France and modern Italy, indicated in the introduction to his work. The real value of his book is that he has studied the MS. *Historiques* of the French regiments. I have, by the kind permission of the French War Office, studied those of the principal regiments, but find no evidence of the truth of Picard's story, beyond a repetition of it in the *Historique* of his own regiment (Paris MS. 20ᵉ, pp. 225, 226), written about the year 1892.

The gallantry of the French army on April 30, and during the siege of Rome in June 1849, was worthy of a better cause—was, in fact, worthy of the nation and the army that delivered Italy in 1796, in 1800, in 1859. May that French army always remain, as it is to-day, the friend of England, and of the Italy which owes so much to French valour. That valour, which no historian of 1849 can possibly deny, does not require to be defended by the belated resuscitation of impossible tales that have long ago died a natural death.

APPENDIX D

TREATMENT OF FRENCH PRISONERS ON APRIL 30

The accusations of ill-usage of the French prisoners by the Italian soldiery and mob on April 30 appear to me to be very doubtful, though *M. Bittard des Portes* (pp. 89, 90) makes great play with them. His authorities are : (1) Balleydier ; (2) *Rapport* du commandant Picard (in the *Moniteur*) ; and (3) Raffet's picture.

1. *Balleydier* is a second-hand partisan authority, whose book the impartial *Mr. Johnston* (p. 319) justly calls ' full of exaggerations and inaccuracies.'

2. Picard is responsible for palming off on the Parisian public such very remarkable statements about April 30 (see Appendix C, above) that all his evidence is, in relation to these events, extremely questionable. It was noted in Rome that while the other French prisoners were friendly he remained sulky (*Koelman*, ii. 22). Unfortunately his story, published in

the *Moniteur* to account to the French nation for the defeat of April 30, became the basis of subsequent French narratives. But be his evidence worth much or little, it does not bear out M. Bittard des Portes' accusation. For Picard does not say that his men were ill-treated or massacred, but only that he himself was insulted and assaulted by the mob as he was being brought into Rome a solitary prisoner. He is quite vague as to what happened to his men after he had left them, except only that he allows somehow or other they were killed, wounded or made prisoner. The *Paris MS.* 20ᵉ *Historique*, p. 226, evidently based on Picard's account, repeats his complaint as regards his own entry into Rome, adding that his men, on the other hand, were taken into Rome under a ' good escort ' (p. 226), and were ' well treated during their short captivity ' (p. 228). And so says *Vaillant*, 11–12 note.

3. The imaginary and sensational picture drawn by Raffet is solemnly quoted by *M. Bittard des Portes* (p. 90, note 1) as an authority. It is only necessary to look at it (either in the original or in the reproduction in *Bittard des Portes*, 90), to see its documentary value. It is, however, worth mentioning that Nino Costa, as Lord Carlisle tells me, was always particularly angry at this picture—which represents priests saving French prisoners from massacre on April 30—because, said Costa, so far from trying to massacre them, ' we gave them cigars.'

In the *Roman MSS. Batt. Univ.*, Andreocci Luigi says : ' La legione menò prigionero il 20 linea passando davanti a noi. Furono rispettati da tutti e non si grido se non *Viva l' Italia*, *Viva l' indipendenza Italiana.*'

Finally, it is to be observed that Oudinot acknowledged in the most grateful terms the extraordinary kindness of the Romans to the French wounded of April 30 (*De Lesseps*, 120, Doc. No. 14), and never complained either of the method in which the prisoners had been captured or of any ill-treatment that they had suffered. This is not without significance. Still more significant is the fact that the French prisoners themselves made friends with their Italian captors. (This is proved not only by the evidence of numerous Italian writers, but by the impartial and neutral observer, Captain Key, of H.M.S. *Bulldog*, on his visit to Rome.) Is it reasonable to suppose that the soldiers of a high-spirited army like the French would, in a few days' time, have made friends with their captors, and have been effusively grateful for the treatment they had received, if they had, in the first instance, been captured by

treachery at the moment of their own victory, and then subjected to massacre and insult after their surrender ?

On June 3 feeling had become much more embittered, and
some French prisoners were on that day massacred by those
to whom they had surrendered, and others insulted and assaulted
by the mob, as I record on p. 189, above. But on April 30 I
do not believe that this occurred.

APPENDIX E

THE COMMAND-IN-CHIEF AND THE VELLETRI EXPEDITION

For the *pros* and *cons.* of the question, see *Hoff.* 61 (a
prejudiced though well-informed witness), and *Roselli passim*
on his own behalf. See also *Loev.* i. 189–191 ; *Roman MSS.,*
F.R. 62. 8, pp. 111–119 ; *Koelman,* ii. 5–7 ; *Mario, Supplement,*
91–95, 100 ; *Pisacane,* 15, 16.

No doubt Europe would have made it yet another charge
against the friendless Republic if she had entrusted the supreme
command to ' the bandit,' and possibly some of the troops in
some of the line regiments would have been mutinous if asked
to serve under him, though I doubt it. But nothing that the
Republicans could have done would have placated Europe ;
and, as the bulk of the troops were volunteers, and the nature
of the operations in the Alban Hills would therefore be a war of
guerillas led straight to the attack of an inefficient regular army
(like the campaign that won Sicily and Naples in 1860), it is
probable that the Romans would have gained more, under the
auspices of Garibaldi, in enthusiasm, dash, and good leadership,
than they would have lost in other respects. And if, indeed,
it was undesirable for diplomatic and political reasons to make
Garibaldi nominal commander-in-chief of the forces of the State,
it would at least have been wiser to send him out with a free
hand for this expedition, in command of all such regiments as
were eager to follow him. Of these he would certainly have
found enough to enable him to knock King Ferdinand's army
to pieces, for it must be remembered that even the Lombard
Bersaglieri, who best represented the regular and conservative
elements in the army, had served under his sole command at
Palestrina, and that their commanding officer, the aristocratic
Manara, was proud to become, on June 4, the chief of Garibaldi's
staff.

APPENDIX F 1

THE FIRST STRUGGLES FOR THE PAMFILI AND CORSINI,
BEFORE GARIBALDI'S ARRIVAL

The best authorities for the conflicts in the Pamfili and
Corsini grounds before the arrival of Garibaldi are : *Paris
MSS.* 33ᵉ and 91ᵉ (16ᵉ *léger*) ; *Gamberini* (one of Pietramellara's
officers on that day) ; *Torre,* ii. 177, 178 ; *Vecchi,* ii. 259 ; *Hoff.,*
114 ; *Gabussi,* iii. 430 ; *Bittard des Portes,* 213–223. The inaccurate statement of the latter that there were 2,000 Italians
defending the grounds of the Villa Pamfili is based on the report of General Oudinot to the Minister of War on June 4
(*Precis Hist. pièce just.,* No. 12). Oudinot, when he wrote, had no
means of guessing the numbers—the villa having been captured
in the darkness. He had every reason for exaggerating, and he
was much given to exaggeration. For example, in the same
despatch he states that the Italians had some 24,000 regular
troops in Rome, and used them nearly all on June 3 in en-
deavouring to recover the Corsini. The truth is that they used
about 6,000, most of them volunteers (see p. 187, above).

Gamberini, who was with Pietramellara on the morning of
the 3rd, gives the number of Italians in the Pamfili at 400 ;
and this is borne out by *Torre,* ii. 177, and *Vecchi,* ii. 259. There
is, therefore, no doubt that there were only 400 defenders in the
Pamfili grounds at the time when the Villa was captured at
three in the morning.

On the other hand, Galletti's whole force was much more than
400 ; some were in the Vascello (*Gamberini,* 14), and, according
to the French accounts, some of Galletti's men came out of the
Porta San Pancrazio, as dawn was growing grey, *after the capture
of the Pamfili,* to the rescue of the Corsini and Valentini, which
they temporarily secured, only to lose them again when the French
came back in greater numbers. This is the account of the matter
given in the French *Historiques* (33ᵉ and 91ᵉ). On p. 158 of the
Historique of the 91ᵉ (16ᵉ *léger*), part of the force under Levaillant, we read : ' Le 2ᵉ bataillon était encore en arrière, retardé
par l'obstacle de la barricade, *le jour commençait à poindre, et
permettait d'apercevoir des troupes ennemies qui débouchaient de
la porte St. Pancrace* (clearly Galletti's men) ; d'autre part on
n'avait aucune nouvelle de la brigade Mollière, qui devait
exécuter l'attaque principale ; cette situation détermina le
Colonel *de faire rétrograder l'avant-garde jusqu'à la villa Pamfili,*

où le 2ᵉ bataillon vint se joindre au premier.' Immediately afterwards (pp. 158, 159) we read of a fierce struggle by part of this regiment for the possession of the Valentini, and on p. 159 we read: 'L'arrivée de la brigade Morlière (Mollière) opéra une heureuse diversion.' (See also *Journal* 16ᵉ, pp. 12–18.) *Gamberini's* recollections (1884) are somewhat different.

The famous patriot Colonel, Marquis Pietro Pietramellara (sometimes called Mellara), was not mortally wounded and captured on this day, as is sometimes said. That fate befell *Captain* Ludovico Pietramellara (*Loev.* i. 216, note), but the Colonel organised the first resistance in the Corsini after the loss of the Pamfili. He was mortally wounded two days later, was taken into Rome, and died there early in July. See the evidence of the eye-witness, *Gamberini* (14, 19, and *passim*), confirmed by *Gabussi*, iii. 434; *Ravioli*, 45, 57; *Bertolini's Pietramellara*, 25–28, 33.

APPENDIX F 2

STRUCTURE OF THE VILLA CORSINI

I have called the Corsini a house of four stories, and I speak of the balcony at the top of the outside staircase as the second floor from the ground, because that was the case as regards the side facing Rome. Hoffstetter and other writers, indeed, call the villa a three-storied building, with the balcony on the first floor, and it was so, as regards the west side. But, as regards the eastern *façade* looking towards Rome, *Werner* represents two stories below the balcony, as well as two above (see illustration, p. 186, above). In this it is borne out by the picture in *Decuppis* (*q.v.* at end of Bibliography, p. 363, below), and in the picture *Miraglia*, 258. In these pictures of Werner, Decuppis, and Miraglia, taken immediately after the siege, the staircase and *façade* are represented as completely blown away by the Italian cannon, so that the internal economy of the house is revealed, and four stories are thus rendered visible. Judging from the picture of the west (Pamfili) side of the villa as given in *Kandler*, there were only three stories (*viz.* only one below the balcony) on that side.

As to my statement that the storming parties could only get into the upper part of the villa from the Roman side by climbing the outer staircase, it is implied by all the detailed accounts of any of the attacks on June 3, especially by *Hoff.*,

121, lines 21–24. The illustration, p. 173, above (*I. L. N.*), shows, indeed, a portal on the ground floor between the two stairways, but apparently it did not connect with the upper stories, merely leading as a gangway through the lower parts of the house into the Pamfili gardens. This is also the impression left by the picture of the west (Pamfili) side of the Corsini, in the panoramic engraving by *Kandler*.

APPENDIX G

GARIBALDI'S USE OF THE BERSAGLIERI ON JUNE 3

The Lombard Bersaglieri, when they fought at Palestrina at the beginning of May, consisted of one battalion of about 600 men. On their return to Rome, between the battles of Palestrina and Velletri, another weak battalion, about 350 strong, succeeded in joining them, having embarked secretly from Spezia.[1]

The first (the original) battalion, 600 strong, consisted of four companies—the 1st under Ferrari, the 2nd under Enrico Dandolo, the 3rd under Massi, the 4th under Rozzat.[2] On June 3 these four companies of the first battalion together comprised 600 men, *minus* their small losses in the Palestrina and Velletri campaigns.

As regards the first attack made by this battalion on the Corsini, there is a discrepancy between the accounts given by Hoffstetter and Emilio Dandolo. *Dandolo*, 237, states that the 1st company was sent by itself to charge the Corsini, and that after it had been repulsed the 2nd company (Enrico Dandolo's) was sent alone on a second charge (pp. 239, 240). But Hoffstetter (who was then present, while Emilio Dandolo was still behind the walls) makes it perfectly clear that the 1st company, to which he himself was at the moment attached, and the 2nd (Enrico Dandolo's) company, were together in the first charge, headed by Manara; this was the charge in which Enrico Dandolo was killed (*Hoff.* 117–121). Hoffstetter also states that Rozzat's company was with them, but this is more doubtful. Rozzat, indeed, was there, but certainly without all, perhaps without any, of his company (the 4th) ; for Emilio Dandolo (242) states that Rozzat went forward alone without his company,

---

[1] *Dandolo*, 216; *Hoff.* 52. [2] *Hoff.* 38, 118.

z

and Emilio Dandolo himself, who was in Rozzat's company, was undoubtedly left behind during the first charge.

To sum up, the first attack by the Bersaglieri on the Corsini was made by a considerable body—the 1st, 2nd, and possibly part of the 4th company of the First Battalion. That is to say, this charge was made by some three hundred men together, and not in small handfuls, as Emilio Dandolo says (pp. 236, 237). But the attack was premature, as the villa had not been subjected to a sufficiently prolonged fire of cannon and musketry. *Hoff.*, 118, puts on Manara the responsibility for the too early beginning of the attack, but it is not possible entirely to exculpate Garibaldi, who was on the spot.

Hoffstetter and Dandolo between them give us an admirable account of the operations of the Bersaglieri on June 3. We have, unfortunately, no such record of the equally heroic charges of the Garibaldian Legion. Where Dandolo and Hoffstetter differ, we must rely on the testimony of that one of them who took part in the event in question. They were apart from each other during the day, except during the tragic scene in the Casa Giacometti, when Manara gave Emilio Dandolo definite news of his brother's death. The correspondence between Hoffstetter's and Dandolo's account of the place and circumstances of that scene, at which they were both present, increases the credit of each as a witness to the details of what he alone saw.

There are two mistakes in detail in the long account given by Hoffstetter of the day's battle. The Bersaglieri arrived on the scene not ' shortly after four o'clock ' (p. 108), but some four hours later ; indeed, Hoffstetter's own statement that they had been kept waiting two hours under arms in the Forum makes it likely that this is a misprint. Secondly, the casual mention of Emilio Dandolo as among the wounded in the first charge (p. 119) is an error. He was then inside the walls, and was wounded in the charge described by himself (*Dandolo*, p. 245).

Possibly Hoffstetter gives himself too much credit for seeing on the spot all that ought to have been done and was left undone by Garibaldi and Manara ; but otherwise he seems to me an admirable witness, and I think his narrative has not always been treated with sufficient consideration by historians.

APPENDIX H

DEATH OF MASINA

I. The first wound received by Masina on June 3 was in the morning, as described p. 176, above. His retirement to the field hospital in San Pietro in Montorio, at Garibaldi's orders, is described by *Koelman*, ii. 77, 85, an eye and ear witness. *Torre*, ii. 185; *Elia*, i. 168; and *Bertolini's Masina*, 23, also mention that Masina was wounded in one of the early attacks, and retired for an hour. *Roman MSS. Roncalli*, f. 156, adds, '*torna in Roma, corre al primo ospedale*,' which can only mean San Pietro in Montorio; so Koelman is well borne out. For Masina, see *R. S. del R.* i. 102–106.

II. The accounts of the later charge in which Masina met his death are somewhat contradictory; but I think that a careful perusal of the leading statements by *Torre, Roncalli, Carletti, Hoff., Koelman*, the *Paris MSS.* 33^e and 66^e, and the document printed in the *R. S. del R.*, will bring out certain facts, not generally recognised, which I epitomise as follows:

(1) Masina's death was in the afternoon, during this confused rush of all the regiments, cavalry and infantry (*Hoff.*, 127; *Koelman*, ii. 88–92), and not in the 'first encounter,' when he was only wounded, and retired to have his arm bound up.

(2) It is certain that in this later charge Masina rode up the steps of the villa on horseback in the sight of the crowd on the walls of Rome; but it is not certain that he received his death wound while so doing.

It is possible that he was killed, as *Torre* states (ii. 185), 'nell' uscir del Casino,' in coming out from the Villa Corsini. For his skeleton was undoubtedly found, on July 5, lying in the garden below, seventy paces from the villa, having lain there during the siege, between the French and Italian lines (*R. S. del R.* i. 110). One witness at the inquest (Lorenzo Bressan) deposed that he had seen Masina fall on the spot where his body was found. *Koelman* (ii. 91) follows the ordinary story, and speaks of him as killed on the steps, though he does not say that he *saw* him fall there. The explanation offered on p. 109 ll. 23, 24 of *R. S. del R.* i. is not good. If he was not killed on the steps, it must have been during the retreat, 'nell' uscir del Casino,' as *Torre*, ii. 85, says.

III. So much (or little) can be said about Masina's own death. As regards the military aspects of the charge, during some part of which his death occurred, there is also considerable difficulty. But I think the following statements can be made :

(1) The cavalry charge ordered by Garibaldi was not—like the expedition of Emilio Dandolo and his twenty men—made against the full force of the French safely ensconced in the villa, but at a propitious moment when the Italian fire had caused a momentary retreat or confusion (*Hoff.* 126 ; *Koelman*, ii. 86–88). Consequently the villa was taken with little loss ('dopo pochi colpi si ritirano i Francesi,' *Carletti*, 274). The French accounts quoted below are in keeping with this.

(2) The cavalry were supported by a rush of many hundreds of men. According to *Carletti*, 274, the cavalry took the Corsini before this rush ; according to *Hoffstetter*, 126–127, they were themselves only a part of the general rush.

(3) This rush consisted partly of the infantry in and about the Vascello (*Hoff.* 126–127), and partly of spent regiments, gunners, and civilians from behind the Porta San Pancrazio, who started without orders or leadership, in a state of great excitement, after they had seen the infantry in the Vascello charge up the slope (*Koelman*, ii. 88–90).

It is very difficult to make out what Garibaldi did or did not do in this affair. It is clear that, as Carletti says, he ordered the *cavalry* to charge the Corsini, and Hoffstetter and Koelman show that he did so because the enemy were momentarily losing hold of the Villa by reason of the Italian bombardment. But Carletti and Hoffstetter say that the *infantry* rush from the Vascello was not ordered, but was the result of a voluntary *élan* on the part of the men ; only when it had begun, Hoffstetter says that Garibaldi sent in every man he could find. Hoffstetter also says that Garibaldi remained at the garden gate of the Corsini, but this is contrary to the evidence of Garibaldi himself (if *Dumas*, ii. 191, is to be taken as Garibaldi's evidence) and to that of Koelman, who says that he saw Garibaldi leading on the infantry from the Vascello, and himself fighting in the Corsini ground, before the rush of the mob began from the Porta San Pancrazio. He also says that he saw Garibaldi on the Corsini Hill, when he (Koelman) had arrived there in the mob. Koelman is a first-hand but not a quite first-rate authority, as he wrote so long after the events.

All this evidence is very contradictory, and probably none of the eye-witnesses who took part in the charge had much time to see what Garibaldi, or anyone else, was doing. But in judging his conduct in the light of such uncertain *data*, it is at least clear that the cavalry took the Villa because their charge was ordered at a propitious moment when the foe were yielding before the bombardment. At what distance the infantry followed, whether they were led by Garibaldi in person, whether he ordered their advance, or whether they started from the Vascello before he had time to organise their advance properly, are points on which authorities differ. It is equally impossible to say whether he is to be blamed for not providing against the rush of the mob from the Porta San Pancrazio, and whether that mob did more harm by adding to the confusion or more good by adding to the numbers of the defenders of the Corsini Hill.

The French *historiques* are rather vague about the fighting on June 3 after the arrival of Garibaldi, as the names of the places, where the fighting described took place, are not often given. But there are passages which clearly refer to this late afternoon attack, and one of them is most valuable as showing that during that attack the convent of San Pancrazio (as well as the Corsini) was momentarily taken by the Italians. The passage is in the *Historique* 33ᵉ (*Paris MSS.*), p. 214 :

' A 4 heures (P.M., as context shows) le 3ᵉ bataillon reçut l'ordre d'aller reprendre les positions que le 66ᵉ avait laissé retomber aux mains de l'ennemi. A l'arrivée du bataillon les Romains étaient descendus près du réservoir de l'aqueduc, mais, comme le matin, le 3ᵉ bataillon les eut bientôt chassés, leur tuant beaucoup de monde. Le 3ᵉ bataillon sous les ordres du Colonel Bonat avait reçu l'ordre de s'emparer de l'Eglise de San Pancrazio occupée par les Romains : cet ordre, malgré la résistance, fut promptement exécuté et l'ennemi refoulé dans la place.'

The *Historique* of the 66ᵉ (MSS., pp. 101–102) merely says the troops were ' exposées à être englouties sous les décombres des maisons qui s'écroulent sous le feu de l'ennemi,' and speaks of ' une sortie en masse appuyée par du canon.'

APPENDIX I

NUMBERS OF THE ROMAN ARMY DURING THE SIEGE

The force under arms in Rome in June was considerably greater than it had been on April 30.

But there is much greater uncertainty as to the numbers of men under arms in Rome than as to the numbers of the French. The French consisted of so many regiments of a regular army, whose numbers it was quite possible to ascertain, and difficult to conceal. Vaillant's statement that there were 30,000 by the end of the siege may be accepted as approximately correct. The defenders of Rome, on the other hand, chiefly consisted of bodies of men of very lax organisation, whose numbers were either fluid or unascertainable, seeing that they are stated differently in every list. Compare, for instance, the three lists given by *Hoffstetter* (at the end of his volume), *Carletti*, 259–260, and *Vaillant*, 185. They are agreed as to the numbers of scarcely any one regiment. For example :

—	Vaillant	Carletti	Hoffstetter
Manara's Lombards	1,000	650	900
Students	300	250	200
Roman Legion	251	800	1,000
Medici's Legion	{ Not mentioned	300	300
First Line Regiment . . .	1,864	1,000	1,200
Second Line Regiment . .	2,000	1,100	1,200
Third Line Regiment . . .	1,493	800	1,000
Artillery	1,574	820	500

In the end, Vaillant gives, as a total of all arms, 21,760 + 12,000 National Guard whom he says were chiefly used for policing the town. Hoffstetter gives 14,790, and mentions that the National Guard were 8,000 or 10,000, but he does not count them in the list ; they had fought on April 30, and now in June patrolled the streets and guarded some parts of the wall. Carletti gives a total of 17,580, including the National Guard (Civica Mobilizzata), whom he reckons at only 1,200, a tenth of Vaillant's estimate.

Hoffstetter, who, next to Garibaldi and Manara, was in a position to know the facts, and was deep in the counsels at head-quarters in the Savorelli and Spada villas, gives a most interesting list of the regiments on the Janiculum on June 29, with the remaining strength of each (*Hoff.* 280–281). The total amounts to 4,170 infantry, *plus* some fifty lancers. I know no reason to think this an under-estimate, if we allow for the several thousands who, he says, had already been killed and wounded (p. 300). This estimate of 4,000 and odd men left on the Janiculum on June 29 is confirmed by *Torre*, ii. 262, and accepted by *Loevinson*, i. 261.

There is no doubt that the bulk of the Roman forces never ascended the Janiculum in June, to judge by the comparatively small number of regiments mentioned in the defence of the Vascello and the walls. The presence of the French outside the Porta del Popolo, the Porta San Paolo, and the Vatican wall, their continual demonstrations against Rome in those quarters, and the need for policing the city, would account for the large numbers kept down below.

APPENDIX J

DAMAGE DONE BY THE BOMBARDMENT INCIDENTAL TO THE SIEGE OF ROME

The protest of the foreign Consuls to Oudinot can be read in *Bittard des Portes*, 343–344, and *Balleydier*, ii. 251–253. It offered ' les remontrances les plus énergiques contre ce mode d'attaque qui non seulement met en danger les vies et les propriétés des habitants neutres et pacifiques, mais aussi celles des femmes et des enfants innocents. Nous nous permettons, Monsieur le Général, de porter à votre connaissance que ce bombardement a déjà coûté la vie à plusieurs personnes innocentes et a porté la destruction sur des chefs-d'œuvre de beaux arts qui ne pourront jamais être remplacés.' The last phrase is exaggerated, unless the buildings on the Janiculum itself are referred to. But the personal injury to the inhabitants is not exaggerated at all, especially as regards the Trastevere.

On this subject see the French defence, *Commission Mixte* (Yellow Book, 1850). Its statements show the limit of the injury done to works of art, but also they show how general was the bombardment, how wide the range of the French missiles all over Rome. To take one example out of many, the Rospigliosi Palace, close under the Quirinal, was hard hit, though its famous ceiling-fresco, Guido Reni's 'Aurora,' was not injured, as was stated by the Liberal press (*Com. Mixte*, 57–58). The actual injury done to the Palace is described in Murray's Guides of the years following—an authority hostile to the defenders of Rome of 1849.

Mr. Marchetti tells me that he recollects, as a boy of five, being taken by his mother into the cellars for several days to avoid the bombardment ; their house was in the Via Borgognona in the heart of Rome (see p. 169, *note* above), and a shell actually entered the room where his brother, who had just come back from a spell of duty on the ramparts, was sleeping.

See also, for the bombardment in general, and in particular the terrible suffering inevitably caused in the Trastevere : *Luzio*, 237 (Borchetta's narrative) ; *Vecchi*, ii. 268–269, 273, 284, 294 ; *Koelman*, ii. *passim*, e.g. 137 ; *Pisacane*, 6 ; *Gabussi*, iii. 458–459 ; *Lazzarini*, *passim*, e.g. 197 ; *Torre*, ii. 231, 263 ; *Dandolo*, 263. And see *Bittard des Portes*, 325–326, 365.

APPENDIX K
THE NUMBERS OF THE KILLED AND WOUNDED

I have indicated (p. 189, above), in reference to June 3, that it is extremely difficult to calculate the numbers of Roman killed and wounded, because :

1. So many wounded may have been taken to private houses, and not to the public hospitals, as noticed by *Torre*, ii. 274.

2. As the numbers of the regiments were fluctuating or unknown (see Appendix I, above), no certain calculations of losses could have been made by counting the survivors.

Hoff., 300, calculates the Italian killed and severely wounded at 4,000 men and 300 officers. Medici (*Beghelli*, ii. 392) says that in the defence of the Vascello alone he lost 300 killed and a much greater number of wounded. The proportion of killed in such an operation would be large, because often only the head was exposed (see *Hoff.* 290). These estimates may be exaggerated, but Hoffstetter and Medici were, at any rate, the people best in a position to know the losses on the whole Janiculum, and at the Vascello respectively.

Torre, ii. 174, calculates the killed and wounded for April 30, the Neapolitan expeditions, and the siege of Rome at about 3,000, basing his estimate on the figures of the hospitals given him by his friend Bertani. This is considered by *Johnston*, p. 310, as the most probable estimate. But Torre makes no pretensions to certainty. *Vecchi*, ii. 298, also calculates the number at 3,000, though with like hesitation. The lists of those who passed through the hospitals (not including the dead on the field of battle or the wounded who were tended in their own homes) give a total of 2,095, from April 30 to the end of the siege (*Ravioli*, 68). *Loev.*, ii. 51, accepts Bertani's very similar calculation (2,063) of the hospital returns.

As regards the *provenance* of the active defenders of Rome, an interesting list of some of the wounded in the hospitals between May 1 and June 30 was published by the restored clerical government in the *Giornale di Roma* on September 15, very similar to the more complete list given by Bertani (*Loev.* ii. 51):

Giornale di Roma (Sept. 15)

Inhabitants of Rome	136
Inhabitants of Roman States . . .	543
Inhabitants of other Italian States . .	322
Inhabitants of foreign countries . .	41
Of origin unascertained . . .	256
	1,298

Bertani's List (*Loev.* ii. 51)

City of Rome	249
Roman States	954
Other Italian States	547
France	10
Other foreigners	46
Unknown	257
	2,063

These lists are probably trustworthy, though we should remember that citizens of Rome would be more likely to be taken to their own houses instead of to the hospitals. But there is no doubt the Ligurians, Lombards, and Romagnuols (the latter citizens of the Roman Republic) were the soul of the defence.

As to the French, we have no certain calculation of their losses. We read in the *Historiques* of the various regiments that they lost, in all, 500 men killed and wounded on April 30, and 250 on June 3. These figures, which do not include prisoners, are admitted by *M. Bittard des Portes* (pp. 95, 235), and represent the lowest probable estimate.[1] If we accept this lowest estimate of the losses on April 30 and June 3, it is difficult to believe that the French lost only 1,024 men in killed and wounded in the whole expedition, as stated by *Vaillant*, p. 159. For it is difficult to see how the losses from June 4 to 30 inclusive could have been under 300 men—*e.g.* M. Bittard des Portes

[1] *Gabussi*, iii. 433, shows there was much doubt entertained as to whether the French lost only 250 on June 3.

(p. 262) admits eighty-three wounded on June 4 and 5 alone. Indeed, there was general incredulity as to the accuracy of the number given by Vaillant (see *Torre*, ii. 275). *Vecchi* (ii. 298) guessed that the French had lost 2,000 killed and wounded.

APPENDIX L

OUDINOT'S GOOD FAITH

(See pp. 164, 165 above)

General Oudinot's much-disputed letter ran as follows :

' GÉNÉRAL,—Les ordres de mon gouvernement sont positifs, ils me prescrivent d'entrer dans Rome le plus tôt possible. J'ai dénoncé aux autorités romaines l'armistice verbal que, sur les instances de M. de Lesseps, j'avais consenti à accorder momentanément. J'ai fait prévenir vos avant-postes que l'une et l'autre armée avaient le droit de recommencer les hostilités. Seulement, pour donner le temps à ceux de nos nationaux [French residents] qui voudraient quitter Rome et, sur la demande de M. le chancelier de l'ambassade de France, la possibilité de le faire avec facilité, je diffère l'attaque de la place jusqu'à lundi matin.

' Recevez, etc.,
' Le général-en-chef,
' OUDINOT DE REGGIO.

' Le 1ᵉʳ Juin, à 5 heures du soir.'

M. Bittard des Portes does not doubt the good faith of this letter, in spite of the attack made on the Pamfili on Sunday, June 3, because he says that the word ' place ' could mean nothing except fortifications of the city built for military purposes, and the ground inclosed by them. Thus, on p. 210, note, he says :

' Cette question semble si peu discutable au point de vue militaire que, dans nos règlements—et on peut ajouter dans tous les règlements des armées européennes sur *le service des places*—" *la dénomination de place de guerre s'applique aux villes fortifiées par une simple enceinte ou par une enceinte avec forts détachés ou par un ensemble de forts détachés.*" Or il ne s'agissait pas de forts, mais de simples villas.'

In view of this plea, I have consulted high military authority as to the natural interpretation of Oudinot's letter. I have received the following reply :

' The letter of General Oudinot is very ambiguous. He says the outposts have been warned they have the right to recommence operations at once, but he guarantees that the " place " shall not be attacked before a fixed time. Technically " place " may be construed to mean the fortress of Rome bounded by its *enceinte*, and not to include any houses or enclosures outside it, and the French commander would then be within his rights in ordering the attack on the Villas Pamfili and Orsini in its suburbs.

' But " place," taken in combination with " attaque," has a wider meaning. The attack on a fortress invariably commences at some distance from it ; it is usual for the garrison to hold certain localities as advanced posts. Oudinot's letter was calculated to deceive and did deceive the Romans ; but they cannot be held blameless, and should have replied that they construed his letter to mean that he would not advance beyond a certain line (between the outposts), and have taken precautions to ensure his not doing so without effectual opposition. . . .

' Good faith is the essence of pacific communications between belligerents in war. . . . The verdict on the case must be that General Oudinot did take mischievous advantages of the wording of his letter, and violated the good faith and spirit of the armistice, and that General Roselli did not take reasonable precautions to ensure the safety of the fortress in his charge.'

And, again, from another high military authority, I have the following opinion :

' General Oudinot wilfully deceived the Romans, as the attack on a fortress may well be held to include attack upon points of vantage outside the actual *enceinte*. On the other hand, General Roselli certainly deserved to be deceived. The agreement was only verbal, and the possibility of the loss of what was really the key to the situation, by an evasion of it, ought to have been foreseen and guarded against by an astute and wide-awake commander.'

For the grave fault of Roselli in this matter, see *Loev.* i. 211 ; *Pisacane, Guerra,* 282 ; *Gamberini,* 6–10 ; and *Gabussi,* iii. 429–430.

The complete security of the Romans as to the interpretation of the letter is shown by a proclamation of the Triumvirs issued on June 2, describing the exchange of letters, and stating that :

' Il Generale Oudinot . . . dichiarò che non solamente considerava rotta ogni tregua e libero il corso alle ostilità, ma che avrebbe assalito la città, non però prima di Lunedì ' (*Roman MSS. Roncalli* 37, *f.* 30).

It never occurred to anyone in Rome to suppose that ' la

città ' or ' la piazza ' would be held to exclude the Pamfili positions.   In their next proclamation, issued after the French attack had been begun, the Triumvirs speak of ' tradimento,' and the violation of the ' promessa scritta ch' è in nostre mani di non assalire prima di lunedì ' (ditto, f. 145).

It must be remembered that Oudinot was living in an atmosphere of the deceits which he was deliberately practising both upon the Italians and upon the French authorities whose instructions he was supposed to obey.   His conduct in this respect has been thoroughly exposed in the recent work of MM. Clermont and Bourgeois (*Rome et Napoléon III*).   Here is a part of M. de Rayneval's letter to Oudinot, written from Gaeta on May 20 :

' Nous sommes entre trois ou quatre formidables écueils. Ménager les susceptibilités de l'Assemblée (the French assembly) tant qu'elle continuera à vivre, avoir l'air d'être ennemi de l'Autriche sans lui faire la guerre, et rester ami du Pape sans en avoir l'air ' (*Clermont*, 97).

The soldier who would receive and act upon such a letter was not likely to be scrupulous about deceiving the Romans in war as well as in politics.

APPENDIX M

ENGLAND AND AUSTRIAN ATROCITIES

(p. 266 above)

The following is a portion of a letter written by Lord Palmerston, then Foreign Secretary, to the representative of England at Vienna :

Panshanger, Sept. 9, 1849.

' MY DEAR PONSONBY,—The Austrians are really the greatest brutes that ever called themselves by the undeserved name of civilised men.   Their atrocities in Galicia, in Italy, in Hungary, in Transylvania are only to be equalled by the proceedings of the negro race in Africa and Haiti.   Their late exploit of flogging forty odd people, including two women at Milan, some of the victims being gentlemen, is really too blackguard and disgusting a proceeding. . . . I do hope that *you* will not fail constantly to bear in mind the country and Government which you represent, and that you will maintain the dignity and honour of England by expressing *openly* and *decidedly* the disgust which such proceedings excite in the public mind in this country ; and

that you will not allow the Austrians to imagine that the public
opinion of England is to be gathered from articles put into the
" Times " by Austrian agents in London, nor from the purchased
support of the " Chronicle," nor from the servile language of Tory
lords and ladies in London, nor from the courtly notions of
royal dukes and duchesses. . . .

'Yours sincerely,
'PALMERSTON.'

In October 1850, à propos of the assault on the Austrian
General Haynau on his visit to Barclay's brewery, London, Palmerston writes to Grey : ' I must own that I think Haynau's coming
here without rhyme or reason, so soon after his Italian and
Hungarian exploits, was a wanton insult to the people of this
country, whose opinion of him had been so loudly proclaimed at
public meetings and in all the newspapers. But the draymen
were wrong in the particular course they adopted. Instead of
striking him, which, however, by Koller's account they did not
do much, they ought to have tossed him in a blanket, rolled him
in the kennel, and then sent him home in a cab, paying his fare
to the hotel.' (*Ashley's Palmerston*, i. 139, 240).

APPENDIX N

HUGH FORBES

Since the appearance of the first edition of this book I have
been fortunate enough to make the acquaintance of Miss Forbes,
the only remaining daughter of Colonel Hugh Forbes. She has
kindly allowed me to consult documents which I refer to in this
edition as the *Forbes MSS.*, and has given me much verbal
information about her father.

Hugh Forbes was the son of a wealthy English gentleman ;
he matriculated at Oxford in 1823, at the age of fifteen, and his
name appears in the Oxford University Calendar as a gentleman
commoner of St. Mary Hall, 1824-6. In 1826 he obtained a
commission in the Coldstream Guards. His first wife, an English
lady, was the mother of his son Hugh, who went through the
Retreat with his father and Garibaldi as described in this book.
But it was his second wife, a foreign lady, *née* Conti, who was his
faithful consort through the troubles of 1848-9. They had been
living for some time in Tuscany, wealthy and prosperous, when
the events of 1848 drew him as a middle-aged man into those

activities on behalf of the liberty of nations in which he was destined to spend his fortune and the energies of the last half of his life. The *Forbes MSS.* show that as early as April 1848 he was serving the Venetian Republic in the Lombard war, while his wife remained at Siena ; he then returned to Tuscany, but from October 1848 to the beginning of 1849 we find him in a high military post under the revolutionary government in Palermo, trying to organise the last resistance there, and writing some-times to his friends the Tuscan Democrats to complain of the weakness and disloyalty which he thought he detected in the revolutionary capital of Sicily, where the way was being pre-pared for *Bomba's* return. From Palermo he also attempted, eleven years too soon, to instigate the raising of a ' British Legion ' in England to assist in the liberation of Sicily.

How long he stayed in Sicily I do not know, but soon after the restoration of *Bomba's* rule in Palermo he reappears, in the late spring or early summer of 1849, taking over from Pianciani the unenviable command of the last forces of the Roman Republic, rapidly dissolving before the Austrian invasion of the Marches. The *Forbes MSS.* tell us that they were attacked at Urbino by the Austrians soon after Forbes had assumed the command, and retreated south by way of Urbania to Terni ; and that Forbes used to keep order among them by causing thieves to wear their coats turned inside out by way of disgrace in the ranks.

Then Garibaldi arrived at Terni, and there followed the events narrated in this book. The *Forbes MSS.* enable me to print Garibaldi's despatch from Prodo (p. 257 above). Young Hugh Forbes seems to have been left at San Marino ; at any rate, he escaped uncaptured. The father, captured at sea, was begged off by his beautiful wife, who travelled about with a pass through the Austrian lines and had a personal interview with D'Aspre.

In the winter of 1849 he was at Genoa, but he retired soon after to the United States. There he took up the cause of the negroes, and in 1857, at the request of the famous John Brown, went west to organise military resistance to the raids of the Southerners in the disturbed border districts. But a most em-bittered quarrel soon arose between the abolitionists and their new ally, whose conduct does not appear to have been above reproach ; these events led to his return to Europe in the winter of 1859-60, in time to play his part in Garibaldi's Sicilian ex-pedition. Of his conduct there I hope to write in a future volume. (*Forbes MSS.* and Admiral Chadwick's *Eve of the*

Civil War, 1907, and F. B. Sanborn's *Life and Letters of John Brown*.)

In 1861-3 this indefatigable friend of human liberty appears on the Polish scene of action, with a sort of commission from Garibaldi ; Forbes also wrote numerous pamphlets to stir up the English nation to a sense of the wrongs of Poland.

His mental activity took many various directions. He was an engineer, and took out patents for inventions. He wrote poetry, and ' Catechisms ' of a highly argumentative character, expressing his own private religion, which was of a Deistic character. Though a strong patriot, and actively connected with the English Volunteer movement, he was not incapable of calling certain sections of his countrymen ' the baptised Pharisees.' He was what is called ' an original.'

He died in reduced circumstances in Pisa, on July 22, 1892. He was not an altogether wise man, but he had incurred obloquy and laid waste his fortune and that of his large family on behalf of one generous cause after another, and these causes he had espoused (except in the case of Garibaldi's Sicilian expedition) at moments when men who follow the beaten track of life shrink from connection with ' disreputable ' associates and ' hopeless ' undertakings. A patriotic society at Pisa decided to go into mourning for three months on the death of Hugh Forbes. They did well ; he had been no fair-weather friend of Italy.

APPENDIX O

CAPTURE OF THE BRAGOZZI AND LANDING OF THE GARIBALDIANS

There is no doubt that the cannonading of the *bragozzi* took place, as I have described it on p. 290, in bright moonlight, but on a stormy sea. The evidence to this effect of the written authorities is borne out by the Austrian picture commemorating the event. That contemporary picture (*Festnahme von 162 italianischen Insurgenten der Legion Garibaldi-Manara in der Punta Maistra am 3 August Nachts durch den kk. Brick Orestes*), dedicated to Gorzkowski, 1849, can be seen in the Museo Civico, Vicenza, Raccolta Fantoni. It represents a small wooden sailing brig (the ' Orestes '), two masts, square-rigged with a very few guns ; and three smaller sailing boats (the pinnaces, *palischermi*, spoken of in the narrative) attacking the fishing fleet. The sailor

Oseladore, in his report (printed in *Citt. Cesena*), says they remained from ten at night to seven in the morning ' always under the fire of the brig's cannon.' This is quite consistent with the Austrian official account, *Benko*, 632.

There is no doubt that 162 prisoners were captured at sea and taken to Pola, as we have the official list with all their names ; but there is conflicting evidence as to the number of boats captured, the number of boats that ran ashore, and the number of Garibaldians who landed from these latter. We may tabulate the conflict of evidence as follows :—

—	Garibaldians who embarked at Cesenatico	Garibaldians who dis-embarked and made off inland	Number of *bragozzi* captured at sea	Number of *bragozzi* whence the Garibaldians succeeded in landing
Report of Commissario of Magnavacca (*Boll. Ris.* ii. 212–3)	260	95	7 + 1 *tartana*	5
Brigadier Sereni, report to municipality of Cesenatico (*Citt. Cesena*)	—	—	—	3
Bonnet . . .	—	—	10	3
Oseladore (one of the sailors pressed at Cesenatico. *Citt. Cesena*)	—	—	—	5
Uccellini's Garibaldi	150 (obviously wrong)	—	8	5
Lt.-Gov. of Comacchio's report (*Gualtieri*, 183), based on Sereni's information	—	150	8	3
Forbes' Volontario, p. 121, *note*	291	—	—	—
Benko (Austrian account)	—	about 100	6 + 1 *tartana*	5

The official (naval) report in *Benko* (631–2) is the best authority, and it states that as many as five *bragozzi* had succeeded in landing the men they contained, three *bragozzi* in one place, and two in another, on the shore. The three that ran ashore together were those which Bonnet saw, and from one of'which Garibaldi landed. There is no doubt whatever, therefore, that some hundred men made off inland, of whom only a comparatively small number were captured. But those few included both Ugo Bassi and Ciceruacchio.

Oseladore's statement (*Citt. Cesena*) is :

'Cinque legni, pure carichi della gente del Garibaldi col Garibaldi medesimo e la di lui moglie (fra i quali legni vi era pure il mio), riuscirono di andare a terra fra Magnavacca e Volana. Lì, in spiaggia, il Garibaldi, la di lui consorte e la sua gente rimasta sbarcono e s'internarono. Seguito lo sbarco stesso, una barcaccia del Brick ci venne incontro ; ed io allora, col mio legno, seguitato da altri due, ci portammo a bordo il Brick, lasciando gli altri due in spiaggia.'

The Brigadier Sereni, prisoner on one of these bragozzi, reported : ' Il Garibaldi sbarcò, insieme con la moglie e diversi suoi seguacì, in faccia al Bosco Eliseo nella mattina del giorno 3 ; sbarcati che furono da soli tre legni, disse a tutti che fossero andati dove credevano, perchè esso Garibaldi non poteva più tenerli presso di sè.' (*Citt. Cesena.*)

APPENDIX P

THE DEATH OF ANITA

The circumstances of Anita's death as she was being carried up the stairs ; the grief of Garibaldi ; the circumstances of her hasty burial in the sand by the peasants ; the subsequent dis-covery of her body by police ; their natural first suspicions that she had been murdered by the peasants ; the complete acquittal of the peasants, and the establishment by the Pontifical Com-mission of enquiry of the facts narrated above, can be found in the following documents :

Museo Civico of Bologna, MSS. entitled ' Garibaldi ' (Anita Ribeyràs) serie B. Dono del Prof. Raffaele Belluzzi.

1. Rapporto del Presidente del Tribunale collegiale di Ravenna al Dicastero di grazia e giustizia di Roma (8 ott. 1849).

2. Lettera scritta dal Presidente sullo stesso argomento in data del 6 novembre 1849.

See also Maria Tavioli's story, *Resto del Carlino*, 9–10 June, 1907, and March 16, 1908. Also letter by G. M. Trevelyan in the *Giornale d'Italia*, March 18, 1908.

LIST OF PRINTED MATTER AND MSS. CONSULTED BY THE AUTHOR

Abbreviations in the notes explained.

[The mark * means that matter concerning the retreat or the escape of Garibaldi will be found in the book or document so indicated. Works not so marked either concern the general history or relate only to events ending with the surrender of Rome.]

I. PRINTED MATTER.

Allocuzione del Sommo Pontefice = *Allocuzione del Sommo Pontefice Pio Papa IX. da Gaeta,* 20 *Aprile* 1849.

*Anita = *Nuova Antologia,* Dec. 1905. Pp. 570–602. Article signed *Sfinge* (= Signorina Codronchi) on Anita Garibaldi. Contains private (family) information, and the genuine portrait by the Italian Gallini taken in 1848.

Ashley's Palmerston = Ashley, Hon. Evelyn. *Viscount Palmerston, 1846–65.*

Balleydier = Balleydier (Alphonse). *Histoire de la Révolution de Rome.* 1851.
(Partisan French. Often inaccurate.)

Beghelli = Beghelli (Giuseppe). *La Repubblica Romana del 1849.* 1874.
(Not of high rank as an authority. Partisan Liberal, and not so fair as *Torre.* The most valuable document in it is Medici's own account of his defence of the Vascello—ii. 387–392.)

Belgiojoso = Barbiera (Raffaello). *La Principessa Belgiojoso.* Milano. 1902.
(Valuable.)

*Bel. = Belluzzi (Raffaele). *La Ritirata di Garibaldi da Roma nel 1849.* Biblioteca storica del Risorgimento Italiano. Serie 1, n. 10. Società editrice Dante Alighieri. Roma. 1899.
(Signore Belluzzi, the late lamented head of the Risorgimento department of the Museo Civico, Bologna, made with great pains, in days when it was not yet altogether too late, a collection of local traditions and personal recollections along the whole route of the retreat, as well as of all relevant printed matter and MSS. Out of this material he composed his *Ritirata di Garibaldi,* the authoritative book on the subject, and left the whole body of papers to the Museo Civico, Bologna. There, according to the liberal custom of the municipality, I have been kindly allowed access to them, and have thus been able to examine at the source the statements which Belluzzi makes in this book, and have had matter by which to check, confirm, and add to *Hoffstetter, Ruggeri,* and the other original authorities on the retreat.)

Bertani = Mario (J. W.). *Agostino Bertani e i suoi tempi.* 1888. (Valuable.)

Bertolini = Bertolini (F.). *Pellegrino Rossi.* Bologna. 1885.

Bertolini's Masina = Bertolini (F.). *Angelo Masini.* Bologna. 1889.

Bertolini's Pietramellara = Bertolini (F.). *Pietro Pietramellara.* Bologna. 1885.

*Bittard des Portes = Bittard des Portes. *Expédition Française de Rome.* 1849. 2nd ed. 1905.

(Valuable for its study of the *historiques* of the various French regiments engaged in the siege. For its limitations see my remarks, end of Appendix C, pp. 329, 330, above.)

Bixio = Guerzoni (G.). *La Vita di Nino Bixio.* 1875.

*Boggio = Boggio (P. C.). *Da Montevideo a Palermo, Vita di Giuseppe Garibaldi.* Torino. 1860.

(For 1849 it is largely a reprint of *Vecchi*, q.v.)

Boll. Ris. ii. = *Bollettino del Congresso Storico del Risorgimento*, No. 2, April 1906. Spadolini, *L'Imbarco di Garibaldi a Cesenatico.*

(Important reports of Papal authorities.)

*Bolsi = Bolsi (Dottore Domingo). *Una memoria ineaita sul passaggio di Giuseppe Garibaldi per Castiglione-Fiorentino nel Luglio del* 1849. Foggia. 1906.

(Good stories about the monks and Garibaldians, reprinted from contemporary MS. of the monk Galassi.)

*Bonnet = Bonnet (Colonnello Gioacchino). *Lo Sbarco di Garibaldi a Magnavacca.* Bologna. 1887.

(Very valuable. First-hand account by the principal actor of the means by which Garibaldi was saved on landing near Magnavacca. Detailed, and there is every reason to think, accurate.)

Bourgeois, vid. *Clermont.*

Brancaleone = Ann. 1, No. 1. Oct. 20, 1906. Roma, Casa ed. Enrico Voghera. Article by *Giovagnoli* (q.v.) on the murder of Rossi. (Further evidence that Luigi Brunetti did it.)

Bratti = Bratti (Dr. Daniele Ricciotti). *I moti Romani 1848-9*, from the letters of Dr. Giovanni Castellani, representative of Venice in Rome, to his Government. (*Documenti Manin.*)

Bresciani = *Opere del Padre Antonio Bresciani*, della compagnia di Gesù. 1866. Vol. vi. = *L'Ebreo di Verona*, racconto storico dal 1846 al 1849. Vol. viii., ix. = La Repubblica Romana e Lionello.

(Picture of parties and movements in the form of a romance, from Clerical point of view. Arguments of the day are given in form of conversational disputes.)

*Brizi = Brizi (Oreste). *Le bande garibaldiane* (sic) *a San Marino.* Arezzo. 1850.

(Brizi was an official of San Marino, of the party unfavourable to Garibaldi. Contains much valuable information.)

Byron, V. = Lord Byron. *The Works of.* Murray. 1901. Vol. v.

(Letters from Ravenna in the old Carbonaro days.)

*Cadolini = Cadolini (Giovanni). *Garibaldi e l' arte della guerra.* Two articles in *Nuova Antologia.* May 1902.

Camozzi, Vecchio = Camozzi. *Documenti della guerra santa d'Italia.* Nov. 1849, vol. iii. fasc. 1. *L'assedio di Roma* di B. del Vecchio, addetto al ministero della rep. rom.

Carducci = Carducci (Giosuè). *Per la morte di Garibaldi.* 1882.

(A fine expression of the central current of Italian feeling about Garibaldi.)

Carletti = Charles Gouraud. *L' Italia. Sue ultime Rivoluzioni. Versione con annotazioni critiche e documenti di Mario Carletti.* Firenze. 1852.

(Carletti's notes and documents are, some of them, most valuable for the siege of Rome, especially that on the Roman Legion.)

Carrano = Carrano (Francesco). *Cacciatori delle Alpi.* 1860.

(First part of book is a life of Garibaldi, containing quotations from the original MS. of his *Memorie* ; the part about the retreat is nearly all taken from Hoffstetter.)

Cianfarani = Cianfarani (N.). *Memorie sul fatto d' arme avvenuto in Velletri.*
(Inhabitant of Velletri, Clerical.) 1900.

Ciceruacchio = Giovagnoli (Raffaello). *Ciceruacchio e Don Pirlone.* 1894. 1 vol. only published.

(By the author of *Pellegrino Rossi.* Most minute study of Ciceruacchio's life, but unfinished.)

Citt. Cesena = *Cittadino di Cesena,* Aug. 5, 1906.

(Article by N. Trovanelli containing important official documents relative to Cesenatico and the landing at Magnavacca. Narrative of one of the fishermen and of Brigadier Sereni who was taken on the voyage.)

Clermont = Bourgeois (E.) and Clermont (E.) *Rome et Napoléon III.* 1907.

(The best work on the French part in the affairs of Rome. The chapters relating to 1849 are by Mons. Clermont.)

Clough's P. R. = Clough (Arthur). *Prose Remains.* 1888. Pp. 144-169.

(Letters from Rome during Republic and siege. Recounts the experiences which inspired the political setting of *Amours de Voyage,* which should also be read.)

C. M. H. = *Cambridge Modern History,* vol. ix. chap. xiv. *The French Dependencies,* H. A. L. Fisher.

(For general effects of Napoleonic régime in Romagna and in the Papal States.)

Cochrane = Alexander Cochrane, M.P. *Young Italy.* Pp. 53-129, on the Roman Republic and siege.

(English reactionary. Inaccurate, but useful as a list of the charges, some true and some false, brought at the time against the Roman Revolutionaries.)

Com. mixte = *Rapport de la commission mixte instituée à Rome pour constater les dégâts occasionnés aux monuments pendant le siége.* 1850.
(French Yellow Book on the subject.)

Corsi = Corsi (Carlo). *Venticinque anni in Italia.* Firenze. 1870. Vol. i.
188-194 contains a valuable first-hand account of enforced journey with Austrian troops in upper Tiber Valley in pursuit of Garibaldi, July 1849.

Costa = Olivia Rossetti Agresti. *Giovanni Costa, his life, work, and times.* 1904.
(Chap. iii. for siege of Rome in which he took part. Contains also important first-hand evidence about Rossi's murder.)

Cuneo = Cuneo (G. B.). *Biografia di Giuseppe Garibaldi.* Genova. 1876 (?)
(Reprint of the Biography of 1850, with Introduction. First-hand authority for Garibaldi's early years. Its value lies in this, that it is prior to and independent of the *Memorie,* which it confirms on many points.)

D' Ambrosio = D' Ambrosio (Gaetano, Capo dello Stato Maggiore Napolitano). *Relazione della campagna militare fatta dal corpo Napolitano,* 1849-1851. 3rd ed. 1852.

(My references are to the third edition. Valuable official narrative, though it suffers from having to make the best of a very poor business.)

Dandolo = Dandolo (Emilio). *The Italian Volunteers and Lombard Rifle Brigade.* Longmans, 1851. English translation of *I Volontarii ed i Bersaglieri Lombardi.* Torino. 1849.

(Very important. First-hand account of siege of Rome by one of its bravest defenders ; gives the point of view of the Lombard Monarchists and their attitude to the Republic and to Garibaldi and his men.)

Dandolo, Vita = Carcano (Giulio). *Emilio Dandolo. I Contemporanei Italiani.* No. 12. 1861.

(Biographical sketch, two years after his death.)

D' Azeglio = D' Azeglio (Massimo). *Degli ultimi casi di Romagna* and Capponi's *Sulle Attuali Condizioni della Romagna.* Lugano. 1846.

(For the state of the Romagna under Papal rule. Politics of the Moderate party.)

De Cesare = De Cesare (R.) *Roma e lo Stato del Papa* (1850–1870). 2 vols. 1907.

(For the restored Papal rule.)

*De Rossi = De Rossi (Eugenio, then Capitano, now Maggiore, 7° reg. Bersaglieri). *La Marcia di Garibaldi da Roma a S. Marino.* Rivista di Cavalleria. Jan., Feb., March, 1902. Casa ed. Italiana, Roma.

(Best account and estimate of the strategic aspects of Garibaldi's retreat, and fullest details of the use of his cavalry. Very valuable, especially to those who wish to judge of Garibaldi's merits as a soldier, who should read also *Gandolfi* and *Nicolosi.* It contains many details, especially as to the time and place of the marches, scouting expeditions, etc. not found elsewhere, derived from notes by Gaetano Sacchi in the possession of Major De' Rossi. Sacchi commanded one of the two divisions on the retreat.)

Della Rocca = General Della Rocca. *Autobiografia di un veterano.* 1897–8. References above are to the English translation, 1899.

*Denkwürdigkeiten = *Garibaldi's Denkwürdigkeiten.* (Elpis Melena.) 1861.

(Part I. consists of an early (German) edition of Garibaldi's *Memorie* up to 1848, with a few facts not mentioned in the Italian edition. Part II. is not by Garibaldi at all, but is compiled from various authors ; it generally follows Hoffstetter as to statistics. Book 4 of Part II. is, however, of great value, as it is written by Garibaldi ; it is a sketch of Anita, chiefly of her conduct in battle in the Rio Grande days.) See below sub. *Mem.*

Diario = *Diario della rivoluzione di Roma.* 1862.

(Clerical history of the revolution compiled from party sources. Detailed, but often inaccurate.)

Don Pirlone = Comic Republican cartoon journal, Sept. 1, 1848–July 2, 1849.

(The original drawings for these famous cartoons are in the possession of Mr. A. L. Smith of Balliol, Oxford ; by his kindness I have been able to reproduce a few specimens in this book.)

Dumas, vid. sub. *Mem.*, p. 362 below.

Duprè = Duprè (Giovanni). *Ricordi Autobiografici.* 1879.

*Dwight = Dwight (Theodore). The Life of General Garibaldi by himself. 1859. New York.

(First edition of the *Memorie.*)

Elia = Elia (A.). *Ricordi di un Garibaldino dal 1847-48 al 1900.* Ed. 1904.

Epistolario = Ximenes (E. E.). *Epistolario di Giuseppe Garibaldi.* 2 vols. Milano. 1885.

Fabrizi = Fabrizi (Alfredo). *Una Pagina della Rivoluzione Italiana. L' Uccisione P. Rossi.* 1898.

*Facchini = Facchini (Didaco). *Biografia di Ugo Bassi*. 2nd ed. Bologna. 1890.

Farini = Farini (Luigi Carlo). *The Roman State from 1815 to 1850*. Translated from the Italian by the Rt. Hon. W. E. Gladstone, M.P. for the University of Oxford. 1852.

(The writer, a moderate Liberal politician of note in these transactions, is hostile both to the Clericals and to the Republicans. Though with a definite point of view which makes him sometimes unfair, he was peculiarly well-informed, and he has a love of true facts.)

*Ferrario = Ferrario (G.). *Il Generale Garibaldi. Vita ed avventure.* 1861.

(Popular brochure, of no real value, though sometimes mentioned as an authority on the Retreat.)

Ferri = Ferri (E.). *Nuova Antologia.* April 1889. *Garibaldi nelle sue Memorie.*

Foglietti = Foglietti (Raffaele). *Garibaldi in Macerata.* 1888.

(From MSS. in the Municipio of Macerata in the Marches, referring to Garibaldi's stay there, Dec. 1848–Jan. 1849.)

Forbes = Forbes (Commander C. S., R.N.). *The Campaign of Garibaldi in the Two Sicilies.* 1861.

(No relation to the Colonel Hugh Forbes of this book.)

*Forbes' Volontario = Forbes (Colonnello Ugo). *Compendio del Volontario Patriotico.* Napoli, dalla stamperia nazionale, 1860.

(Recommended by Garibaldi, and called the 'Volunteers' Bible.' This treatise of the art of war, for the Italian and other volunteers, was composed by Hugh Forbes, partly during the retreat of 1849 between Terni and Cesenatico, as he tells us in the preface. It went through several English and Italian editions.

(On p. 121, *note*, important details about Cesenatico, Aug. 1–2, 1849.)

*Franciosi = Franciosi (Pietro). *Garibaldi e la Repubblica di San Marino.* Bologna. 1891.

Fuller = Margaret Fuller Ossoli, *Memoirs*, vol. iii.

(Contains letters during the siege of Rome. Much the same interest as those of Arthur Clough and diary of W. Story.)

Gabussi = Gabussi (Giuseppe). *Memorie per servire alla Storia della rivoluzione degli Stati Romani.* Genova. 1852. 3 vols.

(An important work, and contains much first-hand knowledge of Rome and its principal defenders during the siege.)

Gaillard = Gaillard (Léopold de). *L'Expédition de Rome en 1849.* Paris. 1861.

(French account: second-hand, but with documents.)

Galeotti = Galeotti (Leopoldo). *Della Sovranità e del Governo Temporale dei Papi.* 1847.

(Liberal pamphlet.)

Gamberini = Gamberini (Cesare). *Schiarimenti sui fatti accaduti a Roma nel Giugno, 1849.* Bologna, 1884.

(Account of the part played by Pietramellara's bersaglieri, by one of his officers on June 3.)

*Gandolfi = Gandolfi (A.). *Garibaldi Generale.* Nuova Antologia. June, 1883.

(Excellent on Garibaldi as a soldier.)

Garibaldi's Cantoni = Giuseppe Garibaldi. *Cantoni il Volontario.* 1870.

(Many incidents of the history of the Legion in 1849 in the form of a bad novel.)

Gavazzi = Nicolini (G. B.). *The Life of Father A. Gavazzi, with three of his orations.*

(Little value historically, except for the orations, as types of his thought and style. There is also a slightly fuller biography of Gavazzi by the same hand, but without the orations.)

For examples of his oratory in the original Italian, see *Il Genetliaco di Pio Nono*, 1847, and *Il Vale Cristiano*, 1848, *Parole del P. Gavazzi, Barnabita, a San Francesco di Paola*, 1847 (*Tre Apostoli*).

*Gavazzi's Bassi = Padre A. Gavazzi. *Elogio Funebre del Padre Ugo Bassi.* Londra. 1849.

(Not authoritative.)

Gavazzi, In Memoriam = Collection of laudatory and biographical notices from newspapers—English, American, German, and Italian—on the death of Gavazzi. 1889.

(Often inaccurate in detail, but gives an idea of his position in the Italian and Evangelical worlds.)

Gazette Médicale de Paris = xix année, série 3, tome 4.

(Number 44, Nov. 3, 1849, contains an interesting first-hand account of a surgeon's experiences under the Vatican walls on April 30.)

Gazzetta di Roma = Official Paper, 1848.

Giornale di Roma = Official paper after the Restoration.

Giovagnoli = Giovagnoli (Raffaello). *Pellegrino Rossi e la rivoluzione Romana.* 1898. One vol. only published.

(Fullest monograph on Rossi and on the problem of his murder, with the only detailed examination of the evidence contained in the extensive documents relating to the trials of those accused. See also *Brancaleone.*)

Gironi = Gironi (Primo). *Anita Garibaldi.* Ravenna. 1896.

(Short life of Anita, and detailed history of movements of the fugitives between the landing near Magnavacca and her death.)

Giuriati = Giuriati (Domenico). *Duecento lettere inedite di G. Mazzini.* 1887.

Gli ultimi sessantanove giorni = *Gli ultimi sessantanove giorni della Republica* (sic) *in Roma.* 1849. tip. Paternò in British Museum. There are various other editions.

(Clerical tract.)

Goppelli = Zeusi Goppelli (Zolli). *La Compagnia Medici e la difesa del Vascello.* 1895.

Gritti = Gritti (Dott. Luigi, Capitano Comm.). *La Marcia a San Marino Servizi logistici.* Rivista di Cavalleria. April 1902.

Gualterio = Gualterio (Di F. A.). *Gli ultimi rivolgimenti Italiani.* 1852.

(Useful for the condition of the Roman States before the revolution : important documents.)

Gualtieri = Gualtieri (L.). *Memorie di Ugo Bassi.* Bologna. 1861.

(Most authoritative of the biographies ; important documents relative to his arrest and execution.)

Guelfi = Guelfi (Dottore Guelfo). *Dal Molino di Cerbaja a Cala Martina.* Firenze. 1885–86. 2nd ed. 1889 is the edition I have used.

(A critical summing-up of *Sequi* and *Ricciardi* (q.v.) and local traditions, as to the last stages of Garibaldi's escape and final embarkation. Very good.)

Guerrazzi = Guerrazzi (F. D.). *Assedio di Roma.* 1864.

(Famous, but often inaccurate.)

Guerzoni = Guerzoni (Giuseppe). *Garibaldi.* Firenze. 1882. 2 vols.

(Standard life of Garibaldi.)

Haweis = Newspaper cutting (anno 1888, name of paper not given), **by Rev** H. R. Haweis, giving personal reminiscences of Garibaldi and Garibaldians. (In possession of Mr. L. Haweis.)

*_Hoff._ = Hoffstetter (Gustav von). *Tagebuch aus Italien 1849.* Zürich. 1st Ed. 1851; 2nd ed. 1860. There is also an Italian translation called *Documenti della guerra santa d' Italia.* Torino. 1851.

(The fullest first-hand authority both for the siege and for the retreat as far as San Marino. Of very great value, as he was on the staff and had every means of filling up his diary accurately. My page references are to the German editions, which are fuller as well as more reliable than the Italian, and contain the next best maps of the siege of Rome, after those in Vaillant.)

Holyoake = Holyoake (George Jacob). *Bygones Worth Remembering.* 1905.

I. L. N. = *Illustrated London News for 1849.*

(The paper had a good artist—George Thomas—in Rome during the siege, who took what are perhaps the best sketches of the garb and appearance of the Garibaldians. By the permission and help of the present editor, I have been able to reproduce some of these.)

*_Itinerary_—Large sheet giving times and places of Garibaldi's embarkation and escape in neighbourhood of Comacchio and Ravenna. Reprinted in pamphlet form, with additions, by *tip.* Mazzini, Ravenna, 1907.

*_Jack la Bolina_ = Vecchi (Vittorio = Jack la Bolina). *La Vita e le Gesta di Giuseppe Garibaldi.* 1882.

(Not very valuable for this period, but represents the Garibaldian tradition. The author was the son of Augusto Vecchi, and the personal accounts of Garibaldi and his sayings in the later part of the book have therefore some authority.)

*_Johnston_ = Johnston (R. M.). *The Roman Theocracy and the Republic,* 1846–49. Macmillan. 1901.

(By the author of the *Napoleonic Empire in Southern Italy.* 1904. This earlier work of Mr. Johnston is more detailed on the political than on the military history of the Republic. Adheres to the views of the Moderate party against Clericals and Democrats.)

Journal 16ᵉ = *Journal Historique du 16ᵉ régiment d'infanterie légère pendant le siége de Rome en 1849.* (Viterbe, 1850.)

(Not quite the same as the *Paris MSS.* Historique, but based on same knowledge.)

Key = Vice-Admiral Colomb. *Memoirs of Sir Astley Cooper Key.* 1898. Commanded H.M.S. *Bulldog* at Cività Vecchia, 1849. (Impartial.)

King = Bolton King. *A History of Italian Unity, 1814–1871.* 1898. **2 vols.** (Standard general history for the English reader, and perhaps the best book of its size on the subject in any language.)

King's Mazzini = Bolton King. *Mazzini.* Dent. 1902. (A good biography, especially on the personal side.)

Koelman = Koelman (Johan Philip). *In Rome, 1846–51.* 1869. te Arnhem bij D. A. Thieme.

A Dutch artist, resident in Rome, who fought on June 3 and remained in Rome during the siege, and saw much of the Garibaldians. His important work appears hitherto to have escaped the notice of Italian and English writers. Some passages appear to me to have been 'written up' somewhat, but the essential truth of most of the personal narrative is beyond question.

I have detected errors here and there, as in all other long personal records of the siege, but I have also verified a great many small details which he could not have got out of books published in the 'sixties, and I believe his memory was in general remarkably accurate. Most of his second-hand narrative, and the words of some of the speeches which he represents himself as having heard, are taken from *Vecchi*.

He himself and his book were both very well known and highly respected in the best literary and artistic circles in Holland, whither he returned in 1857 after a thirteen years' stay in Rome. His reminiscences were first published in the *Nederlandsche Spectator* in 1863. The lapse of fourteen years after the events, before he wrote the book, prevents his narrative from being a first-rate authority, though it is first-hand. For details about Koelman and his book see *Onze hedendaagsche schilders*. C. Vosmaer, The Hague, 1881-85, and *Levensberichten van de Maatschappij der Nederlandsche Letterkunde*, 1893, pp. 109-124. Johan Gram.

* *Kriegsbegebenheiten = Kriegsbegebenheiten bei der Kaiserlich österreichischen Armee in Mittel-Italien und in der Romagna im Jahre 1849.* Wien, 1850.
Part of *Der Feldzug der Österreichischen Armee in Italien im Jahre 1849.*
(For the movements of Austrians during Garibaldi's *Retreat*.)

La Gorce = La Gorce (Pierre de). *Histoire de la Seconde République Française*, vol. i. 1887.
(His account of the Roman expedition is drawn almost entirely from the French authorities, and there is no evidence that he has read the Italian authorities. It is an *ex parte* French statement all through.)

Lanciani = Lanciani (Professor). *Ruins and Excavations of Ancient Rome.* 1897. (For history of the walls.)

La Patria = *La Patria degli Italiani*, newspaper of the Italians in the Plata States, June 19, 1904, and Jan. 9, 1905, containing interesting details of Garibaldi and of Anita in South America.

Lazzarini = *Diario epistolare di G. Lazzarini, ministro nella Rep. Romana.* 1899. (Diary of the siege.)

De Lesseps = Ferdinand de Lesseps. *Ma Mission à Rome.* 1849.
(An account of his negotiations with Mazzini, May 1849, with documents.)

Lessona = Lessona (Michele). *Volere è Potere.* 1869. 2nd ed.

Loev. I. = Loevinson (Ermanno). *Giuseppe Garibaldi e la sua legione nello stato Romano, 1848-49.* Parte Prima. Bibl. Storica del Risorgimento Italiano, Serie III. n. 4, 5. Società ed. Dante Alighieri, Roma. 1902.
(Best scholarly account of movements of Garibaldi before the siege of Rome, and perhaps best modern commentary on military events of the siege. For Garibaldi's part in the siege of Rome *Loevinson* is as indispensable a guide as *Belluzzi* is for his retreat. Signore Loevinson has the qualities of a great scholar.)

Loev. II. = Loevinson (Ermanno). Parte Seconda. Serie IV, No. 6. 1904.
(Best scholarly investigation into composition, equipment, administration, etc., of the Italian Legion, but referring principally to the period before the siege rather than to the retreat.)

Loev. III. = Third part, epistolary, bibliography, index, etc. 1907.

Lushington = Lushington (Henry). *The Italian War, 1848-49.* 1859.
(View of an English sympathiser with Italy, of the Moderate party, who visited Rome soon after the siege.)

Luzio = Luzio (Alessandro). *Profili Biografici.* Milano. 1906.
Contains biographical essays on Mameli (pp. 171-194), and Bixio (pp. 303-316) ; a criticism of d' Annunzio's poem of the siege of Rome (pp. 361-392) ; and a criticism of *Bittard des Portes* (pp. 229-241), contain-ing a narrative by Borchetta (G.), hitherto unprinted.

*Magherini = Magherini (G. Graziani). *Aneddotti e memorie sul passaggio di Giuseppe Garibaldi per l' alta valle del Tevere nel luglio del 1849.* Città di Castello. 1896.

Maguire = Maguire (J. F., M.P.). *Pontificate of Pius the Ninth.* 1870. (Clerical.)

Mameli = Barrili (A. G.). *Scritti editi e inediti di Goffredo Mameli.* 1902. (And see article on *Mameli nella Vita e nell' arte,* by Barrili, in *N. A.* June, 1902).

Mannucci = Mannucci (Michele). *Il Mio Governo in Civitavecchia.* 1850. (See also his *Schiarimenti,* 1849, on the same subject.)

Marchese = Marchese (G. S.). *Garibaldi. I Contemporanei Italiani.* No. 3. 1861. (Not authoritative, but typical of Italian feeling.)

Mario = Mario (Jessie White). *Garibaldi e i suoi tempi.* Milano. Ed. 1884. (Not documented, but she knew the chief actors well. The cheap ' *nuova edizione popolare,*' 1905, with Matania's 100 illustrations, is a fascinating memento of Garibaldi's career.)

Mario, Vita = Mario (Jessie White). *Vita di Giuseppe Garibaldi.* Milano. Ed. 1882.

Mario, Supp. = Mario (Jessie White). *Supplement to English translation of Garibaldi's Memoirs.*
(Contains stray pieces of information not found elsewhere.)

Martinengo Cesaresco = Martinengo Cesaresco (Contessa). *Patriotti Italiani.* Milano. 1890.
(Contains good biographical essays on Mameli and Ugo Bassi.)

Martinengo Cesaresco's Italy = Martinengo Cesaresco (Contessa). *The Liberation of Italy, 1815-1870.* 1895.
(Excellent brief history, perhaps the best introduction for English people to the story of modern Italy. Inspired by personal knowledge of several of the principal actors. Not documented.)

Mazzini V. = Mazzini (Giuseppe). *Life and Writings,* vol. v. Smith and Elder. 1891.

Mazzini I., II. = *Scritti di G. Mazzini,* vol. primo, secondo. Milano. Soc. ed. Sonzogno. 1898.

*Melena = Melena (Elpis), *i.e.* Marie von Schwartz. *Garibaldi, Recollections of his public and private life.* English translation. 1887.
(Chapter IV. contains a first-hand account of his visit in autumn of 1859 to the scenes of his escape near Ravenna.)

**Mem.* = Garibaldi (Giuseppe). *Memorie autobiografiche.* Firenze. 1902. 11th ed.

The *Memorie,* not being a book by a literary man, let out a great deal of truth, and reveal both the strength and weakness of Garibaldi. If the book often displays his want of judgment and of knowledge, it shows also the simplicity and unconscious beauty of his character, his poet's outlook on life, and his unfailing idealism. Without knowing that he is making ' confessions,' he gives himself away as much as Augustine or Rousseau, but the gift is pleasant.

For his South American adventures the *Memorie* are much the most important authority, especially in the versions of *Dumas, Dwight,* and Melena (*Denkwürdigkeiten*). Signor Luzio, in his admirable article in the *Corriere della Sera,* September 15, 1907, points out that *Dumas* is often confirmed on points where his veracity has been called in question, by corresponding statements in *Dwight, Denkwürdigkeiten,* and *Carrano.* All three, like *Dumas,* are based on the original MSS. which Garibaldi cut down in writing his later *Memorie,* the only book now generally known to the public. He cut out, most unfortunately, some delightful adventures of his youth which he thought it bombastic to record, and some passages about the efficacy of prayer, etc., which did not suit his later and more advanced views on religion. But both the adventures and the deistic piety were real facts of his earlier life.

*Military Events = *Military Events in Italy, 1848–49,* translated from the German by Lord Ellesmere. 1851.

(By a Swiss mercenary in Austrian service. Shows the contemporary attitude of the other side towards the Garibaldians and their retreat.)

Minghetti = Minghetti (Marco). *Miei Ricordi.* 1889.

(Valuable for politics of Moderate party, especially at time of Rossi's murder.)

Miraglia = Miraglia (Biagio). *Storia della rivoluzione Romana.* Genova. 1850.

(Contains interesting contemporary coloured pictures, and pp. 305–308 an account of the battle of Palestrina by a captain of Garibaldi's Legion.)

*Mittheilungen = *Mittheilungen des K. und K. Kriegs-Archivs.* Dritte Folge. 1 Band. Wien. 1902.

(Pp. 153–286 = Ereignisse in den Legationen und Marken in Italien in den Jahren 1848 und 1849; good for the occupation of Tuscany, Romagna, and the Marches April to June. The *Kriegsbegebenheiten* (q.v.) is more detailed for Garibaldi's Retreat.)

*Modoni = Modoni (Antonio). *Sul Titano.* Imola. 1879.

(Contains valuable report of Zani's evidence : Zani was Garibaldi's guide from San Marino to Gatteo.)

Moltke = Moltke. *Gesammelte Schriften.* 1892. Vol. I.

(Most interesting criticism by the great soldier of the operations of the siege of Rome, in letters to Humboldt, written while the siege was in progress. He had been in Rome studying the defences, 1845–46.)

Moniteur = *Le Moniteur,* 1849. *Journal officiel de la République Française.*

(For Oudinot's despatches, which are detailed and fairly accurate as regards regular siege operations, but not accurate in descriptions of battles of April 30 and June 3.)

Monitore Romano = Official paper of the Republic.

*Montasio = Montasio (Enrico). *Ugo Bassi.* No. 49 of *I Contemporanei Italiani.* 1862.

(Based on Gualtieri.)

Montor = Artaud de Montor. *La Papauté et les émeutes Romaines, 1849.*

(French clerical author : example of attitude of contemporary pietism.)

Mosto = Mosto (Andrea da). *Nozze Loevinson-Buetow.* 1906.

(A study in the little river war conducted on the Tiber during the siege, from documents in the Archivio di Stato. Dedicated to Sign. Loevinson on the occasion of his marriage.)

N.A. = *Nuova Antologia.* Vid. *Anita, Gandolfi, Ferri, Mameli, Cadolini, Nelson Gay.*

Nelson Gay, N.A. = Article by Mr. Nelson Gay in Nuova Antologia, Feb. 16, 1907, on *L' Italia e gli Stati Uniti.*

Nicolini = Nicolini (G. B.). *History of the Pontificate of Pius IX.* 1851.

(Small value historically, but gives the ultra-revolutionary point of view, especially as to the Rossi and Zucchi affairs.)

Nicolosi = Nicolosi (C.). *L' Arte militare Garibaldina*, Rivista di Fanteria, 1903, pp. 468–508.

(This article, with *De Rossi* and *Gandolfi*, should be read by those wishing to judge Garibaldi's peculiar place as a soldier.)

O'Clery = O'Clery (The Chevalier, M.P.). *History of the Italian Revolution, 1796-1849.* 1875.

(Clerical.)

Ollivier = Ollivier (Emile). *L'Empire Libéral.* 1897.

Orsini = Orsini (Felice). *Memoirs*, written by himself. 1857. English translation.

(Describes his suppression of anarchy and assassination in Ancona, on behalf of the Triumvirate. Valuable documents from Papal archives printed at the end.)

Ortore = Ortore (Bernardo). *Ciceruacchio, o i volontari della Morte.* Adria. 1879.

(Account of Ciceruacchio's capture and death.)

Ottolini = Ottolini (Vittore). *Cronaca della compagnia Medici.* 1884.

(With incomplete list of the regiment. Text approved by Medici.)

Ovidi = Ovidi (Ernesto). *Roma e i Romani, 1848-49.* 1903.

(A most scholarly work : collection of data relative to enrolment and organisation of forces in service of Roman Republic.)

Pallade = Roman Newspaper. 1848-49.

Pasini = Pasini (Giovanni). *Vita del Generale Giacomo Medici.* 1882.

Pasolini = *Giuseppe Pasolini, 1815-1876, memorie raccolte da suo figlio.* Page references in notes above are to the English translation by the Dowager Countess of Dalhousie. Longmans. 1885.

(Valuable on early history of Liberal and Sanfedist movements in Romagna, and on the attitude of Moderate Liberal nobility towards Pio IX, Rossi and his assassins, and the Republican movement.)

Pepe = General Pepe. *Narrative of scenes and events in Italy.* 1850:

(Vol. ii. chap. xii. contains an account by the Roman Deputy Buffoni of the revolution and siege. Not valuable.)

Pianciani = *La Colonna Pianciani.* Bologna. 1852.

(Some details as to the composition and previous history of the men commanded by Col. Forbes at Terni.)

Pisacane = Pisacane (Carlo). *Avvenimenti di Roma dalla salita della breccia al 15 Luglio.* Losanna. 1849.

Pisacane, Guerra = Pisacane (Carlo). *Guerra del 1848-49.* Genova. 1851.

Précis Hist. = *Précis Historique et Militaire de l'Expédition Française en Italie.* Marseilles. 1849.

(Par un officier d'Etat Major : L. Féraud.)

Quarenghi = Quarenghi (Cesare). *Le Mura di Roma.* 1880.
(Historical and military description of the walls of Rome.)

Ranalli = Ranalli (Ferdinando). *Storia degli avvenimenti d' Italia dopo l' esaltazione di Pio IX.* 1848.
(A book of the period of 1846–48. Much information, and reflects the character of that joyous epoch.)

Ravioli = Ravioli (C.). *Notizie dei Corpi Militari Regolari che combatterono a Bologna, Ancona, Roma, 1849.* 1884.
(Valuable information.)

R. G. S. P. = *Royal Geographical Society, Proceedings,* vol. viii., 1886, pp. 354–371. *The Physical Geography of Brazil.* J. W. Wells, F.R.G.S.

R. I. = *Rivista d' Italia.*
(1898, iii. 107–115, 356–358 on Rossi's murder and Ciceruacchio's sons.)

Ricciardi = Ricciardi (Dottore Ricciardo). *Da Prato a Porto Venere.* Grosseto. 1873.
(For the last days of Garibaldi's escape after leaving Prato, but see also *Guelfi*, who is more accurate, as he writes with knowledge of Sequi's evidence, not known to Ricciardi. The real value of Ricciardi is for events at S. Dalmazio and Bagno al Morbo.)

Ritucci = Ritucci (Giosuè). *Attacco di Velletri.*
(Neapolitan narrative of the battle, in some detail.)

Robertson's P. = (J. Parish and W. Parish Robertson). *Letters on Paraguay.* 1838. 3 vols.
(The best book, in English at any rate, on South America and its inhabitants in the early years of the nineteenth century. It is not confined to Paraguay. As a history of events it was sharply and not unjustly criticised by Carlyle in his famous essay on *Dr. Francia,* but it is most valuable as an account of the men, women, and manners among whom Garibaldi soon afterwards found himself, both in the great towns on the Rio de la Plata and up country among the Gauchos.)

Robertson's S. A. = (J. Parish and W. Parish Robertson). *Letters on South America.* 1843. 3 vols.
(Less good than the *Letters on Paraguay,* but much the same sort of book in its scope, merits and defects. The brothers Robertson had lived the best part of their lives not only among but with the natives of South America, and had not kept themselves apart, as did most Englishmen, especially those of the next generation, see vol. iii. pp. 114, 115.)

Roselli = Roselli (Generale Pietro). *Spedizione di Velletri.* Torino. 1853.
(His own statement of his case against Garibaldi.)

R. S. del R. = *Rivista Storica del Risorgimento.*
(Vol. I.; article on Masina's death.)

Rug. = Ruggeri (E.). *Narrazione della Ritirata di Garibaldi da Roma.* Genova. 1850.
(The only other account of the retreat of any length, besides Hoffstetter, written by one who took part in it. Not so detailed as Hoffstetter. Ruggeri took notes in pencil during the retreat. It is of prime importance.)

Rule of the Monk = General Garibaldi. *Rule of the Monk,* or *Rome in the Nineteenth Century.*
(English translation of Garibaldi's melodramatic novel about Clericals and Liberals of Rome. It does more to illustrate the naïveté of the author's

disposition and intellect, his hatred of priests, love of the English, etc., than to throw light on history in any other respect.)

Rusconi = Rusconi (C.). *La Repubblica Romana, 1849-50.*

Rusconi (Ferdinando) = Rusconi (Ferdinando). *19 anni di vita di un Garibaldino.* 1870.

(Personal narrative of author's arrival in Rome and the battle of April 30, in which he took part near the Corsini. The description of the general course of the battle is taken from *Torre*.)

Saffi = Saffi (Aurelio). *Ricordi e Scritti.* 1898.

(One of the Triumvirs. His letters to his mother during the siege, as well as other letters and official documents, very valuable and interesting.)

Salaris = Salaris (Ten. E.). *La Difesa d' Arezzo nel 1849.* Firenze. 1896.

Scampo = Anon. *Scampo del Generale Garibaldi.* Ravenna. 1868. (Local traditions of his escape in the Comacchio and Ravenna district.)

Schoenhals = Schoenhals (Général, Aide-de-Camp de Radetzky). *Campagnes d'Italie de* 1848 *et* 1849. (French translation, 1859.)

(It is perhaps worth noting the opinion of the Austrian headquarters, given on p. 423, ' Garibaldi avait défendu Rome avec courage et habileté.)

Sequi = Sequi (Enrico). *In Val di Bisenzio.* Episodio del 26 Agosto. Firenze. 1882.

(First-hand evidence by Sequi himself of the means by which Garibaldi was put into touch with the patriots of Prato, owing to his chance meeting with Sequi at the mill of Cerbaja. A better authority than *Ricciardi* (q.v.) for events prior to the arrival of Garibaldi at Prato.)

Sforza = Sforza (Giovanni). *Garibaldi in Toscana nel 1848.* 1890.

(A scholarly work.)

Simoncini = Simoncini (Lorenzo). *Giuseppe Garibaldi e Ugo Bassi in San Marino.* Rimini. 1894.

(Valuable. The author was the host of Ugo Bassi and the Garibaldis in San Marino, and perhaps their most active friend in the little Republic.)

Spada = Spada (Giuseppe). *Storia della rivoluzione di Roma.* Firenze. 1869. 3 vols.

(Valuable as the best reactionary account of events which are more usually told by the other side ; not first-hand, but with a tendency to be fair.)

Spaur = Countess Spaur. *Relazione del Viaggio di Pio IX. a Gaeta.* 1851.

(Authentic narrative of the Pope's flight.)

Stocchi = Stocchi (G.). *Un paragrafo inedito della vita di G. Garibaldi.* In *La Rassegna Nazionale*, June 1892.

(Excellent, and only serious historical study of Garibaldi's route and adventures between Modigliana and Cerbaja, August 1849. Contains Teresa Baldini's evidence, cf. to *Mini*, q.v., p. 373 below.)

Story = James (Henry). *William Wetmore Story and his Friends.* 1903.

(Interesting diary during first French attack on Rome, comparable to Clough's Diary.)

Tabarrini = Balzani (Count Ugo). *Marco Tabarrini.* Firenze. 1901.

* *Terrosi* = Terrosi (Pietro). *Garibaldi a Cetona.* Firenze. 1859.

(Brochure sold for ' the million rifles ' fund. No important information.)

Thayer = Thayer (W. R.). *The Dawn of Italian Independence.* Boston. 1893. 2 vols.

(General history, 1814-49.)

Times = Times newspaper, 1849. (Reactionary.)

Tivaroni Aust. = Tivaroni (Carlo). *L' Italia durante il dominio austriaco.* Rome. 1892.

(General history.)

Tivaroni Fr. = Tivaroni (Carlo). *L' Italia durante il dominio francese.*

Torre = Torre (Federico). *Memorie storiche sull' intervento francese in Roma nel 1849.* Torino. 1851–52. 2 vols.

(Vol. ii. contains one of the best first-hand detailed histories of the siege, with good maps; also correspondence of D'Aspre and Oudinot about Garibaldi's retreat. Torre is partisan Liberal, but is creditably accurate as to facts, and often admits facts not pleasing to his own side, wherein he differs both from *Beghelli* and other Liberal writers, and from the French authorities to which his book was meant as a reply.)

Uccellini = Uccellini (Primo). *Memorie di un vecchio Carbonaro Ravegnano.* 1898.

Uccellini's Garibaldi = *Il Generale G. Garibaldi sottratto dai patrioti Ravegnani alle ricerche degli Austriaci.* Ravenna. 1868.

(This very rare tract is known to be by Uccellini, see *Uccellini*, p. xiv. *note.* It contains most important local and personal knowledge of the escape from S. Alberto to Forlì. I did not know it when I brought out the first edition of this book.)

Vaillant = Vaillant (General). *Le siège de Rome en 1849.* Paris. 1851.

(French official history, of very great value, with the most detailed account of the sapping and battery operations. Best maps of the siege, showing date when each parallel was drawn. A very high authority on the successful siege operations of the French. But it omits to describe properly the operations in which the French were repulsed, *e.g.* the recapture of the Pamfili by Garibaldi on April 30 is omitted, and very little is said of the great efforts of the French to capture the Vascello, the failure of which, in the opinion of *Moltke*, protracted the siege so long.)

Valeriani = Valeriani. *Storia della Repubblica Romana.* 2 vols. Rome. 1850.

(An incisive arraignment of the Republican Government on its vulnerable points.)

Varenne = Varenne (Louis de la). *Les Chasseurs des Alpes.* 1860.

(Pp. 353–383 contain some details of, and remarks on, the siege and the retreat of 1849.)

Vecchi = Vecchi (C. Augusto). *La Italia. Storia di due anni 1848–49.* Torino. 1856. 2 vols.

(Vol. ii. contains a most valuable account of the siege, during which the writer was in a high position on Garibaldi's staff. Vecchi's account of June 30, when he closely attended Garibaldi, is particularly important. His narrative of the retreat is not first-hand; it is chiefly drawn from *Rug.* (q.v.); details of the retreat not found in Ruggeri may be presumed to have been related to Vecchi by other Garibaldini, with whom, as with their chief, he was on most intimate terms. For Vecchi, V., see *Jack la Bolina*, above.)

Vecchi's Caprera = Vecchi (C. Augusto). *Garibaldi at Caprera.* 1862.

(The home life and intimate talk of Garibaldi in 1861, by one of his oldest and closest friends. My references are to the English translation, but have studied the Italian *Garibaldi e Caprera*, which is more complete.)

Venosta = Venosta (Felice). *Ugo Bassi.* 1867.

(Life of Ugo Bassi, with account of the retreat.)

Verità = Verità (Don Giovanni). *Brano della narrazione di Don Giovanni*

Verità estratto dal giornale ' Il Timone.' In the Museo Civico, Bologna, Sala del Risorgimento, among the MSS., Serie B, *Trafugamento di Garibaldi.*

(First-hand account by Don Giovanni himself of incidents in the escape, recorded also by Garibaldi in the *Memorie.* But for the complete story as told by Verità, see *MS. Verità.*)

Whitehouse = Whitehouse (H. R.). *A Revolutionary Princess.* 1906.

(A Life of the Princess Belgiojoso.)

Winnington-Ingram = Winnington-Ingram (Rear-Admiral H. F.). *Hearts of Oak.* 1889.

(Memoirs of his life ; chapter vii. about the wars of Montevideo in 1846, with valuable sketches and reminiscences of Garibaldi and the Italian Legion. I have been kindly allowed to reproduce some of the former.)

Wiseman = Wiseman (Cardinal). *Recollections of the last four Popes.*

(Pius VII. to Gregory XVI.)

*Zironi = Zironi (Enrico). *Vita del Padre Ugo Bassi.*

(Popular tract, representative of the Bologna tradition.)

Zucchi = Zucchi (Gen. Carlo). *Memorie.* 1861.

(Valuable for affairs of Bologna and Rossi, Nov. 1848.)

II. MANUSCRIPTS.

I. BOLOGNA MSS.

The following is a list of the MSS. which I have consulted in the Sala del Risorgimento, of the Museo Civico of Bologna, in the collection made principally by Belluzzi. I thank his successor, Signore Cantoni, and the other officials of the Museo for their personal kindness to me, and the Municipio of Bologna for leave to study the MSS. in its possession.]

*Belluzzi's Note-book = The *Note-book* in which Belluzzi jotted down his observations made in travelling over the scenes of the retreat and escape. It is valuable as showing the train of reasoning, or the local information which induced him to make certain statements as to small details in his book on the *Ritirata*, for which the evidence is not apparent there. To one who has been (geographically) over the same ground, it is interesting to see how the various problems presented by the landscape struck his mind.

With regard to the later events, after the relanding near Magnavacca, the *Note-book* is even more important, as foreshadowing the results which he would have given to the world if he had lived to complete his promised *Trafugamento di Garibaldi da Magnavacca a Porto Venere.* But these later jottings do not represent final opinions, and it is evident from the earlier part of the *Note-book* that he sometimes changed his mind on opinions expressed in the *Note-book* (*e.g.* about Poggio Mirteto).

*MS. Bonnet = Bonnet (Cap. Raimondo). *Lettera a Belluzzi.* C. 177, no. 375.

(Describing some details of the retreat, in which he took part.)

*MS. Cesenatico = Municipio di Cesenatico. Serie B. Rit. di Garibaldi.

(Contains a copy of Piva's communication to the *Corriere del Polesine,* first-hand account of the embarkation and capture at sea.)

*MS. Cetona = Corticelli (Carlo). *Copia di documenti ecc. dall' archivio municipale di Cetona relativo al passaggio di Garibaldi.* Serie B. Rit. di Gar. Cetona.

*MS. Coccanari = Coccanari (Luigi). Ricordi personali sul passaggio di Garibaldi per Tivoli. Serie B. Rit. di Gar. Tivoli.

*MS. Franchi = Franchi (Annibale). Racconto del padre suo Giovanni trascritto a memoria. C. 174, no. 372.

(Evidence as to impressment of a few unwilling troops into the Garibaldian column, and their desertion.)

*MS. Manfredini = Manfredini (Francesco). Racconto della ritirata di Garibaldi. C. 176, no. 374.

(Author was in the retreat.)

*MS. Montepulciano = Torsellini (Dottor Dante). Notizie trascritte relative al passaggio di Gar. per Montepulciano. Serie B. Rit. di Gar. Montepulciano.

*MS. Oriani = Estratto dall' opera di Alfredo Oriani ' Fino a Dogali.' Serie B. Trafugamento di Garibaldi.

(Chiefly interesting for the story told by the muleteer nicknamed ' Pio Nono ' of his adventure with Garibaldi and Don Giovanni Verità. ' Pio Nono ' told the story to Oriani twenty years after the event. Are we to believe it? Belluzzi (see Note-book) refused to believe the other story told by Oriani, of Verità carrying Garibaldi over the ford.)

*MS. Piva = Piva (Generale Domenico). Ricordi personali relativi alla ritirata di cui faceva parte. Serie B. Rit. di Gar., no. 12.

(Particularly interesting on the dress, personal appearance, etc., of the principal persons.)

For General Piva's supplement to the Corriere del Polesine see above (sub MS. Cesenatico).

*MS. Poggio Mirteto = Bernabino (L.). Letter of, March 9, 1897.

(Proves where Garibaldians encamped at Poggio Mirteto, and disposes of the idea that they took the road to the left at the Colonna la Memoria, see Belluzzi's Note-book.)

*MS. Roncofreddo = Municipio di Roncofreddo, documents of; August 2, 1849. Serie B. Rit. di Garibaldi.

(Proves that only a few scouts, and not the whole column, passed through Roncofreddo.)

*MS. San Giustino = Lettera del sindaco di San Giustino a Belluzzi. Serie B. Rit. di Gar.

*MS. San Marino = Savini (Dottor Savino). Appunti da lui presi. Serie B. Rit. di Gar. San Marino.

*MS. Savignano = Carteggio del Sindaco di Savignano. Serie B. Rit. Garibaldi.

MS. Savini = Savini (Dottor Savino). Serie B. Rit. di Garibaldi.

(Observations made by author at San Marino during visit of the Garibaldians.)

*MS. Verità = Racconto di don Giovanni Verità del trafugamento di Garibaldi da Modigliana. Serie B. Trafugamento di Garibaldi.

(Report of the story told by Verità on June 12, 1882, and written down the same morning by the hearer. It can be collated with Verità's contribution to ' Il Timone,' see Verità, above, and with Garibaldi's Memorie, pp. 255, 256.)

2. MSS. ROME.

(a) BIBLIOTECA NAZIONALE, VITTORIO EMANUELE. F. R. = Fondo Risorgimento. Batt. Univ. = Andreocci Luigi. Fatti d' arme del Battaglione Universitario nella difesa di Roma. F. R. 6, 3.

B B

(By an eye-witness who took part in the action of the Students'
battalion, on April 30, and the Palestrina expedition.)

F. R. 67, 10. = Account of state of things in Monastery of San Silvestro at
time of departure of the nuns, agreeing well with the story told by
Koelman, i. 310–314, some of which is quoted p. 117 above.

Roncalli = Roncalli, *Cronaca di Roma, documenti stampati.*

(Vol. 37 of this famous *Cronaca*; a very adequate collection of the
proclamations during the siege made by the Government. An important
document about Masina on June 3 is No. 156 of this collection, *Prodezze
de' soldati nelle gloriose giornate del 3, 4, 5 giugno.*)

F. R. 7, 24. Letter of Rossi, when minister, ordering the *Gazzetta di Roma*
not to give more than half a column to the news from Sicily.

F. R. 7, 3. Condemnation and execution (1852–53) of the authors of the
assassinations in S. Calisto, of May 1849.
(The best evidence on the subject of these murders.)

F. R. 7, 17. Communications between Sardinian and Papal Governments,
December 1830, as to the repression of Liberalism in the Neapolitan
and Roman States.

F. R. 6, 2 = Account of Ugo Bassi's conduct during a skirmish near Palestrina,
May 1849.

F. R. 22, 69 = Report of march to Zagarolo, by Colonel L. Calandrelli, commandant of the artillery, dated May 18, 1849.

F. R. 62, 8 = *Memorie autobiografiche del Colonnello Caucci Molara, 1828–60.*
(Contains information of the Velletri expedition and comments on the
siege, Roselli, Garibaldi, etc., pp. 111–119.)

F. R. 36, 23 = Report of the Tuscan Minister at Rome to his government,
May 26, 1849.

MSS. Ris. 90 = (Catalogo Risorgimento, MSS. 90.) Speech prepared by
Rossi to be delivered at opening of Chambers on the day he was killed.
(A good *résumé* of his general political attitude and financial ex-
pedients.)

MSS. Ris. 97 = *Roncalli.* Breve racconto dell' uccisione del Conte Pellegrino
Rossi. V' è unita, nell' originale stampato, la sentenza della Consulta
contro i creduti autori del fatto. (May 17, 1854.)
(The sentence enumerates the reasons for the condemnation of Grandoni (who was really innocent, see p. 81 above), and states that he died
in prison, June 30, 1854.)

(b) ARCHIVIO DI STATO.

Ruoli Gen. = Ministero dell' Armi. Volontari delle campagne di guerra 1848–49.
1ª Legione Italiana Ruoli Generali. 80, 81, 82.

80. Fasc. 1–3 = Chiefly lists of payments made to Legionaries in the
provinces.

80. Fasc. 4 = List of wounded and sick in hospitals of Rome, November
1848—December 1849.

80. Fasc. 5 = Ditto, hospitals in provinces.

81. Lists from which the number of the Legion and particular sections of it,
at various dates, can be made out.

82. Further lists (F. 10–13) about Masina's lancers, and (16) the list of
Garibaldians captured at sea, also printed at end of Belluzzi.
Accounts, etc.

3. PARIS MSS.

(These *Historiques* of the French regiments, in the Ministère de la Guerre, Paris, compiled by officers in recent times, contain valuable information about April 30 and June 3, but are not to be relied on in all particulars of those affairs.)

Paris MSS. 91ᵉ (16ᵉ) = Historique du 91ᵉ Régiment d'Infanterie (ancien 16ᵉ léger). Reçu (au Ministère de la Guerre) 11 décembre 1889.

(Valuable for action of Levaillant's division in capturing Pamfili, early hours of June 3.)

Paris MSS. 33ᵉ = Historique du 33ᵉ Régiment d'Infanterie. Reçu le 10 avril 1891.

(Valuable for April 30 and for June 3.)

Paris MSS. 20ᵉ = Historique du 20ᵉ Régiment d'Infanterie. Reçu le 1ᵉʳ juin 1892.

(Repeats Picard's story about April 30.)

Paris MSS. 66ᵉ = Historique du 66ᵉ Régiment d'Infanterie. Reçu le 18 juin 1875.

(Describes April 30 as a French victory, but gives no details. Some account of June 3.)

4. MS. LANZA.

MS. Lanza = 1. Giornale di Marcia ed operazioni militari della colonna agli ordini del General Lanza mossa dal quartiere generale di Albano il 7 di maggio 1849. (Signed Lanza.)

    2. Comando dei corpi di fanteria dell' esercito di sedizione nello stato Pontificio. (Signed Lanza.)

(These most important reports of General Lanza to his superiors, describing and excusing his defeat by Garibaldi at Palestrina on May 9, were copied from the original MSS. in the Archivio di Stato, Naples, by Captain Paganelli, of the Ufficio Storico, Comando del Corpo di Stato Maggiore at Rome, who invited me to make use of his copy, and to whom I am deeply obliged.)

5. MS. MANARA.

MS. Manara = Private letters of Luciano Manara, 1848–49; the last are from Rome.

(I have taken my notes of these most interesting documents, not from the originals in Milan, but from a copy in the possession of Captain Paganelli, which also he most kindly showed me.)

6. LETTERS TO AUTHOR.

Letters that I have received from various informants in Italy and England are mentioned in their place in the notes or text, and are not noted in this Bibliography.

(I have also to thank *Tenente Generale Saletta*, Head of the General Staff of the Italian army, for his great kindness in presenting me with a *précis* of his lectures on the military aspects of Garibaldi's retreat. This document, together with Major de Rossi's articles in the *Rivista di Cavalleria*, 1902, with which it is in substantial agreement, I have regarded as the best guides to a just opinion on the value of Garibaldi's strategy and method of leadership on this occasion. It is clear that the latest professional opinion regards his generalship during the retreat, and particularly his use of cavalry, as reaching that high degree of excellence which amounts to genius.)

B B 2

F.O. Papers = English. Foreign Office Papers, Record Office.
(I thank the Foreign Office for leave given me to examine the papers for information about Colonel Hugh Forbes.)

III. LITHOGRAPHS, ENGRAVINGS, ETC.

1. *Decuppis* = Atlante generale dell' Assedio di Roma . . . Due carte Militari ed una collezione completa di vedute rappresentanti le rovine degli edifizi più rimarchevoli, etc. Cav. Prof. Decuppis. Roma, 1849. Presso l' editore Giuseppe Ferrini.
(Lithographs. Views of the ruins sketched immediately after the end of the siege.)

2. *Werner* = Similar, but much better and more perfectly reproduced pictures (engravings) of the various ruins, taken at the same period by Carlo Werner. Several of these have been reproduced in this volume.

3. *Kandler* = Panoramic view of the siege of Rome 'dessiné d'après nature et gravé en eau forte par Guillaume Kandler.' 1849. Taken from the French position in Pamfili grounds.

4. *Andrese* = Panorama of the siege of Rome, very carefully done, called 'Vue de Rome, prise du Palais Cafarelli (*sic*) au haut du mont Capitolin dans le mois de juin en 1849 pendant son siège dessinée d'après nature par C. Andrese.' (Published by Spithöver, Place d'Espagne. Engraved by Pulini.)
(These four sets of pictures, the best topographical evidence, were given to me by Lord Carlisle, bound in one volume.)

5. *Raffet = Souvenirs d'Italie. Expédition de Rome.* (Gihaut, éditeur.)
(The pictures are signed Raffet, with the dates ranging from 1851 to 1859. They are not quite so contemporary and authoritative as the works of Werner, etc., mentioned above, but they are most of them more valuable than the famous picture of the priests saving the prisoners on April 30, which is a work of M. Raffet's fine artistic imagination.)

6. *Miraglia* = Coloured pictures of Garibaldi and his Legionaries, and various persons and actions of this period in Miraglia's *Storia della Rivoluzione Romana*. 1850.

7. *Villa Benedetta descritta da Matteo Mayer. In Roma per il Mascardi*, 1677. For pictures cf. Vasiello (Villa Benedetta) at that date.

For *Illustrated London News* and *Don Pirlone* see in list of books above.

IV. MAPS.

The best military maps for the siege of Rome are those attached to *Vaillant, Torre, Hoffstetter, Decuppis*, and *Andrese*.

Rocchi. For old maps of Rome, showing date of the walls, etc., see E. Rocchi, *Le Pianti Icnografiche e prospettiche di Roma nel Secolo XVI.*, reproduced from the originals. And many maps of seventeeth and eighteenth century.
(Mr. Ashby, of the British School, Rome, kindly showed me his collection.)

Pianta del Censo, 1829, is the most detailed map of Rome before the siege.

Carta Grafica del percorso da Cesenatico a Forlì da G. Garibáldi. Ravenna, tip. lit. Ravegnana, 1907, to accompany the *Itinerary* (*q.v.* above).
(For the retreat and escape of Garibaldi, see the Ordnance Maps of the *Istituto geografico militare* for the ground as it is at the present day. Of the older maps, I have mentioned one or two in the footnotes above, *sub. loc.*

Most of my geographical knowledge is first-hand, and gathered on each spot through which Garibaldi passed on his retreat from Rome to Cesenatico. I have also visited Palestrina, Velletri, Comacchio, Mandriole, the scenes near Magnavacca and Ravenna, the scenes of his embarkation in the Tuscan Maremma, and a few of the places passed through in his escape August 7-September 1.)

V. POETRY ETC.

The story told in this book is a subject more suited to poetical treatment than almost any incident of modern history—even of modern Italian history. The retreat appears to have as much attraction for poets as the siege itself.

La Notte di Caprera, XVI.–XIX. Gabriele D' Annunzio.

The Disciples. Ugo Bassi. Mrs. Hamilton King.

Rapsodia Garibaldina, I. Giovanni Marradi.

The Defence of Rome. Ernest Myers. (1880. Macmillan.)

(The siege and the retreat are also the subject-matter of Pascarella's still unpublished but already famous sonnets.)

There is also a modern German romance based on a study of the authorities, *Die Verteidigung Roms*, by Ricarda Huch, 1907.

ADDENDA TO BIBLIOGRAPHY. (FEBRUARY 1908.)

Archibugi = Silvagni (D.). *Eroi sconosciuti*, 1848–9 : *fratelli Archibugi*, 1893.

*Benko = Benko von Boinik. *Geschichte der k. k. Krieges Marine*, 1848–9. 1884. (For Magnavacca).

Bizzoni = Bizzoni (Achille). *Garibaldi nella sua epopea.* 3 vols. 1905.
   (Most beautifully illustrated of the lives of Garibaldi. Text is partisan but contains bits of information and documents not found elsewhere.)

Cavaciocchi = Cavaciocchi (Alberto). *Le prime gesta di Garibaldi in Italia.* 1907. (For 1848.)

Ciàmpoli = Ciàmpoli (Giuseppe). *Scritti politici e militari di Garibaldi.* 1907.
   (Contains some letters not printed in Ximenes' *Epistolario*, but is neither exhaustive nor invariably accurate. The *Ricordi e pensieri* printed at the end, used by Guerzoni, appear for the first time in full.)

Il Progresso = *Il Progresso.* Turin, Aug. 20, 1851. Contains Bixio's letter describing the battle of April 30 and his own capture of Picard.

*Mini = Mini (Giovanni). *Il Trafugamento di Garibaldi dalla pineta di Ravenna a Modigliana.* 1907.
   (Important for itinerary as far as Modigliana. Less good on Filigare and S. Lucia, since the author has not studied *Stocchi* [*q.v.*].)

Nisco = Nisco (Niccola). *Reame di Napoli.* Vol. III. *Ferdinando II.*

Palmer = Palmer (J. Foster). *Spola : Easter Day in Rome*, 1849. Transactions of R. Hist. Soc. N.S. Vol. V.

(Interesting facts relating to religious feeling in Rome, 1849.)

Sassetti = Sassetti (A. S.). *Garibaldi a Rieti.* 1907.

(Interesting account drawn from local records of Garibaldi's relations to inhabitants of Rieti, while his Legion was quartered there early in 1849.)

Stiavelli = Stiavelli (G.). *Garibaldi nella letteratura italiana*, ed. 1907. Partly an anthology, partly a bibliography.

(Useful, but not brought up to date.)

Zamboni = Zamboni (Filippo). Article in the *Pensiero Latino*, July 7, 1907, on Students' Battalion, April 30. (See for Zamboni, *Archibugi*, p. 57.)

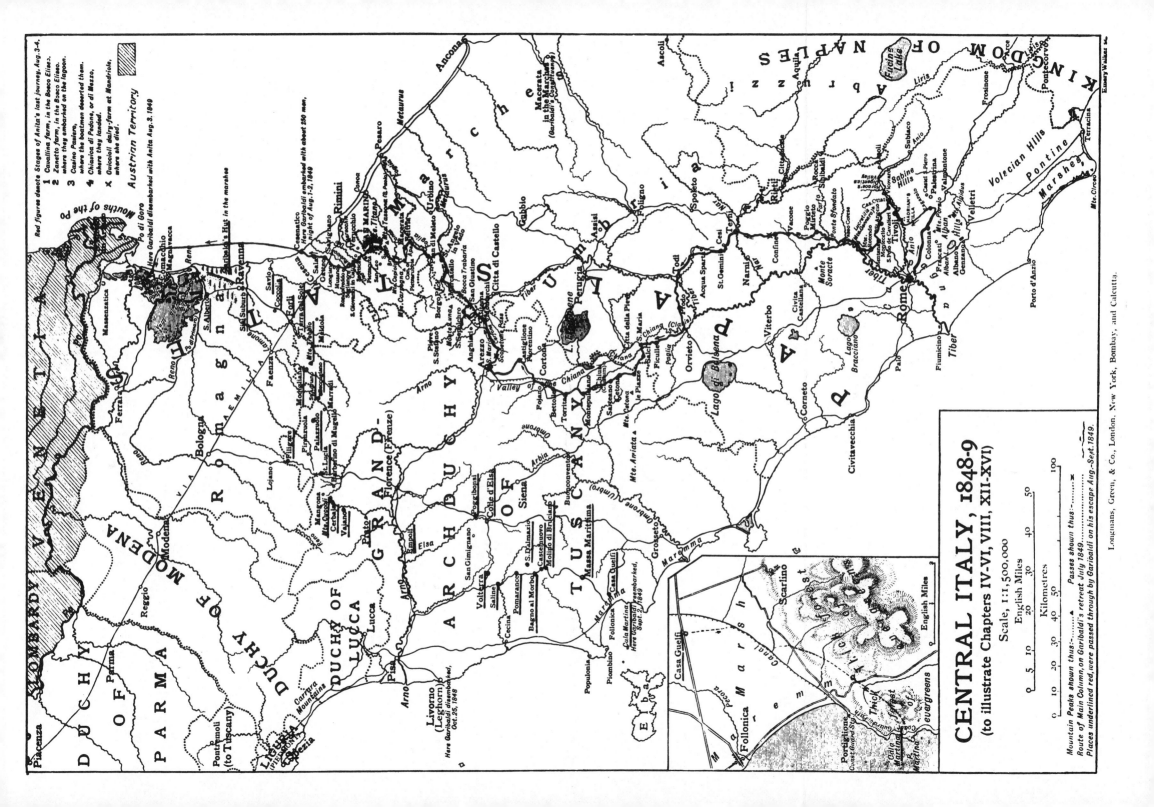

CENTRAL ITALY, 1848-9
(to illustrate Chapters IV-VI, VIII, XII-XVI)

Scale, 1:1,500,000

English Miles

Kilometres

Mountain Peaks shown thus:.......▲
Route of Main Column, on Garibaldi's retreat July 1849.
Passes shown thus:........✕
Places underlined red, were passed through by Garibaldi on his escape Aug.–Sept. 1849.

Red figures denote Stages of Anita's last journey, Aug. 3-4.
1 Cavallina farm, in the Bosco Eliseo.
2 Zanetto farm, in the Bosco Eliseo, where the boatmen deserted them.
3 Casino Panieri.
4 Chiavica di Pedona, or al Mezzo, where they landed.
✕ Guiccioli dairy-farm at Mandriole, where she died.

Austrian Territory

Longmans, Green, & Co., London, New York, Bombay, and Calcutta.

Emery Walker sc.

VENETIA

LOMBARDY, 1848-9

DUCHY OF PARMA

DUCHY OF MODENA

DUCHY OF LUCCA

ROMAGNA

THE MARCHES

UMBRIA

GRAND-DUCHY OF TUSCANY

PATRIMONY

KINGDOM OF NAPLES

INDEX